Dictionary
of
20TH
CENTURY
EUROPEAN
HISTORY

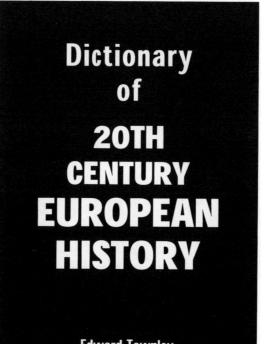

Dictionary of

20TH CENTURY EUROPEAN HISTORY

Edward Townley
Series editor Ian Marcousé

FITZROY DEARBORN PUBLISHERS
LONDON • CHICAGO

Copyright © 1997 Edward Townley

First published 1997 in the United Kingdom by Hodder and Stoughton Educational as *The Complete A-Z 20th Century European History Handbook*

Published in the United States of America by
Fitzroy Dearborn Publishers
919 North Michigan Avenue
Chicago, Illinois 60611
USA

A Cataloging-in-Publication Record is available from the Library of Congress

ISBN 1-57958-127-7

First published in the USA 1999

Typeset by Wearset, Boldon, Tyne and Wear, England and Alacrity, Banwell Castle, Weston-super-Mare, England

Printed in the UK by Antony Rowe Ltd., Chippenham, UK

The *Dictionary of 20th Century European History* is an alphabetical reference book designed for ease of use. Each entry begins with a very brief definition. The information which follows then expands on the topic in relation to its overall historical significance. As well as giving factual knowledge, the entries indicate the historical significance of the subject matter and so enable it to be adapted as part of a wider historical explanation. Topics can be further researched by making use of the cross-referenced entries. For example, the entry on the *Berlin Wall* refers the reader both to *East Germany* and to the *Cold War*. It is intended that readers following up entries in this way will build up both a secure base of historical knowledge and a clear appreciation of their historical significance.

EUROPEAN 20TH CENTURY HISTORY IN CONTEXT

In 1900, world politics centered on the capitals of Europe: Berlin, London, Paris, St. Petersburg, and Vienna. European empires, led by the British and the French, controlled vast stretches of territory across all the continents and seas. In all the major European countries there were expanding pockets of heavy industry, based on steam power, coal, steel and rail transportation, which were transforming both the economic and the military potential of the Continent. Eastern and Central Europe were dominated by three great states: Austria-Hungary, Germany and Russia.

In the course of the twentieth century, Europe was decisively affected by three conflicts:

- the First World War from 1914 to 1918
- the Second World War from 1939 to 1945
- the Cold War from the 1940s to the early 1990s.

Much of the detail of European twentieth-century history only makes sense when it is related to one or more of these conflicts.

By the end of the twentieth century, Europe's position in world affairs had changed totally. This was partly because of events outside Europe, the expanding power of the USA, the development of independent national states across the world, the emergence of China as a world power, and the new economic strength of Asiatic states. The change was also brought about by the destructive effects of the two world wars, which destroyed the economic basis of, as well as the will to defend, Europe's worldwide empires. European history until 1939 can almost be studied as a self-contained unit; after 1941 this is impossible.

The second half of the century was dominated by the two superpowers, the USA and the Soviet Union. The old European empires vanished between 1945 and 1975. Within Europe, the First World War destroyed the Austro-Hungarian Empire and led to communist control of Russia; and the Second World War ended any German dream of domination. This in turn opened the way for the Soviet Union to establish control over Eastern Europe, and led to the political division of Europe into East and West. Only in the last decade of the century was this pattern, established in the 1940s, broken as the Soviet Union disintegrated and the Cold War ended. This process of disintegration seemed likely to open up a new and uncertain phase in European history. In 1914, an event at Sarajevo had marked Europe's plunge into darkness, and in the 1990s, events in Sarajevo again raised the specter of Europe's potential for self-destruction.

Edward Townley

MAPS AND FIGURES

ACKNOWLEDGMENTS

The idea for the *Dictionary of 20th Century European History* came from Tim Gregson-Williams of Hodder & Stoughton in London. He and the editor of this series, Ian Marcousé, provided much help and encouragement during its production, and I am very grateful to both of them.

Ronnie Kowalski of Worcester College of Higher Education provided invaluable help on the Soviet entries, but the opinions, and any errors which have survived in any of the entries, are entirely mine. Simon Townley taught me much about the use of bullet points and how poor a proofreader I am. Finally, I would like also to acknowledge the help provided by the library staff and the library facilities at Worcester College of Higher Education.

The publishers would like to thank the following for permission to reproduce material:

Table p. 94 and table p. 228 © J. Watson, *Success in Twentieth Century World Affairs*, London: John Murray (Publishers) Ltd., 1974; table p. 215 © Cook and Paxton, *European Political Facts 1848–1918*, Basingstoke: Macmillan Ltd., 1978; figure 7, p. 90 reproduced with permission of Punch Ltd.; figure 13, p. 174 © SOLO Syndication Ltd.; figure 18, p. 281 reproduced from Whitaker's Almanack 1997 by permission of the publisher, J. Whitaker and Sons Ltd.

A

abortion controversy: twentieth-century controversy over the practice of terminating pregnancy. Controls against this were relaxed in many countries during the second half of the century, but the Roman Catholic Church remained steadfastly opposed to any form of abortion. In the USA it has remained a matter of passionate argument, but it has been less of an issue in either Eastern or Western Europe – except in certain countries, like Ireland, with a strong Catholic tradition.

Abwehr: the intelligence bureau of the German armed forces. It was strictly part of the *OKW*, the separate personal-command structure for the armed forces devised by Hitler in 1938, when Admiral *Canaris* became its head.

Abyssinia: a country in northeast Africa. (See under *Ethiopia.*)

Acerbo Law: an Italian electoral law introduced by the fascists in 1923 after *Mussolini* became prime minister. It:

- decreed that any party gaining more votes than any of its rivals, and with at least 25 percent of the total vote, would control two-thirds of the seats in the Assembly
- was named after the man who drafted it
- was justified as promoting political stability after a long period when politics had been dominated by fragile coalitions of small parties
- was really intended to strengthen the position of the minority fascist government.

The law was passed only with the help of liberals in Parliament, though with a prominent presence of uniformed *blackshirts* also patrolling outside the building. It illustrates the weakness of Mussolini's opponents, and marks a key stage in the fascists' establishment of total power in Italy.

Action Française: an extreme right-wing French political group of the first half of the twentieth century. Its members, strongly nationalistic and anti-Semitic, wished to restore the monarchy and became openly fascist in sympathy. This, and the movement's close links with the *Vichy* government from 1940, led to its collapse at the end of the Second World War. Its existence illustrates the deep political divisions in the Third French Republic, and is one reason why the French, in the 1930s, found it difficult to provide united resistance to Nazi expansionism.

Adenauer, Konrad: chancellor of the German Federal Republic (GFR – West Germany), 1949–63. He had been both a national politician and mayor of Cologne during the Weimar Republic, but was then removed by the Nazis and later imprisoned.

- He was chairman of the commission which drew up the constitution or *Basic Law* of the German Federal Republic (West Germany)
- After the *Christian Democrats*, whom he led, had won the 1949 election, he became the country's first chancellor at the age of 73
- He was strongly authoritarian towards his party and government

colleagues, and did not hesitate to gain party advantage by smearing his socialist opponents, the SPD, as communists

- Until 1955, he took personal charge of foreign policy, taking a strong anti-communist line which pleased the Western powers, and also developing the first stages of the movement towards European unity by helping to found the *European Coal and Steel Community*.

The Cold War made German rearmament an important and difficult objective, but one which was achieved first within the framework of the Western European Union and later in NATO. In both economic and defense matters, Adenauer worked effectively to maintain and develop good relations with France. This culminated in the *Franco–German Friendship Treaty* of 1963 which underlined the close relations he had developed with the French leader *de Gaulle*.

In domestic politics, however, Adenauer was often authoritarian and inflexible:

- from 1956 to 1968, largely on his own personal initiative, the Communist Party was banned
- he was particularly criticized for not doing enough to reunify the two Germanys, rigorously maintaining the boycott of East Germany established in the *Hallstein Doctrine*
- in old age he clung to office, and his party's popularity suffered as a result
- in 1962, the arrest of the editor of the magazine DER SPIEGEL on a treason charge, after he had criticized the performance of the German army in practice maneuvers, caused an outcry because it seemed so like the tactics employed in the days of the Third Reich. Adenauer's defense minister, *Strauss*, had to resign immediately, and Adenauer's coalition partners insisted that he too must go in 1963
- in the 1960s, as the "economic miracle" slowed, his popularity waned.

Adenauer's great domestic contribution to the GFR was that, despite his authoritarian tendencies, he provided continuity of democratic government across his 14 years in office for a state which had so recently been ruled by a ruthless dictatorship and which had few strong democratic traditions. This, together with the German economic miracle of the 1950s and the moves he encouraged towards European integration, established his state, from the most unpromising beginnings, as a stable democracy.

Aerenthal, Alois: foreign minister of Austria-Hungary, 1906–12. Confident of German support, it was his decision in 1908 to annex Bosnia. The ensuing *Bosnian Crisis* marked a clear step on the way to war in 1914.

Afghanistan, Soviet intervention in: Soviet troops were engaged within Afghanistan, an Asian state to the south of the Soviet Union, from 1979 to 1989, supporting the pro-communist government against Islamic fundamentalist guerrilla forces. This attempt to protect the frontier of its Central Asian Republics, initiated by *Brezhnev*.

- proved both costly and ineffective
- led to much international criticism, including a partial boycott of the 1980 Moscow Olympic Games

- imposed great strains on the Soviet economy, which in turn contributed to the collapse of the Soviet Union in the early 1990s.

Afrika Korps: German troops involved in the *North Africa campaigns* during the Second World War.

Agadir: a Moroccan Atlantic port. In 1911, as the French were establishing their control of the country, a German warship, the PANTHER, visited Agadir to "protect German interests." This pressure on the French was an important example of:

- the growing international tensions of the period up to the outbreak of the First World War
- the aggressive German foreign policy associated with Kaiser *William II.*

It had the unfortunate effect, from a German viewpoint, of annoying the British government and, by driving Britain closer to France, cemented the *entente cordiale.* Eventually, Germany backed down and recognized the rights of the French in Morocco.

Ahnenerbe: the Nazi Institute for Research into Heredity. Ahnenerbe conducted experiments on live prisoners regardless of the cruelty and barbarism involved. Ahnenerbe was described by Schirer, a later historian of the Third Reich, as "one of the ridiculous 'cultural' organizations established by *Himmler* to pursue one of his many lunacies."

AIDS (Acquired Immune Deficiency Syndrome): usually sexually transmitted, a disease of the blood with no known cure. The virus which spreads the infection was given the name Human Immunodeficiency Virus (HIV). From around 1980, it spread across Africa to the USA, and later became established worldwide. Its origins have been extensively debated: outside Africa, it has most seriously affected the homosexual community, and the two most likely routes of its transmission have been identified as anal sex and the shared use of drug needles. Despite great expenditure on research, there had, by the 1990s, been little success in advancing any successful treatment.

aircraft industry: this emerged just before the First World War.

- 1914–18, it expanded rapidly because of war demands, with Britain alone producing 52,000 military aircraft during the war
- Between the world wars, civil aircraft production developed, notably of large seaplanes
- 1930s: US production overtook that of Britain and France; Germany, thanks to its rearmament program, also again became a major manufacturer
- The Second World War stimulated further growth and technical development, including the jet engine. The industry in the USA began to outstrip that of all other countries.

The development of the aircraft industry in the 1930s, often arising from rearmament programs, was an important stimulus to national economies struggling to break out of the worldwide economic recession of the Great Depression. The jet engine had been invented in 1937 in Britain by *Whittle,* but much of its development was due to American engineers during and after the Second World War, when the vast US industry came to dominate civil aircraft markets. In 1962, the British and French embarked on the prestigious but costly Concorde project, and it became increasingly clear that international cooperation within Europe was the only way that the industry there would survive in competition with the USA.

air power: control of the skies, through superior numbers or the superior performance of the air force, became crucial during the Second World War.

- The *blitzkrieg* attacks of 1940, rehearsed during the Spanish Civil War, terrorizing the civilian population of cities and removing defensive obstacles to the advance of tank formations, were as essential an element in the sweeping German advance across Western Europe as they had been in the swift conquest of Poland in 1939
- The achievement of British fighter aircraft in the *Battle of Britain* was equally crucial in denying Hitler the opportunity to invade Britain in the autumn of 1940
- The failure of the German *blitz* on London to break the will to resist of the British people indicated that there were limits to the effectiveness of aerial terror tactics, for casualty figures were never as great as the gloomy pre-war predictions had suggested they would be
- The development of *radar* also provided some hope of constructing a defensive strategy against attack from the air
- The Japanese air attack on Pearl Harbor, and the sinking of the British battleships REPULSE and PRINCE OF WALES by Japanese aircraft in December 1941, marked the end of an era in naval warfare dominated by the great battleships. Aircraft carriers had been built before the war; by its end, they were at the heart of naval strategy.

The Allied advance into Germany in the last years of the war was accompanied by massive day and night bomber raids by the American and British air forces, though, since the war, the effectiveness of these attacks in destroying either the German war effort or the will to fight has been questioned. The use of aerial attacks on essentially civilian targets later raised moral issues that were largely ignored at the time, notably with the bombing of *Dresden* and the 1945 dropping of *atomic bombs* on Japan.

Air power remained crucial in the wars of the second half of the century:

- in the Vietnam War of the 1960s and 1970s, with the use of napalm
- in the Gulf War of the 1990s, with the use of precisely targeted rockets

which added to the deadly potential available to the developed countries. However, air power was still not always decisive: in Vietnam and in the Russian invasion of Afghanistan in the 1980s, determined guerrilla forces held out and eventually triumphed over immeasurably better-equipped opponents. The cost of military aircraft continued to rise and was one factor putting strain on the economy of the Soviet Union in the 1980s. Increasingly, only the USA could afford to produce the prototypes dreamt up by the development scientists.

Alanbrooke, Lord: a British army commander involved in the 1940 retreat from *Dunkirk*. Lord Alanbrooke was a military adviser to Churchill during the Second World War, accompanying him to all the wartime conferences with Roosevelt and Stalin.

Albania: an independent state since the *Balkan War* of 1912. Situated on the Adriatic coast opposite Italy, it was previously part of the Ottoman Empire.

- From 1928 to 1939, it was a monarchy under a local landowner who took the title King *Zog*
- In 1939 Italian troops invaded, and Albania became an Italian protectorate
- In 1941 it was incorporated into Italy.

Partisan fighters led by the communist Enver Hoxha liberated much of the country in 1944–45. At the end of 1945, Hoxha established the Communist People's Republic of Albania, and the country moved into a period of extreme political isolation. After a rift with the Soviet Union in 1958, Albania moved closer to communist China and then into isolation from the rest of the world until the late 1980s.

- From 1988, diplomatic relations were reopened with other European states, the USA and the Soviet Union
- In 1990, this was accompanied by the relaxation of internal restrictions.

This did not totally prevent demonstrations for further changes, and political unrest continued. The treatment of Albanians living in the Kosovo region of Yugoslavia also caused tensions within Albania in the 1990s.

Alcalá Zamora, Niceto: president of the unstable Spanish Republic from 1931 to 1936.

Alexander I: king of Yugoslavia from 1921 to 1934. He had a distinguished military career in the Balkan Wars and in the First World War. He and his prime minister, *Pašić*, strove from 1921 to 1926 to eliminate ethnic, religious and regional rivalries in the country, but thereafter Alexander could only maintain order by imposing a dictatorship with army support. His formal title, as king of the Serbs, Croats and Slovenes, hints at the nature of the problems he faced. In 1929, he renamed his country Yugoslavia. Civil unrest and economic depression continued to plague the country, and in 1934, he was assassinated by a Croatian terrorist. His political career nicely illustrates the difficulties faced in providing political stability or democratic government in the newly independent nations of Central Europe which succeeded the Austro-Hungarian Empire after the First World War.

Alexander, Earl: a British army commander in the Second World War. In 1942 he stopped the German advance on Egypt. In 1943 he was deputy to Eisenhower in the *North Africa campaign*, and in 1944 he commanded the Allied invasions of Sicily and Italy. A much-respected military figure, he had earlier commanded at Dunkirk and in Burma.

Alexandra, Tsarina: the German wife of Tsar *Nicholas II* of Russia. She was a firm believer in tsarist autocracy and an obstacle to any political concessions or reforms in Russia, repeatedly urging her husband to rule as well as reign. She later fell under the influence of the court adviser *Rasputin* and, after September 1915, when her husband had taken command of the army at the battlefront, interfered with both the government of the country and the war administration, with disastrous consequences. In contributing to the unpopularity of both the war and the monarchy, she helped to bring about the end of the *Romanov* dynasty in the February

Revolution of 1917. Along with her husband and family, she was assassinated in 1918 by the Bolsheviks.

Alfonso XIII: king of Spain from 1886 to 1931. His mother ruled as regent until 1918. His reign was increasingly autocratic and troubled by internal disorder, during which he survived five assassination attempts, and in 1923 he accepted *Primo de Rivera* as dictator. After the dictator's resignation in 1930, the Spanish people voted overwhelmingly for a republic. Alfonso refused to abdicate the throne, but in 1931 he left Spain, and at this point Spain became a republic.

Algeciras Conference: a 1906 international conference held in Spain. It settled the future of Morocco as a French protectorate after disputes between France and Germany had caused tension among the European powers, and followed on from provocative statements on the part of the German Kaiser William II at *Tangier*. At the conference, Britain backed France, and the kaiser thus unintentionally strengthened the *entente cordiale* between them. Tension reappeared in the area in 1911, when the German warship PANTHER visited *Agadir*.

Algeria: a North African country colonized by the French in the nineteenth century. It was politically incorporated into Metropolitan France, but its Arab population had few rights.

- The first organizations committed to ending French control emerged in the 1930s
- In the Second World War, it was freed from German occupation in 1942
- The political promises then made to its native population were not honored, and this led to growing unrest and violence.

Algeria is a powerful example of how the Second World War marked a crucial stage in the disintegration of European overseas empires, both by promoting the aspirations for independence of its native population and by undermining the ability of the imperial power to resist its demands. In:

- 1952, the discovery of oil in the country raised the stakes for all the parties
- 1954, the nationalists launched the full-scale *Algerian War* of independence, which lasted for eight years and created a major crisis in France in 1958, bringing *de Gaulle* back into office and so ending the *Fourth French Republic*
- 1963, Algeria ceased to be part of Metropolitan France and became an independent nation.

Algerian War: the struggle from 1954 to 1962 of Algerian nationalists to secure independence from France. It was marked by atrocities on both sides and, at its height, by the commitment of most of the French army to the struggle. French settlers were determined to keep Algeria part of Metropolitan France, and the recent discovery of oil deposits increased their resolve. The cost, length, losses and barbarity of the war alienated much of French public opinion, and the crisis led to the return of de Gaulle and the end of the Fourth French Republic. Through the *Évian Agreements*, Algeria then secured its independence.

Allied powers: shorthand term:

- in the First World War, for Britain, France and Russia; also, in the last months of the war, for the USA
- in the Second World War, for Britain, Russia and the USA.

The term usually also embraced the other powers who fought on the same side as the above.

Allies, the: another shorthand term for the Allied powers, above.

All-Russian Congress of Soviets: the national forum for delegates from *soviets* across Russia. The *Bolsheviks*, thin in numbers outside the big cities, were in a minority among the delegates called to the October 1917 meeting of the Congress. *Lenin* was determined to show the delegates that the Bolsheviks controlled Petrograd, and so launched *Trotsky* on the course of action which brought about the *October Revolution.*

Alsace-Lorraine: a region on the west bank of the river Rhine with many iron and coal deposits, and of great strategic importance to both France and Germany.

- In 1871, it was ceded by France to Germany after the latter's defeat in the Franco-Prussian War
- In 1919, it was restored to France by the Treaty of *Versailles*
- During the Second World War, it was reoccupied and made part of Germany once more
- 1944–45, it was liberated, and since then has been part of France.

ambassador: a diplomat sent by one state to another, usually as its permanent representative there, or occasionally on a specific mission.

Amnesty International: an international pressure group founded in 1961 to promote respect for human rights.

amphibious: in military terms, an operation landing forces from the sea.

anarchism: the belief that government and law should be abolished.

Andropov, Yuri: Soviet politician.

- In 1956, he helped to crush the *Hungarian Revolution*
- From 1967 to 1982, he was head of the KGB, where his firm handling of dissident movements enhanced the reputation for toughness he had earned in Hungary
- In 1983, he succeeded *Brezhnev* as chairman of the Communist Party, and despite his hard-line reputation and his ill health at the age of 68, he tried to introduce reforms decentralizing decision-making and attacking the corruption which had marked Brezhnev's last years.

This realization, from a member of the Soviet old guard, that the communist system needed reform, was never put into practice, for Andropov died in February 1984. He promoted the career of *Gorbachev*, but was himself succeeded by another member of the old guard, *Chernenko*. Relations with the Western powers worsened during Andropov's period in office with the mistaken shooting down of a Korean civil aircraft by the Soviets, and also as a result of the West's deployment of intermediate-range missiles in Western Europe.

Anglo–Japanese Treaty: a 1902 defensive alliance between Britain and Japan. It marked a first move by Britain away from both relative isolation and the avoidance of international commitments, and towards the series of international agreements which it made prior to the First World War. The alliance:

- was entered into as a form of protection for British imperial interests in Asia in the event of its becoming entangled in a European conflict
- was based on growing British uneasiness about commercial and naval rivalry from Germany
- arose from British sensitivity about the problems it could face in a future European conflict, which was one consequence of the military difficulties and international hostility it had experienced during the *Boer War*.

Anglo-Russian Entente: a 1907 understanding between Britain and Russia. It removed sources of friction between the two countries. The two powers:

- agreed to respect the independence of Afghanistan and Tibet
- divided Persia (Iran) into zones of influence.

The entente, following on from the 1893 alliance between France and Russia and the 1904 *entente cordiale* between Britain and France, was encouraged by fear of German power and intentions. It marked the end of British nineteenth-century suspicion of Russian expansionism and also completed the two systems of alliances and understandings which divided Europe prior to the outbreak of the First World War.

animal rights movement: during the twentieth century, a great number of national and international societies were established either to protect animals from cruel treatment or to safeguard endangered species of animals.

- In the Western world generally, protests against the use of animals in laboratory experiments, including some use of violent methods, became common in the 1980s.
- In Britain in the 1990s, this extended to protests against the export of live animals, especially young calves, for slaughter. The type of protester, often female, middle-class and quite elderly, was very different from that normally encountered in political protest demonstrations.

annex: to incorporate territory into one's own. It usually implies doing this without any right to do so, as in "the annexation of the Sudetenland by Nazi Germany."

Anschluss: the wish for union between Austria and Germany, which in practice came into being in 1938. It had its origins in the nineteenth century and arose from their common language and cultural inheritance. Until 1918, Austria's role at the head of the multi-national Austro-Hungarian Empire had made its fulfillment unlikely, but Austria's loss of its non-Germanic lands as a result of the First World War gave the matter a renewed impetus. Anschluss had, however, been specifically forbidden by the Treaty of *Saint Germain,* part of the Paris Peace Conference.

- In 1931, a proposed customs union between the two countries was blocked by France
- From 1933, Anschluss figured prominently in Hitler's dreams for a greater Germany
- In 1934, *Mussolini* mobilized Italian troops on the Austrian border to prevent Hitler exploiting a coup by Austrian Nazis aimed at bringing it about

- In 1938, Hitler exploited unrest fomented by the Austrian Nazis to put pressure on the Austrian chancellor *Schuschnigg* to take the Nazi leader *Seyss-Inquart* into government.

In order to forestall a referendum on the issue of union with Germany, the Austrian Nazis then invited Hitler to send in German troops to keep order. The Austrian people gave the Germans and Hitler personally such a warm welcome that he was encouraged immediately to declare Austria's union with Germany rather than be content with setting up a puppet Nazi government there. Rather than the Anschluss being part of a master plan, Hitler was carried along by events. His success was made possible by:

- the new closeness between fascist Italy and Nazi Germany which, in 1938, led Mussolini to accept the Anschluss which he had prevented in 1934
- Britain being content, despite the dire warnings of the likely consequences from Churchill, simply to lodge a token protest at the breaking of the treaty terms
- the French being, again, in the middle of a government crisis and unable to act
- a general opinion in Europe that the Austrians had simply exercised their rights to *self-determination* which they had been denied in the earlier peace treaty.

The most dramatic consequence of the Anschluss was that it opened up the southern frontier of Czechoslovakia to German pressure. The Czechs' formidable frontier defenses with Germany had been outflanked. (See map, p. 110.)

anticlericalism: opposition to organized religion. It usually applies to opposition to the Catholic Church. Anticlericalism was rife in many countries in nineteenth-century Europe, and was also politically important in undermining the stability of the Spanish Republic of 1931–36.

Anti-Comintern Pact: in 1936–37 between Germany, Japan and Italy. It was originally a pact in November 1936 between Germany and Japan, the countries agreeing to work together against international communism. Italy signed in 1937. It was seen, by democratic nations, as an ominous joining together of right-wing militaristic powers.

anti-nuclear protests: in the 1950s and 1960s, a series of movements in the Western world challenged both the morality and the safety of reliance on nuclear weapons. They were inspired by the *Pugwash Manifesto* issued by prominent scientists, and they included the British *Campaign for Nuclear Disarmament.* There were persistent rumors in the 1950s that a nuclear incident had occurred at a British airfield, with a plane loaded with a nuclear bomb crashing. These rumors resurfaced in the 1990s but continued to be denied by the British authorities. The continued proliferation and deployment of nuclear weapons, and the increased sophistication of the means of delivering them, led to the growth in the 1980s of the European Nuclear Disarmament (END) movement, which formed links with groups in Eastern Europe, particularly the Czech *Charter 77*. In the 1980s, women's protest groups also came to the fore, particularly in Britain, where direct-action protests were centered on the US base at Greenham Common in Berkshire. The relaxation of Cold War tensions suggested that the nuclear threat had receded, but the ominous growth in the number of states with nuclear capability, and also the question of the safety of the vast Soviet stockpile of nuclear weapons when the Soviet Union disintegrated, indicated that nuclear disaster was still possible.

Opposition to the dangers inherent in the disposal of nuclear waste also led, in the 1980s and 1990s, to demonstrations against this, and against the nuclear-power industry in general, in several European countries. Such protests increased in the aftermath of the 1986 *Chernobyl* nuclear-reactor disaster, which provoked particular concern in West Germany. Only the French, with their extensively developed nuclear-power industry, seemed immune from popular protest on the issue.

anti-Semitism: hostility towards Jews. Its origins lay in religious differences, but in nineteenth-century Europe, it also developed through envy of Jewish success in business.

- In France, the *Dreyfus Affair* from 1894 to 1906 was one notorious example of anti-Semitism
- In Russia and other East European countries, there were many instances of state persecutions, or *pogroms*, against Jews, which exploited popular resentment of them, often in order to distract the people from other grievances
- The Nazi *Holocaust* during the Second World War was based on the Nazis' own notions of racial superiority but was also sustained by the hatred or distrust felt by many others towards Jews, both in Germany and in German-occupied countries
- At the end of his life, anti-Semitic feelings were one of the motives behind Stalin's continued pursuit and persecution of alleged troublemakers, notably in the so-called Jewish *Doctors Plot* and in the *Slansky Trial.*

Antonescu, Ion: Romanian dictator, 1940–45. He promoted a pro-Nazi policy in the Second World War, sending troops to help the 1941 German invasion of the Soviet Union. Romania switched sides in the war after it had been invaded by the Red Army in 1944. Antonescu was then tried and shot.

Anzio: a Second World War battle in the *Italian Campaign.* In January 1944, some 50,000 Allied troops were landed from the sea behind enemy lines in order to bypass the stubborn German resistance and move swiftly on Rome. They failed to exploit their initial advantage and became pinned down in a series of German counter-attacks.

Aosta, Duke of: a cousin of King Victor Emmanuel III of Italy. He was, in 1922, a fascist sympathizer who helped to smooth away any royal opposition to *Mussolini* taking over the government. It has also been argued that the king hesitated to take strong action against Mussolini because he was afraid that the duke might then lead a right-wing coup against him. During the Second World War, Aosta commanded the Italian garrison in Ethiopia, and in 1941 surrendered to the British, paving the way for the return of *Hailie Selassie.*

appeasement: making peace by concessions or by satisfying demands. During and after the Second World War, it was used in a derogatory sense to describe the

TIMELINE: INTERNATIONAL AFFAIRS, 1931–41

1931 Japanese attack on Manchuria. League of Nations failed to act

1932

1933 Hitler came to power in Germany

Germany withdrew from international disarmament talks

1934 Mussolini moved troops to discourage German pressure on Austria

1935 Stresa Front set up by Britain, France and Italy

Naval Agreement between Britain and Germany

Italo–Ethiopian War started (to 1936): failure of League and its members to take effective action

1936 German troops moved back into the Rhineland in defiance of the Versailles Treaty

Spanish Civil War began (to 1939)

1937

1938 Anschluss (union of Austria and Germany)

Munich Agreements handed the Czech Sudetenland to Germany

1939 March – Germany seized the remainder of Czechoslovakia and occupied Memel

August – Nazi–Soviet Pact

September – Germany invaded Poland

France and Britain declared war on Germany

1940 German conquest of most of Continental Western Europe

Dunkirk and Battle of Britain "saved" Britain

1941 June – Germany invaded the Soviet Union

December – Japanese bombed Pearl Harbor, USA declared war on Japan

Germany and Italy declared war on the USA: European war became a world war

efforts, especially those of the British prime minister *Chamberlain*, to keep peace with Nazi Germany from 1937 to 1939, most notoriously by the *Munich Agreements* to which the French prime minister *Daladier* was also a party. The sharpest critic of the policy was *Churchill* and, as war did in fact come in 1939, his view of the folly of the policy held sway for 20 years after the end of the Second World War. Only after that time was a more considered view taken, by historians such as *A. J. P. Taylor*, suggesting that Hitler may not have had such a clear-cut master plan for European conquest as Churchill had insisted. A defense of appeasement as a rational policy at the time is possible on the following lines:

- British and French public opinion was overwhelmingly in support of the policy because of its fear of the effects of war following on from the horrors of the First World War, and in the conviction that, in any future war, these would be multiplied by the development of aerial bombing
- a costly rearmament program could only be at the expense of urgently needed economic and social spending to lift the Western democracies out of the effects of the Great Depression
- neither the USA nor the British dominions were anxious to adopt a strong commitment to resisting Hitler

- both the British and the French would have the greatest difficulty in defending their empires in the event of a European war
- it could be argued that Germany had been harshly treated by the *Versailles* Treaty and that some of the steps taken by Hitler were, in the light of this, not unreasonable. The decision to rearm, the reoccupation of the Rhineland and even the Anschluss could be seen in this way
- to right-wing politicians, a greater threat to international stability than fascism was posed by communism, and indeed Hitler could be seen as a useful block to the ambitions of the Soviet Union to spread communism across Europe
- the British and French governments did not have the benefit of hindsight. Chamberlain, his government and the British people did, however, have many good reasons not to trust Churchill, the main critic of appeasement
- only after Munich did Hitler's full ambitions emerge. Then at least the people of France and Britain could see that war was inevitable and in September 1939 went to war united. This would not have been the case a year earlier, at the time of Munich.

April Theses: the statement of Bolshevik strategy for seizing power, produced by *Lenin* in April 1917. The Theses:

- required the party to make an early bid to take power by not cooperating with the Provisional Government or helping with the war effort
- developed the strategy of pressing for power to be passed to the *soviets*, where the Bolsheviks would build up their influence
- presented a radical political program of nationalization of land and banking
- proposed the abolition of the army, the police and the civil service.

The boldness of the proposals shocked the Bolshevik Party leaders, but they eventually accepted them. The Theses set the agenda that led to the *October Revolution*, and demonstrated the importance of Lenin's role in bringing the Bolsheviks to power.

Ardennes Campaign: the German Second World War military offensive of December 1944 and January 1945, the last German counter-attack of the war. It is also known as the Battle of the *Bulge* from the large but temporary dent which the German advance created in the Allied lines.

- Despite initial surprise success against the advancing US forces, the attack failed to break out from the Ardennes forest region and reach its objective, the Belgian port of Antwerp
- The Allied counter-attack in early January 1945 regained the ground lost and inflicted 120,000 casualties on the German forces.

armaments reduction: see the entry under *disarmament*

Armenia: a region spanning the borders of Turkey and the Soviet Union. Independence movements in Turkish Armenia from 1915 to 1923 led to widespread massacres and mass deportations of the Armenian population, with millions dying.

For a brief period at the end of the First World War, the collapse of the Ottoman Empire offered a prospect of Armenian independence, notably at the Treaty of *Sèvres* in 1920. This was frustrated by the revival of Turkish power and the creation of the Republic of Turkey so that, at the Treaty of *Lausanne* in 1923, there was international agreement that most of Armenia should be part of Turkey. The Soviet Union gave up its claims to Turkish Armenia in 1920 and in 1922 incorporated Russian Armenia into the Transcaucasian Soviet Republic. Armenians on both sides of the international border continued to dream of separate nationhood and this was a source of continuing tension in the region. In 1991 Armenia became a founding member of the *Commonwealth of Independent States.* Memories of the mass slaughter of so many of the Armenian population from 1919 to 1923 made the issue of Armenian nationalism a very emotive one in the Republic of Turkey.

armistices, 1917–18: the agreements to cease fighting prior to the negotiation of the peace treaties which ended the First World War. The most famous of these armistices was that of 11 November 1918 on the Western Front between Germany and the Western Allies. Germany had still not been invaded, and later the myth was developed by right-wing groups in Germany that, by agreeing to the armistice, the politicians who had inherited power from the kaiser only two days earlier had stabbed the German army in the back. In fact, *Ludendorff,* who had planned the German 1918 offensive, had already advised the kaiser to sue for peace because the German military situation had become untenable.

arms race: a term used during the Cold War to describe the rivalry between the Soviet Union and the Western powers to establish their supremacy in arms production. It led to vast defense budgets and, by the 1980s, was imposing unacceptable strains on the Soviet economy.

Army Law: the Nazi German law of July 1933 which restored the powers of the officer class within the army to what they had been in Imperial Germany. Coming so soon after the Nazis had come to power, it did much to encourage the military leaders to support the new regime.

Arnhem: a Second World War battle in Holland in September 1944. The combined land and air operation was intended to enable the Allies to force a crossing of the lower reaches of the Rhine. The advancing land forces were unable to support those dropped from the air and, after heavy losses, most of the gains had to be abandoned.

Article 48: of the constitution of Weimar Germany. It gave the president the right to take emergency powers to preserve public safety and order. It was increasingly used in the early 1930s at the behest of von *Papen*'s and *Brüning*'s governments, and eventually by Hitler to undermine the democratic state that it had been devised to protect.

artillery: heavy guns used for fighting on land.

artillery barrage: concentrated fire from heavy guns. It was usually designed to open a breach in enemy defenses and was a feature of the attacks, like in the Battle of the *Somme,* intended to end the stalemate on the *Western Front* in the First World War.

Aryan race: the name promulgated by the Nazis for the "superior" European race which formed the basis of their nonsensical racist philosophy.

Asquith, Herbert: British prime minister from 1908 to 1916. In 1915, his Liberal government formed a coalition with the Conservatives, but his conduct of the First World War continued to be seen as lethargic and he was replaced by *Lloyd George*. The criticism of his wartime record and the manner of his fall, which marked a crucial stage in the disintegration of the British Liberal Party, illustrate the pressure put on democratic states by the demands of total war.

Atatürk: the title meaning "Father of the Turks" taken in 1934 by Mustafa Kemal, president of Turkey from 1923 to 1938. He had earlier:

- played a key military role in resisting the Treaty of *Sèvres* proposals both for an independent Armenia and for Greek control of much of western Turkey
- through his military successes, enabled the Turks to retain these areas at the Treaty of *Lausanne.*

As first president of the republic founded in 1923, he worked to create a secular state, rejecting the Islamic legacy of the Ottoman Empire. He encouraged the Westernization of Turkey through:

- industrialization
- the emancipation of women
- the adoption of the Western alphabet and the metric system
- social policies which abolished polygamy, banned the fez and the veil, and established civil marriage and divorce.

He created an efficient modern state, but ruled it in a highly autocratic way.

Atlantic, Battle of the: the most important *sea warfare* battle of the Second World War, fought to keep open the vital supply lines from the USA to Britain. These were threatened mainly by German U-boat attacks, which sank nearly 3,000 ships. The critical period was from 1940 to early 1943, after which improvements in *radar* and in the range of both escorting ships and planes, together with the breaking of German codes, turned the battle in favor of the Allies. The end of the battle came in 1944, when the U-boat bases were captured by the Allied armies which had invaded the Continent.

Atlantic Charter: a declaration of principles for the future conduct of world affairs. It was issued jointly by President Roosevelt and Winston Churchill after a meeting at sea in August 1941, before the USA had entered the Second World War. The principles included:

- freely chosen governments
- international free trade
- freedom of the seas
- disarmament of the aggressor states.

These ideas later served as a basis for the *United Nations*, but in 1941 the charter was mainly important as an indication, at a crucial stage of the war, of the developing US support for the British war effort.

atomic bomb: the first two atomic bombs, and the only ones ever used in actual conflict, were dropped on Japan in August 1945. The bomb had been developed in the USA during the Second World War, and the two dropped on Japan caused some 100,000 deaths and appalling injuries to many more.

Possession of the bomb appeared to give the USA an enormous military advantage in the early stages of the *Cold War*. It fuelled Soviet suspicion of the West until, in 1949, the former developed its own atomic bomb, which in turn worried many in the West. In these ways, the atomic bomb contributed to the deepening of the Cold War, but may also have deterred the powers from attempting a military solution to their differences. Britain had its own bomb by 1952, and China and France soon followed. Its potential for destruction and as a *nuclear deterrent* against attack was soon eclipsed by the development of the *hydrogen bomb*.

Attlee, Clement: British prime minister, 1945 to 1951. He served loyally and effectively as deputy prime minister in Churchill's 1940–45 coalition government. His post-war Labour government:

- undertook major social reforms, with the introduction of a welfare state
- carried out the nationalization of major industries and transportation undertakings
- had to cope with the problems of post-war economic reconstruction
- was faced with the crises and costs of the developing Cold War between the communist and capitalist worlds.

In its 1945 election victory, Labour had made great play of being able to work with the Soviets, but as the Cold War developed, Attlee's government, encouraged by the foreign secretary, *Bevin*, proved a staunch ally of the USA. It:

- accepted the *Marshall Plan*
- played a full part in the *Berlin Airlift*
- helped to form *NATO*
- sent troops to the *Korean War.*

Auschwitz: the most infamous, and by far the largest, of the Nazi *death camps* set up to bring about the *Final Solution* to the "Jewish Problem." Towards the end of the war its gas chambers were killing 6,000 people a day. Estimates of the total number of victims who died at Auschwitz alone have varied from 1 to 4 million, with the later estimates tending to accept the lower figure. After the war, parts of the exter- mination camp were preserved as a memorial to the victims and as a permanent reminder of the *Holocaust*. It is located in southern Poland.

Austria: a republic first founded in November 1918 following the defeat of the Austro-Hungarian Empire, and with its borders agreed at the Treaty of *Saint Germain*. It had a troubled internal history, with its political life deeply divided between left and right and its economy grossly distorted by the loss of the industrial towns of the old empire but with the retention of the vast imperial capital, Vienna, within its borders. In 1934, political unrest led to over 300 deaths and culminated in the local Nazis' assassination of the chancellor, *Dollfuss*.

The Treaty of Saint Germain had forbidden Austria to join with Germany, but in 1938 German troops entered the country and *Anschluss* (union) was proclaimed.

- During the Second World War, Austria remained part of Germany
- In 1945, it was restored as an independent republic
- In 1955, it achieved full sovereignty with the withdrawal of occupation troops after the signing of the *Austrian State Treaty*.

Since 1955, Austria has become increasingly prosperous, with tourism and trade with Germany its two main economic assets. In 1986, its president, Kurt *Waldheim*, was accused of anti-Semitic activity during the Second World War, but although this became an international issue, it did not affect his status in Austria. In 1995, the country became a member of the European Union.

Austrian State Treaty: an international treaty of 1955 signed by Britain, France, the USA and the Soviet Union. They agreed to end the post-war occupation of Austria and to recognize the republic. It was one of the few signs of any softening in the *Cold War*, and it enabled Austria, while maintaining a neutral stance politically, to develop a Western economy and society.

Austro-Hungarian Empire: founded in 1867, as the successor to the Austrian Empire, with Austria and Hungary as separate countries but both ruled by the *Habsburg* monarchy. It is sometimes referred to as the *Dual Monarchy*. Foreign policy was decided by ministers common to both countries. The empire contained many separate national groups, Croats, Czechs, Poles, Romanians, Serbs and Slovaks, who increasingly wanted some form of self-rule.

- In 1908, the largely Slav-inhabited provinces of *Bosnia and Herzegovina*, under Austrian protection since 1878, were formally *annexed*
- In 1914, it was Serb nationalism in Bosnia which, with the assassination of *Franz Ferdinand*, began the sequence of events which led to the outbreak of the First World War.

The firm Austrian response to Serbia, in which it was backed by Germany, transformed its rivalry with Serbia into a European war. The long-serving emperor *Francis Joseph* died in 1916, and the empire, defeated in war, was broken up into separate national states by the Allies at the treaties which formed part of the Paris Peace Conference of 1919:

- of *Saint Germain* with Austria
- of *Trianon* with Hungary.

autarky: the policy of economic self-sufficiency. It was the policy attempted by Nazi Germany in the late 1930s, aiming at relying totally on home production and excluding all imports.

authoritarian: favoring or requiring obedience to authority. Usually, it is used in political terms as the opposite of "liberal," and to identify stern and repressive government.

autocracy: absolute rule by one person, a dictatorship.

autonomous: self-governing or independent.

Aventine Secession: the 1924 departure of many opposition deputies from the Italian Parliament in protest at the murder of *Matteotti* by fascist thugs. King Victor Emmanuel III had refused to take action because he feared that it would help the socialists, whom he disliked more than he did the fascists. The walk-out was later seen as a naive response and a missed opportunity to challenge *Mussolini*, who bluffed his way past the murder charges and then turned on the opposition, introducing press censorship and banning meetings of opposition parties. When the deputies tried to return, they were told they had forfeited their seats by their "revolutionary secession." Mussolini went on to introduce further laws against any possible form of opposition. The episode was one of the key stages in Mussolini gaining dictatorial power.

Axis: a term used first by Mussolini to describe Italy's new, cordial relationship established in 1936 with Nazi Germany.

Axis powers: a term used in the late 1930s and during the Second World War to identify Germany and its allies, chiefly Italy and Japan. It derives from the Rome–Berlin Axis proclaimed by Hitler and Mussolini in November 1936.

Azaña, Manuel: president of the Spanish Republic during the *Spanish Civil War* from 1936 to 1939. From 1931 to 1934, he had been the republic's first prime minister.

Baader-Meinhof Gang: a common name applied to the terrorist group the *Red Army Faction*, prominent in the 1970s and 1980s. Led by Andreas Baader and Ulrike Meinhof, both of whom were to commit suicide in prison, they were a gang of urban guerrillas at war with capitalist society. They carried out terrorist acts including bombings, kidnapping and murder, operating mainly in West Germany. In 1976, in their most famous exploit, they combined with Palestinian guerrillas in hijacking an Air France plane, and had it flown to Entebbe.

background to the First World War: see *First World War*, background to

Badoglio, Pietro: Italian field marshal. He took command of the army after the First World War defeat at *Caporetto*, and was from 1928 to 1933 governor of Libya. He returned to the army to lead it to victory in the 1935–36 *Italo-Ethiopian War*. In 1940, he opposed Italy's entry into the Second World War but was then commander-in-chief in the disastrous 1940 campaign against Greece. In 1943, he briefly succeeded Mussolini as prime minister, leading a non-fascist government which negotiated peace with the Allies and then declared war on Germany. He resigned office when leading Italian partisans refused to serve under him, and died in 1956.

balance of payments: the difference in value between the amount paid by a country for its imports and that paid to it by other countries for its exports.

balance of power: a situation in which major states or groups of states have roughly equal power, so that no one power can dominate. The theory of maintaining the balance of power was behind Britain's closer relations with France from 1904 to 1914, its objective being to prevent Germany from becoming so dominant, through its industrial and military might and its alliances, that it would upset the balance of power in Europe.

Baldwin, Stanley: British prime minister, 1923–24, 1924–29 and 1935–37. In British domestic politics, he was involved in all of the major issues of the inter-war period, including

- the 1926 *General Strike*
- the formation in 1931 of the National Government
- the abdication of King Edward VIII in 1936.

On defense issues and foreign affairs:

- he was later accused of having done too little to resist Hitler's aggressive policies, notably with regard to the German remilitarization of the *Rhineland*
- his government's failure to prevent Italian aggression against Ethiopia in the *Italo-Ethiopian War*, and to back the League of Nations in the crisis, is often seen as a major cause of the worsening international relations in the late 1930s
- he followed a policy of non-intervention in the Spanish Civil War, which allowed Franco's nationalist forces, aided by Germany and Italy, to over-

throw the elected republican government and replace it with a fascist-style regime

- he was, during the Second World War, frequently accused of having neglected British defenses. His comment that "The bomber will always get through" is often quoted to illustrate the widespread fear of another war, which did so much to encourage the policy of *appeasement*
- although he had a horror of the effects of modern warfare and was fully aware of the British public's reluctance to contemplate vast expenditure on arms, from 1935 he quietly laid the basis for later rearmament, including – most importantly – the re-equipping of the air force and the building of the *radar* network.

Balfour, Arthur: British prime minister, 1902–5. He helped to establish the *entente cordiale* with France in 1904. From 1916, he was foreign secretary in Lloyd George's wartime coalition government and, in 1919, was a leading British representative at the Paris Peace Conference. He gave his name to the *Balfour Declaration.*

Balfour Declaration: a letter of 1917 in which the British foreign secretary, Balfour, committed Britain to supporting a national home for the Jews in Palestine. The declaration was confirmed by the Allies and became the basis of Britain's League of Nations mandate over Palestine which led in 1948 to the creation of the state of Israel.

Balkan League: of 1912, comprising Bulgaria, Greece, Montenegro and Serbia. It has been seen as a Russian creation to dismember the Ottoman Empire in Europe, but although the Russians welcomed it as a check on Austro-Hungarian power in the Balkans, it was more a vehicle for Serb and Bulgarian ambitions against the Ottoman Empire. Its creation led to the *Balkan Wars.*

Balkan Pact: a 1933 attempt by King *Alexander* of Yugoslavia to form a defensive alliance among the Balkan nations. It broke down in 1940 as these nations adopted different policies towards the growing power of Germany.

Balkan Wars: of 1912 and 1913. In the First Balkan War, between the *Balkan League* and the *Ottoman Empire,* the Turks lost all their European lands except Istanbul and three coastal forts. Both Italy and Austria-Hungary were concerned at these gains by the League countries, especially at the prospect of *Serbia* gaining a foothold on the Adriatic coast.

- Austria-Hungary mobilized its army to oppose this, and the Russians theirs in order to defend Serbia
- Their allies, Germany and Britain, urged caution
- In the 1913 Treaty of *London*, the great powers imposed a division of the spoils of war among the victorious League members, crucially denying Serbia its Adriatic coastline.

The Second Balkan War was between the previous members of the Balkan League, each trying to secure more territory than they had gained in the Treaty of London. The Bulgarians attacked first but, when Greece and Serbia were joined by Romania and the Turks, they were soon defeated and lost territory, at the Treaty of *Bucharest,* to all the victors.

The main consequences of the Balkan Wars were:

- an increase in both the strength and the pretensions of all the members of the Balkan League except Bulgaria
- Serbia's expansion and its unsatisfied Adriatic ambitions now posed a serious threat on Austria-Hungary's southern border
- an increased possibility that the great powers, especially Austria, would be drawn into any future conflict in the region
- the prospect that, although the Balkan Wars had been confined to the small states of the region and the diplomacy of the great powers had prevented a larger conflict, their outcome had created even greater tensions in the Balkans which the great powers would not in future be able to control.

In all of these ways, the Balkan Wars represented a step towards the outbreak of the *First World War*.

Baltic Republics: the three republics of *Estonia, Latvia* and *Lithuania*.

- Until the end of the First World War, they had been part of the Russian Empire
- In 1919, they became independent states
- At the end of the Second World War, they were reabsorbed back into the Soviet Union
- In the 1990s, they regained their independence once more with the disintegration of the Soviet Union
- The Soviet Union formally recognized the independence of all three countries on 10 September 1991.

Barbarossa (Operation Barbarossa): the code name for the June 1941 German invasion of the Soviet Union.

Barcelona: a Spanish city. It was held by the republicans during much of the *Spanish Civil War*, suffering many bombing attacks. It was captured by the nationalists in January 1939.

Basic Law: the 1948 law which defined the constitution of the Federal Republic of Germany (West Germany). It had been devised by a committee chaired by *Adenauer*, and helped to provide political stability by excluding from the Bundestag all parties which, under the system of proportional representation, received less than 5 percent of the total votes cast.

Basic Treaty: the 1972 treaty between East and West Germany. The two countries agreed:

- to develop normal relations
- to respect each other's independence
- not to concede full recognition of the other's sovereignty.

The treaty opened up East Germany for visits by those who had earlier fled to the West, and was the culmination of the *Ostpolitik* pursued in the late 1960s by the West German Brandt government which had sought to overturn Adenauer's policy of isolating East Germany diplomatically.

Basques: a race living across the Franco–Spanish border. In the period of the Spanish Republic from 1931, their wish for autonomy seriously weakened the republic as tension grew prior to the Spanish Civil War. A Basque republic was declared in 1936 but was destroyed by Franco. In the 1970s and 1980s, continued Basque demands for independence were spearheaded by the terrorist organization *ETA*.

Battle for Births: an Italian fascist campaign, started in 1927, to increase the population from 37 to 60 million. The greatness of the nation was held to be dependent on this. High taxes on bachelors and prizes for mothers were two of the tactics adopted, but the birth rate remained disappointingly static. The population rose to 44 million in 1939, largely because of both a steep decline in emigration, brought about by US immigration limits imposed from 1921, and a fall in the death rate.

Battle for Grain: an Italian agricultural and propaganda campaign of the 1920s and 1930s to make Italy self-sufficient in wheat production:

- Mussolini was featured in films driving a tractor
- new land, notably the *Pontine Marshes*, was brought into cultivation
- the most productive farmers were awarded medals.

Wheat production doubled from 1922 to 1939, but imports were still necessary and, because of subsidies, the cost of grain remained high. Marginal land which could have been better used for fruit or olives was turned over to grain; on the other hand, little was done to improve farm sizes or to reduce the iron grip of large landowners. Despite these shortcomings, Mussolini's agricultural policies achieved more than any other of his economic policies.

Battle for Land: a campaign in fascist Italy to change the pattern of landowning. It intended to benefit the great number of small farmers at the expense of the vast estates, and was accompanied by much propaganda, but in practice it achieved nothing in the way of land redistribution. In 1940:

- the peasants, comprising nearly 90 percent of the farming population, still owned only 13 percent of the land
- the richest 0.5 percent of the population owned over 40 percent of the land.

These proportions had scarcely changed over the period of fascist rule. This failure indicated how conservative a force Italian fascism was in the social and economic spheres, and how dependent it was on the privileged classes whose support had helped bring it to power. The greatest achievement of the Battle for Land was the draining of the *Pontine Marshes*, which brought hundreds of thousands of acres of wasted land into production. Even here, the impact of the war meant that much had to be retrieved once more after 1945.

Battle of Britain: see *Britain, Battle of*

Battle of the Bulge: see *Ardennes Campaign*

Battle of the Atlantic: see *Atlantic, Battle of*

Baudouin I: king of the Belgians from 1951 to 1993. He succeeded his father

Leopold III when the latter abdicated because of his controversial role during the Second World War. Baudouin was successful in using loyalty to the monarchy as a means of containing, but not ending, the deep divisions in Belgium between French and Flemish speakers and regions.

Bavaria: until 1918, a kingdom within the German Second Empire, and then a republic within the Weimar Republic. In November 1918, *Eisner* established a short-lived Bavarian socialist republic, and in April 1920, the *Spartacists* set up a communist state which was crushed by the *Freikorps* in October 1920. Bavaria then became a center for right-wing political movements and uprisings, notably the 1923 Nazi *Munich Putsch*. In 1948, Bavaria became a state within the Federal Republic of Germany (West Germany).

Bayar, Mahmud: president of Turkey, 1950–60. He was imprisoned after a military coup in 1960, but was released in 1964.

Beck, Josef: a Polish politician who served as foreign minister under *Pilsudski*. He:

- arranged a pact with Germany in 1934
- failed to persuade the French to resist German militarization of the Rhineland in 1936
- sought territory at the expense of Czechoslovakia at Munich in 1938
- signed a military alliance with Britain on 25 August 1939, two days after the *Nazi–Soviet Pact*.

These shifts in policy give some indication of why Poland was open to German pressure and then aggression in 1939. When war came, Beck fled to Romania, where he was imprisoned and died in 1944.

Beer Hall Putsch: see *Munich Putsch*

Belgian Congo: a Central African colony of Belgium until it was granted independence in 1960. The Belgians had done little to prepare the country for self-rule and, fearful of the costs of a war against the Congo's nationalists, rushed through the granting of independence in a few months. The result was chaos and great loss of lives. At one point, Belgium tried to support a puppet government in Katanga, a mineral-rich province, but this failed, as did UN attempts to restore order. The area was in reality abandoned to its problems, which continued through to the 1990s. It is the classic example of the gulf between the theory of European imperial responsibility to the governed and the reality of exploitation and neglect. For the context, see the entries on *European Empires* and *decolonization*.

Belgium: an independent kingdom of great strategic importance, having common frontiers with France and Germany, and being situated directly across the English Channel from the Thames estuary. Its neutrality had been guaranteed by international treaty in 1839.

- In 1914, it became the German *Schlieffen Plan* invasion route to attack France, which helped to bring Britain into the First World War. The Belgians fought on the Allied side, and the Western Front straddled the country, causing immense destruction to its towns and countryside
- In 1940, when the Germans invaded again, the Belgian king, Leopold III, at once surrendered and spent the war as a prisoner, his country occu-

pied by the German army. The continuing unpopularity of his surrender forced him to abdicate in 1951

- During the Second World War, a Belgian government in exile continued to organize resistance from London, and Belgium was liberated following the Allied invasion of the Continent in 1944.

The monarchy survived the abdication of Leopold and, under his son *Baudouin I*, provided a focus of loyalty as post-war divisions between French- and Flemish-speaking parts of the country became more acute. Concessions on the dual use of language on public signs and more regional autonomy did not automatically remove ethnic tensions.

Belgium was, from the first, an active participant in the moves to closer European integration, joining the Benelux Customs Union from which emerged the European Community, later the European Union. Brussels became the site of the headquarters of the European Commission and other agencies. Belgium was a founding member of NATO in 1949, but ceased to be an imperial power with the granting of independence both to the *Belgian Congo* in 1960 and to its League of Nations mandated territories, Rwanda and Burundi, in 1962.

Belsen: infamous Nazi German *concentration camp*. The medical experiments conducted on prisoners there were the subject of post-war trials at Nuremberg.

Benelux Union: a customs union formed in 1948 by *Belgium, Holland* and *Luxembourg*. In 1960, it became the Benelux Economic Union between the three countries, which allowed free movement of people and capital as well as trade. It marked one of the first moves towards European economic union.

Beneš, Eduard: president of *Czechoslovakia*, 1935–38 and 1945–48:

- In the First World War, he helped to organize a Czech army to fight on the side of the Western Allies
- From 1919, he was Czech foreign secretary until he succeeded *Masaryk* as president, and was throughout a strong supporter of the League of Nations
- In 1938, he resigned as president in protest against the *Munich Agreement*
- During the Second World War, he led a Czech government in exile, returning to Czechoslovakia in 1945
- In 1948, he refused to sign the communist constitution imposed on the country by *Gottwald*, and resigned, dying later in the year.

Berchtesgaden: a village in the Bavarian Alps which became Hitler's favorite place for rest and relaxation, and where he stayed regularly with close followers both before and during the Second World War.

Beria, Lavrenti: the ruthless head of the Soviet *NKVD* secret police from 1938, taking a major role in the *Great Purge* of the late 1930s. He organized Soviet concentration camps for Stalin. After Stalin's death in 1953, he was caught up in the leadership struggle. He was arrested, tried secretly on a charge of conspiracy against the state, and executed.

Berlin: capital of the German Second Empire, 1871–1918. The *Weimar Republic* restored Berlin as the capital after the initial constitution-making sessions at Weimar which had given the new state its name. The Nazis adorned Berlin with grandiose architectural projects, notably the stadium where the 1936 Olympic Games were held. At the end of the Second World War, the city had been largely reduced to rubble, and the final acts of the Third Reich were played out there as Soviet troops fought street by street to occupy it and leading Nazis, including Hitler, committed suicide in the city.

After 1945

Berlin was well within the Soviet *zone of occupation* of Germany but was itself divided into four occupation zones: Soviet, American, British and French.

- It was the setting in 1948 for one of the most dramatic episodes of the developing *Cold War*: the *Berlin Blockade* and associated *Berlin Airlift*
- As the Cold War became more intractable, the three Western zones worked more closely together and handed over internal city administration to elected German leaders but did not incorporate their Berlin zones into the German Federal Republic (West Germany), from which they were separated by the Soviet zone of occupation
- The Soviet zone in Berlin was treated by its occupying force as the capital of the German Democratic Republic (East Germany), which had been formed in 1949 from the Soviet zone of occupation of Germany
- The frontier across central Berlin became one of the most sensitive in the Cold War, and in 1961 the city was physically divided when the East German authorities built the heavily fortified and guarded *Berlin Wall* along it in order to stop the flight of so many of their citizens to the West.

In 1989, as reform swept the Soviet bloc, the East German regime opened the wall and the crowds streamed across it in the most powerful of all the symbols of the end of the Cold War. Citizens from both sides of the wall then proceeded to knock it down, stone by stone. By 1990, the two Germanys were reunited, and a decision was taken that Berlin would, by 2000, again become the seat of government of a united Germany.

Berlin Airlift: the US and British response, from August 1948 to May 1949, to the Soviet *Berlin Blockade* of land transport to the American, British and French occupation zones. The air forces, despite some Soviet harassment and several air crashes, ferried in 2 million metric tons of food and fuel and enabled the Western presence in Berlin to be maintained. Despite the fact that in May 1949 Stalin had called off the blockade, which had become a major trial of strength and determination between East and West, the episode hardened *Cold War* attitudes on both sides.

Berlin–Baghdad Railway: a German engineering project, running through the Ottoman Empire, which caused international alarm before the First World War. It was once seen as an important factor in bringing about the war, but in fact both Britain and Russia had earlier been satisfied that their own interests were not endangered. Only a small part of the railway as originally projected was ever built.

Berlin Blockade: the Soviet blockade of the land routes to the Western zones of Berlin. It lasted from August 1948 to May 1949, and was an attempt to prevent Western reform of the German currency, which the Soviets did not wish to allow into their occupation zone. It was seen in the West as a Soviet Cold War attempt to drive them out of Berlin. The blockade led to the *Berlin Airlift*.

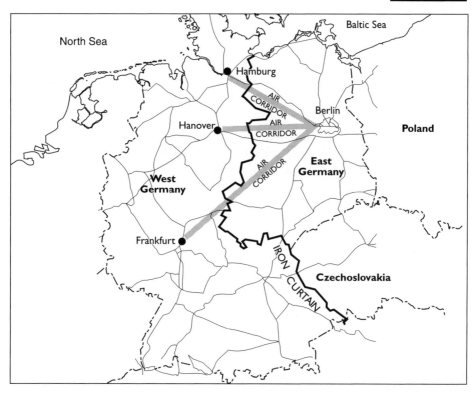

| *The Berlin Airlift*

Berlin Bunker: the underground headquarters of Hitler in the center of Berlin. On 30 April 1945, with Soviet troops only one street away, he committed suicide there.

Berlin Treaty: of 1926, between the Weimar Republic and the Soviet Union. It strengthened the cooperation first established at the treaty of *Rapallo.* At Berlin, each power pledged to remain neutral in the event of the other being involved in a war with other powers. The treaty, part of *Stresemann*'s policy of improving relations with both East and West, was widely welcomed in Weimar Germany and marked a further stage in the improved international status enjoyed by the Weimar Republic in the late 1920s.

Berlin Wall: the wall along the frontier between East and West Berlin. It was built by *East Germany* in 1961 at the height of the *Cold War* in order to stop the flight of increasing numbers of its citizens to the West. The wall:

- was heavily fortified with barbed wire, minefields and sentry boxes manned by armed troops and police
- caused many deaths as East Berliners persisted in trying to cross it
- led to the brutal physical division of the city, becoming a potent symbol of a Europe divided by the rivalries of the Cold War.

By 1989, the flood of East Germans crossing the Austrian frontier to the West became unstoppable, and the East German government abandoned the need for exit visas and opened crossing points in the wall. Amid emotional scenes of rejoicing, citizens of the two parts of Berlin mingled. They then started to tear down the wall, and soon official plans were drawn up for its total destruction. The end of the wall symbolized the collapse of the Soviet communist empire in Eastern Europe, and could never have happened without that collapse.

Berlusconi, Silvio: Italian prime minister, May–December 1994. The millionaire television-station owner promised a new political start for Italy, but his government collapsed when he faced corruption charges – and this after much had been made of the radical reorganization of the political system between 1992 and 1994. Berlusconi's career seemed to sum up the chronic political instability that had plagued Italy for so long.

Bernadotte, Count Folke: a Swedish diplomat who carried out international humanitarian work for the Red Cross during both world wars. In 1945, Himmler asked him to take peace proposals to the Allies. After the Second World War, he worked for the UN, and was murdered by Israeli terrorists in 1948.

Bethlen, Count István: prime minister of Hungary, 1921–31. He was a leading supporter of Admiral *Horthy*, and followed reactionary policies aimed at maintaining aristocratic privileges. He died, a Soviet prisoner, in 1944.

Bethmann-Hollweg, Theobald von: chancellor of the *German Second Empire*, 1909–17. He was inexperienced in foreign and military affairs, which allowed the military leaders undue influence over policy. He sought unsuccessfully from 1909 to 1912 to restrict *Tirpitz*'s naval building program in the hope that this might lead to better relations with Britain. His government greatly increased the German army, and he believed that a war on at least one of Germany's frontiers was inevitable, which led him, in July 1914, to promise support to Austria-Hungary. It was for this reason that the German historian Fritz *Fischer* held him responsible for the outbreak of war. He mistakenly hoped that Britain would not become involved, and to this end, and even as the armies moved forward, he was promising both to restore Belgian independence and not to annex French territory. Once war came, his position was undermined by the growing power of the German military leaders, and his tentative peace feelers to Russia came to nothing. He retired in 1917 and died in 1921.

Bevin, Ernest: British foreign secretary, 1945–51. He had been a pre-war trade-union leader, and from 1940 served in Churchill's wartime coalition government. Soon after the Second World War, he became strongly opposed to Soviet policies in Europe.

- He saw Western Europe as being wide open to communist subversion and to the advances of the Red Army
- With Prime Minister Attlee, he worked to keep an American presence in Europe to meet this threat
- He committed British troops in the *Greek Civil War* to help the Greek royal government against the communist partisans who had fought the German army of occupation and who now sought to take control of the country.

When Britain could no longer provide the military and economic help needed in Greece, it was Bevin who pressed the US government to take on the protection of the free nations of Europe, and this in turn led to the *Marshall Plan* and the *Truman Doctrine*, to both of which Bevin gave prompt and firm support. Bevin was important in the founding of *NATO*, but his American links and his strong feelings for the Commonwealth left him cold towards the idea of European union. In all these respects, he was a key formulator of British foreign policy in a number of important areas. It was also largely his decision in 1947 to end the British mandate in Palestine.

Bidault, Georges: prime minister of France during the Fourth Republic in 1946, 1949–50 and 1958. He supported moves towards European cooperation but opposed de Gaulle over the Algerian War and, accused of plotting against the security of the state, went into exile from 1962 to 1968.

bilateral: involving two parties – for example, a trade treaty between just two countries.

Bismarck, Otto von: arguably the founder of the *German Second Empire* in 1871. After the unification of Germany, he built up an elaborate alliance system to keep France isolated and so unable to take revenge for its military defeat and the loss of Alsace-Lorraine in 1870. He retained alliances with both Austria-Hungary and Russia, though rivalry between these two countries meant that the Russian alliance looked increasingly precarious. He was abruptly dismissed in 1890 by Kaiser *William II*. German foreign policy then took a more adventurous turn, and Russia drew closer to France. Bismarck's alliance with Austria-Hungary, however, survived his fall and took both countries into the First World War. Bismarck died in 1898.

Björko, Treaty of: a 1905 treaty signed by Kaiser William II of Germany and Tsar Nicholas II of Russia while on the former's yacht. They agreed to give each other full support in the event of war. Neither German nor Russian diplomats approved of this hasty piece of personal diplomacy, and the French, who were supposed to be brought into it, were hostile, saying that an agreement of this sort with Germany was impossible. The treaty was never ratified, and relations between Germany and Russia worsened.

Black Hand: a Serbian terrorist organization founded 1911. It was committed to gaining the Austrian provinces of Bosnia and Herzegovina, annexed in 1908, for Serbia by any means, and by this contributed greatly to the poor relations between Serbia and Austria-Hungary. It has been held responsible for the 1914 assassination of Archduke *Franz Ferdinand*, but its members were not involved – though its founder, the head of Serbian intelligence, Colonel *Dimitrievitch*, had recruited and armed those who were.

blackshirts: a popular name given to the *Squadristi*, the paramilitary supporters of *Mussolini*. They wore blackshirts as a military-style uniform, and from 1919 used street violence to fight left-wing opponents. They became the volunteer militia of the Italian Fascist Party, and were important in helping Mussolini both to intimidate potential opponents and to impress the lukewarm with the virility of fascism.

Blair, Tony: prime minister of Britain, 1997–. He led the Labour Party to a landslide election victory in May 1997, ending 18 years of Conservative government.

However, Britain's relationship with Europe, which had bitterly divided the previous Conservative administration, continued to be a major preoccupation.

blitz: a British term, derived from *blitzkrieg*, used to describe German bomber attacks on British cities, particularly on London in 1940–41.

blitzkrieg: meaning "lightning war," used to describe German military tactics in the early stages of the Second World War. The tactics were based on the use of swift-moving tanks and motorized infantry on a narrow front, splitting the enemy lines and allowing rapid penetration to the unprotected territories beyond. Supported by *dive-bombers*, the tactics were used to great effect in the invasions of Poland and France in 1939 and 1940.

bloc: a combination of countries or parties, to promote some interest that they have in common.

Blomberg, Werner von: commander-in-chief of the German army, 1933–38. He congratulated Hitler on the events of the *Night of the Long Knives* and supported him loyally thereafter. In 1938, Hitler reluctantly dismissed him over a personal scandal relating to his wife, and then took the opportunity to assume personal command of the armed forces and to establish the *OKW* as his own command structure over the military.

Bloody Sunday (Northern Ireland): the name given to the incident when, on 30 January 1972, British troops, facing growing disorder, opened fire on a Catholic civil-rights march in Northern Ireland, and 13 people were killed.

Bloody Sunday (Russia): the name given to the events outside St. Petersburg's Winter Palace in January 1905. Following days of strikes, and against the background of defeat in the *Russo–Japanese War*, a crowd of over 200,000, led by Father *Gapon*, gathered outside the royal palace.

- It was a peaceful demonstration intent on presenting a petition to Tsar Nicholas II for social and constitutional reforms, and many sang hymns and carried pictures of the tsar, who had in fact left the palace the previous day
- The palace guards panicked, tried to break up the crowd with whips and then swords, and finally opened fire.

Even official figures admitted to 130 dead and 300 wounded, and the massacre destroyed much of the popular respect for the tsar. It was followed by widespread strikes and street disorder in the cities and peasant uprisings in the countryside, and led on to the *Potemkin Mutiny* and unrest in Poland. The nationwide troubles resumed in the autumn and became known as the *Revolution of 1905*.

Blum, Léon: prime minister of France in 1936 and 1946–47. His 1936 government was a left-wing *Popular Front* coalition of the radicals, the socialists and the communists. The disagreements between the coalition partners over what action, if any, to take over the Spanish Civil War illustrate the difficulties that even committed opponents had in taking a stand against fascist expansionism. The radicals refused to support intervention, and the communists left the government because of the failure to intervene. During the Second World War, Blum, a Jew, was interned in German concentration camps. After the war, he was again briefly prime minister and played a part in establishing the *Fourth French Republic*.

Boer War: the war between Britain and the Boer republics in South Africa, 1899–1902. It required a major and prolonged commitment of men and resources, including the creation of the first concentration camps for civilians, for Britain to defeat the Boers.

- Many of those who volunteered to join the British army were found to be unfit to serve
- International, and particularly German, opinion openly favored the Boers
- The war provided a sharp jolt to British imperial complacency, and was one reason for a renewed interest in searching for allies, which led to the Anglo–Japanese Treaty of 1902.

The course of the Boer War gave some of the earliest indications that the great days of European imperial expansion might not be indefinitely prolonged.

Bolshevik: a member of the majority wing of the Russian Social Democratic Party which, from 1903, favored revolutionary tactics in the search for political power. It is often more loosely used by opponents to describe any socialist extremist.

Bolshevik Party: the Russian political party founded by *Lenin* in 1912. At a London meeting of the exiled Russian Social Democratic Party in 1903, the majority, the Bolsheviks, voted to follow Lenin's view that the party should be an élitist one of dedicated revolutionaries rather than a mass party committed to gradual change as advocated by the minority, or *Mensheviks.* The party then split, with both branches calling themselves Social Democrats until, in 1912, Lenin founded the Bolshevik Party.

- In the *April Theses* of 1917, Lenin spelled out both the party's strategy to gain immediate power and its radical political program
- Party membership increased tenfold to a quarter of a million in the next months
- The Bolsheviks seized power in Russia in the *October Revolution* of 1917.

The term "Communist" was added to the party's title in 1919, and, increasingly referred to as the Communist Party and structured around the principles of *democratic centralism,* it ruled the Soviet Union until 1990, dropping Bolshevik from its title in 1952.

bolshevism: a common term to describe what opponents see as extreme socialism.

Bonhoeffer, Dietrich: a German Protestant theologian. He became the leading Christian spokesman against the Nazi regime. He left Germany in 1933 but returned in 1935 to work within the German Confessional Church until, in 1937, this was closed down by the Nazis – and this after most of the larger German Christian churches had made agreements with the Nazi regime. He then became involved in the German resistance movement and, in 1943, carried secret unofficial peace proposals to the Allies on behalf of Admiral *Canaris,* which were rejected. He was hanged in 1945 for alleged involvement in the 1944 *July Plot.* His reputation as a Christian thinker, based on his many books, grew rapidly after the Second World War.

Bonomi, Ivanoe: prime minister of Italy, June 1921–February 1922, immediately prior to *Facta* whose fall led to Mussolini taking office. His brief, impotent ministry illustrates the drift among democratic politicians as post-war Italy grappled with disillusionment and corruption.

Bormann, Martin: a German Nazi leader. He was an extremist on racial issues, advocating the extermination of the Jews and other "inferior races" and also leading the Nazi attack on the Christian churches. He joined Hitler's staff in 1928 and later worked for Hess, succeeding him as head of the chancellory in 1941. Bormann disappeared in 1945, and there were persistent rumors that he had escaped to South America. In 1973, however, his skeleton was identified in Berlin, and the West German government declared itself satisfied that he had, in 1945, followed Hitler's example and committed suicide.

Bosnia and Herzegovina: a Balkan province legally under Turkish sovereignty but occupied and administered by the *Austro-Hungarian Empire* from 1878 and formally annexed to that empire in 1908. It had a large *Slav* population, and the annexation led to the *Bosnian Crisis*, a significant step in the deteriorating international relations in the Balkans prior to the First World War.

- In 1914, after the assassination of *Franz Ferdinand* at *Sarajevo*, the capital of Bosnia, events quickly escalated into the First World War
- From 1919, Bosnia and Herzegovina formed part of the Yugoslav kingdom and were, during the Second World War, the scene of much bitter fighting by Yugoslav partisans against the German occupying army
- From 1945, the province formed one of the six republics which made up the communist federal state of Yugoslavia.

After the death of Tito in 1980, strong separatist tendencies emerged in Bosnia, as elsewhere in Yugoslavia. The republic declared its independence in 1991, which was supported by a 1992 referendum. Independence had been supported by two ethnic groups, the Muslims and the Croats, but was rejected by the Serbs, who made up one-third of the population and who wanted to be part of a Greater Serbia.

Civil war, accompanied by mass atrocities, famine and much material destruction, began in 1992.

- For a long time, the initiative lay with the Serbs, and outside intervention, both by the UN and then by NATO forces, could provide no basis for restoring peace
- In 1993–94, economic sanctions on the rump of the Yugoslav Republic, centered on Belgrade, forced the Serbs there to cease equipping the Serbs in Bosnia and persuaded them to put pressure on the latter to accept a compromise territorial settlement.

In 1996, NATO negotiated and set out to police a peace deal between the ethnic groups. Among the most intractable problems they faced in maintaining a desperately fragile peace were:

- the status of Sarajevo, the old provincial capital, which none of the parties wished to abandon but where they were unable to live at peace with one another
- the wish to identify and prosecute alleged war criminals for the atrocities committed. In practice, this came to center on alleged Serb atrocities and

a repeated demand that the Bosnian Serb leader *Karadžić* stand trial. The Serbs were unlikely to agree to this.

Events after 1990 illustrated both the structural weaknesses there had been across Tito's Yugoslavia and also how remarkable his achievement had been in building and holding the state together for so long.

Bosnian Crisis: the Balkan crisis of 1908–9. Austria-Hungary decided to absorb its protectorate of *Bosnia* and *Herzegovina*, with its largely Slav population, into its empire, and Germany gave full backing to this, if necessary to the point of war. This was a dangerous extension of its commitments to Austria-Hungary, which ended in a blunt German ultimatum to Russia that it must accept the annexation or face the consequences. The outcome of the crisis was that:

- the annexation was completed but Russia was left deeply humiliated
- relations between Serbia and Austria-Hungary were further soured
- tensions in the Balkans and between the great powers were greatly increased.

It would have been difficult, if not impossible, for Russia to back down again in its commitment to the protection of the Slav race, and following the 1914 assassination of *Franz Ferdinand* at *Sarajevo*, this commitment was to prove decisive in the sequence of events leading to the outbreak of the First World War.

bourgeoisie: the middle class. "Bourgeois" means "associated with the middle class" or "conventional." The term is usually used in a derogatory sense arising from Marxist writing contrasting the bourgeoisie with the proletariat, or working class, to whom the future belonged.

Brandt, Willy: chancellor of West Germany, 1969–74. Milestones in his political career included:

- his public opposition to the Nazis, which forced him to live in exile from 1932 to 1945, during which time he linked up with the wartime German resistance movement from neutral Sweden
- living in West Berlin after 1945, and becoming its mayor from 1957 to 1966, having to cope in 1961 with the crisis surrounding the building of the Berlin Wall
- being chairman of the West German *Social Democratic Party* (SPD) from 1964 to 1987. The party had been kept out of office since the foundation of West Germany by Adenauer's Christian Democratic Party (CDU). Brandt, with his record of opposing communism in Berlin, played a key role in making the SPD more electable throughout West Germany as it shed its pro-Marxist image
- becoming foreign minister in 1966 in a coalition government under Kiesinger of the CDU.

The SPD's success in the 1969 election owed much to the public's perception of Brandt's leadership qualities, and he was able to form a coalition government with the Free Democrats, ending the CDU's domination of political power.

As chancellor, his most distinctive achievement was the development of the policy of *Ostpolitik*, which marked a more cordial relationship with the countries of Eastern Europe. In:

- 1970: he agreed with the Soviet Union to accept the political frontiers drawn across Eastern Europe at the end of the Second World War, something Adenauer had always refused to do
- 1971: he reached an agreement with the Soviet Union on the status of Berlin
- 1972: he acknowledged Poland's western frontier along the *Oder–Neisse Line* and signed non-aggression pacts with both Poland and the Soviet Union
- 1972: in the *Basic Treaty*, he recognized the existence of the German Democratic Republic and opened diplomatic relations with it.

In domestic matters, there was more emphasis on continuity with the policies pursued by Adenauer. He felt forced to resign in 1974 over a spy scandal in his political office. In 1980, he gave his name to the international *Brandt Report* on development issues.

Brandt Report: the 1980 report to the UN on the state of the world economy. The commission which drew it up was chaired by the West German political leader Willy *Brandt*. Its formal title, NORTH AND SOUTH: A PROGRAM FOR SURVIVAL, indicated its central message that urgent action must be taken to reduce the gross imbalance in wealth and trade between the rich north and the poor south. When little was done about the recommendations, the commission's members, in 1983, issued a second, even gloomier report.

Brauchitsch, Walter von: commander-in-chief of the German army during the *blitzkrieg* attacks of 1939–40 and an enthusiastic supporter of Hitler. He was dismissed by Hitler in 1941 because of the German failure to capture Moscow.

Braun, Eva: Hitler's mistress from the early 1930s. He married her in 1945, just hours before their joint suicide in the *Berlin Bunker*. She played no part in the public life of the Nazi state, and apparently had no influence on Hitler's attitudes or actions.

Brest-Litovsk, Treaty of: a treaty in March 1918 between the new Bolshevik rulers of Russia and the governments of Germany and Austria-Hungary. It ended the war on the *Eastern Front*.

- In order to secure peace, the Bolsheviks had to surrender nearly half of Russia's European lands, including Finland, the Baltic Republics, Poland and the Ukraine
- The treaty was declared void at the *Paris Peace Conference*, but the Bolsheviks managed to regain only the Ukraine
- The terms of the treaty pushed the western frontier of Russia hundreds of miles further east than it had been in 1914.

This was a price that Lenin and Trotsky, the chief Russian delegate at the peace conference, were prepared to pay to end the war and be free to consolidate the Bolshevik state. For the Allies on the Western Front, the treaty was seen as a betrayal and became one more grievance against the Bolsheviks.

Bretton Woods Agreement: an agreement reached in 1944 to stabilize world currencies and provide credit for international trade after the Second World War.

At the conference, plans were laid for the creation of the *World Bank* and the *International Monetary Fund*, both of which became agencies of the UN.

Brezhnev, Leonid: a Soviet politician. In 1964, he succeeded *Khrushchev* as first secretary of the Communist Party and soon became the key figure in the government of the Soviet Union, though he shared power with *Podgorny* until 1977 and with *Kosygin* until 1980. These three men initiated policies of cautious change in the Soviet Union. Brezhnev condemned many of Khrushchev's reforms as adventurism, but:

- civil liberties which did not injure society were guaranteed
- Khrushchev's attacks on religion came to an end
- welfare facilities were improved
- peasant standards of living in particular were raised
- the average hours worked in industry fell sharply.

The *command economy* and the Communist Party's monopoly of political power were, however, preserved and both agriculture and industry remained inefficient. In lean years, the Soviet Union became increasingly dependent on grain imports. Military expenditure remained a great burden on the economy and restricted the opportunity to invest elsewhere. Few of the country's economic problems were addressed, and Brezhnev and his compatriots sought political stability by:

- maintaining a prison- and labor-camp population of around 2 million
- strict control of the press and other media so that the people learned only that which the authorities wished them to know.

They were prepared to pay the price of economic stagnation in order to achieve political quiet. It was only some years after Brezhnev's death, when *Gorbachev* wished to pursue radically different policies, that his achievement began to be questioned in the Soviet Union.

Brezhnev was especially interested in foreign policy:

- In 1968, he was largely responsible for the Warsaw Pact decision to invade *Czechoslovakia*, preferring this to any disintegration in the Soviet hold over Eastern Europe, and promulgating the *Brezhnev Doctrine* to justify the action
- In the early 1970s, he contributed to the policy of détente which led to the 1972 *SALT* I agreement
- In 1979, he sent Red Army troops into *Afghanistan*, in what became a lengthy, and ultimately unsuccessful, commitment to help the communist government there and so protect the Soviet Union's long Central Asian frontier. This Afghanistan adventure revived all the bitter hostilities of the *Cold War.*

Brezhnev's legacy

This long period of rule by old men who evaded their responsibility to modernize the Soviet Union, along with the strain of the defense budgets necessitated by the Afghanistan War, made a major contribution to the problems facing their successors, and indeed contributed to the eventual disintegration of the Soviet Union from 1989 onwards. Brezhnev died in 1982, and only more than 10 years later did it emerge that since 1973 he had been seriously ill with cerebral sclerosis and that he had been fed excessive doses of tranquillizers for this condition, which had in turn damaged his central nervous system. *Andropov* and others had covered up his state of health lest they be accused of political conspiracy against him. His illness contributed to the state of drift at the top of the Soviet Union government in that period.

Brezhnev Doctrine: this asserted the right of socialist states to interfere in any state where the socialist system was threatened. The doctrine was developed by the Soviet politician Brezhnev to justify the 1968 invasion of Czechoslovakia by the *Warsaw Pact* countries at the time of the *Prague Spring*, but was tacitly abandoned by Gorbachev when, in 1989, Soviet control over the communist countries of Eastern Europe disintegrated.

Briand, Aristide: eleven times prime minister of France and a major 1920s figure in European international relations.

- In 1921–22, he criticized French demands for retribution against the Germans, and his government fell as a result
- He was largely responsible for two of the most successful international initiatives of the decade, the *Locarno Pact* of 1925 and the *Kellogg–Briand Pact* of 1929, and thus played a large part in restoring stability to relations between European states.

His plan for a Union of European States remained a dream, and he died in 1932 just before the fragile nature of his work for peace was cruelly exposed by the new adventurism of Hitler and Mussolini.

Britain: the brief form of *Great Britain*, and often also for the *United Kingdom*.

Britain, Battle of: the air battles of August to October 1940 between the British Royal Air Force and the German Luftwaffe. They followed the surrender of France and the retreat from *Dunkirk*.

- German planes attacked shipping and targets in southern England, and were resisted by some 700 Hurricane and Spitfire fighters
- Many German bombers and fighters were shot down, though British claims on numbers made at the time were exaggerated
- In the early stages, military installations, and particularly airfields, were prime bombing targets
- After more than 50 bombers were shot down on 15 September, Hitler ordered the attacks to be switched to British cities, first by day and then, as losses remained high, by night
- In the battle, the British lost 900 planes, while the numerically superior Luftwaffe lost almost 1,700. The newly installed *radar* system had played a large part in the British victory.

The German attempt to destroy British air power had failed, and in October, Germany's invasion plans had to be postponed. They were never reactivated. The German defeat, its first in the Second World War, meant that it was not able to capitalize on its earlier triumphs on the Western Front. It also meant the indefinite prolongation of the war, with the resources of both countries totally committed to victory. *Churchill*, the master propagandist, in perhaps his most famous speech to the British House of Commons, summed up the results of the battle and the British debt to those who had won it in a few words: "Never in the field of human conflict was so much owed by so many to so few."

British: an adjective used to identify Great Britain or the United Kingdom, as in "the British government." It is not interchangeable, as the Scots, Welsh and some Northern Irish will quickly point out, with "English." Unfortunately, some similar usages have become so established – for example, the "Anglo–Japanese Treaty of 1902" or the "Anglo–French Entente," both of these the work of the British government – that to change them to any other form would cause confusion.

British Empire: British possessions overseas which, at their zenith after the First World War, covered a quarter of the world.

- Before 1900, responsible government had been granted to Australia, Canada, New Zealand and South Africa
- By 1931, all these had become self-governing dominions with control of their own foreign policy.

The territories with significant numbers of non-white inhabitants, however, continued to be governed as colonies by London-appointed administrators, with the *British Raj* in India having quite separate and distinctive relations with Britain from those of the other territories. In the late nineteenth century, the main imperial expansion had been in Africa, but dreams of controlling all the land from the Cape of Good Hope to Cairo faded after the *Boer War* of 1899–1902. After the First World War, German and Turkish territories, particularly in Africa and the Middle East, were added as *mandates* to the empire, which at that point reached its maximum size.

In the 1930s, the issue of how to defend its imperial possessions if Britain became involved in another European war caused great concern and encouraged the government in its policy of *appeasement*. The empire had begun to be seen as a burden, as well as a source of pride and strength. From 1931, the empire was commonly referred to as the *Commonwealth of Nations*.

After 1945

The Second World War weakened Britain's ability, and perhaps also its will, to continue shouldering imperial responsibilities, and after 1945 a process of *decolonization* began, which was virtually complete by 1980. This paralleled Britain's somewhat reluctant search for a new role in Europe.

- In 1947, British India was granted independence by the new Labour government
- In 1948, Britain pulled out of its troublesome Palestine mandate
- Britain fought a successful jungle war to prevent a communist takeover of Malaya, but as part of the strategy of denying the communists control, it was then happy to concede independence to the country in 1957.

The outcome of the 1956 *Suez Crisis* destroyed many of Britain's imperial illusions, and the pace of decolonization quickened:

- From 1957 to 1966, 11 British colonies in Africa were granted independence

- From 1962 to 1966, so were all the significant island colonies of the West Indies. The smaller West Indian islands and the small Pacific island colonies followed in the 1970s.

By the 1970s, the world's greatest empire had all but disappeared. The white settlers of Rhodesia created a hiccup, but had become part of an independent Zimbabwe by 1980. Gibraltar remained to trouble relations with Spain, the Falkland Islands to provoke war with Argentina in 1982, and Hong Kong to be surrendered to China in 1997.

The end of the British Empire can be explained by:

- the build-up of demands for independence in the colonies
- the realization in Britain that, in the aftermath of the Second World War, it could no longer afford to defend its colonial territories against the aspirations of their own inhabitants
- the loss of will to continue as an imperial power once the decolonization process had begun. This does much to account for the rapid decolonization of the 1960s
- the fact that the ending of the British Empire was part of a wider movement affecting all the *European empires.*

British Expeditionary Force (BEF): an army group formed in August 1914 from the territorial reserve army created by *Haldane* in 1906. The BEF fought in France and Belgium in the autumn of 1914, halting the German advance to the Channel ports and suffering a very high level of casualties.

British Raj: a term for the British Empire in India:

- it was headed by a viceroy with direct access to the British cabinet
- it involved a vast bureaucracy and a large standing army to rule some three-fifths of the Indian subcontinent
- the remaining areas were ruled by independent princes, who were bound by treaties with the British crown.

In the 1920s and 1930s, movements emerged to press for Indian independence, and these were much strengthened during the Second World War. Britain withdrew totally in 1947, when the independent nations of India and Pakistan replaced British India. This marked the first significant decline from the high watermark of empire so recently reached.

brownshirts: members of the *SA*, a Nazi paramilitary movement.

Brüning, Heinrich: chancellor of the *Weimar Republic*, 1930–32. He was leader of the Catholic Center Party. His unpopular deflationary policies failed to solve the economic problems arising from the worldwide onset of the Great Depression. After the 1930 election, he frequently had to rule by undemocratic means through emergency decrees under *Article 48* of the Weimar constitution. After losing President Hindenburg's support, he was forced to resign in 1932. Both his methods and his failed economic policies played a part in Hitler's rise to power. He left Germany in 1934, returning only in 1951. He died in 1970.

Brusilov, Aleksei: a Russian general who, in 1916, launched the so-called *Brusilov Offensive.* During the February Revolution of 1917, he persuaded Tsar Nicholas II not to bombard Petrograd. He became supreme commander of the armies of the Provisional Government and later held senior rank in the Bolshevik Red Army, dying in 1926.

Brusilov Offensive: a Russian attack in 1916 on the Austro-Hungarian forces on the southern section of the *Eastern Front*. It was an attempt to relieve pressure on France and Britain on the *Western Front* which proved costly but was partially success-ful. The even heavier losses inflicted on the Austro-Hungarian forces did much to undermine their will to continue the war.

Brussels Treaty Organization: set up in 1948 between Belgium, Britain, France, Holland and Luxembourg to promote defense and economic cooperation. It was superseded by the *Western European Union* in 1954.

Bucharest, Treaty of: the treaty which, in 1913, ended the Second *Balkan War*. This was largely at the expense of Bulgaria, which had been defeated by its former allies in the Balkan League.

buffer state: a small country between two powerful ones. Its existence was thought to reduce the chance of war between them.

Bukharin, Nikolai: a Soviet leader and thinker. Active in the *October Revolution*, he became a close friend of Lenin. He wrote many books on communist theory and strongly defended the *New Economic Policy*, arguing, as at that time did Stalin, against the collectivization of agriculture.

- In 1928, Stalin changed his views on collectivization; Bukharin opposed him and was expelled from the Politburo
- In 1937, at the time of Stalin's notorious purges of political opponents, Bukharin was expelled from the Communist Party
- In 1938, in the first trial of the *Great Purge*, he was tried for espionage and executed.

Bukharin was later regarded as perhaps the most famous and most able of the victims of Stalin's lust for total power.

Bulganin, Nikolai: a Soviet politician. Once a member of the Cheka secret police and, in the 1930s, mayor of Moscow. He organized the city's defense during the Second World War, and from 1946 was Soviet minister of defense. He was Soviet premier from 1955 to 1958, when he shared power with Khrushchev, attending an international summit meeting in 1955. He was displaced by Khrushchev in 1958.

Bulgaria: until 1908, part of the Ottoman Empire; from 1908, an independent Balkan state. It fought on the German side in both world wars. From 1946, it was a communist state firmly established within the Soviet bloc until, in 1989, popular disturbances led to the collapse of the communist regime, after which:

- in 1990, other political parties were made legal, and the forces of repression, like the secret police, were disbanded
- following the 1990 elections, a multi-party coalition government even-tually emerged and embarked on a program of economic and political reform
- in 1992, this was replaced by a second, weak, reforming coalition govern-ment

- in 1994, with its reforms incomplete, this was in turn defeated by the Bulgarian Socialist Party, made up largely of ex-communists.

The future direction of the state was at that point far from clear.

Bulge, Battle of: a Second World War battle fought at the end of 1944 as the result of a German counter-attack into Belgium. It is also known as the *Ardennes Campaign.*

Bülow, Bernhard von: chancellor of Germany, 1900–09. In foreign policy he:

- turned down unofficial overtures from Britain for a defensive alliance in 1900–01, fearing that Germany would have to bear the brunt of any war against Russia, and swayed by the strong anti-British feeling in Germany
- pandered to Kaiser *William II*'s wish for glory abroad and supported *Tirpitz*'s naval building programs, arguing that the latter was needed to protect Germany's overseas trade and colonies
- forced the French in 1906 to accept the *Algeciras Conference* on Morocco, only to see this diplomatic triumph turned to ashes when the main result of the conference was to bring Britain and France closer together
- assured Austria-Hungary in 1908 that it could rely on German support for whatever action was felt necessary against Serbia in the *Bosnian Crisis,* persuading Kaiser William II that this was essential. This marked a dangerous extension of Germany's commitment to Austria. It also antagonized Russia, and in 1914, left Germany with little choice but to back the Austrians again as events raced towards the First World War.

Bülow also had difficulty holding together support in the *Reichstag,* and found an active foreign policy a convenient way of keeping support both there and among the electorate. His political career illustrated the way in which, in the years before 1914, domestic and foreign policies came together to create international tension in Europe. After losing the confidence of the kaiser, he resigned in 1909, expecting to be recalled, but this did not happen and he was succeeded by *Bethmann-Hollweg.*

Bundestag: the lower house of the West German Parliament. In practice, as the fully elected house, it retained the initiative in all political matters. Its membership and powers were established by the *Basic Law* of 1948.

C

cabinet: a group of ministers responsible for implementing government policy. It is a British political term for the inner group of senior ministers, and does not comprise the full government.

Cadet Party: a Russian liberal political party at the beginning of the century, Cadet equals KD, translating as Constitutional Democrat. In 1905, it had supported the efforts of the workers who were seeking political reforms, but it then broke ranks and accepted the reforms offered by Nicholas II in the *October Manifesto*, taking part in all four *Dumas* but having little influence on the course of events. The difficulty it had in working with the parties of the left weakened the opposition to the tsarist government. The party became disillusioned by the government's conduct of the war and frustrated at the tsar's refusal to contemplate radical changes in the composition of his government, and thus it welcomed the setting up of the *Provisional Government*. In the December 1917 election following the October Revolution, the party polled only 2 million of the 30 million votes cast, but in any event was barred by the Bolsheviks from attending the only meeting of the *Constituent Assembly* on the grounds that it was a bourgeois party.

Cambon, Paul: the French ambassador to Britain, 1898–1920. He played a large part in the improvement in relations between the two countries, from the depths of the *Fashoda Crisis* of 1898 to the formation of the *entente cordiale* in 1904. He was then deeply involved both in the developing understanding between the two countries, and in the critical days of August 1914 when, to the French government, it seemed that Britain was hesitating to honor its commitments to France.

Cambrai: the place where, on the *Western Front* in November 1915, the first-ever example of successful *tank warfare* occurred. British tanks broke the German lines, but the advantage gained was never exploited and the Germans regained the ground captured.

Campaign for Nuclear Disarmament (CND): a British pressure group, founded in 1958, committed to securing the abandonment of British nuclear weapons.

Canaris, Wilhelm: a German admiral and one-time Nazi. He was, from 1938, the head of German military intelligence, the *Abwehr*, and in this position became leader of the secret German wartime resistance to Hitler. Dietrich *Bonhoeffer* was one of his agents and tried unsuccessfully to open peace negotiations with the Allies for him. He was hanged in 1945, just before Soviet troops entered Berlin, for helping to organize support for the *July Plot* against Hitler.

capitalism: an economic system in which trade and industry are controlled by private owners and for profit. It is also used to refer to a system of society based on this type of economy, and can be contrasted with the state-controlled and -directed economies of communist countries.

capitulation: surrender.

Caporetto, Battle of: a German–Austrian victory in late 1917 against the Italians. It opened up the prospect of an invasion of northern Italy, but the Italians managed to regroup. It is evidence that, even at this late stage of the First World War, there was nothing inevitable about the speed of the eventual Allied victory.

Carmona, Antonio: president of Portugal, 1927–51 and a colleague of the dictator *Salazar.*

Carol II: king of Romania, 1930–40. He set up a fascist-style regime in 1937 but, in 1940, was forced by Hitler to surrender territory to the Soviet Union under the terms of the Nazi–Soviet Pact. He then abdicated.

cartel: the name given to a group of producers who make an agreement to limit output in order to keep prices high. To be able to do this, they must dominate the market for the goods in question. Cartels of great firms were seen as dominating German heavy industry before and after the First World War, and were later held to have had undue political influence. They have been blamed for Germany's desire to build up great armaments prior to 1914, and for their support of right-wing parties, including the Nazis, in the inter-war years.

Casablanca Conference: a conference held in Morocco in January 1943. Churchill and Roosevelt met to plan Second World War strategy and agreed that they would only accept "unconditional surrender" from Germany.

Casement, Roger: an Irish patriot hanged for treason in 1916 by the British. Having failed to obtain German help for an uprising to establish an independent Ireland, he had landed in Ireland from a German submarine in an attempt to have the *Easter Rising* postponed, but was then captured.

Catalan: an inhabitant of the Spanish province of Catalonia. Catalan separatists sought an independent state based on Barcelona; they jealously guarded local customs and deeply distrusted the central government in Madrid. The source of much political violence in the 1920s and 1930s, they were a major destabilizing influence on the 1931–36 Spanish Republic, but once the Spanish Civil War began, they solidly supported the republican side against Franco's forces.

Caudillo, El: the title assumed by *Franco* in 1937 as leader of the nationalist forces in the Spanish Civil War. In Spanish it means "the leader," and from 1947 it was used to indicate Franco's role as the head of the Spanish state.

Cavell, Edith: an English nurse in German-occupied Belgium during the First World War. She helped British and French troops to escape to neutral Holland. She was executed by the Germans in October 1915, an act which attracted international attention, was disapproved of by Kaiser William II and was treated by the Allies as illustrating German barbarity.

Ceaușescu, Nicolae: president of *Romania*, 1967–89. He took an anti-Soviet line which was admired in the West; for example, he opposed the 1968 invasion of Czechoslovakia by the Warsaw Pact nations. His regime:

- was very authoritarian
- was based on an elaborate spy system
- centered on an extravagant personality cult
- came to an end in the *Romanian Revolution.*

He opposed Gorbachev's liberalization policies, and in 1989 savagely repressed popular demonstrations. When the army switched sides, he and his wife were captured, summarily tried and shot in December 1989.

censorship: the suppression of all or part of books, newspapers, films, etc. on the grounds of obscenity or security risks or, particularly in *totalitarian* states, simply because the political views expressed are not acceptable to the state authorities.

Central powers: in Bismarck's *Triple Alliance* of 1882, the term applied to Germany, Austria-Hungary and Italy. During the First World War, when Italy stayed neutral and then joined the *Allies* in 1915, the term was used to describe Germany and Austria-Hungary, and their allies Bulgaria and the Ottoman Empire.

center: usually a reference to middle-of-the-road political parties rather than to the *left* or the *right* in politics.

Center Party: a right-wing but democratic political party in Weimar Germany which relied heavily on the Catholic vote. It was dissolved by the Nazis in 1933.

Cernik, Oldrich: the Czech prime minister, 1968–70. He was associated with *Dubček* in the *Prague Spring* and survived its failure, but only for two years.

Chamberlain, Houston: an English-born author who became a naturalized German in 1916. He was a committed supporter of the idea of the superiority of the *Aryan race*. In his writings, the Germans had a mission to strengthen the Aryan race and to rule over the inferior races, especially the Slavs to the east. His ideas were the inspiration for much of Hitler's half-baked racial theory, though the latter added his own unique form of virulent anti-Semitism.

Chamberlain, Neville: British prime minister, 1937–40. He sought an understanding with Hitler over the latter's territorial demands against *Czechoslovakia*. There was a general desire at the time to avoid war, and Chamberlain's efforts to reach a compromise were hugely popular with the British public. However, when, despite his efforts, war resulted in 1939, this policy of *appeasement* was bitterly condemned to such an extent that the word itself took on a new, loaded meaning as a craven policy which would inevitably lead to disaster.

- In 1938, Chamberlain went three times to Germany to meet Hitler in order to prevent a German military takeover of Czechoslovakia
- At Munich, he and the French prime minister *Daladier*, without consulting the Czechs, made concessions which handed over the western half of the country to Germany
- Deserted by their only potential allies, the Czechs had no choice but to accept the arrangement.

Faced at the time of Munich, and again in the first half of 1939, with Nazi expansionism, Chamberlain's government failed to attempt serious negotiations to bring about an alliance with the Soviet Union. He did nevertheless pledge military support to *Poland*, and this committed Britain to declaring war on Germany in September 1939. The war in the West started quietly, but Chamberlain's complacency was exposed when, in April 1940, Germany invaded Norway and British troops and ships sent there were routed. Many of his own Conservative Party supporters rebelled against him, and he was forced to resign.

His successor, *Churchill*, was the chief author of the case against appeasement, and for decades his criticisms of it held sway. The argument that appeasement was, in the circumstances of the time, a perfectly sensible policy needs to be considered in any judgment on Chamberlain's foreign policy, especially given that Britain in the late 1930s was ill-prepared for war.

Chanak Crisis: an international crisis of 1922 arising from the resurgence of Turkish power. At the Treaty of *Sèvres*, the Turks had been stripped both of large areas of European Turkey west of the Dardanelles strait and of the city of Smyrna (later Izmir) on the western coast of Turkey. Under Mustafa Kemal (later Atatürk), they recaptured Smyrna and moved in on the Dardanelles strait, threatening to cross and retake the lost territories in European Turkey. There was a small British garrison on the strait at Chanak, and the British prime minister *Lloyd George* seemed prepared to use it to resist the Turkish advance. A compromise led to the Treaty of *Lausanne* replacing, to the advantage of the Turks, the terms agreed at Sèvres. His adventurism in this crisis was one reason why Lloyd George lost office.

chancellor: the head of the German government, and the equivalent of the British prime minister. From 1934 to 1945, Hitler combined this post with that of president, using the title of Führer.

Charles I (Karl I): the last Habsburg emperor of Austria-Hungary, 1916–18. Both his reform and his peace attempts failed, and he fled to Switzerland. His empire was broken up into separate national states at the *Paris Peace Conference.*

Charter 77: a Czechoslovak dissident movement demanding greater respect for human rights by the communist authorities in the country. It was named after a petition inspired by the 1975 *Helsinki Agreement* affirming the importance of human rights, and was presented to the Czech government in 1977. Despite persecution, the petition attracted hundreds of signatures. It acted as an inspiration both for later dissident East European groups and for the successful Czech Revolution in 1989.

Charter of the United Nations: the foundation document of the United Nations, ratified in 1945.

Chechenia: a region within Russia close to the Caspian Sea. Following a nationalist coup, it declared its independence from Russia in 1991, a move which the Russian government refused to accept. Civil war between nationalist and pro-Russian groups broke out in 1994. The latter were backed by Russia, which surrounded and then invaded Chechenia, subjecting its capital Grozny to heavy bombardment. The Chechens seized Russian hostages, but in June 1995 an uneasy ceasefire was negotiated. In 1996, Chechenia's political future remained unresolved and fierce fighting resumed, though it seemed unlikely that any Russian government could accept an independent and potentially hostile state within its borders.

Cheka: the Bolshevik secret-police force set up by Lenin in 1917. Its purpose was to protect the outcome of the October Revolution in the critical period of the Russian Civil War and, led by *Dzerzhinsky*, it carried out interrogations under torture and executions of opponents of the Bolsheviks. The scale of these activities made its headquarters, the Lubyanka prison in Moscow, notorious, but its ruthless efficiency helped to ensure the survival of the Bolshevik state. In 1921, the Cheka was replaced by the *OGPU*.

chemical warfare: this occurred on both Eastern and Western Fronts in the First World War, and involved the use of both chlorine and mustard gas. Its use produced no breakthroughs in the trench-warfare stalemate, but did lead to troops having to wear gas masks. The League of Nations outlawed its use, and chemical warfare through the use of *poison gas* did not feature in the usually less static military operations of the Second World War.

Chernenko, Konstantin: a Soviet politician. He was promoted by *Brezhnev*, served under *Andropov* and, on the latter's death in 1984, became chairman of the Soviet Communist Party. Within months, he became seriously ill and an elaborate façade was maintained to keep news of this from the Soviet people. Along with Brezhnev and Andropov, he was a member of the generation of elderly Soviet leaders, plagued by ill-health, which failed to deal with the growing crisis in the Soviet economy. He died in 1985 and was succeeded by *Gorbachev*.

Chernobyl: the scene of the 1986 Soviet nuclear-power-station disaster. It caused many radiation deaths and long-term illnesses, particularly in the Ukraine and Belorussia, and its effects on farming spread across much of Europe. Among those economically affected in Western Europe, sheep farmers in North Wales and the English Lake District were particularly badly hit, with the prospect of the sheep from affected pastures being denied access to the market for decades. The disaster raised further doubts about the safety of nuclear power in general, though Western governments continued to insist that their safety standards were far higher than those employed at Chernobyl. The question of the safety of other Soviet nuclear-power stations, after the disintegration of the Soviet Union, remained unanswered.

chetniks: Serbian nationalist guerrillas who fought against German occupation of *Yugoslavia* in the Second World War. They were also fiercely opposed to Tito's communist partisans, whom in the end even Britain and the USA preferred to back as they provided more effective resistance against the Germans. As the war ended, many of the chetniks were shot as collaborators by the Soviet Red Army as it drove the Germans back.

Chirac, Jacques: president of France, 1995–. He served as prime minister under *Giscard d'Estaing* from 1974 to 1976, and from 1986 to 1988 he was the right-wing prime minister with socialist *Mitterrand* as president, the first time that this had occurred in the *Fifth French Republic*. The latter usually outmaneuvered him in any disputes, and defeated him in the 1988 presidential election. Chirac was then the architect of a right-wing alliance between the Gaullists and other conservative groups which won the 1993 National Assembly elections, and then secured his 1995 presidential-election victory.

Christian Democrats: moderate Roman Catholic political parties, favoring social reform but hostile to socialism. In West Germany, the Christian Democrats, the CDU, were the party of *Adenauer* and *Kohl*.

Churchill, Winston: British prime minister, 1940–45 and 1951–55.

Career to 1939

He was, in the 1930s, the leading critic of the policy of *appeasement*, and in his HISTORY OF THE SECOND WORLD WAR, published in the late 1940s, he wrote a blistering attack on it, justifying his own pre-war stance. The chief victims of his version of history were *Baldwin* and *Chamberlain*, and it was fully 20 years after the end of the war before the case for appeasement could get a fair hearing. Churchill argued that:

- Hitler had from the start expansionist ambitions, which he pursued relentlessly and ruthlessly
- the Western powers should have rearmed more vigorously
- they should also have rejected Hitler's demands, for example over the *Rhineland*, concerning the *Anschluss* and above all at Munich, since every concession they made simply fed Hitler's appetite.

Churchill was less forthcoming about his more ambiguous attitude in the 1930s towards Mussolini's aggression, about the need for Britain to back the League of Nations, and about the value of Britain making an alliance with the Soviet Union. Until early 1939, appeasement commanded general support in Britain, and there were also many reasons, relating to Churchill himself, as to why he was not listened to. These included:

- his two switches between political parties made loyal Conservatives see him as a career opportunist
- Labour, the main opposition party, distrusted him for his provocative industrial policies, using troops against strikers prior to 1914, and proposing aggressive action during the 1926 General Strike
- he had lost office in the early 1930s because of his belligerent opposition to any form of Indian self-rule
- he was flamboyant and aggressive in his general reputation and in his attacks on government policy, and so could easily be dismissed as a warmonger.

A later history of his career to 1939, when he was 65, was entitled A STUDY IN FAILURE. War came in 1939, and with his warnings now justified, his reputation was restored and he was recalled to government and put in political charge of the navy.

The Second World War

In May 1940, when Chamberlain resigned following defeats in Norway, Churchill became prime minister, leading a coalition government, with his own reputation surprisingly unaffected by the military and naval calamities in Norway. Within hours as prime minister, he in any case faced far greater disasters in France and Belgium. He proved an inspirational war leader, having without consultation committed his country to total victory at whatever cost, and this at the darkest moment of the war. Notable features of his wartime leadership were the skillful way in which he worked to win US support for Britain and, from December 1941 when the USA entered the war, his close cooperation with President Roosevelt through wartime conferences. The first of these was held aboard ship off Newfoundland in August 1941, when the *Atlantic Charter* was issued, and another at *Casablanca* in January 1943. The two leaders were joined by Stalin at subsequent conferences held at *Tehran* in November

1943 and *Yalta* in February 1945. Churchill also attended the opening sessions of the *Potsdam Conference* in July 1945.

Career from 1945

After the end of the war in Europe, his Conservative Party lost the general election of July 1945 and he resigned office. In March 1946, in a famous speech made at Fulton in the USA in the presence of President *Truman*, he analyzed the threat to the West from the ambitions of the Soviet Union and popularized the concept of an "Iron Curtain" stretched across Europe between the Soviet and the Western areas of influence. During his second term as prime minister, from 1951 to 1955, he lacked his earlier vigor, but stressed the need for Western unity and for a special relationship between the USA and Britain. He died in 1965 after a long illness.

Ciano, Count Galeazzo: the Italian foreign minister, 1936–43. He negotiated the pre-Second World War agreements with Nazi Germany but, in 1943, voted for the deposition of Mussolini. After capture by the Germans, he was handed over to still-loyal Italian fascists and shot.

cinema: the mass medium of entertainment in the first half of the twentieth century. It became the first cheap, mass, working-class form of entertainment, and in Western European countries in particular, millions would attend the cinema each week. The brief newsreel films allowed these millions to catch a glimpse of events worldwide, but much that was offered was quite superficial entertainment.

Cinema provided a valuable propaganda opportunity for regimes like those led by Hitler – with the German *Riefenstahl* perhaps the most gifted film director of her age – and by Mussolini, but some of the most chilling messages came from the factual material showing the devastation wrought by German aircraft in operation against the cities of republican Spain.

The British cinema industry during the Second World War produced a series of useful, morale-boosting films and some invaluable propaganda for the British cause aimed at the American market. In the 1950s and 1960s, cinema increasingly began to give way to the more immediately available television pictures, and it ceased to be the mass-entertainment medium.

CIS: the *Commonwealth of Independent States* made up of former member states of the Soviet Union.

Clemenceau, Georges: prime minister of France, 1906–09 and 1917–20. In 1917, he injected new vigor into the French war effort and secured *Foch*'s appointment as commander of the Allied forces on the Western Front. He chaired the 1919 *Paris Peace Conference* where, backed by the anger of the French people at the losses and damage caused by the war and by their determination to prevent any repetition of German aggression, he pressed hard for full compensation for France against Germany, arguing that the latter should pay the total cost of the war. When these demands could not be fulfilled, his popularity in France waned and he took little part in post-war politics. He died in 1929.

CND: the *Campaign for Nuclear Disarmament*

Cod War: the term used to describe the dispute over fishing rights between Britain and Iceland in the 1970s.

Cold War: the period of international tension from the end of the Second World War in 1945 to the collapse of the Soviet domination of Eastern Europe circa 1989. The term was coined by the press to distinguish it from what might happen in a real, or "hot," war, perhaps involving atomic weapons.

- Soon after the end of the Second World War, the anti-Nazi alliance crumbled into mutual suspicion as communist regimes took over in the liberated states of Eastern Europe
- It seemed to Western observers that both Greece and Turkey risked the same fate. British troops were involved in fighting the communists in

THE COLD WAR
The origins of the Cold War

1945 Yalta Conference, end of Second World War in Europe, Potsdam Conference, atomic bombs dropped on Japan, Japanese surrender

1946 Greek Civil War, Churchill's "Iron Curtain" speech

1947 Truman Doctrine, Marshall Plan, Cominform

1948 Communist coup in Czechoslovakia, Berlin Airlift

1949 Soviet atomic bomb, NATO formed, China fell to communists

1950 Korean War (to 1953)

1953 Death of Stalin

Crises of the Cold War		Attempts at détente	
1956	Hungarian Revolution	**1963**	Test Ban Treaty
1961	Berlin Wall	**1968**	Non-proliferation Treaty
1968	Czech rising (Prague Spring)	**1970–73**	West German pacts with Poland and
1962	Cuban Missile Crisis		the Soviet Union
1979–89	Soviet invasion of	**1972**	SALT I
	Afghanistan	**1973–75**	Helsinki Conference
		1979	SALT II
		1987	INF Treaty

The end of the Cold War

1985 Gorbachev came to power in the Soviet Union, and concentrated on internal reforms

1989 The Soviet Union failed to support communist governments in Eastern Europe against popular uprisings. The Berlin Wall destroyed by the people. The Soviet army left Afghanistan

1990 Gorbachev agreed to the reunification of Germany

1991 August – after a failed coup against Gorbachev, power in the Soviet Union went to the leaders of the separate republics

September – the Soviet Union recognized the independence of the three Baltic Republics

December – Gorbachev resigned as president. The Soviet Union formally ended and was succeeded by independent republics, later grouped in the CIS

Greece, but the costs seemed insupportable to *Bevin*, the foreign secretary

- Western Europe was exhausted and apparently open to takeover by the victorious *Red Army*
- Britain was particularly concerned that, with victory in war assured, the Americans should not withdraw totally from Europe as had happened at the end of the First World War.

In 1947, the USA made its commitment to Europe, through the *Marshall Plan* and the *Truman Doctrine*, that it would bring both economic stability and military aid to nations threatened with a communist takeover. The lines were ever more sharply drawn with the formation of *NATO* and *Comecon* in 1949 and the *Warsaw Pact* in 1955, following the expansion of NATO to take in West Germany. The Cold War reached beyond Europe as the West's perception of a worldwide communist conspiracy seemed to be confirmed by:

- the communist takeover of China
- the attack on South Korea by communist North Korea, which led to the *Korean War*

2 Europe after 1945

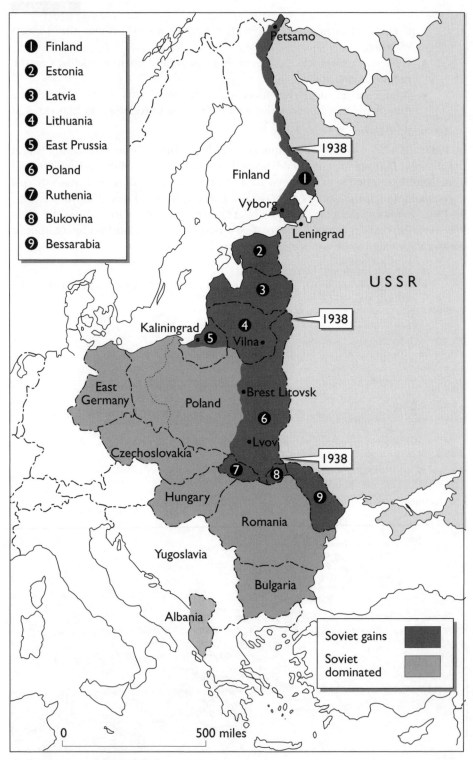

Key:
1 Finland
2 Estonia
3 Latvia
4 Lithuania
5 East Prussia
6 Poland
7 Ruthenia
8 Bukovina
9 Bessarabia

Petsamo

1938

Finland

1

Vyborg

Leningrad

USSR

2

3

1938

Kaliningrad

4

5 Vilna

East Germany

Poland

Brest Litovsk

6

Czechoslovakia

Lvov

1938

7 8

9

Hungary

Romania

Yugoslavia

Bulgaria

Albania

Soviet gains

Soviet dominated

0   500 miles

3 Soviet land gains, 1940–45

- a series of crises ranging from spy scares inside Western countries to the electoral successes of the communists in Italy
- the brutal reimposition of Soviet control over *Hungary* in 1956 and *Czechoslovakia* in 1968
- the *Cuban Missile Crisis* of 1962.

The Soviet Union's view was that in Eastern Europe it was creating a defensive buffer zone to protect itself from further invasions like that launched by Nazi Germany in 1941. The Soviets pointed to US possession of the *atomic bomb*, and later

---

COLD WAR CHRONOLOGY 1945–91

1945	Second World War ended. Potsdam Conference	**1970**	
1946	Churchill's "Iron Curtain" speech. Greek Civil War	**1971**	East–West Treaty on Berlin
1947	Truman Doctrine. Marshall Plan. Cominform	**1972**	SALT I, USA and Soviet Union. West German pacts with Poland and Soviet Union
1948	Coup in Czechoslovakia. Berlin Airlift	**1973**	
		1974	
1949	Soviet A-bomb. NATO. China went communist	**1975**	Helsinki Conference
		1976	
1950	Korean War (to 1953)	**1977**	
1951		**1978**	
1952	UK A-bomb	**1979**	SALT II. Soviet invasion of Afghanistan
1953	Stalin died		
1954		**1980**	Olympic boycott
1955	West Germany entered NATO. Warsaw Pact formed	**1981**	
		1982	
1956	Polish unrest. Hungarian Revolution. Suez Crisis	**1983**	US cruise missiles in UK
		1984	
1957		**1985**	
1958		**1986**	
1959		**1987**	INF Treaty
1960	French A-bomb	**1988**	Strikes in Poland
1961	Berlin Wall built	**1989**	Eastern European governments fell. Berlin Wall down. Baltic separatism emerged
1962	Cuban Missile Crisis		
1963	Test Ban Treaty	**1990**	Gorbachev agreed to German unification
1964			
1965		**1991**	September – Soviet Union accepted Baltic States' independence. December – Gorbachev resigned, end of Soviet Union
1966	France withdrew its troops from NATO		
1967			
1968	Non-proliferation Treaty. Warsaw Pact countries invaded Czechoslovakia (Prague Spring)		End of Cold War? Peace dividend?
1969			

---

of the hydrogen bomb, and to the ring of NATO bases, in Turkey for example, which threatened their security. Attempts to reduce tension, like the *Rapacki Plan* or the *SALT* agreements and the *Helsinki Conference*, had only limited success but produced a short period of *détente* in the 1970s. The Cold War continued, however, with the build-up of Western nuclear missiles in Europe and the Soviet invasion of *Afghanistan* in 1979. Only after 1985 did tension in Europe ease as the Soviet Union started to pull out of Afghanistan and discontinued its involvement in Africa. By 1989, the communist regimes in Eastern Europe were collapsing, and even the *Berlin Wall* was being broken down.

The Cold War had its origins in Europe, but its later history can only be understood as part of a global conflict involving:

- different philosophies
- contrasting economic systems
- clashing national interests
- mutual suspicions and misunderstandings between the great *superpowers* – the USA and the Soviet Union.

With the end of the "*Iron Curtain*" and the tensions which surrounded it, the countries of Europe seemed destined to be the main beneficiaries of the end of the Cold War, but events after 1989 soon demonstrated that the post-Cold War world would also have its tensions and complexities.

collaborator: someone who supports an enemy occupier of a country. The term was commonly used during the Second World War. *Laval* in France was one example of a collaborator, while *Quisling* in Norway gave his name to the role.

collective security: securing international security by the joint effort of several countries working together to deter action against one of their members.

collectivism: a social and economic system based on the idea that economic resources should be owned and operated by and for the benefit of the community.

collectivization: the confiscation of private land-holdings in order to create collective, or cooperative, farms. The best-known example came from Stalin's policies in the Soviet Union in the 1930s, where its ruthless implementation caused great suffering, with millions of the better-off peasants, or *kulaks*, dying from destitution. The policy was also enforced after 1945 in many of the countries of Soviet-dominated Eastern Europe.

colony: a territory subordinate to, and ruled by, another state.

Comecon: the Council for Mutual Economic Assistance, formed in 1949 among the Soviet bloc countries. Its purpose was to promote both trade and, from 1960, international economic planning. It ceased to operate with the collapse of the Eastern European communist bloc in 1989.

Cominform: a body founded in 1947 by Stalin to coordinate communist-party activity throughout Europe. Yugoslavia was expelled in 1948 after Tito's quarrel with Stalin. Cominform was abolished by Stalin's successors in 1956 in an effort to improve relations with the West.

Comintern: an abbreviation of Communist International, an international organization for all national communist parties, also known as the *Third International,* established by Lenin in 1919. Its organization owed much to the work of *Zinoviev,* who was its leading figure from 1919 to 1926. It sought to ensure that all national parties copied the Soviet model. Stalin abolished it in 1943 as a goodwill gesture towards his wartime allies.

command economy: an economy controlled by central planning, as opposed to a free-market, capitalist economy. It was a characteristic of the Soviet Union and its satellite countries. In the 1980s, command economies proved inflexible and inefficient, and their weaknesses contributed largely to the political collapse of the Soviet Union.

common agricultural policy: European Union economic policy subsidizing farmers via a common agricultural fund contributed by the member states. The difficulty of controlling the cost and auditing the payments made under the policy made its allegedly wasteful use of money increasingly controversial. On the other hand, it was argued that the policy was responsible for the European Union's flourishing agriculture and food surplus.

Common Market: a general term in Britain, from the 1950s to the 1980s, for the *European Community,* which in turn became the *European Union.*

Commonwealth of Independent States (CIS): the group of 12 independent states which were formerly republics making up the Soviet Union. (See map on p. 52.) The CIS:

- was formed in December 1991, though the three *Baltic Republics* declined to join
- acts to coordinate the foreign, defense and economic policies of the otherwise independent states.

Disputes between the states in the aftermath of the collapse of the *Soviet Union* rendered the CIS generally ineffective in its first two years, though it did secure mutual recognition of frontiers and central control of nuclear weapons. The four republics with nuclear weapons agreed to implement the Soviet–US *START* terms to reduce the stockpile of strategic nuclear weapons. In both non-nuclear military matters and on economic issues, cooperation was quite limited, with considerable suspicion aroused by Russian dominance within the CIS. Ten of the republics had, by 1995, agreed to accept Russian troops in their country; the Ukraine, which was in dispute with Russia over the future control of the Black Sea fleet, had refused to agree. Western economic aid to the republics had been made conditional on their cooperation within the CIS, and this increased its significance.

Commonwealth of Nations: the loose association of states made up from former members of the *British Empire.* The term was first used in the 1920s and was given official status in 1931 at the same time as the full independence of the "white dominions" was recognized. Its political influence, and still less its political power, has been difficult to assess since 1945. There have been withdrawals and, in particular in the case of South Africa, returns, but the main impact on Europe has been to encourage in Britain a nostalgia for the empire and a resistance to full membership of European institutions, which has produced friction with European partners.

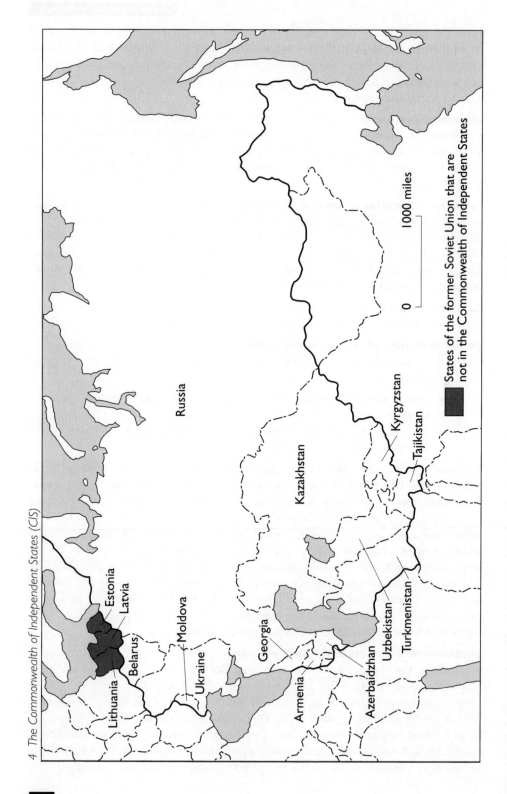

4 *The Commonwealth of Independent States (CIS)*

States of the former Soviet Union that are
not in the Commonwealth of Independent States

Russia

Kazakhstan

Kyrgyzstan

Tajikistan

Estonia
Latvia
Lithuania
Belarus
Moldova
Ukraine
Georgia
Armenia
Azerbaidzhan
Uzbekistan
Turkmenistan

0   1000 miles

communism: an egalitarian political theory according to which all property should be owned by the community and labor organized for the common benefit. It emerged in the nineteenth century, owing much to the writings of Karl Marx.

communist parties: the first communist party was so titled in 1919, when Lenin proposed the addition of the name to that of the triumphant *Bolshevik Party*. Its organization and its role in the state were based on Lenin's principles of *democratic centralism*. Communist parties were then quickly founded in most European countries, and by 1939 existed in most countries of the world. In the late 1980s and the 1990s, communist parties, particularly in Europe, were on the defensive as their record in economic matters and civil liberties came increasingly under attack when it became clear that the *command economies* of the Soviet Union and its associates were in a state of collapse. In Western Europe after 1945, only the Italian communist party had ever looked close to achieving power in an open election, though the French communist party became a minor partner in a coalition government from 1981 to 1983, the only such occasion since 1947.

concentration camps: these were first used by the British in the Boer War, but are particularly associated with Nazi Germany from 1933 to 1945. By 1939, there were six German concentration camps, intended to confine "anti-social" members of society. Trade unionists, communists, Gypsies and Jews figured prominently among the early inhabitants. The camps were run by the *SS*, and their number increased to 30 after the outbreak of war, when the policy of exterminating the Jews (the *Holocaust*) and other "undesirables" was introduced both in Germany and in German-occupied Europe. Among the most infamous of the specially designed *death camps* were *Auschwitz* and Treblinka. At least 4 million Jews died in this systematic genocide, as well as half a million Gypsies. But in another sense, all the concentration camps, such as Belsen, Buchenwald and Dachau, were death camps in which, in appalling conditions, millions died from torture, starvation and disease.

Conditions in the concentration camps were so bad, deliberately so, that many millions of Polish and Soviet *prisoners of war* also died in them.

concordat: meaning "agreement." A concordat was added to the *Lateran Treaties* of 1929 between fascist Italy and the papacy. By it:

- Catholicism was the state religion, and all schools were to give religious instruction
- the papacy gave up all claim to Italian lands outside the *Vatican City*
- the papacy accepted the state's right to object to Church hierarchy appointments.

The concordat was politically important because it ended a bitter split between the papacy and the Italian state going back to 1870. The new agreement helped to win the loyalty of devout Catholics to the fascist regime, and must be regarded as one of *Mussolini's* most constructive acts of statesmanship. It also saved the Catholic Church in Italy from the sort of persecution that its German counterpart suffered at the hands of the Nazis.

In July 1933, there was also a concordat between the newly installed Nazi regime in Germany and the Catholic Church there, but this was soon ignored, and there was then regular Nazi persecution at any sign of disagreement with Nazi policy on the part of either the Church or individual churchmen.

Condor Legion: an aircraft unit of over 100 planes sent by Hitler to help Franco in the Spanish Civil War. Early in the war, it did him invaluable service by shipping his troops from Morocco to Spain, and then provided a link between his northern and southern forces. It later became notorious for its bombing of both republican lines and civilian targets, most notoriously the town of *Guernica.*

Conference on Security and Cooperation in Europe Treaty: at first, this was a continuous conference between *NATO*, the *Warsaw Pact* and non-aligned European states following on from the *Helsinki Conference* of 1975. However, following the end of the Cold War, it was, from 1990 to 1992, turned into a formal institution to coordinate security, economic and human-rights issues across the Continent, and in 1994 it changed its name to the Organization for Security and Cooperation in Europe. By 1995, there were 53 participating states.

conscientious objectors: people who, for reasons of conscience, object to military service. The objection often has a religious basis, as with the Society of Friends. Objectors were often callously treated by all states during the First World War but, in non-totalitarian states at least, had a slightly more sympathetic reception in the Second World War. They were frequently offered essential alternative employment to military service but were often put in great danger, working for example as ambulance men or stretcher bearers for the wounded in battle.

conscription: the compulsory enlistment of civilians for military service. It was common during the nineteenth century in Continental Europe but was only, and controversially, introduced into Britain under pressure of *total war* in 1916. Hitler defied the Versailles Treaty to reintroduce conscription in 1935. Britain reintroduced conscription early in 1939, before the coming of war. Under the guise of National Service, it survived until 1960. It lasted longer in many Continental countries – until 1996 in France, for example – but as armies came to rely more on sophisticated technology than on weight of numbers, its military value was increasingly questioned.

conservatism: the political philosophy of the *right*, based on the wish to preserve and keep intact institutions, practices and traditions.

Constantine II: king of Greece, 1947–73. He owed his throne to the assistance he received between 1945 and 1949 from Britain and the USA in resisting the attempt of the communist partisans of *ELAS* to take over the Greek state. In 1967, he at first mistakenly supported the military coup of the "*Greek Colonels*" but then went into exile. In 1973, the "Colonels" declared Greece a republic and, after their fall in 1974, a referendum confirmed their action.

Constantinople Agreement: a secret Allied agreement of 1915 to the effect that, at the end of the First World War, Constantinople (Istanbul) should become part of tsarist Russia. In 1918, the Bolsheviks greatly embarrassed the Western Allies by publishing its details. The terms became a great spur to the revival of Turkish strength under Mustafa Kemal (*Atatürk*).

Constituent Assembly: the body summoned by the *Provisional Government* to provide Russia with a constitution following the abdication of Nicholas II. Elections were called for December 1917 but were overtaken by the events of the *October Revolution*. The Bolsheviks allowed the elections to continue, but when the Assembly met in January 1918, they were in a minority, and at that point they forcibly abolished the Assembly and set out to construct the communist state through their control of the soviets.

constitution: the arrangements by which a state is organized and governed. These may be formally laid down in one document, as with the constitution of the *Weimar Republic* or the *Basic Law* of West Germany, or they may have developed over time, as with the British constitution.

constitutional government: government according to, usually written, rules. Its historical use implies the sharing of power with a role for an elected parliament and the protection of individual rights through the rule of law. All this is in contrast to a *dictatorship* or an *autocracy*.

contingency plan: a plan drawn up to meet unforeseen circumstances.

Control Commission: an organization set up by the Allies after the First World War to supervise German demilitarization.

Control Council: an organization set up by the Allies after the Second World War. Its chief function was to coordinate policy with regard to the administration of Germany. It consisted of the four supreme Allied military commanders of the *zones of occupation* into which Germany had been divided.

Conventional Arms in Europe Treaty (CFE Treaty): a treaty, signed in 1990 by *NATO* and *Warsaw Pact* countries, placing limits on non-nuclear weapons and providing for its enforcement by the inspection of weapon sites. The agreement was one of the first results of the end of the Cold War.

convoys: the practice in *sea warfare* of merchant ships sailing in groups with armed escorts. In the First World War, the German U-boat offensive had, by 1917, made Britain's supply situation desperate. Lloyd George compelled a reluctant admiralty to introduce a convoy system, and this was so successful that it was in general use by the end of the war. It was used by Britain throughout the Second World War in the crucial Battle of the *Atlantic*.

Corfu Incident: this arose from the 1923 murder of Italian peacekeepers on the Greek island of Corfu. *Mussolini* defied the League of Nations in invading the island to obtain compensation but, under pressure from Britain and France, then withdrew. It enabled Mussolini to gain glory at home but also raised early doubts about the effectiveness of the League.

corporate state: a term from *fascist Italy* denoting the attempt to incorporate all the organized economic interests under the direct control of the state.

- The economy was organized around corporations based on occupations in which employers and workers, represented in separate syndicates, came together
- The system originated in the *Rocco Law* of 1926 but was not fully in operation until 1934
- The corporations were supervised by a ministry of corporations, and normal trade-union activity ceased, so that economic disputes were settled by civil servants and strikes became illegal.

The system appeared to be decentralized, but in practice policy remained in the hands of the government, and it was government appointees who made the important decisions within the corporations. There were eventually 22 corporations set up, which represented all major areas of Italian economic life. All this extended fascist control of everyday life but, because of internal corruption and muddle, did not promote great improvements in economic efficiency; indeed, the vast bureaucracy involved encouraged both waste and monopoly. In 1939, the corporations were made the basis of national political life, as Parliament was replaced by a Chamber of Fasces and corporations. The reorganization of economic activity had social parallels in the close control of education, youth organizations and even adult leisure, with:

- school textbooks being rewritten to reflect the fascist message and to inspire loyalty to Mussolini
- a comprehensive system of fascist youth organizations being set up, with their members taking dramatic oaths of loyalty to the state, and leading on to full membership of the Fascist Party
- an organization, the Dopolavoro, was created to control and promote all aspects of adult leisure through cinemas, libraries, orchestras, sporting bodies and even holiday arrangements.

In all of this, the corporate state took on many aspects of *totalitarianism*, seeking to control both the institutions within the state and the daily lives of its citizens. In the late 1930s, Mussolini also began to copy Nazi anti-Semitic legislation in terms of social and economic discrimination, though Italy's Jews were spared the full rigors of the *Holocaust*.

Cosgrave, William: president of the Irish Free State, 1922–32. He was a strong supporter of the *League of Nations*.

Coty, René: president of the *Fourth French Republic*, 1953–59. His ability to provide France with stable government was seriously restricted because of the few powers granted to the president under the constitution. Unable to resolve the Algerian crisis, and faced by the possibility of a revolt by the French army, he took the initiative in recalling de Gaulle to power and so brought the Fourth Republic to an end.

Council of Europe: an organization of European democratic states set up in 1949 to promote unity based on a common cultural heritage. One of its principal achievements was the establishment of the *European Court of Human Rights*. The Council is quite separate from the *European Union*, and in 1995 had 34 members.

coup: a successful stroke or move. In politics, it often refers to a sudden move against the power of established authority. It comes from the French "coup d'état," meaning a sudden change of government by force, a seizure of power.

course of the First World War: see *First World War*, course of the war

course of the Second World War: see *Second World War*:

- under the various subheadings identifying and describing the different theaters of the war
- the end of the entry for information on other useful general entries.

covenant: a formal agreement or pledge. It has religious overtones, implying something particularly solemn and binding. The most famous covenant was that of the *League of Nations*, entered into at the *Paris Peace Conference* in 1919.

Creditanstalt: the leading Austrian bank. Its collapse in 1931 was partly as a result of French financial pressure intended to stop closer economic ties between Austria and Germany, but was also brought on by the depression in world trade after the *Wall Street Crash*. It marked the beginning of a series of financial crises across capitalist Europe, which in turn caused great social unrest and political turmoil.

Crete: a Mediterranean island. It was once within the Ottoman Empire but has been part of Greece since 1913. In 1941, during the Second World War, it was the scene of savage fighting against British Commonwealth troops when it was successfully invaded by the Germans.

Croatia: once part of the Austro-Hungarian Empire but, from 1921, part of *Yugoslavia*. This was after the failure of an attempt to set up an independent Croatia in 1918. Strong anti-Serb feeling made many Croats support the German invaders in the Second World War, when many anti-Serb atrocities were committed and a Nazi kingdom, with an Italian duke as king, was set up. After Germany's defeat in the war, Croatia became a republic within communist Yugoslavia.

As Yugoslavia began to disintegrate, a movement for an independent Croatia was founded, based on strong anti-Serb feeling. In 1991, Croatia announced its independence as a separate nation. A full-scale war with Serbia followed. It lasted until the beginning of 1992, when the UN and the European Community arranged an uneasy ceasefire based on a partition of Croatia between its separate ethnic groups. The Serbs living in Croatia proved reluctant to accept these arrangements, but international pressure on Serbia helped to maintain an uneasy peace.

Croce, Benedetto: an historian, and Italy's most notable intellectual figure of the first half of the twentieth century. While still living in the country, he openly opposed Mussolini's regime from 1925, most remarkably in his book HISTORY AS THE STORY OF LIBERTY, and yet was tolerated by the regime. His ability to do this indicates the less oppressive nature of the Italian fascist state compared with that in Hitler's Germany or with Stalin's Soviet Union. From 1943, he helped to rebuild democratic institutions in Italy. He died in 1952.

Crystal Night: see *Kristallnacht*

Cuban Missile Crisis: arose in October 1962 when the US government discovered that Soviet missiles with atomic warheads were being installed on the island of Cuba. US President Kennedy ordered a blockade of the island to stop further missiles reaching it, and demanded the removal of the Soviet weapons. Soviet merchant ships headed towards the blockade in perhaps the worst crisis of the *Cold War*. The crisis cooled when *Khrushchev* ordered the ships to turn back and later removed the Soviet weapons. When, in the 1990s, Soviet and US official papers were made available it became clear that:

- the number of Soviet nuclear weapons already in Cuba was far greater than the US government had realized; they could have caused enormous damage to US cities
- senior US military men of the time were almost anxious for a nuclear showdown with the Soviet Union.

The world was much nearer to a full-scale nuclear war than had been generally recognized. Those members of the British *Campaign for Nuclear Disarmament (CND)* who had, to general amusement, fled to southwest Ireland in an effort to avoid nuclear disaster were wiser than their critics had realized.

Curzon Line: proposed in 1920 by the British foreign secretary, Lord Curzon, as the frontier between Poland and the Soviet Union, but not adopted.

- Soviet weakness in the *Russo–Polish War* of 1919–21 enabled the Poles to push the frontier hundreds of miles to the east of the Curzon Line
- In 1939, the line became the border between Nazi Germany and the Soviet Union, when those two powers jointly swallowed up Poland following the *Nazi–Soviet Pact* of August 1939
- Red Army successes in the later stages of the Second World War allowed the Soviet Union to push its frontiers far to the west, back to the Curzon Line, which has, since 1945, fulfilled the role originally envisaged for it as the frontier between Poland and the Soviet Union.

Its history in the intervening 25 years is a sharp reminder of the changing balance of national power in Eastern Europe since 1914. The mass involuntary population movements which the frontier changes involved simply added to the other human costs of the wars in the region.

customs union: nations combining together to promote trade with each other by such devices as favorable import duties.

Cyprus: an east Mediterranean island. Until 1878, it was part of the Ottoman Empire, but in the first half of the twentieth century it was controlled by Britain and was formally declared a British colony in 1925. The island has been plagued by ethnic tensions between its Turkish and its majority Greek inhabitants. Among the latter, there was a strong desire for *enosis*, i.e. union with Greece, and in the 1950s a terrorist campaign, led by *Grivas*, sought to bring this about. In 1959, independence and membership of the Commonwealth were instead accepted as a compromise by Archbishop *Makarios*, political leader of the Greek Cypriots. The complex constitution, with separate seats for Turks and Greeks, and with a Greek president and a Turkish vice-president each elected by the separate ethnic communities, did not work well.

- In 1964, amid growing ethnic violence, a UN peacekeeping force was placed on the island
- In 1974, a coup to bring about enosis was backed by the *"Greek Colonels."* It removed Makarios but in turn provoked a Turkish invasion and the division of the island into Greek and Turkish areas
- When the coup collapsed, Makarios returned, but the island remained divided and the Turkish area, with a large Turkish military presence, declared itself an independent state: the Republic of North Cyprus. It is recognized only by Turkey, and relies on a large force of the Turkish military for its defense.

The partition of Cyprus, with the frontier running through the island's main town Nicosia, continued to be a source of tension between Greece and Turkey, which caused problems for their fellow members of *NATO*. UN mediation has also failed to resolve the issue, and in mid-1996 violence flared up again when pro-Greek demonstrators tried to force their way into North Cyprus. Two British military bases have been retained on the island as part of the West's *Cold War* strategy in the eastern Mediterranean.

Czech Legion: a military unit formed in 1917 from Czech prisoners of war held by the Russians, mainly in Siberia. They at first planned to return west via Vladivostock but then turned against the Bolsheviks and entered the Russian Civil War on the side of the *White Russians*. They were a serious threat to the survival of the Bolshevik government, for they controlled much of the *Trans-Siberian Railway*. It was the disintegration of the other White armies which ended the Czech threat.

Czechoslovakia: a republic, *Prague* its capital, created from part of the Austro-Hungarian Empire at the *Paris Peace Conference*.

Events 1919–39

Czechoslovakia formed alliances with Romania and Yugoslavia in the *Little Entente* in 1920–21; and an alliance with France in 1924. It was economically well advanced, and militarily:

- to the west, it had easily defensible frontiers with Germany
- it had a large army backed by the massive Skoda arms works.

The new state had, however, serious internal political problems. Relations between the Czechs and the Slovaks were often strained, and tensions arose in relation to other national minority groups – Hungarians, Poles, Ukrainians and especially the large number of Germans in the west of the country. The state's national mix illustrated how difficult the notion of national self-determination, so much in vogue at the time of the Paris Peace Conference, was to implement on the ground. Throughout most of the inter-war period, the country was well served by Tomaš *Masaryk* as president and *Beneš* as foreign minister, but after the former's retirement in 1935, Czechoslovakia in the late 1930s became a victim of Hitler's expansionist ambitions:

- in early 1938, the *Anschluss* had left the Czech southern frontier open to German attack
- Hitler quickly applied diplomatic pressure on the Czechs, exploiting unrest among the German minority in the west, the *Sudetenland*, much of it deliberately fostered by the Nazi Party in the region led by Konrad Henlein
- the *Munich Agreement* made by Britain and France with Hitler in September 1938 handed the Sudetenland to Germany, with the deserted Czechs impotent spectators.

In this most infamous example of the policy of *appeasement*, peace in Europe was, temporarily, saved, at the expense of the Czech state. It did not, however, save Czechoslovakia from further plunder by Nazi Germany. In March 1939, the Germans occupied the provinces of Bohemia and Moravia, including Prague, and all this territory became part of the Third Reich. *Slovakia* became a German Nazi puppet state.

Events after 1945

At the end of the Second World War, Prague was the last great city to be liberated from German occupation, and an independent democratic Czechoslovakia was then re-established. In 1948, the communists, led by *Gottwald*, seized control and remained in power until 1989.

In 1968, the communist government under *Dubček* introduced a program of reforms in the *Prague Spring*, but its attempts to break away from Soviet domination led to the country's occupation by Warsaw Pact troops and the return of hard-line government. In a well-remembered incident, a Czech student, Jan *Palach*, burned himself to death in protest at this repression. Each year, the January anniversary of his death was made the occasion for further public demonstrations. From the late 1970s, the *Charter 77* movement also kept reforming dreams alive. In November 1989, street protests were mounted, and after overcoming brutal suppression, these led to the downfall of the communist government. Vaclav *Havel*, the leading spokesman of the street protesters, was elected president, and the border with non-communist Austria was thrown open.

Nationalist feelings in both the Czech and the Slovak regions of the country then developed rapidly and, following a year of negotiations in 1992, the country was, at the beginning of 1993, divided into two separate states, the *Czech Republic* and the republic of Slovakia.

Czech Republic: a republic founded in late 1992. It had been part of the Austro-Hungarian Empire until 1919, and then part of Czechoslovakia, with parts taken into Nazi Germany from the 1938 Munich Agreement until 1945. Its foundation followed both the collapse of the communist regime in 1990 and the inability of the Czech and the Slovak politicians to work together. Its foundation is a classic, if relatively peaceful, example of the revival of the forces of nationalism in Eastern Europe following the collapse of Soviet domination of the region.

D

Dachau: a Nazi concentration camp set up before the war to house opponents of the regime. The treatment of prisoners there during the Second World War, including mass killings and medical experiments, was the subject of charges at the *Nuremberg Trials.*

Daladier, Édouard: prime minister of France in 1933, 1934 and 1938–40. He was himself a pacifist, supporting the policy of *appeasement* and, with *Chamberlain*, in 1938, he signed the *Munich Agreement* with Hitler. When he was then received with acclaim on his return to France, he indicated privately that he had no faith in the permanence of the deal he had struck. During the Second World War, his attempts to undermine the *Vichy* government led to his imprisonment. He died in 1970.

D'Annunzio, Gabriele: an Italian hero of the First World War. He had argued for Italian intervention in the war with a view to Italy gaining territory at the expense of the Austro-Hungarian Empire. Such hopes were dashed at the Paris Peace Conference and, in 1919, volunteer troops under his command, early *blackshirts*, seized the Adriatic port of *Fiume.* He imposed a fascist-style government on the port, which he held for over a year until starved into surrender by the liberal Italian government of *Giolitti.* His actions:

- illustrate Italian dissatisfaction at the *Versailles* Treaty terms
- indicate the strength of right-wing nationalist feeling in Italy
- provided an inspiration for those who supported *Mussolini*'s rise to power.

D'Annunzio welcomed this, but from 1922 took no further part in politics. He died in 1938.

Danzig: (from 1945, *Gdansk*) a Baltic port. Part of East Prussia until 1919, it then became a *free city* under the League of Nations and provided Poland with access to the Baltic Sea. A local Nazi attempt to reunite it with Germany helped to bring about the outbreak of war in 1939. After its capture by the Red Army in 1945, it became part of Poland, and its German population was expelled. Its massive shipyards were, in 1980, the birthplace of the Polish trade union *Solidarity*, whose strikes and political demands led to the collapse of the Polish communist regime.

Dardanelles: the strait between the Aegean Sea and the Sea of Marmara, linking the Mediterranean Sea with the Black Sea and dividing Turkey in two. In 1914, under German pressure, the Ottoman Empire closed the strait to all shipping. This cut Russia off from her wartime allies, France and Britain. The latter decided to force a passage through the strait, and this was attempted in February 1915, when severe losses were inflicted on the Allied navies by land-based Turkish gun batteries. There was then a two-month delay before troops were landed at *Gallipoli* in what was to be an equally unsuccessful operation to force a passage.

In 1922, the Dardanelles strait was the setting for the *Chanak Crisis.*

Darlan, Jean: an admiral appointed commander-in-chief of the French navy in 1939. After the French capitulation in 1940, he became naval minister in the *Vichy*

Government. He had ordered the French fleet to be prepared to scuttle their ships if the Germans should try to seize them, but the British did not trust French intentions and bombarded units of the French fleet at Mers el Kebir. Darlan then actively cooperated with the Germans and became vice-premier in the Vichy government. After the Allied invasions of North Africa, Darlan negotiated with Eisenhower and ordered the Vichy French forces there to stop fighting. He was assassinated in 1942, shortly after being declared head of state in French Africa.

Dawes Plan: the 1924 US plan to enable *Weimar* Germany to keep up its reparations payments. It:

- provided loans to stabilize the German economy
- fixed an annual reparations payment in gold raised from taxation, rather than in goods
- enabled Germany to meet its revised reparations commitments until 1929
- contributed to the general stabilizing of European international relations in the second half of the 1920s.

It was succeeded in 1929 by the *Young Plan.*

death camps: the extermination camps set up by the Nazis to carry out the *Holocaust.* By far the largest and most infamous of these camps was *Auschwitz*, with four huge gas chambers and adjoining crematoria. Treblinka, Belzec, Sobibor and Chelmno, all situated in Poland, also used gas chambers to kill their victims. Five smaller death camps, again in Eastern Europe, killed by shooting rather than by use of gas. Death camps had a special, sinister reason for their existence, but all of the 30 or so Nazi concentration camps were death camps in which millions died from torture, starvation or disease. It seems all too probable that as many as 4 million Jews and 3 million others, mainly Slavs and Gypsies, died in the death camps.

D day: 6 June 1944, when the Western Allies invaded German-occupied Europe in the Second World War. The largest fleet ever assembled took the invasion force across the English Channel to the Normandy beaches. By the end of the day, the troops had moved inland and were opening the *Normandy Campaign* and the *Second Front.*

Debré, Michel: a French politician. He played a large part in drawing up the constitution of the *Fifth French Republic* and was appointed by de Gaulle as its first prime minister. He died in 1996.

decolonization: the ending of the colonial empires of the European powers. The term began to be commonly used in the 1950s when the process had its first impact on the *European empires*, including the *British Empire*. It was encouraged by the disapproval of imperialism of the USA and, less directly, by the hostility of the Soviet Union, as well as by the great strains which had been imposed on all of the imperial powers by their experiences in the Second World War.

- Britain withdrew from the Indian subcontinent in 1947, and from nearly all of its African and West Indian colonies in the 1960s
- France, after vain attempts to resist nationalist demands by military force, released its colonies in Indo-China, Algeria and Tunisia in the 1950s and early 1960s, and granted virtual independence to its African possessions

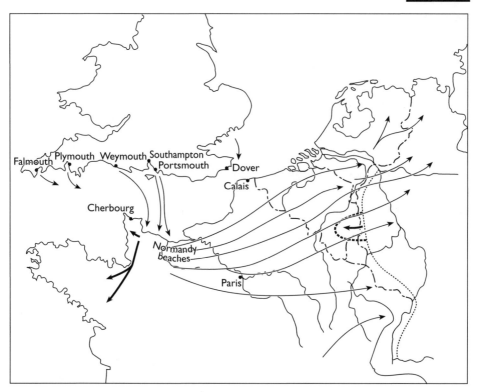

5 D day, 6 June 1944

in the same period
- Belgium, Holland and, belatedly, Portugal had all relinquished their colonies by the late 1970s.

Decree on Land: the decree enacted by the Bolsheviks in November 1917, immediately after they took power in Russia. It abolished all private ownership of land and placed it under the control of peasant committees. It simply sanctioned the peasant seizure of the land which had already taken place in many parts of the country, and encouraged many peasant soviets to vote Bolshevik. Under the pressure of the Russian Civil War, peasant control of the land was replaced by state direction of production as part of the policy of *war communism*.

defensive alliance: a commitment by one state to go to the aid of another if, and only if, the latter is attacked. If the ally opens the war, then there is no obligation to assist. The 1902 *Anglo–Japanese Treaty*, for example, set up a defensive alliance between these two countries.

deflation: a reduction in the amount of money in circulation, having an adverse effect on the demand for goods etc. This can lead to price reductions and a decline in economic activity.

De Gasperi, Alcide: prime minister of Italy, 1945–53. He had been an opponent of Mussolini. After the Second World War, he:

- played a key part in creating the Christian Democrat Party as a vehicle for Italian Catholic opinion
- opposed communism, both internationally and within Italy (opposing the activities of the strong communist party there)
- was in favor of European cooperation and, as prime minister, took Italy into NATO, the Council of Europe and the European Coal and Steel Community.

He was one of the most significant of the founding fathers of the movement towards a united Europe.

de Gaulle, Charles: president of France, 1959–69. From the 1940 invasion of France by the Germans until his death in 1970, he was politically the most important Frenchman.

During the Second World War

In 1940, on the French capitulation, he fled to Britain and proved a valuable but difficult ally, whose views about the role and status of the French required sensitive handling by Churchill and others. He was leader of the *Free French* forces, and he marched at their head when, in 1944, they returned to a liberated Paris. He objected to France's exclusion from the *Potsdam Conference* and came to resent the overwhelming American presence in the Allied war effort, as well as the close relations forged between the Americans and the British.

Fourth French Republic

In the aftermath of the war, de Gaulle formed a provisional government which ruled from 1944 to 1946. In 1945–46 he also served as provisional president, but retired from politics when he disagreed with the proposed constitution of the new *Fourth French Republic*. In particular, he believed that both the limited powers given to the president and his mode of election, by members of the Parliament, would prevent him from ensuring strong government. In 1947, he formed a new right-wing political party, the RPF or Rally of the French People, to keep his ideas before the people and to challenge the threat from the left. He personally remained aloof from political life, and in 1953, when the party was disbanded, his moment seemed to have gone. He re-entered politics in 1958, when the Algerian crisis was at its height. It seemed possible that the army might take power in order to stiffen French resolve to retain *Algeria* as part of *Metropolitan* France, and President *Coty*, to avert that danger, asked the military hero of the Second World War to form a government which the army would support. De Gaulle would only return if given the full executive powers he had felt necessary in 1946, and when the French Parliament conceded these powers to him, the Fourth Republic was dead.

Fifth French Republic

De Gaulle founded the *Fifth French Republic*, and became its first president in January 1959. He showed himself to be more radical than his record up to that point had suggested. With regard to the Algerian problem, he:

- conceded independence to Algeria and to France's African colonies, so ending the costly and dangerous *Algerian War*
- resisted the threat of a colonists' rising against him headed by the *OAS* under *Salan.*

De Gaulle was keen to establish France's international role and its reputation as an independent power. He had a vision of Europe as being less under the influence of the USA and its ally, Britain. To help bring this about, he:

- dominated the *European Economic Community*, blocking British attempts to join
- developed the independent French nuclear deterrent
- in 1966, took France out of NATO so that its military power could be deployed independently
- vainly tried to develop links with the countries of Eastern Europe, which included a triumphant state visit to the Soviet Union in 1966
- succeeded in forging close links with *Adenauer*'s Germany
- was anxious to demonstrate France's independence of the USA, and so, in 1964, recognized communist China
- asserted French interest in the future government of Quebec, the French-speaking province of Canada, in a controversial visit to the city of Quebec in 1967.

At home, problems loomed in 1968 with student uprisings and strikes by industrial workers. De Gaulle was forced into unwelcome concessions to both groups but, as conservative elements rallied at the threat of disorder, his supporters did well in the Assembly elections, and he seemed secure once more.

In 1962, he had proposed the direct election of the president by the people, and used a referendum to alter the constitution to this effect. On several later occasions, he again appealed to the electors over the heads of the politicians through a referendum. His personal prestige had always carried him triumphantly through, though in 1965 he was re-elected president only after a second ballot. In 1969, on a minor constitutional matter, he unnecessarily called another referendum which, after recent unrest, became a vote of confidence in his leadership. The vote was lost, by 12 million votes to 10.5 million, and de Gaulle immediately, and finally, resigned. He died in 1970.

Delcassé, Théophile: French foreign minister, 1898–1905, 1914–15. He was a key figure in promoting the *entente cordiale* with Britain, bringing to an end the rivalry between the two countries in Africa when faced with a common concern about German intentions.

democracy: government by the people. In the twentieth century, this has invariably been through the election of representatives to a parliament rather than directly. Even in countries normally regarded as democratic, some groups of people may be denied the vote. In Britain, for example, women did not vote at all in parliamentary elections until 1918, and on equal terms with men only after 1928; and it was only in the 1970 election that people between 18 and 21 in Britain obtained the vote for the first time.

democratic centralism: the political principle on which *Lenin* based the Bolshevik, later the Communist, Party.

- In theory, the election of leaders and the determination of policy were the product of democratic debate conducted at all levels of the party; once agreed, decisions became binding on all party members
- In practice, leaders and policy were imposed on all lower levels of organization by the largely self-appointed party Central Committee
- The party so constructed was the real source of power in communist states, so rendering ineffective the apparently democratic powers granted to the soviets, from the grass roots upwards, in the constitution
- Lenin's organization of the Soviet Union on these lines, with the Communist Party as the repository and guardian of the true interests of the proletariat, was one of his major contributions to Marxist theory and practice.

demographic change: changes in population.

- In the nineteenth century, despite large-scale emigration, Europe's population had increased greatly
- In the first half of the twentieth century, the birth rate slowed down, causing particular concern in France, where it was seen as a problem affecting the country's international status. Deaths in the First and Second World Wars also checked population growth
- In the second half of the twentieth century, the birth rate in most European countries dropped further and, despite immigration and improvements in medical science, the Continent's population rose much less sharply than that of the other continents
- Projections in the 1990s indicated that Europe's population would fall in the twenty-first century from 730 million in the year 2000 to around 680 million by 2050. This is also in distinct contrast to the likely experience of the other continents.

de-Nazification: the process undertaken by the Allies at the end of the Second World War. Courts were established to check on the records of those Germans suspected of war crimes or crimes against humanity, with a view to ridding German society of this evil presence. The most important individuals received justice at the *Nuremberg Trials*, but below this was a vast network of courts and summary inquiries where, inevitably rough, justice was meted out. *Niemöller*, the most outspoken and courageous of Hitler's German critics, nevertheless repeatedly objected to the arbitrary nature of the de-Nazification process.

Denikin, Anton: a Russian general. He served both the tsar and, in 1917, the Provisional Government. After the Bolsheviks seized power in October 1917, he became commander of a "White" army of counter-revolutionaries in the Russian Civil War, succeeding *Kolchak* in command of the Czech forces in Siberia. After successes in southern Russia in 1918, he was defeated by the Red Army under Trotsky, and in 1920 his army disintegrated.

Denmark: a north European kingdom. In the Second World War, it was occupied by the Germans from 1940 to 1945. Denmark joined NATO in 1949, the European

Free Trade Area (EFTA) in 1960 and, with Britain, the European Community in 1973.

deportation: the removal of an unwanted person from a country.

Depression, the Great: a trade depression in the early 1930s following on from the *Wall Street Crash* of 1929. Its features included:

- large stocks of unsold goods
- a slowdown in production
- personal and company bankruptcies
- soaring unemployment
- a series of national financial crises.

The Great Depression affected all the capitalist countries of Europe, but hit Weimar Germany especially sharply, with 6 million people unemployed by 1933. There, it had serious political consequences in assisting the advance of the Nazis to power. For many years, as national economies struggled to recover, the nations of the world became more concerned with domestic social and economic problems than with taking a decisive line on pressing international political issues. Only in the second half of the 1930s was economic recovery clearly discernible. Ironically, this was assisted in part by expenditure on armaments as Europe moved towards war.

de-Stalinization: the demolition of the cult of personality which had grown up around the Soviet dictator Stalin. This was started by *Khrushchev* in a speech to the Twentieth Congress of the Soviet Communist Party in 1956, three years after Stalin's death.

détente: a term in political history indicating the easing of strained relations between states. It became widely used from the 1970s to describe improvements in relations between the Soviet Union and the USA. The *Helsinki Agreement* of 1975 was an instance of general détente between the Western and communist nations.

de Valera, Eamon: an Irish nationalist leader, president of the Republic of Ireland, 1959–73. He was an important influence in the 1920s in the creation of an independent Ireland. He rejected the 1921 division of Ireland and the exclusion of *Ulster*, and took part in the Irish Civil War against those who had agreed to these. In 1924, he renounced violence and created a new political party, Fianna Fáil, becoming leader of the opposition and later prime minister. He played an important role, both in 1937 when Ireland repudiated its allegiance to the British crown, and in 1949 when it left the Commonwealth. As prime minister, he kept Ireland neutral in the Second World War, and after the war he was twice more elected prime minister and twice president of the Republic of Ireland. He died, aged 93, in 1975.

dictator: a ruler with unrestricted power.

dictatorship: a system of government involving the rule of a dictator.

Dieppe Raid: an ill-organized and disastrous Allied *amphibious* raid on the French port of Dieppe in August 1942. The bulk of the casualties were Canadian, and over 100 Allied aircraft were lost. The lessons learned contributed to later, more successful seaborne invasions. It also contributed to Britain's determination not to concede to Soviet pressure to open a *Second Front* by launching a full seaborne invasion of German-occupied Europe, until everything had been carefully planned.

Dimitrievitch, Dragutin: a Serbian head of intelligence. He was founder of the *Black Hand* terrorist organization. It is generally accepted that Dimitrievitch organized the 1914 assassination of *Franz Ferdinand* which led, via Austrian pressure on Serbia, to the outbreak of the First World War. He had recruited some of the young Bosnians, not members of the Black Hand, who made up the assassination group, and provided them with Serbian arms.

direct action: exerting pressure on a community or government by action, such as a strike, sabotage or intimidation, seeking an immediate effect rather than acting by parliamentary means. It became increasingly common in the second half of the twentieth century and, at its most extreme, as with the *Baader-Meinhof Gang* or the Provisional *IRA*, it involved acts of open terrorism which cost many lives.

disarmament: after 1918, it was believed that the build-up of armaments prior to 1914 had helped to bring about the First World War. By the *Versailles Treaty*, limits were put on Germany's future armed strength, but other nations made few efforts to reduce their own armed power. Between the two world wars, attempts at promoting international disarmament were undertaken by the League of Nations, and the *Washington Conference* of 1921–22, attempting to limit naval forces, had some success, but the League's Disarmament Commission made little further progress, even in the more stable political situation of the late 1920s. A 60-nation conference from 1932 to 1934 sought a general reduction in arms, but the Soviet Union was skeptical about capitalist intentions and the French were still suspicious of Germany, and so it achieved little. In 1933, Hitler came to power and Germany withdrew from the conference. For the remainder of the 1930s, the emphasis in Europe was on rearmament.

Since the Second World War, disarmament has been largely concerned with nuclear weapons. There has been more success in limiting their proliferation than in promoting actual disarmament. Steps taken have included:

- the 1968 *Non-proliferation Treaty*
- the 1972 and 1979 Strategic Arms Limitation Talks leading to *SALT I* and *SALT II*
- the 1975 *Helsinki Conference*
- the 1982 Strategic Arms Reduction Talks (*START*), suspended in 1983, resumed in 1987
- the 1987 Intermediate-range Nuclear Forces (*INF*) *Treaty*
- the 1990 *Conventional Arms in Europe (CFE) Treaty* between NATO and the Warsaw Pact countries.

The end of the Cold War in the early 1990s brought the hope of a general reduction in arms with the prospect of a *peace dividend* in which resources could be used for more productive ends. When new areas of tension emerged in the Middle East and in Yugoslavia, this began to look a more remote possibility, as military men and others called for caution in the abandonment of national protection.

dissidents: those who refuse to conform to the beliefs and practices of the society in which they live. As a political term, it was used mainly in communist countries to identify those whose ideas were not acceptable to the state authorities. *Sakharov* and *Solzhenitsyn* were well-known Russian dissidents.

dive-bombers: aircraft able to fly low and either shoot up or drop bombs on specific targets on the ground. They played a central part in the German *blitzkrieg* offensives of 1939–40:

- in destroying any attempts by enemy troops to make a stand against the advancing German ground forces
- by creating terror and panic among the civilian population, forcing many to flee and thus disrupting enemy defense strategies.

Djilas, Milovan: a dissident Yugoslav politician and writer. He was imprisoned by the communist authorities in the 1950s and 1960s. He remained a committed socialist, but foresaw the likely collapse of the communist system in Eastern Europe.

Doctors Plot: 1953 allegations by the Soviet authorities that a group of doctors, mostly Jewish, had been working for the USA and had murdered Soviet leaders who had been their patients. At the expense of the lives of two of the nine accused, confessions were obtained from the doctors. It seemed that this was to be the opening phase of a major purge of the Soviet leadership, but at that point Stalin died. His successors declared that there was no truth in the allegations, and the doctors were released. The "plot" illustrates:

- the arbitrary terror exercised by Stalin right until the end of his regime
- the strong feelings of *anti-Semitism* which marked the dictator's last years, especially as it was exposed only two months after the *Slansky Trial* of Czech Jews which Stalin is generally believed to have instigated.

Dodecanese: Aegean islands controlled by the Ottoman Empire but conquered by Italy in 1912. After the First World War, Italy refused to implement an earlier promise to hand them over to Greece. Mussolini saw them as the basis of an eastern Mediterranean empire and fortified them heavily. After German occupation in the Second World War, they finally became Greek in 1947.

Doenitz, Karl: a German admiral. In the 1930s, he organized the *U-boat* building program. He became naval commander-in-chief in 1943. In April 1945, after Hitler's suicide, he became German head of state and immediately agreed to an unconditional surrender. He was sentenced to 10 years' imprisonment at the Nuremberg Trials.

Dolfuss, Engelbert: chancellor of the Austrian Republic, 1932–34. He had limited success in dealing with the economic and social problems brought about by the Great Depression, or in curbing political extremists, i.e. communists on the left and nationalists seeking *Anschluss* with Germany on the right. Amid scenes of civil war in which 300 people were killed, he introduced a new constitution giving greater powers to the chancellor and had secret talks with Mussolini about introducing an authoritarian regime able to protect Austria's independence. Before he could act on these plans, he was assassinated by Austrian Nazis in 1934, and was succeeded by *Schuschnigg.*

dominions: self-governing nations of the *British Empire*, later the British Commonwealth, they were mainly countries controlled by white settlers, such as Australia, Canada, New Zealand, South Africa. The term fell into disuse after the Second World War.

dreadnoughts: a popular name for the class of heavy battleships that formed the heart of the British and German naval building programs which made up the *Naval Race* prior to the First World War.

Dresden Raid: successive air raids on the historic German city of Dresden by British and American bombers in February 1945. Despite the knowledge that the city housed some 200,000 refugees, it was seen as strategically important for the continued Allied advance into Germany. The scale of the destruction and killing led to the action being much criticized after the war. It was the most devastating example of the later controversial Allied bombing offensive against Germany. The scale of the tragedy is still much debated, with estimates of the number of dead ranging from 50,000 to 400,000.

Dreyfus Affair: a French military scandal from 1894 to 1906. It revealed the deep strain of anti-Semitism among right-wing elements in French society. Captain Dreyfus was a Jewish officer in the French army who:

- in 1894, was convicted of selling military secrets to Germany
- in 1898, continued to be held guilty by the French authorities, preventing the reopening of the case, even after it had become clear that other officers were responsible
- in 1899, was retried and again found guilty but with extenuating circumstances
- in 1900, received a pardon
- in 1906, had his conviction set aside and his military rank restored by the French Parliament.

The long-running case produced a bitter rift in French society and politics between those, mainly of the political left, who supported Dreyfus, and those of the right who supported the army authorities. It is often cited as evidence of the fragile nature of French internal unity under the Third Republic.

Dual Monarchy: the Austrian Empire, reorganized in 1867 as the *Austro-Hungarian Empire.*

- Budapest and Vienna were the empire's joint capitals
- The Habsburg ruler was crowned separately as ruler of Austria and of Hungary
- Each country had a separate government, but certain issues, notably foreign policy, war and finance, were decided by ministers who were members of the governments of both countries
- Its establishment was a tribute to the strength of the Magyar peoples of the empire, but in practice government power tended to lie with the Austrian elements of the state.

Dubček, Alexander: a Czech politician. He rose to become first secretary of the Czechoslovak Communist Party in 1968, and was one of a group, the *Prague Spring* movement, within the government and outside, who tried to ease the rigid controls over Czech society and the economy which had been imposed since the communist takeover in 1948. He suspended the old Stalinist leaders, including *Novotný*, from office, abolished all censorship and encouraged freedom of speech. Soviet pressure on the Czechs failed to break their support for these reforms, which were backed by a program of passive resistance and public demonstrations. Dubček then promised a gradual restoration of democracy and the pursuit of an independent foreign policy. This was unacceptable to the Soviet Union, and led to:

- the issuing of the *Brezhnev Doctrine*
- the Warsaw Pact invasion of Czechoslovakia
- Dubček being summoned to Moscow and forced to disown his reform proposals, and being required to broadcast his recantation over the radio on his return to Prague.

Dubček was then removed from office in disgrace, working for many years as a clerk, but re-emerging with the collapse of the communist state in 1989, when he was elected chairman of the Czechoslovak Parliament.

Duce: the title assumed by *Mussolini*. In Italian it means "leader."

Duma: the Russian Parliament reluctantly set up by *Nicholas II* in 1906 in order to quell the unrest of the 1905 Revolution.

First Duma, 1906

A week before the first Duma met, Nicholas issued the *Fundamental Law* reserving to himself powers – to appoint the members of the government, veto legislation, conduct foreign policy, raise loans, control the army, govern by decree whenever the Duma was not in session – which ensured that his autocratic authority was preserved. When, despite the decision of most of the left-wing groups to boycott it, the Duma proved hostile to the government and called for reforms, Nicholas dismissed it after only 10 weeks.

Second Duma, 1907

This was also dissolved by Nicholas after only three months of inter-party rivalry and propaganda, with no achievements to its credit.

Third Duma, 1907–12

The number of those entitled to vote in the election of the Duma was sharply reduced, leaving 50 percent of the vote in the hands of the landowners and 2 percent in the hands of the urban working class. This produced a more docile Duma with which the chief minister *Stolypin* was able to work, and one which achieved some modest reforms in education, the administration of justice and insurance for workers. For the first time, Russia had a political forum in which such matters could be discussed. On the other hand, the tsar's autocratic powers were not dented.

Fourth Duma, 1912–17

This body was as narrowly elected as the third Duma, and until 1914 continued the same program of modest social reforms. Once the First World War started, it was rarely allowed to meet. When it did, there was growing discontent among even the most loyal of its members, like the *Octobrists*, to the tsarist government's conduct of the war. In the *February Revolution* of 1917, the fourth Duma brought about the end of tsardom when it resisted Nicholas's attempt to dissolve it and instead formed a provisional government, under Prince Lvov, which persuaded the tsar to abdicate.

Like so much else in pre-1914 Russia, the tentative Duma experiment in representative government was choked by the pressure of the war. It does, however, seem unlikely that Nicholas II would ever have willingly agreed to share political power with his people. Russia in 1914 was not on the eve of an experiment in democracy or even constitutional government.

Dunkirk Evacuation: the evacuation to Britain of defeated troops in May–June 1940. The German *blitzkrieg* had trapped great numbers of British and French troops in Dunkirk, cutting them off from the main French forces to the south. From 26 May to 4 June, 330,000 men, mainly British, were evacuated by naval and merchant ships, aided by hundreds of small private boats which had sailed across the Channel. The dramatic escape from the beaches, aided by German hesitation in pressing home the attack, was widely portrayed as a triumphant rescue of an army now vital to the defense of Britain. The considerable loss of arms and equipment was often forgotten. The romance of "the little ships" also led to less than justice being done to the rescue work of the British navy.

Dutch East Indies: thousands of islands in the Pacific which formed the most important part of the Dutch overseas empire. In the Second World War, they were invaded and conquered by the Japanese. After the war, Holland was unable to re-establish its authority against the growing nationalist movement and in 1949, after four years of fighting, it recognized the independence of the islands, which became the Indonesian Republic.

Dzerzhinsky, Felix: head of the Soviet *Cheka*, the secret police. He had been prominent in the *October Revolution*, and later worked ruthlessly, and with no regard for individual civil rights, to suppress any opposition to the Bolsheviks, organizing the detention of thousands in prison camps. In the struggle to succeed Lenin, he supported Stalin. He died in 1926.

E

East Berlin: the name given to the former Soviet occupation zone in Berlin. From 1949, the communists treated it as the capital of East Germany (GDR). In 1961, it was physically divided from West Berlin by the *Berlin Wall*. Its separate existence ended with the reunification of Germany in 1990.

Eastern Bloc: the term used to identify as a group the communist states of Eastern Europe from the end of the Second World War to the 1980s. With the collapse of the Soviet Union's power from 1989, the "bloc" lost much, if not all, of its cohesion.

Eastern Front, First World War: campaigns between Russia and the *Central powers.*

- In 1914, the Russians advanced into East Prussia but then suffered costly defeats at *Tannenberg* and the *Masurian Lakes*
- By 1915, they had to surrender Warsaw and withdraw from Poland
- In 1916, at the request of their Western allies, they made a successful but costly attack in the south against Austria-Hungary in the *Brusilov* Offensive
- Better-equipped German reinforcements turned the attack around and started a massive advance, taking Romania and advancing, along the shores of the Black Sea, to the Crimea in the south, and almost to Petrograd in the north.

The pressures of war led, in 1917, to the abdication of the tsar, and the efforts of the Russian Provisional Government to stem the tide of defeats proved vain. It was left to Lenin and the Bolsheviks, after the October Revolution, to negotiate a difficult peace at *Brest-Litovsk.*

Eastern Front, Second World War: mainly the campaigns between Germany and the Soviet Union. In 1939–40, following the *Nazi–Soviet Pact*, the two countries combined to attack and conquer Poland, with the bulk of the country going to Germany and the eastern third to the Soviet Union, which also occupied the three Baltic Republics.

In June 1941, Hitler launched his surprise attack on the Soviet Union in *Operation Barbarossa.*

- Employing blitzkrieg tactics, the Germans advanced hundreds of miles to besiege *Leningrad* in the north and almost reached the outskirts of Moscow on the central front
- Winter then stopped the advance in the center and the north, but in 1942 a new German offensive in the south reached the Crimea on the Black Sea and *Stalingrad* on the Volga.

The turning point of the war in the east came in February 1943, when the Red Army managed to consolidate its lines and then counter-attacked at Stalingrad in a battle in which the Germans lost 300,000 men. A further German attack in the south was defeated at *Kursk*, and the Red Army began the advance that was to end in Berlin in May 1945.

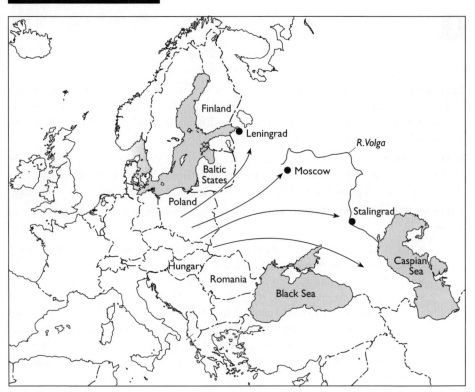

6 Operation Barbarossa, 1941

- In 1944, Leningrad was relieved and the Red Army crossed the Russian frontiers into Poland, Romania, Bulgaria and Hungary
- In January 1945, the Red Army entered Germany and linked up in April with the Allied armies from the west.

At least 20 million Soviet soldiers and civilians died as a result of these campaigns, which involved far greater numbers, covered much wider territory and occasioned more systematic brutality and indifference to human suffering than anything seen on the Western Front.

Eastern Orthodox churches: Christian churches of Russia and the Balkans. They trace their history back to the earliest Christian times, and are quite separate from either the Roman Catholic or the Protestant traditions. The patriarch (head) of the Russian Orthodox Church was closely linked to tsardom, and often had considerable political influence.

East Germany: the common name for the German Democratic Republic (GDR). It:

- was set up by the Soviet Union in 1949, based on the Soviet *zone of occupation* and incorporating *East Berlin* as its capital

- was a one-party state on the model of the Soviet Union, and had a *command economy*
- was fully integrated into the Soviet East European Bloc economically and militarily
- had its political life dominated by two long-serving politicians, *Ulbricht* and *Honecker.*

In the 1950s, relations between East Germany and Adenauer's West Germany were bad, culminating in the East's 1961 decision to build the *Berlin Wall.* In 1972, the two parties agreed, in the *Basic Treaty*, to work together to improve this situation but stopped short of full recognition of each other. With the collapse of the Soviet Empire in Eastern Europe, East Germany was formally joined with West Germany in October 1990 with the signing of the *Treaty on the Final Settlement With Respect to Germany.*

East Prussia: part of Germany until 1945. It was geographically separated from the rest of the Weimar Republic from 1919 when, in the Treaty of *Versailles*, Poland was given German land, the *Polish Corridor*, to give it access to the Baltic Sea, and *Danzig* became a free city. Other land was lost at the same time to Lithuania and to create the free city of *Memel*, which by 1923 had been incorporated into Lithuania. Hitler seized Memel in March 1939, reintegrating it into East Prussia. The other lost lands were reconquered by Germany in the opening stages of the Second World War, but at its end, with Germany defeated, the land that had formed East Prussia was absorbed into Poland and its Germanic population was expelled.

Easter Rising: an Irish nationalist rising in 1916 at the height of the First World War. Roger *Casement* came to Ireland to advise its postponement but it nevertheless went ahead. Fifteen hundred men seized strategic buildings in Dublin, most famously the General Post Office. The rebels proclaimed an Irish Republic but commanded limited public support, for many Irishmen were fighting in the British army. After some sporadic fighting, the rebels surrendered unconditionally. Fifteen of the leaders were executed by the British authorities and 2,000 followers and sympathizers were imprisoned. The rigors of war were claimed to defend this severity, but in fact it swung Irish public opinion firmly behind the nationalist cause. After the end of the war, Ireland became ungovernable, and Irish independence from Britain came in 1921.

Ebert, Friedrich: president of the *Weimar Republic*, 1919–25. He had been the last chancellor of the German Second Empire, and on 9 November 1918, two days before the armistice on the Western Front, he proposed setting up a republic. He led the new state through difficult times:

- his signing the *Versailles* Treaty was seen by right-wing opponents as a betrayal of Germany, and one for which he was constantly attacked and sneered at in right-wing circles
- his crushing of the attempted *Spartacist* uprisings, after agreeing the *Ebert–Groener Pact* with the army, lost him the support of the left.

By the time of his death in 1925, however, the worst of the crises seemed over, with the Weimar Republic more stable and winning international respect. All this owed much to his patient support of democratic institutions.

Ebert–Groener Pact: a 1919 deal between *Ebert*, president of the Weimar Republic, and General *Groener*. It gave Ebert army support against the *Spartacist* uprising, though the Freikorps rather than the army were used to crush the Spartacists.

Ebro: the crucial battle of the *Spanish Civil War*, which took its name from the River Ebro. In the autumn of 1938, the republicans attempted to retrieve their fortunes with a desperate counter-attack. Their defeat in the battle led swiftly to the fall of first Barcelona and then Madrid, marking the end of the war and the nationalist victory.

economic miracle: see *German economic miracle*

ECSC: see the *European Coal and Steel Community*

Eden, Anthony: British foreign secretary, 1935–38, 1940–45, 1951–55, and prime minister, 1955–57. He resigned from office in 1938 in protest over Chamberlain's failure to take a stronger line on Mussolini's successful aggression against Ethiopia. As a member of Churchill's wartime government, he played a central role in decisions about the war. His record in opposing *appeasement* in the 1930s led him, in the 1950s, to identify President Nasser of Egypt as a dictator who had to be resisted. This led to the *Suez Crisis* of 1956, in which he lost the support of his American ally and caused great controversy in the Commonwealth and in Britain itself. This and poor health led to his resignation.

Edward VII: king of the United Kingdom, 1901–10. His love of France and his popularity there may have helped to create a favorable climate for the improved relations between the two countries at the beginning of the century. It is clear, however, that he had little or no influence over the conduct of British foreign policy at that time, and that the new cordiality actually rested on solid grounds of mutual interests rather than on the whim of the monarch.

egalitarian: an egalitarian policy is one which advocates equality. The term comes from the French "égalité."

Egypt: from 1882 to 1956, there was a British military presence in Egypt. In the 1956 *Suez Crisis*, Egypt was attacked by Israel, France and Britain, attracting worldwide support as the victim of imperialist aggression.

Ehrhardt, Hermann: a German *Freikorps* leader. His brigade led the march into Berlin at the time of the *Kapp Putsch*, but he avoided arrest when it collapsed. He later organized an assassination group targeting Weimar politicians, notably *Rathenau*. His activities and his lenient treatment by the authorities, including protection by *Seeckt*, the army commander-in-chief, illustrate the threat to the stability of the Weimar Republic posed by right-wing extremists.

Eichmann, Adolf: a Nazi administrator. From 1942, he was responsible for organizing "the *final solution* to the Jewish problem": he arranged the transport of Jews to the death camps and built gas chambers for mass extermination. He escaped Allied custody in 1945 but was traced by Israeli agents and taken to Israel, where he was tried and executed in 1962.

Einstein, Albert: a physicist of Jewish stock. He fled from Nazi Germany to the USA in 1933. By 1939, he was warning President Roosevelt about German research intended to build an atomic bomb. After 1945, he became alarmed at the threat to human existence from atomic warfare and helped to found *Pugwash*. He died in 1955.

Eisenhower, Dwight: president of the USA, 1953–61. In 1942, during the Second World War, he had been appointed commander of the US troops in Europe.

- In November 1942, he commanded the Allied landings in the *North Africa Campaign*
- In 1943, he was appointed Supreme Commander of the Allied Expeditionary Force, in which role he planned and coordinated the *Second Front*
- In 1944, he commanded the Allied landings in *Normandy* and the subsequent campaigns in Western Europe.

During his period as president, he sought vainly to improve relations with the Soviet Union, but his hopes were shattered in 1960, when a US high-level U2 "reconnaissance" plane was shot down over the Soviet Union and the Soviets broke off all talks.

Eisner, Kurt: a German politician. On 7 November 1918, as the German Second Empire disintegrated, he led a revolution in Munich and proclaimed an independent socialist republic of Bavaria. This was crushed by right-wing supporters, and Eisner was murdered, by monarchists, in 1919.

El Alamein: a decisive battle of the Second World War in North Africa. In July 1942, the German advance into Egypt was halted there, and in the autumn the British army, now under *Montgomery*, defeated the German forces under *Rommel*, driving them back into Libya.

ELAS: Greek communist *partisans*. They fought the German army of occupation in the Second World War and, at its end, controlled much of the country. They then engaged in a bitter three-year civil war against the forces attempting to re-establish the Greek monarchy. Their defeat owed much to Stalin's refusal to help them, in contrast to the abundant aid that their opponents received from the USA.

Enabling Act: an act passed by the German *Reichstag* in March 1933 granting *Hitler* dictatorial powers for four years. Under its terms, the government could rule for that time without consulting the Reichstag on any matter. As an amendment to the constitution, it needed to be passed by a two-thirds majority, and two-thirds of the members also had to be present for the vote. This requirement was made easier by the earlier expulsion of the communist members and by a rule change which meant that absent members were counted as present unless specifically excused. The presence of rowdy gangs of *SS* and *SA* members in the building meant that those who spoke against the bill required great courage. In fact, the center and right-wing parties supported the measure, and democracy disappeared from Germany by a vote of 441 to 94; all the minority votes came from the socialist SPD. The act was the key piece of legislation allowing Hitler to establish the Nazi tyranny. Technically at least, it had been passed quite legally and by a large majority. Its powers lasted not the four years provided for in the act, but for as long as the Nazi Reich that it helped to create.

England: a country which, together with Scotland and Wales, forms Great Britain and, with Northern Ireland added, the United Kingdom.

English: the inhabitants of England. Used as an adjective of nationality, it does not mean the same as *British*.

enosis: the term (in Greek, "union") used to describe the aim of the Cypriot movement seeking the political union of *Cyprus* and Greece. In the 1950s, enosis was the aim of the *EOKA* terrorist movement under *Grivas*. In 1974, an attempted coup to achieve enosis, supported by the "*Greek Colonels*," backfired, and the north of the island was instead first occupied by the Turkish army and then turned into a separate Turkish Cypriot state.

entente: (from French) an understanding. An agreement between nations that falls short of a formal alliance, notably the Anglo–French Entente of 1904, which was often referred to as the *entente cordiale*, and the *Anglo–Russian Entente* of 1907.

entente cordiale: a popular term for the understanding between France and Britain reached in 1904. It settled outstanding colonial questions between the two countries. Stated simply:

- Britain was to have a free hand in Egypt
- the French were to have the same in Morocco.

Previously, relations between the two countries had been far from cordial; indeed, they had seemed close to war over colonial rivalry in the Nile Valley in the *Fashoda Crisis* of 1898. The entente arose from German heavy-handed diplomacy which had brought a clearer understanding of what each country's true national interests were. Since the defeat of 1870, the French had seen Germany as their natural enemy, but it took the German naval building program, its growing industrial might, its tactless support for the Boers in the Boer War and its belligerence with regard to Morocco, to make the British see that the issues which divided them from France might be of less importance than this new threat. Edward VII played a part in creating the more friendly atmosphere, but the roles of the British foreign secretary Lord *Lansdowne*, the French foreign minister *Delcassé* and the French ambassador to London *Cambon*, were more significant. For the French, the entente was a triumph to add to their alliance of 1893 with Russia: France was clearly no longer isolated in Europe. The entente cordiale involved no military commitment for either party but it was the basis for later joint military and naval talks which inevitably tied Britain closer to the French connection, which was to prove impossible to break when war came in 1914.

envoy: a diplomatic representative sent by one government to another to conduct political business.

EOKA: a Greek–Cypriot terrorist movement of the late 1950s. It was led by Colonel *Grivas* and aimed to force a British withdrawal from Cyprus as the first step to securing *enosis* with Greece.

Erhard, Ludwig: economics minister of West Germany, 1949–63, and *chancellor*, 1963–66. As economics minister, he was given much of the credit for the *German economic miracle* of the 1950s, with a trebling of gross national production during his 14 years in office. In 1949, West Germany was still devastated by war; by 1963 it had arguably the strongest economy in Europe. With regard to the economy, Erhard:

- benefited from the country's internal political stability, for which *Adenauer* deserved much of the credit

- benefited also from the expanding European market resulting from both the recovery of national economies and the development of European trading communities
- nationalized the railways
- gave tax incentives to encourage investment in productive industries
- encouraged workers' councils to participate in running businesses, and made labor relations in German industry a model for other countries
- met labor shortages in the rapidly expanding economy by encouraging immigrant workers from Turkey and other areas of Eastern Europe
- coined the term "social market economy" to describe his achievement with the German economy, which combined considerable economic freedom with a wide range of social-service provisions.

As chancellor, following Adenauer, Erhard lacked his predecessor's political skill both in Parliament and with the electorate, and resigned in 1966 when tax increases undermined the popularity of his Christian Democrat government.

Eritrea: a country in northeast Africa. From 1889 it was an Italian colony, and prior to that part of Ethiopia. It was the base from which the Italians, in 1935–36, launched their invasion of Ethiopia. From the 1970s, it was the setting for civil war and famine.

Erlander, Tage: prime minister of Sweden, 1946–68. His government further developed Sweden's extensive social-welfare provisions and continued to promote its neutrality during the sharpest period of the Cold War.

escalation: increasing the intensity or range (of a conflict).

espionage: spying, or the use of spies.

Estonia: one of the three *Baltic Republics*. It:

- was part of tsarist Russia until, in 1917, it gained its independence at the time of the Bolshevik Revolution
- was occupied in 1940 by Soviet troops acting in accordance with the terms of the 1939 *Nazi–Soviet Pact*
- welcomed the German army in 1941 when it was invaded as part of *Operation Barbarossa*
- was reoccupied in 1944 by the Red Army and became a republic within the Soviet Union.

For over 40 years within the Soviet Union, Estonian national feeling survived, and in late 1989 popular pressure led the Estonian Supreme Soviet to declare the country a sovereign independent state. Independence was overwhelmingly supported in a 1991 referendum and was accepted by the Soviet Union on 10 September of the same year.

ETA: the initials of the *Basque* terrorist group in Spain. It aimed to force the concession, from the Spanish state, of a separate Basque republic in northern Spain, so restoring the short-lived republic of 1936–37 destroyed by Franco. In the second half of the twentieth century, it was responsible for many acts of political terrorism.

Ethiopia: a country in northeast Africa. It is also called Abyssinia and was, in the early twentieth century, one of only two countries in Africa which were not ruled by the European empires. Its ruler in the 1930s took the title of Emperor *Haile Selassie*. In 1935–36, the country was conquered and occupied by Italy in the *Italo-Ethiopian War*, the emperor's appeal to the League of Nations for help falling on deaf ears. Ethiopia was liberated from Italian rule by British forces in 1941, and its emperor was restored to the throne.

Euratom: short for the European Atomic Energy Community, which was set up in 1957 to encourage cooperation in the development of nuclear energy, and became part of the European Community in 1967.

Eurocommunism: the individual communist parties in Western European states after the Second World War pursuing their own policies and paths to power without – as had happened between the two world wars – control from the Soviet Union. They sought separate national identities and power through elections rather than by plotting revolution and the overthrow of the capitalist state. One of their most successful exponents was the Italian communist leader *Togliatti*, but elsewhere the tactics produced very limited electoral success.

European Coal and Steel Community (ECSC): founded in 1951 on the basis of the *Schuman Plan* to merge the coal, iron and steel industries of the Benelux countries, France, Italy and West Germany. It became part of the *European Community* in 1967. Its creation was a triumph for post-war reconciliation and the first major step towards European economic union.

European Commission: the executive arm of the *European Union*. It was set up in Brussels in 1957, and its paid officials were given extensive powers to run the then *European Economic Community*'s affairs.

European Community (EC): formally established in 1967 when the European Atomic Energy Community (*Euratom*), the *European Coal and Steel Community* (the ECSC), and the *European Economic Community* (the EEC) merged. Its purpose was to develop economic and political integration as planned in the *Rome Treaties* of 1957. Prior to 1967, the constituent bodies had already established an overarching framework of control and consultation, and in this respect it can be argued that the community originated in 1958 with the implementation of the *Rome Treaties*.

European Convention on Human Rights: promulgated by the Council of Europe in 1950 to give protection against the abuse of human rights by the governments and courts of member nations of the council. The council set up the *European Court of Human Rights* and the European Commission of Human Rights to administer the convention.

European Court of Human Rights: created in 1950 by the Council of Europe to administer the *European Convention on Human Rights*. It acts as a court of appeal from the law courts of the member nations and has proved a valuable protector of citizens against arbitrary acts of government and unjust legislation. As such, it has often been unpopular with these governments, not least the British government. It amalgamated with the European Commission of Human Rights, set up to administer the same convention, in 1993.

European Defense Community: a French plan of the early 1950s for a common defense policy among the West European nations making up the *European Coal and*

Steel Community. Britain was reluctant to become involved, and the plan was over-taken by the expansion of NATO and the creation of the *Western European Union* in 1955.

European Economic Community (EEC): created by the Rome Treaties in 1957. It became one of the constituents of the *European Community* in 1967 and the *European Union* in 1993. It was often referred to as the *Common Market.*

European empires: territories outside Europe, often of vast size, controlled by European nations as colonies.

- Many colonial possessions, particularly in Asia and the West Indies, trace their origins back to the sixteenth and seventeenth centuries
- Several of the empires expanded greatly in the Pacific, and above all in Africa, in the nineteenth century
- With the addition of League of Nations *mandates* after the First World War, these empires were territorially at their height in the 1920s and 1930s
- The great imperial powers of the twentieth century were Belgium, Britain, France, Holland and Portugal. Germany had colonies in Africa and the Pacific, but these were taken from it by the 1919 Versailles Treaty.

The first signs of pressure on the empires began to appear in the inter-war years, with nationalists wanting independence active in some Asian colonies, and with the cost of the empires, and particularly their defense in any future European war, becoming an important consideration. After the Second World War, the European empires began to disintegrate, and the process of *decolonization* set in. By 1980, this process was virtually completed, and the centuries-old domination of the world by the countries of Europe was at an end. (For the fate of the European empires after the Second World War, see the entries under *Belgian Congo, British Empire, Dutch East Indies, French Empire* and *Portugal.*)

European Free Trade Area (EFTA): created in 1959 as an alternative trading area to the *European Economic Community* (EEC). At its height, it consisted of Austria, Britain, Denmark, Norway, Portugal, Sweden, Switzerland, Finland and Iceland. It became clear that EFTA could not create an effective economic area to rival the EEC, and this led in 1972 to the withdrawal of Britain and Denmark, both of which joined the EEC. This further reduced EFTA's significance, and in 1977 it entered into trade agreements with the EEC. By 1995, all the EFTA countries except Iceland, Norway and Switzerland had become members of the *European Union,* the eventual successor to the EEC.

European Parliament: the parliament of the *European Union,* originally set up as part of the *European Coal and Steel Community* and meeting alternately in Luxembourg and Strasbourg. Since 1979, it has been elected directly by the citizens of the union and has increased its powers in financial and constitutional matters. The *Single European Act* of 1986 gave it some powers over the separate national parliaments of the European Union member states.

European Union: formally constituted in 1993 by the *Maastricht* Treaty. It is the successor of the *European Community* and its constituent organizations. The following countries were members in 1998 (with dates of accession):

- Austria (1995)
- Belgium (1958)
- Denmark (1973)
- Finland (1995)
- France (1958)
- Germany (1958) – i.e. West Germany, with East Germany joining on reunification in 1990
- Greece (1981)
- Ireland (1973)
- Italy (1958)
- Luxembourg (1958)
- Netherlands (1958)
- Portugal (1986)
- Spain (1986)
- Sweden (1995)
- United Kingdom (1973).

In 1985, Greenland withdrew from membership, and in 1994, the Norwegian people, in a referendum, rejected membership.

The origins of the European Union are in the period of reconstruction after the Second World War. Key figures in its early development were *Monnet* and *Schuman* of France, *Spaak* of Belgium, *De Gasperi* of Italy, and *Adenauer* and *Erhard* of West Germany. They were motivated by their experience of the economic and social ills of the 1930s and by the destruction brought about during the Second World War by aggressive nationalism. The enthusiasm of the three smallest original members, Belgium, Holland and Luxembourg, stemmed directly from their role as wartime victims of the expansionism of a larger neighbor. Key stages in the development of what became the European Union were:

- 1948: Belgium, Holland and Luxembourg formed the *Benelux Union*
- 1950: Schuman proposed that France and Germany pool their coal and steel industries
- 1951: the *European Coal and Steel Community* (ECSC) founded by Belgium, France, Holland, Italy, Luxembourg and West Germany (the "Six")
- 1957: *Rome Treaties*, signed by the Six, established the *European Economic Community* (EEC) and *Euratom*
- 1958: the European Parliament and European Court of Justice established for the ECSC, the EEC and Euratom. The EEC established the European Commission and the Council of Ministers
- 1962: a *common agricultural policy* was set up
- 1967: the ECSC, EEC and Euratom merged to form the *European Community* (EC) with one council of ministers and one commission
- 1970: the foreign policies of member states began to be coordinated
- 1971: a common fisheries policy was agreed
- 1972: the Social Fund was set up
- 1979: the first direct elections of members of the *European Parliament* were held
- 1979: the European Monetary System (EMS) was founded

- 1986: the *Single European Act* was passed
- 1991: the *Maastricht* Treaty was signed
- 1992: the European Union was officially founded with the implementation of the Maastricht Treaty.

Évian Agreements: agreements reached in 1962 between the French government of *de Gaulle* and the Algerian nationalists, agreeing to referendums, in both *Algeria* and France, on the future of Algeria. The agreements, when implemented and ratified in both countries, ended the *Algerian War* and led to the independence of Algeria. They were savagely attacked by the *OAS* as a betrayal of the interests of the French settlers in Algeria.

executive: in political terms, the government of the country. It should not be confused with the legislature, or law-making body.

Facta, Luigi: prime minister of Italy, 1922. With the Italian government paralyzed, he wanted to make a stand against the threats and bluster of Mussolini and the fascists. The unions had called a general strike to force the government to take action against fascist violence in the cities, and the fascists had retaliated violently in order to break the strike. Facta's government was divided between those who wanted to challenge the fascists and those who wanted to do a deal with them against the socialists. Facta:

- established that the army would remain loyal
- reinforced the garrison in Rome
- asked the king, *Victor Emmanuel III,* for emergency powers to block the fascist *March on Rome.*

The king at first approved of Facta's resolution but within hours changed his mind and refused his request. Facta then resigned, and after further political negotiations, the king appointed Mussolini as prime minister.

faction: a small group with special aims within a larger group.

fait accompli: a thing that has been done and is past arguing against. It comes from the French and could be applied to such events as the abrupt seizure of power in a state, as in the October Revolution in Russia bringing the Bolsheviks to power.

Falange: a right-wing Spanish political movement founded in 1933. During the civil war it opposed the Spanish Republic, and afterwards was used by Franco as the basis for the political life of the fascist state.

Falkenhayn, Erich: a German general who commanded the 1916 attack on *Verdun.* He intended a war of attrition which would bleed the French dry in defense of the town. In practice, casualties were so heavy on both sides that, after four months, he called off the attack and was then relieved of his command on the Western Front. His battle strategy illustrates how insensitive First World War generals were to the losses incurred among the troops they commanded.

Farinacci, Roberto: an Italian fascist politician. As party secretary, he made the Fascist Party more efficient in the late 1920s and so did much to help consolidate Mussolini's position, doing the necessary mundane work which Mussolini lacked the will to tackle. He was little known and made little impact on national politics, and his career perhaps illustrates the mediocre, anonymous quality of the men around Mussolini, in contrast to the notorious figures around Hitler. Farinacci was captured and shot on the same day in 1945 and by the same group of Italian partisans who killed Mussolini as they tried to flee to Switzerland.

fascism: a term generally applied to authoritarian and *Nazi* movements during and since the 1920s and 1930s, when it first came to prominence.

- The term originated in Italy (the fasces, bundles of sticks, were symbols of authority in the ancient Roman Empire) and was used by *Mussolini* to depict the nationalist, authoritarian and anti-communist movement which brought him to power

- Since then, it has become widely, and too loosely, used by opponents to describe almost any extreme right-wing regime, party or individual of which they disapprove
- Its use is best limited to its original historical context, namely the emergence of right-wing authoritarian regimes in Europe between the First and Second World Wars.

In this context, fascism was a response to:

- the collapse, at the end of the First World War, of the great European empires
- the failure of the parliamentary regimes which succeeded them to solve vast economic and social problems
- the emergence of the new communist state set up in the Soviet Union in 1917.

Fascism was an emotional response to the political problems of these years, and it never developed into a coherent philosophy, as Marxism did. Its energy appealed to ex-servicemen cast adrift at the end of the war, and most fascist movements were linked to paramilitary organizations. Fascism contained both radical and conservative elements within it. Hitler relied on the support of conservative interests in Germany, but constructed a far-reaching reorganization of the German state. Mussolini's propaganda stressed radical change, but in Spain Franco set up a deeply conservative regime. There was great diversity among fascist regimes, but they had in common:

- a stress on national identity
- vehement opposition to communism
- single-party politics
- the maximum control of all aspects of life within a *totalitarian* state.

fascist Grand Council: a new constitutional body of the 1920s in Italy. In theory, it would decide the succession to the throne or to the office of prime minister. In practice, it remained a cloak for the personal dictatorship of Mussolini.

fascist Italy: topics and issues which are important to historians here include:

- reasons for the post-war dissatisfaction with the democratic parties and politicians
- nationalist resentment at Italy's treatment at the Paris Peace Conference
- why *Mussolini*'s 1922 bluff succeeded in making him prime minister
- the appeal of fascism for many Italians
- the means by which Mussolini established totalitarian power between 1922 and 1926
- the reasons for the ineffective opposition to Mussolini's growing power after 1922
- the structure and the domestic achievements of the *corporate state*
- Mussolini as European statesman, 1922–35
- Mussolini and the Italian Empire in *Ethiopia*, 1935–36
- Mussolini and the alliance with Nazi Germany
- Italy's role in the Second World War.

Fashoda Crisis: the 1898 crisis between Britain and France. A French force, after a cross-desert march, occupied a fort on the Nile and so challenged Britain's

FASCIST ITALY – KEY ISSUES

Background		The 1920s
Disillusion with Italian democracy	The events of 1922	The consolidation of power
The fascist appeal		Lack of opposition

Fascist Italy 1922–43

Foreign policy	The role of Mussolini	The corporate state
Imperial policy		Battles for Grain, Land and Births
Second World War		Propaganda

Assessing what was achieved:
political life
the economy
society
empire
foreign affairs
war

previously undisputed presence in Egypt and the Sudan. Neither government would at first back down, but fortunately there was no actual conflict at Fashoda. This was the low point of Franco–British relations, and the crisis ended when the French backed down in return for British recognition of their claims in Morocco, which in turn led to the *entente cordiale* and the opening of a new stage in relations between the two countries.

The incident also illustrates the attitude of the European imperial powers, then at their height, towards the exploitation and division of vast areas of Africa as a matter of right.

February Revolution: the 1917 Russian revolution which overthrew tsardom. Soldiers joined rioters, protesting in Petrograd over food shortages and the war, having first refused orders to fire on strikers. This refusal to obey orders was the crucial difference from the events of the 1905 Revolution when the army had remained loyal to the tsar. There were no recognized leaders of the revolution, and for a moment *Nicholas II* thought of shelling his own capital, but was dissuaded by his generals. The liberal politicians in the fourth Duma, who had set up a *Provisional Government* under Prince Lvov, wanted constitutional reform, and many of them would have been happy to retain a reformed monarchy. Nicholas was not prepared to compromise his own authority as tsar and preferred to abdicate. When his brother, the Grand Duke Michael, refused the throne, the imperial monarchy simply disappeared. These events occurred between 8 and 15 March in the Gregorian calendar in operation in Western Europe, but the Julian calendar then still applied in Russia – hence the February Revolution. After the revolution, the Provisional Government ruled until the Bolshevik takeover in the *October Revolution* of 1917.

federal: a system of government in which states combine into one nation but retain considerable powers over their own internal affairs. The balance of power between the central and the state governments may, of course, change over time and usually in favor of the central government, though the case of Yugoslavia after the death of Tito is a notable exception.

Federal Republic of Germany (FRG): more commonly referred to as *West Germany*.

fellow traveler: usually used for someone who is a sympathizer with the Communist Party but is not a member of it. There is usually a hint of criticism attached to its use.

field marshal: an army officer of the highest rank.

fifth column: a Second World War term used to describe secret enemy sympathizers. It was coined during the Spanish Civil War when, with four nationalist military columns closing in on Madrid, it was claimed that the civilian inhabitants would form a fifth column of support for the advancing fascists.

Fifth French Republic: set up by *de Gaulle* in 1958 at the height of the crisis brought on by the *Algerian War*. The central feature of its constitution, in contrast to the *Fourth French Republic*, was the creation of a powerful presidency. The president:

- appoints the prime minister
- can order new Assembly elections to break any deadlock there
- has considerable emergency powers
- can put issues direct to the people in a referendum.

De Gaulle became the first president, and in 1962 used a referendum to effect a sweeping change in the constitution whereby the president would in future be elected directly by the people. All this reflected de Gaulle's personal view of government and his distrust of the French political class. Political parties changed their titles on several occasions under the Fifth Republic, but the main groupings were:

- on the right, the Gaullists Union for the New Republic (UNR) and their frequent allies, the Popular Republican Movement (MRP), with *Debré*, Pompidou and Chirac prominent supporters. They fought the 1995 election as an alliance between the RPR (Rassemblement Pour la République) and the UDF (Union Pour la Démocratie Française), between them winning 474 of the 577 National Assembly seats
- the Center Party (from 1987, the UDF) of Giscard d'Estaing and its allies
- the Socialist Party of Mitterrand
- the Communist Party of *Marchais*, briefly in office as coalition partners, from 1981 to 1983, for the first time since 1947
- a neo-fascist movement led by Le Pen which had some limited success in national and local elections in the 1980s through exploiting immigration and race issues.

The republic survived the tensions caused by the end of the French Empire, particularly in Algeria, and played a full part in moves towards European union, making a particular virtue of the close relationship with West Germany. When, in 1969, de Gaulle lost a further referendum on a quite minor constitutional matter, he resigned.

Presidents since 1969 have been:

- 1969–74: Georges *Pompidou*
- 1974–81: Valéry *Giscard d'Estaing*
- 1981–95: François *Mitterrand*
- 1995– : Jacques *Chirac*

film: together with the radio, one of the two most important mass-communication media developed in the first half of the twentieth century. Pre-1914 developments were chiefly in France, but during and after the First World War its use spread widely, particularly in the USA. Though much of the output was simply for mass-entertainment purposes, film in the *cinema* had, between the wars, significant effects on politics, both in terms of providing vivid information and as deliberate propaganda. From the 1950s in Western Europe, it increasingly took second place to television.

Final Solution: the term increasingly used during the Second World War by leading Nazis to identify the policy of exterminating the Jewish population of Germany and German-occupied countries.

Finland: an independent Baltic state since 1919. It had previously been controlled by Russia, and independence came as a consequence of the 1917 Bolshevik Revolution. Soviet troops invaded the country in the *Finnish–Russian War* of 1939–40, and the defeated Finns lost much territory at the end of that war. From 1941, Finland fought on the German side in the Second World War, but by 1944 had to surrender once more to the Soviet Union, switching sides as late as March 1945 and declaring war on Germany. After 1945, Finland sought good relations with the Soviet Union and took a neutral stance in international affairs. This satisfied the Soviet Union, which did not attempt to draw it into the Soviet bloc of East European communist states. In 1961, Finland joined EFTA and, in 1995, the European Union.

Finnish–Russian War: the war of November 1939–February 1940. After some early success in holding the Soviet army at bay, Finland was, after fierce fighting, forced to make peace on Soviet terms, losing land on its eastern frontier. In Britain and France, two countries already at war with Germany, there was much sympathy for the Finns, though it was probably fortunate for the future conduct of the Second World War that it proved impossible to send troops to help them against the Soviets.

First World War: the war from 1914 to 1918 which took place in Europe.

Background to the war

The war was brought about by growing national rivalries, particularly in the Balkans between *Serbia* and the *Austro–Hungarian Empire*. The rival systems of alliances, the *Triple Alliance* and the *Triple Entente*, made it into a European-wide conflict between the *Central powers*, principally Germany, Austria-Hungary, the Ottoman Empire and Bulgaria, and the *Allied powers*, principally Britain, France, Russia, Belgium and Serbia; but with Greece, Italy, Portugal, Romania and the USA joining in during the course of the war. The period from 1900 to 1914 had been marked by an arms race between the powers and by a series of diplomatic crises, notably the *Bosnian Crisis* of 1908, which created a situation in which neither Austria-Hungary nor Russia felt it could back down in 1914 in the aftermath of the assassination of the Archduke *Franz Ferdinand.* Alliance obligations then came into play to entangle, with varying degrees of willingness, Germany, France and Britain. (The origins of the war are analyzed at greater length in the next entry in this handbook.) /

Course of the war

The early German advance into Belgium and France was checked, and the fighting on the *Western Front* turned into a static war, with a decisive breakthrough coming only in the last weeks of the war. The *Eastern Front* produced more movement and, by 1917, a decisive victory for Germany against Russia, followed by the Treaty of *Brest–Litovsk.* The *Dardanelles* Campaign failed to create a new front against the Ottoman Empire, but in the Middle East the British and their Arab allies mopped up Turkish possessions. The *Salonika Campaign,* north from Greece, and the Italian attacks in the Alps made little progress until Austria-Hungary was crumbling from other pressures.

- *Air power* played little part in deciding the outcome of the war
- The only great naval battle was *Jutland,* and the inability of the German fleet to dominate the seas denied it any hope of victory against Britain
- The German *U-boat* offensive in the Atlantic, however, came close to cutting Britain off from vital war supplies and food.

End of the war

By November 1918, the German army on the Western Front was in full retreat, the German fleet was in a state of mutiny and there were food riots in the streets of the major German cities. On the Eastern Front, the Austrian army had disintegrated or was in headlong retreat. The German army commanders Hindenburg and Ludendorff advised Kaiser William II to surrender. Instead, he abdicated and the new government surrendered two days later.

Results of the war

- In total, some 9 million people were killed during the course of the war, and perhaps twice that number were wounded
- The influenza epidemic at the end of the war may well have killed as many as the war dead and wounded together
- The war contributed to the downfall of tsardom in Russia
- Defeat brought about the end of the German Second Empire, as well as subjecting Germany to the humiliations of the *Versailles* Peace Treaty
- Defeat also ensured the end of the Austro-Hungarian and Ottoman empires
- At the *Paris Peace Conference,* a host of new nations emerged across Central and Eastern Europe to replace them.

First World War, the debate on its origins: the war from August 1914 to November 1918 which took place in Europe. At the Paris Peace Conference in 1919, the Allies formally declared Germany to have been guilty of starting the war and required Germany to accept that this was the case, and outside Germany, this view prevailed in the inter-war years.

(Cont. p. 93)

BRAVO, BELGIUM!

7 The cartoon that helped to bring Britain into war in 1914 (reproduced with permission of Punch Ltd.)

ORIGINS OF THE FIRST WORLD WAR

The political issues of the period

- National aspirations in the Balkans: Serbia and Austria-Hungary, Russia as protector of the Slavs
- The French wish for revenge for 1870 and for the restoration of Alsace-Lorraine
- German unification and industrial and military might upsetting the European balance of power
- Colonial and commercial rivalry between the powers
- A popular acceptance of war, social Darwinism, jingoism.

Rival alliance systems	The arms race	International crises
Triple Alliance	Conscription and mass armies	Morocco
versus	Artillery and machine guns	Bosnia, 1908
Triple Entente	Railways for fast deployment	Balkan Wars
	Anglo–German naval rivalry	

The events of 1914

28 June Assassination of the Archduke Franz Ferdinand, heir to the throne of Austria-Hungary; assassins linked to Serbia

5 July Austria notified Germany of its intention to deal firmly with Serbia, which it held responsible

6 July Germany assured Austria of its support

23 July Austrian ultimatum to Serbia. Serbian conciliatory reply rejected

25 July Serbia accepted all the Austrian demands except one

28 July Austria, with the backing of Germany, declared war on Serbia and bombarded Belgrade

30 July Russia mobilized its armed forces, ignoring German warnings

1 August Germany declared war on Russia, which requested French help under the terms of the 1893 alliance. The French mobilized their armed forces

3 August Germany declared war on France

4 August Germany implemented the Schlieffen Plan and invaded Belgium in order to secure a swift route to victory against France

5 August Britain declared war on Germany

Comments

- Austria-Hungary's determination to end the threat to its multinational empire from Serbian nationalism was the trigger for war
- Germany's rash backing of Austria, as in the Bosnian Crisis, 1908, encouraged this boldness
- Russia's role as protector of the Slavs and its wish not to see Austria powerful in the Balkans meant that, after the 1908 humiliation, it felt it had to back Serbia
- The French could not ignore Russia's appeal for help without destroying the anti-German alliance built up over 20 years
- Britain, despite its understanding with France, hesitated to get involved, but the German attack on neutral Belgium convinced the doubters that it too had to honor the obligations it had drifted into under the entente cordiale
- The speed of events in late July prevented second thoughts or the pursuit of other solutions
- There was throughout Europe a willingness, among the public and many leading politicians, to go to war, the length and the horror of which had not been foreseen
- In the event, colonial rivalries may have encouraged the rival alliance systems, but they played no part in the events leading to war in 1914.

MILITARY FORCES AND SPENDING IN THE FIRST WORLD WAR

	War expenditure (1913 prices) (billions of US dollars)	Total mobilized force (millions)
British Empire	23.0	9.5
France	9.3	8.2
Russia	5.4	13.0
Italy	3.2	5.6
United States	17.1	3.8
Other Allies (Belgium, Romania, Portugal, Greece, Serbia)	−0.3	2.6
Total Allies	57.7	42.7
Germany	19.9	13.25
Austria-Hungary	4.7	9.0
Bulgaria, Turkey	0.1	2.85
Total Central powers	24.7	25.10

TIMELINE: THE FIRST WORLD WAR – PRINCIPAL MILITARY ENGAGEMENTS

1914 War began

Germans checked Russian advance at *Tannenberg* and pushed them back at the *Masurian Lakes*

French checked German advance at the *Marne*

First Battle of *Ypres* checked German advance to seize the Channel ports

Beginning of trench warfare on the *Western Front*

1915 The *Dardanelles* Campaign, Gallipoli

First use of tanks, by British at *Cambrai*, failed to break Western-Front deadlock

1916 German offensive against *Verdun*

The Battle of the *Somme*

The Brusilov Offensive on the *Eastern Front* followed by German advances

The naval battle of *Jutland*

1917 The Battle of *Vimy Ridge* produced only a dent in the German defensive lines

Mutinies in the French army

The Battle of *Passchendaele* produced no breakthrough despite enormous losses

1918 German spring offensive blocked at the Marne (as in 1914)

Allied August offensive, using tanks and aircraft, produced the first breakthrough on the Western Front. German resistance quickly crumbled

November Armistice ended the war in the west

Since then, the causes of the war have been much debated by historians. An arguable explanation of the origins of the war could be offered on the following lines:

- There was a widely held view at the time that any war would be a short one. No one envisaged the total commitment needed in, and the total devastation caused by, the actual war, so there is no need to explain why statesmen were prepared to embark on such an appalling conflict: they lacked the imagination to see what a war backed by science and technology might be like in reality
- The war started as a Balkan war between Austria-Hungary and Serbia, and this is where the explanation should start
- This Balkan war arose from Austrian fears that Slav nationalism, headed by Serbia, threatened the existence of its own multinational empire
- Serbia's power and territory had greatly increased in the *Balkan Wars* of 1912–13, and its leaders had ambitions to create a greater Serbia which would include Slavs living in the Austro-Hungarian Empire. Austria had

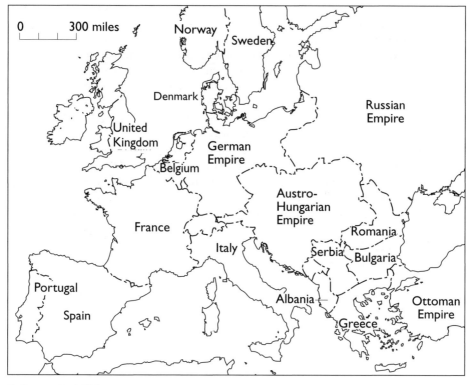

8 Europe in 1914

THE DEAD IN THE FIRST WORLD WAR

Allies	Dead	Central powers	Dead
Russia	1,700,000	Germany	1,773,700
France	1,357,800	Austria-Hungary	1,200,000
British Empire	908,371	Turkey	325,000
Italy	650,000		
Romania	335,706		
United States	116,516	Total all belligerents	8,367,093

been a spectator in those wars and felt it could not afford to allow further Serbian expansion

- The assassination of Archduke *Franz Ferdinand* at Sarajevo gave Austria an excuse to check Serbia, even at the risk of a Balkan war. An ultimatum to Serbia was followed within days by the bombardment of the Serbian capital Belgrade, and the "short Balkan war" had begun
- The danger to Austria-Hungary was that the greatest Slav power, Russia, would support its fellow Slavs, and so the Austrian government might not have risked war but for the firm guarantees of support that it had received from Germany
- Germany's role and the existence of two Europe-wide rival alliance systems, the *Triple Alliance* and the *Triple Entente*, are central to an explanation of why the Balkan hostilities became a European war
- There was a view in Germany that a European war was at some stage likely and could be used to break the encirclement of Germany by the Entente powers. *Fischer*, the German historian, later argued that the military, Kaiser *William II* and even Chancellor *Bethmann-Hollweg* were in favor of war both for this reason and also because it would strengthen their power within Germany against the socialists
- Russia was the first state to mobilize its troops, in order to put pressure on Austria. It had been humiliated in the *Bosnian Crisis* of 1908 and felt that its international standing would not survive a second retreat when challenged by Austria
- Germany's war strategy rested on the *Schlieffen Plan*, which required a knock-out blow against France prior to an expected longer war against Russia. Faced with its commitments to Austria-Hungary and Russia's mobilization, Germany demanded that France surrender border forts to guarantee French neutrality. The French, unsurprisingly, refused and Germany invaded, driving through Belgium to secure the Schlieffen Plan's quick victory
- In this explanation of the war, France's only role was to react to unreasonable German demands
- Britain, morally committed under the *entente cordiale* to help France, hesitated, but the German invasion of Belgium swung opinion in favor of war

- Many factors which had created the rival alliance systems played no part in the short-term causes of the war. It was not about imperial rivalries overseas, nor, as Marxists would have liked, about rival capitalist countries fighting over markets and raw materials. The arms race did not cause the war, it simply made the bloodshed more terrible once it came. Even the alliance-system obligations could have been evaded: Britain almost tried to evade these obligations; Italy did, and remained neutral until 1915, when it deserted its Triple Alliance partners and came in on the Allied side

- It is worth repeating that no one anticipated the long and terrible war that developed. In the tense, jingoistic atmosphere of pre-1914 Europe, a small war producing significant diplomatic gains may well have seemed a reasonable extension of normal diplomacy; such may well have been the feelings in Austria-Hungary and Germany. However, once the alliance systems began to extend the scope of the conflict, the powers felt they

---

TIMELINE: EUROPE 1890–1914
International affairs

1890 Death of Bismarck, creator of the German Second Empire and of the Triple Alliance
1891
1892
1893 Franco–Russian defensive alliance
1894
1895
1896
1897 First German Navy Law to expand its battle fleet
1898 The Fashoda Crisis between France and Britain
1899 Boer War (to 1902)
1900 Second German Navy Law
1901
1902 Anglo–Japanese defensive alliance
1903
1904 Russo–Japanese War (to 1905)
Entente cordiale between France and Britain
1905
1906 Algeciras Conference over Franco–German dispute in Morocco
German Navy Law to widen and deepen the Kiel Canal
1907 Anglo–Russian Entente
1908 Bosnian Crisis
1909
1910
1911 Agadir Crisis
1912 Balkan War
1913 Second Balkan War
1914 Outbreak of the First World War

could not afford to desert their allies and face future isolation – this was the situation faced by France and Britain.

Fischer, Fritz: a German historian who argued that the outbreak of the First World War in 1914 was a premeditated act of aggression by the German kaiser, his military advisers and the chancellor, Bethmann-Hollweg. His argument did not convince all other historians, but certainly drew attention to the clear belief in top German circles that a great European war was likely, and that this encouraged both military preparations and also a reckless willingness to back Austria-Hungary in the 1914 crisis. To this limited extent at least, Germany was "guilty" of starting the war.

Fisher, Lord: the British first sea lord from 1904 to 1915, after service in the navy since 1854. He was responsible for the decision to build *dreadnought* battleships in response to German naval building plans. He resigned over differences with his political master, Winston Churchill, and in protest against the Dardanelles expedition. He died in 1920.

Fiume: the principal Adriatic port of the Austro-Hungarian Empire. In 1919, it was claimed by both Italy and the new kingdom of Yugoslavia. Allied plans to make it a free city foundered when D'Annunzio occupied it for Italy. Most of the area was incorporated into Italy by Mussolini in 1924. At the Treaty of Paris in 1947, it was ceded to Yugoslavia.

Five-Year Plans: a feature of the *command economy* of the Soviet Union from 1928.

- The First Plan for the *Soviet economy*, organized by the central planning authority *Gosplan*, concentrated on the collectivization of agriculture and on developing heavy industry and power supplies
- Collectivization was largely complete by the end of the First Plan, and the Second and Third Plans, in 1933 and 1937, concentrated again on heavy industry, transport and power. The proposed production of more consumer goods in the Third Plan was overtaken by the expansion of the armaments industry
- The Fourth Plan, in 1946, successfully concentrated on the post-war reconstruction of agriculture and heavy industry, which was again the emphasis in the Fifth Plan of 1951.

Gosplan continued to plan development and production targets, controlling prices and wages as part of the process, and its powerful planning bureaucracy became an obstacle to necessary economic reforms which neither *Khrushchev* nor *Gorbachev* was able to overcome.

Flanders: a region of Belgium which was the scene of some of the most bloody fighting of the First World War.

Foch, Ferdinand: the leading French soldier of the First World War. In 1914, he fought the Battle of the *Marne* and, in 1916, commanded the French troops at the Battle of the *Somme*. His belief in the need to attack the enemy led, in the era of trench warfare, to high casualties. After the British agreed, in 1918, to accept him as Allied commander-in-chief, the previous distrust between the military men of the two Allied nations, which had impeded effective prosecution of the war, ended and Foch's summer offensive led directly to the German surrender in November. At the

Paris Peace Conference, he was one of the hawks pressing for very tough terms to be imposed on Germany.

Food and Agriculture Organization: a specialized agency of the UN.

foreign currency reserves: the quantity of foreign currency held by a country. It is one measure of how healthy a nation's trading position is. In times of economic or political crisis, foreign investors may well withdraw their investments and so deepen the crisis by depleting the reserves, and this acts as a powerful weapon forcing the government to correct the situation. In 1956, this was one factor forcing Britain and France to bring the Suez Crisis to a speedy end.

Fourteen Points: principles of the peace program of US President Woodrow Wilson. When the USA entered the First World War, Wilson was determined that the Allies' war aims be defined and that their role in fighting the war be given a moral basis. In January 1918, he produced his Fourteen Points, each of which sought to provide future solutions to the sorts of dangerous issues which had led to the outbreak of war in 1914. He then pressed these on the Allies and tried to insist that they become the basis for peace negotiations at the *Paris Peace Conference*. In practice, it did not prove simple to apply all the points to the complex arrangements necessary at the end of the war, and in any event the French were determined that revenge for their suffering and protection against future German aggression be of at least equal importance. The Fourteen Points were:

- all treaties and international diplomacy to be open
- freedom of navigation of the seas
- the removal of economic barriers between nations
- armaments reduction to the lowest point consistent with domestic safety
- colonial rivalries to be settled by negotiation, and the interests of the colonial people to be borne in mind
- all Russian territory to be evacuated and its people allowed to decide their own future
- Belgian independence to be restored
- Alsace-Lorraine to be returned to France
- national determination to decide the line of Italy's frontiers
- autonomous development for the people of the Austro-Hungarian Empire
- the territorial integrity of the Balkan states to be restored, and this to include access to the sea for Serbia
- the Ottoman Empire to be broken up and Turkish areas to form an independent state, with autonomous development for the other peoples of the empire; the Dardanelles strait to be permanently open to all shipping
- an independent Poland to be created, with access to the sea
- an international association to be set up to guarantee the independence and territorial integrity of all nations.

Whenever, at the Paris Peace Conference, the application of the first thirteen points proved difficult or impossible, Wilson took comfort from the fourteenth point, for once the international association existed, all the other weaknesses of the peace treaties could eventually be rectified through its beneficial offices. His tragedy was that his fellow Americans rejected precisely that point in the peace arrangements, and the USA never became a member of Wilson's creation, the *League of Nations*.

Fourth French Republic: set up in 1946 after the Second World War, it survived until 1958. Its constitution, established in 1946, set up:

- a National Assembly which could only be elected every five years
- a council as a second chamber of the Parliament with few powers
- a weak presidency chosen by the members of the Parliament.

De Gaulle, fearing that this was a recipe for weak, short-lived coalition governments, at this point withdrew from politics. His fears proved to be well-founded: only one government of the 23 formed in the next 12 years was drawn from a single party: this was Blum's socialist ministry of only two months' duration at the end of 1946.

The system of proportional representation in Assembly elections produced a large number of parties there. From the political right to left, the main ones were:

- the Poujadist Movement in the mid-1950s: the neo-fascist party of *Poujade*
- the Rally of the French People (RPF), a short-lived *Gaullist* party which was disbanded in the early 1950s
- the Popular Republican Movement (MRP): with *Schuman* and *Pflimlin*
- the Socialist Party: the party of Blum and *Mollet*
- the Radical Socialists: with *Mendès-France*
- the Communist Party: with *Thorez*.

In these circumstances, all governments other than Blum's were coalitions, formed after much inter-party haggling made more prolonged by the constitutional clause that new Assembly elections were not possible until the five-year interval had been completed. Elections in 1947, 1951 and 1956 failed to break the deadlock between conservative parties strong in rural France and left-wing parties strong in the indust-rial cities. In the late 1950s, the neo-fascist party led by *Poujade* further complicated the business of government-making. Even the republic's most active reforming prime minister, Pierre Mendès-France, failed to provide government stability.

The underlying economic and social record under the republic was, however, more impressive:

- there was a good recovery from the disruption of war on the basis of both the five-year *Monnet Plan* and *Marshall Plan* funds
- economic growth was strong and unemployment usually low
- France, guided by Robert Schuman, played the leading part in founding the *European Coal and Steel Community* in 1952, and this led on to the sign-ing of the *Treaties of Rome*, establishing the *European Economic Community*, in 1957
- family allowances, to encourage population growth, retirement pensions and health care, were improved.

Nevertheless, there were successive economic crises, usually arising either from consumption exceeding production – thus leading to inflation and to repeated devaluations of the franc – or from imports exceeding exports – thus leading to a balance-of-payments deficit.

The republic suffered military defeat in 1954 at Dien Bien Phu in French Indo-

China, when besieged French troops had to surrender; 3,000 had been killed in the fighting and at least another 10,000 died in captivity. The attempt to hold on to the French colony cost 74,000 lives and had a terrible effect on national morale. The humiliation of the *Suez Crisis* followed in 1956, and another imperial crisis, this time in *Algeria* in 1958, led to the recall of de Gaulle and the end of the Fourth Republic.

France: a republic continuously since 1870.

- The *Third French Republic* lasted from the defeat by Germany in 1870 to the surrender to Germany in 1940. Technically it survived until 1946, but in the years 1940 to 1944 France was ruled in part by the collaborating *Vichy* government and in part directly by the German army of occupation
- The *Fourth French Republic* was established in 1946, following the Allied victory in the Second World War, and lasted until the Algerian Crisis of 1958
- The *Fifth French Republic* was founded at the beginning of 1959.

franchise: the right to vote in a state election.

Francis Joseph (Franz Josef): Emperor of Austria-Hungary, 1848–1916. He resisted the demands of the peoples of his empire for greater self-rule and was also a strong opponent of Slav nationalism in the Balkans. The 1914 assassination of his heir at Sarajevo made him more determined in this and so contributed to the events leading to the outbreak of general war in Europe. The empire survived him by only two years.

Franco, Francisco: Spanish general, head of state, 1939–75. By 1936, he was chief of the general staff and governor of the Canary Islands. At first he hesitated to become involved in the military conspiracy against the newly elected left-wing government, but after he led troops from Morocco to Spain in July 1936, he became the key figure on the nationalist side in the *Spanish Civil War*. His authoritarian control molded his nationalist forces into an effective army, in distinct contrast to their republican opponents.

After the nationalist victory in the war, Franco became dictator of Spain. He:

- banned all political parties other than the *Falange*, which became the political arm of his rule
- kept Spain neutral during the Second World War, and this despite his Civil War debts to the Axis powers
- in 1947, took the title of El Caudillo (the leader)
- relied on the support of right-wing forces in the country, in particular the army, the large police force, the landowners and the Catholic Church, to maintain his repressive and authoritarian rule
- maintained a socially conservative regime based firmly on a religious code of morals, even down to a strict code of dress
- continued to repress Catalan and Basque separatist movements

Spain under Franco was not allowed into the UN, but its anti-communism produced a thaw in relations with the West during the Cold War, when NATO airbases were set up in the country. Franco proved surprisingly willing to grant independence to Spain's fragmentary African possessions, retaining only the Spanish Sahara for its mineral deposits. In 1969, he declared that *Juan Carlos*, the grandson of the last

Spanish king *Alfonso XIII,* would succeed him, and this happened without incident on Franco's death in 1975.

Franco–German Friendship Treaty: a treaty of 1963. For *Adenauer,* chancellor of West Germany, it was the culmination, right at the end of his period of office, of his policy of re-establishing his country in Europe by pursuing closer relations with France. For *de Gaulle,* president of France, who had just blocked British entry into the European Economic Community, it was proof of his central importance in European affairs, and also a step towards building a closely integrated Europe in which American influence would be more limited.

Franco–Russian Alliance: a defensive alliance formed in 1893. Each country agreed to provide troops to aid the other if:

- Germany, or Italy aided by Germany, attacked France
- Germany, or Austria-Hungary aided by Germany, attacked Russia.

The alliance marked the end of French isolation in Europe and also Russia's breaking away from the alliances which had until recently linked it to Germany. It was a serious diplomatic setback for Germany and a significant move in the division of Europe into two hostile camps prior to the First World War.

Frank, Anne: a German–Jewish concentration-camp victim at the age of 16. Her family had fled to Holland but was overtaken by the German occupation of the country. The family hid in a sealed-off back room from 1942 until betrayed to the Gestapo in 1944. She died in 1945 in Belsen concentration camp. The diary she had kept during her confinement in the room was later found, published, dramatized and made into a film. In this way she became the unbearably poignant symbol of anonymous Jewish suffering under Nazi tyranny.

Franz Ferdinand: archduke and heir to the throne of Austria-Hungary. He and his wife were assassinated on 28 June 1914 at *Sarajevo,* precipitating the chain of events that led, a month later, to the outbreak of the First World War.

free city: a self-governing city outside the control of the state. *Danzig* was, from 1919 to 1939, a free city under the supervision of the League of Nations. An attempt to make *Fiume* a free city on similar lines failed when it was incorporated into Italy.

Free Democratic Party (FDP): a West German political party favoring individual freedom. Since the creation of West Germany in 1949, the party has had undue influence, despite its limited electoral success, because of the deals it has struck with the other parties in the Bundestag. Until 1974, it worked in coalition with the Christian Democrats (CDU) but then entered a coalition with the Social Democrats (SPD) under *Schmidt* until it forced the collapse of the government in 1982 when it switched its support back. The party reached its peak in the 1961 election, and even then captured only 12 percent of the vote. Later, with 6.8 percent of the vote in 1983, it was dangerously close to falling below the 5 percent minimum vote which parties must reach to be allowed seats in the Bundestag. In the united German elections of 1994, however, the Free Democrats obtained 47 Bundestag seats.

Free French: the organization of exiled French people in the Second World War. It was set up in 1940 by General *de Gaulle* following the surrender of France. It played a part in the liberation of French North Africa and formed a provisional government which moved to Paris when the city was liberated in 1944.

free trade: international trade free from restrictions such as tariffs. It became unfashionable in the late nineteenth century as governments moved to protect their industries from foreign competition. Britain was the last country to retain open markets, but it too reverted to *protectionism* between the two world wars. Since 1945, the Bretton Woods Agreement, the International Monetary Fund and *GATT* have been the basis of repeated international attempts among Western nations to promote economic growth by freeing world trade from tariffs and other restrictive practices.

free world: a term used in the West to describe the non-communist world.

Freikorps: German right-wing vigilante groups in the early 1920s. They were mainly made up of ex-servicemen, often unemployed, and felt betrayed by the Armistice and the Versailles Peace Treaty. They had no loyalty to the Weimar Republic but were fiercely opposed to the communists, with whom they fought battles for control of the streets, and in this way helped the republic by defeating the *Spartacist* uprising. They attracted the support of some members of the German army and, in 1920, tried to seize control of Berlin as a first step to restoring the monarchy, in what became known as the *Kapp Putsch*.

French Community: the association of France, its overseas possessions and ex-colonies in Africa which formally lasted only from 1958 to 1961. Despite a number of states breaking away from formal membership, the various territories once belonging to France continue to maintain close cultural links and have financial, technical and economic agreements with it. France, for its part, also continued to provide military assistance to its ex-colonies in periods of internal political instability.

French Empire: developed in the nineteenth century.

- In North Africa were the colonies and protectorates of Algeria, Morocco and Tunisia, and to their south, French West Africa
- Elsewhere in Africa, possessions included the tropical colonies of Dahomey, French Somaliland, Senegal, Guinea, Ivory Coast, Congo and the island of Madagascar, as well as the mandates of Togoland and Cameroon granted to France after the First World War
- In the Middle East, Syria and Lebanon became French mandates after the First World War
- In the Far East, there was the colonial territory of French Indo-China which was occupied in the Second World War by the Japanese.

By 1945 it was evident, if not to all French people, that in North Africa and Indo-China, the events of the Second World War had created a difficult situation for France as an imperial power. Its own defeat and occupation during the war further weakened its ability to maintain a worldwide empire.

- In Indo-China, war against the nationalists lasted from 1946 to 1954 and ended in the *French Fourth Republic*'s abject defeat at Dien Bien Phu, which led to the recognition of the independence of Cambodia, Laos and Vietnam

- Despite the commitment of almost all its army in the late 1950s, France was no more successful in trying to quell armed revolt in favor of independence by *Algeria*, and by 1962 it too was granted independence by de Gaulle as president of the Fifth French Republic
- De Gaulle, after an attempt in 1958 to create a French Community of African colonies and ex-colonies which soon foundered, also recognized the complete independence of the French colonies in Africa
- By 1961, only the French islands in the Pacific remained as the last remnant of the empire.

French Foreign Legion: a French volunteer military force made up mainly of foreigners and employed chiefly in defending the country's imperial territories.

French Union: arose from a 1946 reorganization of the French Empire, which lasted until 1958 when it was replaced by the *French Community*.

Freud, Sigmund: the founder, with *Jung*, of psychoanalysis. He was a Jew from Vienna who died in 1939 in London, an exile from the Nazis. His work earlier in the century, which transformed the understanding of human psychology though his emphasis on the psychosexual origins of neuroses, was later challenged, by Jung among others.

Frick, Wilhelm: the Nazi minister of the interior. He had been with Hitler since the Munich Putsch of 1923, and after 1933 was responsible for banning trade unionism, ending the freedom of the press and promoting anti-Semitism. He was sentenced to death at the Nuremberg Trials in 1946.

Fritsch, Werner von: commander-in-chief of the German army, 1934–38. After the *Night of the Long Knives* and the death of Hindenburg in 1934, he took a per-sonal oath of loyalty to Hitler, which helped the latter to become Führer. He subsequently failed to see how the rise of the Nazi state had undermined the political power of the army. In 1938, he protested at Hitler's plans for an expansion-ist foreign policy and was dismissed and smeared as a homosexual in Hitler's reorganization and subordination of the army command structure, which included the setting up of the *OKW*.

Führer: (from German, meaning "leader") a new title used from 1934 to denote Hitler's status in the German state. It followed his amalgamation of the offices of chancellor and president after the death of Hindenburg. It had been used by his followers since the early 1920s to denote Hitler's role in the Nazi Party.

fundamentalist: one who strictly maintains traditional orthodox religious beliefs which are held to be fundamental to, i.e. an essential foundation of, true faith.

Fundamental Law: Russian laws to protect the autocratic power of the tsar against the *Duma*. They were issued in 1906 as part of the new constitution just one week before the first Duma met. The most important was Article 87, which allowed the tsar to rule by decree whenever the Duma was not in session. Other articles of the law allowed the tsar to appoint the members of the government, veto legislation, conduct foreign policy, raise loans and control the army. The law:

- limited drastically the scope of the reforms agreed to by Tsar Nicholas II following the *Revolution of 1905*

- indicated how little the tsar was prepared to concede to the need for reform
- ensured that the autocratic power of tsardom was preserved.

Funk, Walther: a German Nazi politician. In the 1930s, he helped persuade fellow businessmen to back Hitler. He succeeded *Schacht* as minister of economics in 1936, and as president of the Reichsbank (the state bank) in 1939. He was responsible for the wartime economic exploitation of the German-occupied territories, and was sentenced to life imprisonment at the Nuremberg Trials.

G

Gallipoli: a First World War military campaign from April 1915 to January 1916. After the failure of the *Dardanelles* naval expedition to force a passage through to the Black Sea, Allied troops were landed at Gallipoli with the aim of fighting their way to Istanbul.

- The delay since the naval attempt and poor security were fatal to their prospects
- The steep hillsides were fully fortified by Turkish troops armed with German heavy guns, and the Allied troops were pinned down close to the sea in the bitter fighting which ensued
- The Allied forces lost 36,000 dead and more than twice that number wounded or captured before withdrawing.

They had never remotely looked likely to achieve their objective, and the disaster dented the reputation of Winston Churchill, whose idea it had been.

Gamelin, Maurice: a French general. He served with distinction in the First World War, but in 1940, as commander-in-chief of the Allied forces, was totally unprepared for the German thrust through the center of the Allied lines which led to the retreat to Dunkirk and to the surrender of France.

Gapon, Father: a Russian priest of peasant origins. He led the crowd at the 1905 *Bloody Sunday* demonstration outside the tsar's Winter Palace in St. Petersburg. There were allegations that he had been a tsarist government agent, and in 1906, he was the victim of a left-wing assassin.

GATT (General Agreement on Tariffs and Trade): a specialized trade agency within the UN from 1948 to 1995. It began in 1948 as an agreement between 23 nations to promote international trade until the UN could create a formal agency. This was never done, and GATT evolved into a semi-permanent agency developing its own procedures and rules. With its headquarters at Geneva, and eventually reaching a membership of 90, it was committed to the removal of barriers blocking international trade. It conducted a series of "rounds" of negotiations to this end, most recently the *Uruguay Round*, which lasted from 1986 to 1994, from which measures will not be fully implemented until 2002. The final act of the Uruguay Round was to establish the *World Trade Organization* which superseded GATT at the end of 1995.

Gaullists: members of French right-wing political parties formed to support *de Gaulle* or to continue his policies.

- In 1947, during the Fourth French Republic, de Gaulle founded the short-lived Rally of the French People (RPF) to keep his ideas alive after he had withdrawn from daily political life
- In the Fifth French Republic, with de Gaulle its first president, the Union for the New Republic (UNR) was another such party, working in coalition with other parties to form a right-wing government
- *Pompidou* and *Chirac*, both later president, were Gaullists.

Gdansk: a Polish port on the Baltic. Under its Germanic name of *Danzig*, it played an important part in the origins of the Second World War. The trade union *Solidarity* began in the 1980 strikes in the Gdansk shipyards. Despite the later political importance of Solidarity, the vast shipyards could not be protected indefinitely from international competition in shipbuilding, and in 1996 the Polish government decided to close them.

General Assembly: of the *United Nations Organization.* It:

- is the main debating body of the UN, holding one regular meeting each year but with emergency sessions possible at any time when peace is threatened
- has a membership which has grown from 51 states in 1945 to 185 in 1998, mainly as a result of the entry of many Third World countries. Each member state is entitled to a delegation of five, and each state has only one vote, regardless of size.

In the early years, the West could usually rely on a majority in the debates, but the expansion of membership made this less predictable, particularly in debates on aid, development and colonial issues. The intensely democratic nature of the Assembly's voting procedures is balanced by the powers reserved for the *Security Council* and by the veto on any action which is enjoyed by the permanent members of that body.

General Relations Treaty: a 1972 agreement between East and West Germany made on the initiative of West German Chancellor *Brandt.* In it, he recognized the legal existence of East Germany, and diplomatic relations were established between the two countries.

general strike: a strike of workers across the economy. The idea was favored by exponents of *syndicalism,* who saw it as an effective means of putting pressure on the state authorities to alter policies, or even as a weapon in workers taking over the state. The 1926 General Strike in Britain, however, was a half-hearted affair intended to show sympathy with striking miners. The government stood firm, and after 10 days, the strike was called off.

Geneva Agreements: 1954 agreements on the future of French Indo-China. They followed the French defeat at Dien Bien Phu and recognized Cambodia, Laos and Vietnam as independent nations. They thus marked the end of the *French Empire* in Asia.

Geneva Conventions: international agreements on the treatment of the victims of war dating from 1864. They laid down rules for the treatment of wounded soldiers and prisoners of war and were extended and elaborated in 1906, 1929 and 1949. In the Second World War, the conventions greatly assisted the work of the *Red Cross* in protecting the status of prisoners whose countries had ratified the agreements, and they partly explain why British and US prisoners in German hands were better treated than Soviet prisoners. It was the failure of several countries to apply the conventions during the Second World War which led to the 1949 revisions, which also extended their protection to civilians in enemy-occupied territories.

Geneva Protocol: a 1924 scheme to strengthen the *League of Nations.* It would have involved those who signed it in accepting arbitration of disputes and helping to enforce arbitration decisions. It had been drafted by the Czech, *Beneš*, and was promoted by the British Labour leader, MacDonald. It lapsed after a change of government in Britain, and the League remained as impotent as ever if serious disputes arose between members.

genocide: the deliberate extermination of a people or nation, as in the Nazi *Holocaust.*

Gentile, Giovanni: an Italian philosopher who became the intellectual spokesman for the fascist regime. He also held ministerial office under Mussolini. He attempted to construct a philosophy of fascism, but its intellectual basis remained unconvincing. He planned the 35-volume ITALIAN ENCYCLOPEDIA, which became Italian fascism's most important intellectual achievement. In 1944, he was assassinated by communist partisans.

German Democratic Republic (GDR): more commonly referred to as *East Germany.*

German economic miracle: a shorthand term for the remarkable economic progress made by Germany as it recovered in the 1950s and early 1960s from the destruction of the Second World War.

German Federal Republic (FRG): more commonly referred to as *West Germany* (1949–90).

German history, 1919–39: the most studied period of the nation's history. Topics and issues which interest historians include:

KEY ISSUES IN GERMAN HISTORY, 1919–39

1919–23: Weimar's survival	**1924–30: Weimar's stability**
Armistice	Stresemann
Versailles	Dawes Plan
Spartacists	Young Plan
Kapp Putsch	International stability
Ebert	Prosperity
Munich Putsch	Extremists limited support
Hyperinflation	

German history, 1919–39

Origins of the Nazis, 1921–28	**Hitler's rise to power, 1928–33**
The appeal of nationalism	The effects of the Great Depression
The role of Hitler	Improved election results, 1928–32
The build-up of the Nazi organization	Deals with other right-wing parties
Playing on the fear of communism	Nazi vigor and propaganda

1933–39: the Nazi state	**1933–39: Hitler's foreign policy**
Assuming absolute power	Repudiated Versailles; rearmed
Night of the Long Knives	Rhineland, Anschluss, Munich
Persecution of opponents	Prague, Memel, Poland
Anti-Semitism	Product of a master plan,
The totalitarian state	or of opportunism and miscalculation?

- the many problems and weaknesses of the *Weimar Republic*, 1919 to 1923
- the factors enabling the Weimar Republic to survive in these years
- the reasons for the greater stability and prosperity from 1924 to 1929 – how soundly based was this?
- the origins and appeal of the *National Socialist Party*
- the reasons for the dramatic advance of National Socialism from 1929 to 1933
- why was *Hitler* able to gain power legally in 1933?
- the consolidation of Nazi power in 1933–34
- the main features of Nazi rule during the *German Third Empire* (Third Reich)
- how fully did the Nazis satisfy the hopes of the German people from 1933 to 1939?
- the nature and extent of the opposition in Germany to the creation of the Nazi state
- Hitler's foreign policy: a master plan or the skillful seizing of opportunities?

Once Germany had embarked on the Second World War, a further and wider range of issues need to be considered.

German industry: this developed rapidly following the unification of Germany in 1870, and by 1914 had helped make the country militarily the most powerful in Europe.

- Traditional industries such as iron and steel, along with coal and the development of railways, grew rapidly and overtook those of Britain, which had been the first industrial nation
- New industries, like the chemical, electrical and automobile industries were pioneered in Germany
- Industry was dominated by a few large firms such as the steel, armaments and engineering combine, *Krupp* of Essen, and the chemical giant *I. G. Farben*
- Large industrial areas developed, as in the *Ruhr* and parts of *Silesia*
- Germany's export trade tripled between 1890 and 1914, and the competition it provided for other nations became a source of international tension.

German Second Empire (Reich): formed in 1871 and survived until 1918. Its kaiser (emperor) from 1888 to 1918 was *William II.* By 1900, the state had become the major industrial and military power of the Continent and had gained a colonial empire in East Africa. After the 1890 resignation of its first chancellor, *Bismarck*, its military and industrial potential and its adventurous foreign policies created increased tension in Europe. Its two most important political leaders in the early twentieth century were *Bülow* and *Bethmann-Hollweg.*

German foreign policy:

- was based on the need to isolate France
- made it become a close ally of Austria-Hungary, which it backed in the 1908 Bosnian Crisis and after the assassination of Archduke *Franz Ferdinand* at Sarajevo in 1914, so leading directly to the First World War

- led to worsening relations with Britain in the early twentieth century as a result of its naval building program and its clumsy attempts to provoke crises in Morocco which brought France and Britain closer together.

In the alliances and ententes from 1893 to 1907, its potential enemies, France, Russia and Britain, began to develop closer links, and Europe became divided into two camps. Defeat in the First World War led in November 1918 to the abdication of Kaiser William II and the end of the empire just two days before Germany signed the armistice agreement ending the war. The Second Empire was succeeded by the *Weimar Republic*.

German Third Empire (Reich): the Third Reich is the term used to describe the *Nazi* dictatorship in Germany, 1933–45. Its creation and operation is the central issue in *German history, 1919–39*. The Third Reich was in fact proclaimed by *Hitler* in 1934 when the fragile democracy of the Weimar Republic was swept away. The new state was centralized and authoritarian.

- Political parties other than the *National Socialist Party* were closed down and all their assets confiscated. Non-Aryans were removed from public office and the elected provincial assemblies were replaced by Nazi governors. "Unreliable" members of the civil service were dismissed. Under the process known as *gleichschaltung*, the Nazi Party created a large number of organizations to run and control the life of the state and its individual citizens
- The legal system was used to persecute enemies of the regime in secret trials, with the accused often sent to the newly founded *concentration camps*
- Personal liberty was restricted and the Christian churches were attacked. Education was organized, and censorship applied to it, so as to enable it more effectively to present the Nazi message, biology and history being curriculum subjects particularly prone to distortion for this purpose. The *Hitler Youth* movement was set up to indoctrinate the young
- Trade unions were closely regulated or closed down, to be replaced by official labor organizations linked to the German Labor Front. The professions were controlled by Nazi "fronts," and only those working within that structure could continue to work in their professions
- The press was closely censored, papers opposing the Nazis were soon closed down by the minister of the interior, *Frick*, and the radio became an effective instrument of state-controlled propaganda
- in the most radical feature of the regime, anti-Semitism was rigorously imposed through the *Nuremberg Laws*.

The regime was, however, supported by many Germans and tolerated by even more. Three groups stand out:

- German industrialists and financial leaders, who in the early 1930s had seen the Nazis as a protection against the advance of communism, had their trust confirmed in 1934 by Hitler's purge of the radical *SA*. They also welcomed the stimulus that the regime gave to the economy through the program of public works and the rearmament program, as well as approving of its taming of the power of the trade unions

- the Catholic Church reached a *concordat* with the Nazi regime which in theory protected its privileges but in practice left it tied to the regime. The Lutheran (Protestant) Church agreed to the setting-up of a state church, which left it equally powerless. It was left to individual Christians, like *Niemöller* and *Bonhoeffer*, working within the German Confessional Church until it was closed down in 1937, to continue a lonely and courageous opposition to the regime on grounds of conscience
- the army was in favor of Nazi nationalist aims; it wanted rearmament, expansion of the armed forces and an active foreign policy. It had welcomed the *Army Law* passed in July 1933, and in 1934 was also among those who had been reassured by the action taken against the SA. In 1934 it was required to take an oath of loyalty to the Führer, but it was only in 1938, after the dismissal of General *Blomberg*, that Hitler imposed his own command structure on the army.

The Nazi economy

During the 1930s, the economy recovered and employment prospects improved from the depths of the Great Depression, and this aided the regime's popularity with urban workers. In 1933, there had been 6 million unemployed; by the end of the first four-year economic plan, there were only 1 million. This had been achieved by:

- a vast program of public works such as motorway-building, afforestation schemes and dam-building projects
- encouraging the intensive use of labor instead of labor-saving machinery
- introducing conscription in 1935
- paying marriage allowances to women to encourage them to leave work, and by propaganda urging women to make home and family the center of their existence.

In 1936, a second four-year economic plan, headed by *Goering* but really the work of *Schacht*, set out to make Germany self-sufficient in the event of war by schemes to produce synthetic oil and rubber and to protect the German steel industry in order to exploit the country's vast resources of low-grade iron ore. It was never totally successful, and by 1939 Germany was still dependent on oil and raw material imports. Nevertheless, the German *gross national product* (GNP) had doubled between 1933 and 1939.

The Nazi appeal

The restoration of national pride and the conquest of unemployment by the Nazi regime gave many Germans what they most wanted. Lives were more controlled, for example by the Hitler Youth, but even here there were compensations, with heavily subsidized holidays and sporting and cultural facilities. Most were prepared to accept the restrictions on their freedom imposed by the totalitarian regime and also the reduction in real wages which accompanied the conquest of unemployment. It was also possible, with the encouragement of the vast propaganda machine,

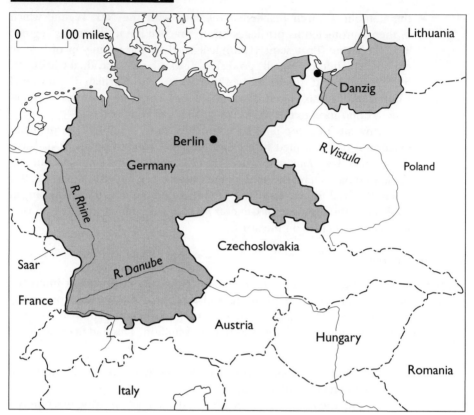

9 Germany in the 1930s

for Aryan Germans to turn a blind eye to what was happening to their Jewish neighbors.

The cultural achievement during the Nazi period was mediocre at best, with the regime stamping out "modern" experiments in art and music and encouraging only the most monumental and pretentious of architecture. Only in the cinema, notably with the work of *Riefenstahl*, was anything of lasting interest produced, and even here works of propaganda dominated the output.

Foreign policy

This was frankly expansionist and was explained in terms of overthrowing the unjust *Versailles* Treaty and uniting all Germans in one state.

- In 1933, Germany walked out of the international disarmament talks
- In 1935, the *Saar* coalfield region was regained after a plebiscite of its inhabitants
- In 1936, the army moved back into the *Rhineland*, contravening the Locarno Treaty
- In 1938, *Anschluss* with Austria and the annexation of the *Sudetenland* were both achieved

- In 1939, the rest of *Czechoslovakia* and *Memel* were occupied in March, and the signing of the *Nazi–Soviet Pact* in August led to the invasion of *Poland* in September.

The Second World War

As a result of remarkable military successes on both the Eastern and Western Fronts, Germany had, by the end of 1941, built up an enormous European empire stretching from the Spanish border with France to the North Cape at the tip of Norway, and from the English Channel to the suburbs of Moscow. Much of North Africa was also under German control. From 1943, however, the Germans were forced on the defensive, and the Third Reich ended in May 1945 with Hitler's suicide in the rubble of a Berlin occupied by the Red Army. (For the history of the German Third Empire from 1939 to 1945, see the *Second World War* entry.)

Gestapo: the secret state police of Nazi Germany, first formed in 1933 by *Goering* to be the secret police in Prussia. *Himmler* became its head in 1934, and later it became part of the *SS*. It had great powers, which were extended into countries occupied during the war, including that of executing without trial those disloyal to the Nazi regime. It ran the German *concentration camps*, and by 1945 had 40,000 members.

Gheorghiu-Dej, Gheorghe: virtual dictator of communist Romania from 1948 and its president from 1961 to his death in 1965. An ally of Khrushchev, in 1961 he persuaded the Soviet Union to withdraw its troops from Romania.

Gibraltar: a British colony on the southern tip of Spain, which claims it as part of its national territory. It has been the source of a long-running dispute between the two countries, with the Spanish closing the border and imposing customs restrictions on several occasions. Self-government was granted in 1964, and in a 1967 referendum the inhabitants voted to stay British.

Gierek, Edward: a Polish politician who, in 1970, succeeded *Gomulka* as first secretary. He promised economic reforms and embarked on an industrialization program. This led the country into debt, causing economic dislocation, and he was ousted from office in 1980 when the *Solidarity* strikes and protests began.

Giolitti, Giovanni: an Italian prime minister on five occasions between 1892 and 1922. He was a master of the art of *transformismo*, or forging coalitions of politicians to form governments which did little to meet Italy's pressing social and economic problems but which were devoted to maintaining his own grasp on office. In 1921, continuing this practice, he made an electoral pact with Mussolini, and as a result turned a blind eye to the increasing street violence of the fascist *blackshirts*. His 1921–22 government was unable to deal with the economic problems facing the country or to suppress political extremism from either the communists or the nationalist supporters of D'Annunzio. Its collapse brought anarchy to Italy and so led, following *Facta*'s short-lived government, to the king's invitation to Mussolini to become prime minister. His career illustrates the weakness, self-seeking and drift within Italian democracy which made fascism attractive to many Italians.

Giscard d'Estaing, Valéry: president of France, 1974–81. He:

- held government posts under both de Gaulle and Pompidou
- worked with the Gaullists as a fellow conservative politician, but had an uneasy personal relationship with *Chirac*
- narrowly defeated *Mitterrand* in the 1974 presidential election
- faced serious economic problems after 1974 from recession, unemployment and inflation, as France's rate of economic growth slowed down.

He promoted active intervention in the internal affairs of ex-French colonies in Africa, and his reputation was damaged by charges that he had corruptly accepted gifts from the notorious Bokassa, president of the Central Africa Republic. He lost the 1981 presidential election to Mitterand.

gleichschaltung: the 1930s process of coordination in Nazi Germany. It concentrated power in the hands of the central government at the expense of the Land governments and led to a great tightening of Nazi power, helping to create a *totalitarian* state. The Nazi Party had a large number of organizations devoted to running and controlling the life of the state, but this did not lead to more efficient government, since the hierarchy of authorities overlapped and frequently fell into conflict. The Nazi hierarchy has been described as riddled from top to bottom with bitter rivalries and feuds.

Gobineau, Joseph: a French nineteenth-century writer who wrote about the inequality of the races and has been described as the originator of the idea of racial superiority and the cult of the superman. With Houston *Chamberlain*, he provided the ideas which led on to Nazi theories of race.

Goebbels, Josef: a leading German Nazi. He was remarkable for his gifts as an orator and manipulator of *propaganda*, staging mass parades and meetings, notably the *Nuremberg Rallies*, to enhance the Nazi appeal. From 1933 to 1945, he was minister of public enlightenment and propaganda, with control over the press, radio and all aspects of culture. During the Second World War, his responsibilities and power over German domestic policy and society greatly increased. In August 1944, he was put in charge of the total mobilization of resources for one last effort to win the war. He:

- tried to whip up enthusiasm for the war effort by tales of the terrible fate awaiting the German people in the event of an Allied victory
- backed this up by savage repression of anyone who appeared critical of the Nazi conduct of the war.

Goebbels was close to Hitler right until the end of the Third Reich, and in April 1945 he killed his wife and six children before committing suicide in the ruins of Berlin.

Goerdeler, Carl: one of the conspirators in the *July Plot* of 1944 to kill Hitler. He had been a Nazi politician who had resigned office before the war. When the plot failed, he was put to death.

Goering, Hermann: a leading German Nazi. A First World War fighter-pilot ace, he was wounded when taking part in Hitler's 1923 *Munich Putsch*. He was one of the 12 Nazi deputies elected to the Reichstag in 1928. He entered the Nazi government in 1933 as prime minister for Prussia, founding the *Gestapo* in 1933, and as Reich minister for air he worked to build up the *Luftwaffe.* In 1936, he was put in charge of the second four-year plan, which aimed at *autarky.* He was appointed foreign minister in 1937 and Hitler's deputy in 1938, reaching the height of his popularity and power in 1940 with the overwhelming successes of the Luftwaffe in 1939 and early 1940, a period of triumph marred only by its failure in the *Battle of Britain.* As the war progressed, Goering's interference in military operations and his erratic personal behavior, combined with the all-too-evident failure of the Luftwaffe to sustain control of the skies, led to him losing all influence, and in 1945 he was dismissed. He was sentenced to death at the *Nuremberg Trials* but committed suicide before the sentence could be carried out.

gold reserves: the quantity of gold held by a national government. When a country is on the *gold standard,* these reserves can become depleted in times of crisis, as foreign traders sell their holdings of the currency for the greater security of gold. Even when a country is not on the gold standard, a financial crisis can force a government to defend the value of its currency by using its gold reserves and its *foreign currency reserves* to buy up its own unwanted currency on the international markets in order to protect its value.

gold standard: this occurred when a country backed the value of its currency with gold, and would exchange gold for its currency when asked to do so. In 1900, all major currencies were based on the gold standard. *Witte* had placed the Russian rouble on the gold standard in 1897 in order to give confidence to the foreign investors whom he was anxious to attract. Most countries came off the standard during the First World War and, although some returned to it after the war, the Great Depression of the 1930s led to its general abandonment. It had provided a convenient way of measuring the relative values of currencies but, in times of war or depression, its *deflationary* effects were unacceptable.

Gomulka, Wladyslaw: a Polish politician, first secretary of the Polish Communist Party, 1956–70. He was distrusted by the pro-Stalinist Polish government and was imprisoned from 1951 to 1955. A supporter of Khrushchev, he was returned to favor following the latter's speech of 1956 denouncing Stalinist extremism; he promoted more liberal social and economic policies, particularly on individual rights and on religious liberty, than had been possible in the Stalin era. In 1970, public disorder in *Gdansk,* brought on by economic hardship and in protest at continued instances of repression, forced his resignation. He died in 1982.

Gorbachev, Mikhail: a Soviet statesman who, in 1985, became general secretary of the Communist Party. He replaced *Chernenko* and ended a long period of rule by elderly communist politicians reaching back to *Brezhnev.* Repression had lessened under *Khrushchev* and Brezhnev, but the supreme role of the Communist Party and the command economy remained intact in 1985. (See the entry *Soviet economy after 1945.*) It was Gorbachev who brought all this to an end, but at the eventual price of also bringing the Soviet Union itself to an end. He:

- introduced policies of perestroika (restructuring) and *glasnost* (openness) with the dual aim of regalvanizing the stagnant economy and weeding out corruption and inefficiency

- aimed in foreign policy to ease the tensions of the Cold War and so reduce the burden of defense spending
- allowed private ownership of property and permitted some private businesses to develop, so beginning to allow a market economy to replace the communist command economy
- released political prisoners
- abolished the guaranteed leading role of the Communist Party.

The policy of glasnost released pent-up ethnic and nationalist demands, and perestroika led to a communist backlash as the economic and administrative restructuring began to undermine the privileged position of the communist bureaucracy. In August 1991, a hard-line communist coup attempted to reimpose communist control, but mass street demonstrations, especially that led in the full glare of television cameras in Moscow by *Yeltsin*, coupled with the reluctance of army units to support the rising, resulted in its failure.

Gorbachev had apparently been briefly held by associates of the plotters, but was then released and returned to Moscow. His credibility was, however, seriously damaged, and the political initiative passed to the leaders of the separate republics, especially Yeltsin, who began to announce the withdrawal of their lands from the Soviet Union, which at this point began to disintegrate. Gorbachev resigned as president on 25 December 1991, and the Soviet Union formally ended the next day.

In foreign affairs, Gorbachev's role was of crucial importance. When dissidents in the Soviet satellite states in Eastern Europe began, in 1989, to challenge the communist authorities there, he made no attempt to apply the *Brezhnev Doctrine* to bolster communist regimes like that of Honecker in East Germany, which in consequence quickly collapsed. In this sense, he had a permanent impact on the political structure of all of Europe. This was symbolized by his 1990 acceptance of the *Treaty on the Final Settlement with Respect to Germany*, which allowed the reunification of that country, and also, in 1990, by his agreement that the newly reunited Germany could be a full member of NATO.

Goremykin, Ivor: a Russian conservative politician. He was appointed chief minister to *Nicholas II* when Witte was dismissed in 1906. This was a move designed to limit the scope of the reforms that the tsar had been forced to concede after the 1905 Revolution.

Gosplan: the state planning commission of the Soviet Union, founded in 1921. It:

- became the route through which the Communist Party imposed planning priorities on the economy
- was responsible for constructing and imposing the *Five-Year Plans* of the Stalinist era, interfering across the entire economy.

In the Khrushchev and Brezhnev periods, Gosplan became a major obstacle to economic reform and flexibility. By 1985, with the arrival of Gorbachev, it was much criticized for its obstructionism and for its interference in economic details. Its strength had lain in the development of heavy industry and the economic infrastructure in earlier decades, but by the 1980s it was denying the Soviet economy any chance of being flexible and innovative. Its record in developing and utilizing computers, for example, was lamentable, and it came to represent Soviet bureaucratic economic inertia at its worst.

Gottwald, Klement: president of Czechoslovakia, 1948–53. He spent the Second World War in Moscow and was, from 1946 to 1948, prime minister in a coalition government with *Beneš*. He became president after the 1948 communist coup which he himself had masterminded. He was a hard-line Stalinist, employing concentration camps, forced labor, purges and show trials to establish a totalitarian communist state. He even accepted Stalin's *Comecon* plan to make the considerable Czech industrial base subordinate to that of the Soviet Union.

government: the group of persons governing (running) a state. It should not be confused with *parliament.*

glasnost: a Russian term meaning openness. It was used from 1985 by *Gorbachev* to describe his policy of encouraging intellectual freedom and general questioning, particularly about the errors of the past, within the Soviet Union. Glasnost led to the voicing of long-suppressed ethnic and nationalist demands, which were to destroy Gorbachev's work. These were made worse by an outburst of criticism of the workings of the communist regime, which became a flood when promised economic improvements did not materialize, and this too helped to undermine Gorbachev's efforts to preserve the existence of the Soviet Union.

Great Britain: this consists of England, Wales and Scotland, which, together with Northern Ireland, then make up the United Kingdom.

Great Patriotic War: a Soviet propaganda term to describe the war against Germany from 1941 to 1945. It was linked to promoting the notion of Stalin as the savior of the state.

Great Purge: the persecution of alleged dissidents during the late 1930s in the Soviet Union. It is usually known as *Yezhovshchina* after N. I. Yezhov, its most vigorous proponent.

Greece: an independent kingdom up to 1924, a republic 1924–35, the monarchy restored in 1935, and a republic again from 1973.

In the Second World War, Greece repulsed a 1940 Italian invasion from Albania, but in 1941 was defeated by German troops. British Commonwealth troops sent to help the Greeks were forced to withdraw after bitter fighting on the mainland and the island of Crete. At the end of the war, Greek resistance movements were sharply split between those loyal to the monarchy and the communist-controlled *ELAS* resistance groups. This led, after 1945, to the *Greek Civil War*, which lasted until 1949.

In 1967, the "*Greek Colonels*" seized power in a military coup led by *Papadopoulus.* They:

- abolished the monarchy in 1973
- encouraged the 1974 adventurism which tried to bring *enosis* between Greece and *Cyprus.*

When this ended in failure following the invasion of northern Cyprus by the Turkish army, the colonels were overthrown and democracy, but not the monarchy, was restored. Because of the Cyprus issue, relations with Turkey remained difficult after 1974. Greece joined the European Community in 1981.

Greek Civil War: fought from 1944 to 1949 between *ELAS* communist partisans and royalists seeking to restore the monarchy. First Britain and then the USA provided aid to the royalists, whose forces, led by *Papagos*, were victorious. The war was an important episode in the developing Cold War, for when Britain could no longer support the royalists, it turned to the USA to take on the burden. It was the specific issue of help for Greece (and Turkey) against communist subversion which led to the promulgation of the *Truman Doctrine* in 1947. There were claims in the West that the ELAS fighters were receiving help from Moscow, and that this was part of the continuing advance of Soviet communism across Eastern Europe to the Mediterranean. In fact this was not so, for Stalin, honoring an assurance to Churchill that after the Second World War was over Greece would come into the Western zone of influence, provided no aid to the ELAS fighters.

"Greek Colonels": a term describing the military regime in Greece from 1967 to 1974. It was brutally repressive to any sign of discontent:

- torture and imprisonment were used systematically for political ends
- censorship was rigorous
- the 1973 student protests were brutally suppressed.

In 1974, the regime promoted a scheme to bring about *enosis* (union) with *Cyprus* by deposing *Makarios*. This plan failed when the Turkish army intervened in Cyprus and, as a result, Greece was close to civil war. The military resigned and constitutional government was restored.

After first welcoming the colonels' coup, King Constantine II went into exile, and in 1973 the military, led by *Papadopoulus*, declared Greece to be a republic. A referendum after the restoration of constitutional government confirmed at least this part of the colonels' work.

green movement: the emergence during the 1970s of pressure groups working for action on environmental issues. Their greatest impact was in West Germany where success in elections forced the government to take action on a variety of issues, if only to blunt the political threat of the "Greens." The German Green Party became more left-wing in the 1980s as it concentrated on the nuclear-defense policies of NATO and took in a range of other causes such as gay rights and women's rights. Green parties also emerged, though with less electoral success, in most other Western European countries.

Greenpeace: an international anti-nuclear pressure group, founded in 1971 with its headquarters in Holland.

Grey, Edward: the British foreign secretary, 1905–16. He:

- was responsible for bringing Britain, France and Russia together in the *Triple Entente* of 1907
- permitted further talks between British and French military leaders while insisting that these did not commit either nation to joint action in the event of war.

In practice, the division of naval commitments, with the French navy to safeguard the Mediterranean and the British the North Sea, meant that the entente had become a military alliance which Britain would find difficult to evade when war came. In 1914, Grey persuaded the reluctant British cabinet to go to war because

Germany had invaded Belgium despite international guarantees on its neutrality. His pre-war diplomacy, with its implications withheld even from fellow members of the British government, was typical of the secrecy with which international relations were conducted prior to 1914. This secret diplomacy was much criticized after the war as having contributed to the heightened tensions and misunderstandings of the time.

Grivas, George: the leader of the militant *EOKA* group campaigning, often by the use of terror, for *enosis* (union) between *Cyprus* and Greece. He fought first against the British presence in Cyprus, which he left in 1959 to a hero's welcome in Greece. In 1971, he returned to independent Cyprus to become a thorn in the side of Makarios' government, directing a terrorist campaign for enosis until his death in 1974 at the age of 76.

Groener, Wilhelm: a German general. His pact with President *Ebert* in 1919 helped to save the Weimar republic from the *Spartacist* uprising.

gross national product (GNP): the value of all the production of a country plus its income from abroad. It is usually the most easily understood measure of national economic growth, and so is much used by historians to illustrate economic trends.

Guchkov, Alexander: a Russian politician. He came from the merchant class and was, after 1905, leader of the *Octobrists* in the Duma and, in 1917, minister of the interior in the Provisional Government.

Guernica: a Spanish town, the main center of *Basque* culture. In 1937, at the height of the Spanish Civil War, it was heavily bombed by German planes practicing the dive-bombing techniques later used to devastating effect in the *blitzkrieg* offensives of the Second World War. Newsreel film of the devastation shocked cinema audiences across Europe, adding to the general horror at the thought of another war and strengthening the appeal of pacifism.

guerrillas: people taking part in irregular fighting by small groups acting independently. Guerrilla warfare was common between 1940 and 1945 in Nazi-occupied Europe, with such groups as the *ELAS* fighters in Greece, Tito's *partisans* in Yugoslavia and the *Maquis* in France being particularly noteworthy.

Gulag: a Soviet labor camp.

Gulf War: this war followed the invasion of Kuwait by Iraq in 1990. A UN force, largely from the USA but also with British and French forces involved, liberated the country in February 1991. Years later, there were persistent claims that some Western troops involved in the war had contracted debilitating diseases as a result either of the "cocktail" of medical injections they had been given prior to the campaign, or of the deliberate or accidental use of poison gas during the course of the fighting.

Haakon VII of Norway: king of Norway, 1905–57. He was elected by the Norwegian Parliament when Norway separated from Sweden. After the German invasion in 1940, he fled to London, where he led a government in exile.

Habsburgs: the ruling house of the *Austro-Hungarian Empire* until 1918. Francis Joseph was emperor from 1848 to 1916.

Haig, Douglas: a British field marshal. In 1915, he became commander-in-chief of the British forces on the *Western Front*. He failed to break the deadlock of opposing trench warfare and fought a war of attrition, incurring very heavy casualties in the battles of the *Somme* and *Passchendaele*. He had the reputation of being a stern disciplinarian, never hesitating to sign the death warrants for those, including the shell-shocked, who had deserted in the face of the enemy. He was deputy to *Foch* in the final successful breakthrough in 1918, and after the war worked to create the Poppy Day charity appeal in Britain to provide money for the care of the wounded.

Haile Selassie: emperor of *Ethiopia*, 1930–74. He earlier ruled as regent. The Italian invasion of 1935 interrupted his reign, and his emotional speech for intervention by the League of Nations failed to sway the members to take effective action. He lived in exile in London until, in 1941, he was restored to the throne by the Allies. He then ruled autocratically until he was deposed a year before his death, in 1975.

Haldane, Richard: a British politician. He was secretary for war, 1905–12, when he carried out major army reforms. He:

- created a small expeditionary force capable of being deployed swiftly and backed by a territorial force, based on the British regions, capable of rapid expansion
- was responsible for Britain establishing for the first time an imperial general staff to be responsible for planning and conducting military strategy.

These reforms were stimulated by growing fear of German rearmament, and he deserves the credit for Britain having, in 1914, a relatively modern army to send to war.

Halder, Franz: a German general. He:

- planned the *blitzkrieg* offensives of 1939 and 1940
- was dismissed in 1942 when he opposed Hitler's decision to attack Stalingrad
- was imprisoned in a concentration camp by the Nazi government after the *July Plot* of 1944.

He survived the war, avoided prosecution at the Nuremberg Trials and died in 1972.

Halifax, Lord: a British politician. He was a supporter of the policy of *appeasement*, and as foreign secretary from 1938, he accepted both the *Anschluss* and the *Munich Agreement*. He would not go to Moscow in 1939, thus losing the chance of an understanding with Stalin and pushing the latter towards the Nazi–Soviet Pact with Hitler. In 1940, on the fall of Chamberlain, he declined the opportunity to form a government but served instead under Churchill.

Hallstein Doctrine: a West German doctrine, promulgated in 1957, that any state, other than the Soviet Union, which recognized East Germany could have no diplomatic relations with West Germany. It was named after a West German foreign-office official and illustrated the very poor state of relations between the two Germanys in the 1950s and 1960s. Adenauer, determined to see a reunited Germany, insisted on its full application, and under it relations were severed with Yugoslavia in 1957 and with Cuba in 1963. Only the introduction of Brandt's *Ostpolitik* from 1966 saw the doctrine fall into disuse.

Hammarskjöld, Dag: Swedish secretary-general of the UN, 1953–61. He was responsible for establishing emergency UN forces in the Middle East after the 1956 Suez Crisis, and also directed the work of the UN in the Congo in 1960–61. His independence antagonized the Soviet Union and also Western mining interests in Africa, and there was considerable speculation that the air crash which killed him was not an accident.

Havel, Vaclav: president of Czechoslovakia, 1989–92, president of the Czech Republic from 1993. He was a dissident Czech writer who became the main voice for political liberalization in Czechoslovakia in the last years of communist rule there. He was made president by the Parliament when Husak, the communist president, was forced to resign. Havel was re-elected, this time by popular vote, in 1990. With the separation of the Czech and Slovak republics at the beginning of 1993, he became president of the Czech Republic.

Hayek, Friedrich von: a right-wing Austrian political and economic philosopher, born in 1899. After the Second World War, he became the most famous proponent of the importance of self-regulating free-market mechanisms as the best safeguard of political liberty and economic progress. In this, he inspired the reduction in the economic role of the state carried out by the British Conservative governments of Margaret *Thatcher* from 1979 and later copied by other European states.

Heath, Edward: British prime minister, 1970–74. He had earlier led the 1960s negotiations for Britain's entry into the European Economic Community which were vetoed by de Gaulle, but in 1973 successfully negotiated Britain's entry into the European Community. During the years of Thatcher- and Major-led Conservative governments from 1979, he remained the most enthusiastic British supporter of the European ideal, even when many in his party became increasingly skeptical about the direction that the *European Union* was taking.

hegemony: the leadership or dominance of one state in a federation.

Helsinki Agreement: an international agreement reached at the 1975 *Helsinki Conference* session which:

- made proposals to prevent accidental crises between the power blocs
- made arrangements for international economic and technological cooperation
- issued a declaration on human rights embracing freedom of conscience, religion and thought.

The practical results were disappointing, since the stockpile of nuclear weapons continued to grow, and Western complaints about the failure of the Soviet Union to act on its human-rights promises did nothing to ease the lot of Soviet dissidents but certainly worsened relations between East and West. If anything, the Cold War entered an even colder phase in the years after 1975. One positive consequence was the inspiration it gave to civil-liberties groups in East European states, notably *Charter 77* in Czechoslovakia.

Helsinki Conference: international meetings, resulting from a Soviet initiative, in 1973 and 1975 to discuss a range of difficulties between the powers. They resulted in the *Helsinki Agreement* and were followed by unproductive meetings in Belgrade, 1977–78 and Madrid, 1980–83.

Henlein, Konrad: leader of the *Sudetenland Nazi Party*. He pushed for the Sudetenland to be incorporated into Germany and so enabled Hitler to put pressure on Czechoslovakia, which led to the *Munich Agreements* of 1938.

Herzl, Theodor: the founder in the late nineteenth century of *Zionism* as a political movement. The anti-Semitism evident in the Dreyfus case inspired him to advocate the remedy of creating a separate Jewish state. His work came to fruition with the creation of the state of Israel in 1948.

Hess, Rudolf: a German Nazi leader. He took part in the 1923 *Munich Putsch* and is reputed, in prison, to have taken down Hitler's testament, *Mein Kampf.* From 1934, he was Hitler's deputy. In 1941, he flew secretly, and on personal impulse, to Britain in an effort to negotiate peace. He was imprisoned there for the rest of the war. At the Nuremberg Trials, he was sentenced to life imprisonment, a term which, despite his growing eccentricity, he was forced to serve to the full, dying in 1987.

Heydrich, Reinhard: a Nazi SS general who, in 1938, initiated *Kristallnacht,* the smashing of the windows of Jewish houses and shops which led to the destruction of synagogues and the dispatch of thousands of Jews to concentration camps. In 1939, he stage-managed a hoax Polish invasion of Germany to provide a pretext for the German attack on Poland. In 1941, he was made protector of the Nazi-occupied regions of Bohemia and Moravia in what had been Czechoslovakia. He was assassinated by Czech terrorists in 1942, and, in reprisal, the Nazis razed the village of *Lidice* and slaughtered all its male inhabitants.

hijack: to seize control of a vehicle or aircraft, especially in order to force it to a new destination. It, and any crew and passengers, then becomes a bargaining counter to be set against some political demand. In one famous instance, the *Baader-Meinhof Gang* and Palestinian terrorists in 1976 hijacked an Air France plane and flew it to Entebbe in Uganda. A daring raid by Israeli commandos then released the captives, despite the failure of the Ugandan government to assist.

Himmler, Heinrich: a German Nazi leader and police chief. He was involved in the 1923 *Munich Putsch* and was, in 1929, made leader of the *SS.* In 1934, it was this force, under his personal supervision, which carried out the murders of the *Night of the Long Knives.* In 1934, he became head of the *Gestapo,* and in 1936 of all the police, ruthlessly persecuting anyone perceived as being an enemy of the Nazi state and building up an elaborate system of spies, concentration camps, torture and murder for this purpose. From 1940, this role was extended outside Germany into the occupied countries. He was responsible for the relentless pursuit of anyone suspected of involvement in the 1944 *July Plot* against Hitler and was the single individual most responsible for the program of genocide – the *Holocaust* – against the Jews. In 1945, he tried to negotiate a peace deal with the Allies, and when this was discovered, he was expelled from the Nazi Party and fled. He was captured by British troops and committed suicide.

Hindenburg, Paul von: a German First World War general and president of the *Weimar Republic*, 1925–34. In 1914, he led the German army in the defeat of the Russians at *Tannenburg*. He played a key role in negotiating the Treaty of *Brest-Litovsk* with the Bolsheviks and in launching the final German offensive on the Western Front in the spring of 1918, and when the latter failed he advised the kaiser, *William II*, to try to make peace. He was on the right politically but reluctantly accepted the Weimar Republic and became its second president. In the early 1930s, he:

- did not oppose the rise of the Nazi Party
- appointed Hitler chancellor in January 1933 on the advice of von *Papen*
- continued in office until his death in 1934, thus giving an air of continuity and aiding the emergence of the Third Reich from the ashes of the Weimar Republic.

Hitler, Adolf: dictator of Germany, 1933–45. His rise to power and his creation of the German Third Empire (Third Reich) is the dominant theme both in *German history, 1919–39*, and in his conduct of German policy during the *Second World War*.

Early years

Hitler was born in Austria in 1889.

- In 1914, he joined the German army and was decorated for bravery
- He joined the anti-Bolshevik German Workers Party in 1919, which soon changed its name to the National Socialist Workers Party (or *Nazi Party*)
- As a minor political figure but impressive public speaker, he attacked the evils of the *Versailles* Peace Treaty, and through it attacked the politicians of the Weimar Republic, the Jews and Marxists, all of whom he held responsible for the humiliation which Germany had suffered
- In 1923, he attempted the unsuccessful *Munich Putsch* and was imprisoned.

In prison, he wrote *Mein Kampf* ("My Struggle"), setting out his political program for Germany based on simple but clear proposals:

- rearmament
- economic self-sufficiency
- the suppression of communism
- the extermination of the Jews.

There has been dispute among historians as to how far the book can be taken as evidence that Hitler had made long-term plans for the German expansion which occurred in the 1930s and led to the Second World War. *Churchill* claimed that the

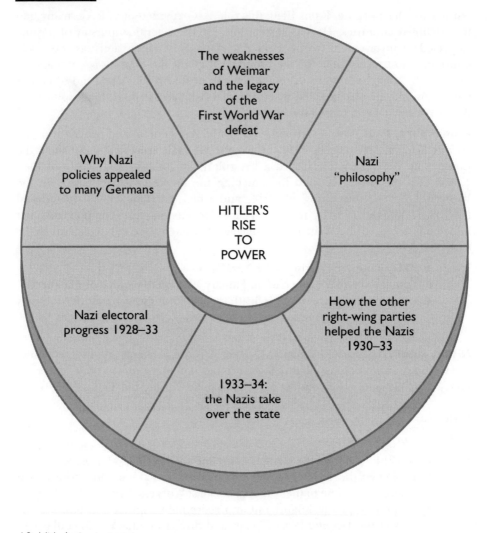

10 Hitler's rise to power

work fully substantiated this charge, but A. J. P. *Taylor* considered that MEIN KAMPF should not be taken seriously, regarding it as the idle dreams of a failed revolutionary.

Rise to power

Released from prison after serving nine months of a five-year sentence for leading the Munich Putsch, Hitler established himself as the unrivaled leader of the Nazi Party, now setting out to gain power by constitutional rather than revolutionary means. In 1925, he set up a private bodyguard, the *SS*, as an addition to the *SA* which had been founded as the Nazi Party's paramilitary arm in the early 1920s.

Party membership rose rapidly in the aftermath of the Great Depression, when democratic parties seemed incapable of providing solutions to pressing economic and social problems. The Nazi Party's vigor and clear message, and even its violence, seemed to offer a better way forward.

- The 107 seats won in the 1930 Reichstag election made it the second largest party
- In the July 1932 election, this number rose to 230
- In January 1933, President *Hindenburg* appointed Hitler chancellor, with von *Papen* his deputy.

Whatever he did subsequently, he had become head of the German government quite legally. Once in power, he acted ruthlessly to establish his power on a permanent and totalitarian basis:

- he took advantage of the *Reichstag Fire* in February 1933, portraying it as part of a communist plot in order to carry out arbitrary arrests of left-wing opponents and disbar communist deputies from the Reichstag
- the March 1933 Reichstag election was marked by systematic violence, including use of the police, against political opponents
- he used intimidation of the members of the Reichstag to pass the *Enabling Act*, which transferred full law-making and government power to Chancellor Hitler for a period of four years.

The Enabling Act marked the end of democracy and the rule of law in Germany.

His position after 1933

- Political parties other than the Nazis were closed down
- In the *Night of the Long Knives*, he both purged his own party of his opponents and won the support of the German army for his regime
- After Hindenburg's death in 1934, Hitler added the office of president to that of chancellor, and took the title of *Führer* ("Leader").
- He declared that the Weimar Republic was dead and inaugurated the Third Reich (see *German Third Empire*).

The history of the Third Reich from 1933 to 1945 was closely tied to Hitler's personal vision of the purpose of the state and its position in Europe. His propaganda skills, at the *Nuremberg Rallies* or on the radio, united the mass of the people behind that vision; an important and controversial example of how he personally directed the domestic and international strategy of the Nazi state is revealed in the *Hossbach Memorandum* of 1937. His entry into Vienna in 1938 at the time of the *Anschluss* was a personal triumph. Later that year, he dominated the *Munich Agreement* negotiations.

The Second World War

- In 1939, he personally made the decision to attack Poland and so started the Second World War
- He insisted, against hesitant military advisers, on the daring and totally successful 1940 attack on France and the use of *blitzkrieg* tactics

- His most fateful wartime decision was to launch *Operation Barbarossa* against the Soviet Union, once more ignoring the doubts of senior generals.

Hitler came increasingly to despise the German military leaders and became convinced of his own intuitive military skills, and this led him into increasingly reckless decisions as the war progressed, notably the decision to commit major resources to the attack on Stalingrad, in which he was opposed by General *Halder*, who had planned Germany's earlier victories on both the Eastern and Western Fronts. When the war began to go wrong, he blamed the military leaders and ultimately the German people, who had failed to live up to his vision. He survived an assassination attempt in the *July Plot* of 1944 and took ruthless revenge on all those remotely suspected of involvement. He also had personal involvement in devising the "Final Solution" to the "Jewish problem" which led to the deaths of millions in the *Holocaust*. His hold over Germany remained remarkable even when defeat was inevitable. Almost to the end, he believed the "Grand Alliance" against Germany would fall apart. With Soviet troops only streets away from his underground bunker in Berlin in April 1945, he married his mistress, Eva Braun, and both then committed suicide.

Hitler Bomb Plot: see *July Plot*

Hitler Youth: the youth movement of the *Nazi Party*, founded in 1933. In 1936, all other youth movements were abolished. The movement sought to bring up the German youth to accept Nazi values. Boys were subject to military discipline, and girls, through the League of German Maidens, were to be prepared for their domestic duties. By 1938, there were nearly 8 million members of the Hitler Youth, but despite all the pressure to join, this still left 4 million young people outside it. In March 1939, in a move which illustrated the *totalitarian* nature of the Nazi state and its disregard for individuals, a law conscripted all young people into the movement. Parents were warned that their children would be removed to orphanages unless they enrolled.

Hoare, Samuel: a British politician. He was appointed foreign secretary in 1935, just as the Italian attack on Ethiopia was beginning. With the foreign minister of France, *Laval*, he devised the *Hoare–Laval Pact*, which was intended to partition Ethiopia.

Hoare–Laval Pact: the 1935 pact between Hoare, the British foreign secretary, and his French opposite number Laval to partition Ethiopia between Italy and the government of Haile Selassie at the time of the *Italo–Ethiopian War*. Public outrage at this pandering to aggression forced the British prime minister, Baldwin, to disown the pact, and Hoare resigned.

Holland: strictly, one of the provinces making up the kingdom of The *Netherlands*. The outline national history of the country is included under that heading but, following common practice, in all other entries the state itself is identified as Holland.

Holocaust, the: the name given to the killing of over 4 million, and perhaps as many as 6 million, Jews by the Nazis during the Second World War. Until 1941, the persecution of the Jews in Germany had been limited to loss of civil rights, the confiscation of businesses, restrictions on occupations and random violence such as that on *Kristallnacht* in 1938. This persecution was to promote Nazi ideas on racial purity by encouraging true Germans to hate and fear the Jews and also to encourage the latter to emigrate.

From 1941, the persecution took a much more sinister form, including forced labor, mass shootings, and confinement in *concentration camps*, some of which, like *Auschwitz* and *Treblinka*, were set up as mass-extermination or *death camps*. This was the Nazi "Final Solution" to the "Jewish problem," and its application was extended to countries occupied by the German army, particularly in Eastern Europe. Some historians see a cold-blooded master plan behind the Holocaust, while others emphasize the makeshift nature of the appalling enterprise as the first idea of shipping the entire Jewish population into Siberian Russia foundered on the successful resistance of the Soviet army to the German advance.

The numbers of those slaughtered are inevitably intelligent estimates at best. In descending order of total numbers, they include:

- Poland: 2.5 million of the 3 million Jews were killed
- Soviet Union: 1.2 of 2.5 million (but see below)
- Romania: 400,000 of 850,000
- Germany: 180,000 of 250,000
- Hungary: 200,000 of 400,000
- Holland: 110,000 of 150,000.

With the active cooperation of the Vichy government, between 65,000 and 130,000 of France's Jewish population of 300,000 were sent to their deaths. In each of Austria, Greece and Yugoslavia, some 60,000 from 70,000 were killed. In contrast, thanks in part to the courage and obstruction of Denmark's non-Jewish citizens, only 100 of 9,000 Jews died there. In Italy, illustrating the relative inertia of the fascist regime in pursuing its Jewish populace, 10,000 from 75,000 were killed. Even at the end of the century, the figures are a subject of debate. One recent suggestion is that the Soviet Union figures should be much higher, with 2,200,000 killed of a total Jewish population of 4,700,000. Perhaps this idea that somehow historians had lost sight of over 1 million brutal murders does something to indicate the scale of the horror perpetrated.

Honecker, Erich: head of state of East Germany (GDR), 1976–89. His resistance to the Nazis led to his being held in a concentration camp from 1935 until his release by the Red Army in 1945. He was effectively in control of the state from *Ulbricht*'s death in 1973 and then took repressive measures against dissent to maintain the full totalitarian authority of the communist state. In international affairs, he usually closely followed the official Soviet line. He lost office with the collapse of the communist regime and, though accused of corruption, was too ill to stand trial.

Horthy, Miklós: the fascist-style dictator of Hungary, 1920–44. In 1919, he overthrew Béla Kun's communist regime. Technically, he was regent on behalf of the monarchy, but he never allowed it to be restored. He was an authoritarian ruler who maintained a reactionary social order in the country. In 1920, he agreed to the Treaty of *Trianon*, by which Hungary lost much of its pre-war land, and which left some 3 million Magyars under foreign, mainly Romanian, rule. The *Vienna Awards* of 1940 restored two-thirds of what had been lost. In the 1930s, Horthy's rule became increasingly dictatorial, and in 1941 he became an ally of Hitler, declaring war on the Soviet Union. In 1944, when he tried to negotiate a separate peace with the Allies, German troops invaded Hungary and he was imprisoned. He was taken by the Allies in 1945, released in 1946 and lived in exile until his death in 1957.

Hossbach Memorandum: the minutes of a November 1937 meeting, addressed by Hitler, which were kept by Colonel Hossbach. During the meeting, attended by the heads of armed forces and the foreign ministry, Hitler stressed the necessity for *lebensraum* and stated that, because he believed that German military superiority would only last until 1943–45, he was determined to solve the problem of living space by those dates at the latest. The minutes, read alongside his earlier autobiography *Mein Kampf,* have been seen as the clearest indication that Hitler had, from an early date, planned a general European war to achieve his goals. However, among British historians, A. J. P. *Taylor* in particular challenged this interpretation, making the point that the "memorandum" survives as a copy of a copy of the original, which Hossbach had in any event written from memory, days after the conference. Taylor wrote of the memorandum that "far from being an official record [it] is a very hot potato." He went on to argue that the Hossbach conference was called to discuss future rearmament, not war plans, and to outmaneuver *Schact* and his financial scruples over the cost of the proposals involved. In this view, the memorandum is worthless as evidence of Hitler's war plans and fits in with Taylor's wider thesis that Hitler, far from having a master plan in foreign affairs, was an unscrupulous opportunist, taking advantage of circumstances as they arose.

Hugenberg, Alfred: leader of the German Nationalist Party and a prominent industrialist. He led the party to the right, increasingly opposed to the very existence of Weimar, and in 1929, gave Hitler massive publicity in his vast newspaper network as part of a joint campaign against the *Young Plan.* His willingness in 1933 to take office in Hitler's government was important in persuading President Hindenburg to appoint the Nazi leader as chancellor. He was, with von *Papen,* a member of the small group of reactionary politicians who thought they could manipulate *Hitler* for their own purposes, and it was this mistaken belief that helped Hitler to achieve power legally.

Hungarian Revolution: the October–November 1956 rising against the communist regime in Hungary. It arose in the aftermath of *Khrushchev*'s denunciation of Stalin, which had created high hopes of reforms in Hungary, and began with student demonstrations in Budapest, leading to a popular uprising against the repressive government of Gero. Soviet troops had to withdraw from Budapest, and a new government was set up under *Nagy* and *Kádár.* This:

- introduced liberal reforms, for example the legalizing of political parties
- released Cardinal *Mindszenty* from house detention
- announced both the withdrawal of Hungary from the Warsaw Pact and its future neutrality, like that of neighboring Austria.

This last move was the work of Nagy and it caused Kádár to switch sides, leading Soviet troops and tanks into Budapest to crush the rising. Kádár was then installed as the head of a new communist regime. The crushing of the rising and the hopes it represented caused great anger in the West and led to an emergency UN debate but, faced with a massive Soviet military presence in Hungary, there was no way in which the rebels could be helped. The rising was one of the most dramatic events of the *Cold War* in Europe, and demonstrated the determination of the Soviet Union to maintain firm control over its East European satellites.

Hungary: up to 1918, part of the Dual Monarchy of the *Austro-Hungarian Empire*. This was in effect a German–Magyar alliance against the other nationalities of the empire. After its defeat in the First World War, Hungary lost over half its territory. A short-lived communist regime under Béla Kun was replaced from 1920 to 1944 by the increasingly authoritarian rule of Admiral *Horthy*. In the Second World War, Hungary fought on the Axis side and, in 1944, was invaded and occupied by the Red Army.

After the war, a communist republic on rigidly Stalinist lines was imposed on the country, with first *Rákosi* and then *Nagy* as prime minister. The *Hungarian Revolution* of 1956 was crushed by Soviet intervention, and *Kádár*, at first a Soviet puppet but later the introducer of some limited liberal social reforms, headed the government through to 1988. In 1988–89, as the Soviet bloc began to disintegrate, other political parties were formed in Hungary, and at the end of 1989 even the Communist Party was reorganized under internal pressure and took the name of Socialist Workers Party. Hungary then officially became a multi-party state. The 1990 elections led to the formation of a non-communist government, the Hungarian Democratic Forum. There was a territorial crisis with Romania, and economic liberalization led to falling living standards for many. The 1994 election was won by the former Communist Party, which gained 209 of the 386 seats, and the future political and economic direction of the state was thrown into doubt.

hydrogen bomb: an immensely powerful bomb based on the explosive fusion of hydrogen nuclei. The first bomb was exploded by the USA in 1952 and represented greater explosive capacity than all the bombs used in the Second World War in total. In addition, there was a widespread and highly dangerous fall-out of radio-active material. By prompting fears of total destruction of the planet, the hydrogen bomb encouraged the emergence of campaigns for nuclear disarmament in many countries. The Soviet Union had the hydrogen bomb by 1953, Britain by 1957, China by 1967, France by 1968. The bomb raised the stakes in the *Cold War* to unbearable heights, but its destructive potential perhaps also ensured that the powers would never use it.

hyperinflation: a rise in prices which becomes totally out of control, as in Weimar Germany in the early 1920s.

I

I. G. Farben: a large German chemical firm. Its development of synthetic oil and rubber, as part of the Nazi drive towards economic self-sufficiency in the 1930s, was later invaluable to the German war effort. The killer gas used in the extermination camps had been patented by them, and the firm was a major employer of slave labor drawn from concentration camps such as Auschwitz.

IMF: see *International Monetary Fund*

Imperial Conferences: meetings of the prime ministers of Britain and the British dominions, held in London from 1911 to 1937.

imperialism: empire-building, the gaining of colonies. The opening of the twentieth century marked the great period of *European empires*. Belgium, Britain, France, Germany, Holland and Portugal were the leading imperial powers. After the First World War, the British and French empires continued to expand through the acquisition of League of Nations *mandates*, giving them control of both former German colonies and lands previously belonging to the Ottoman Empire. From this high watermark, European imperialism began to be challenged by the first beginnings of national movements in European colonies, for example in British India. However, the dismantling of empires, i.e. *decolonization*, came after 1945 and was much encouraged by the weakening of the imperial powers in the course of the Second World War.

imperial preference: a system of economic protection which gives preference by charging tariffs on goods from other parts of an empire that are lower than those charged on foreign imports.

inflation: a general rise in prices. There were two dramatic instances of runaway inflation, or hyperinflation, in the first half of the century:

- in 1918, the Soviet Union deliberately printed vast amounts of money in order to destroy the market economy and citizens' savings so that *war communism* could be imposed
- in the early 1920s, chronic inflation in Weimar Germany destroyed the savings of many middle-class and better-off working-class people, and so encouraged support for right-wing politicians like Hitler.

Inflation of a less spectacular sort became a more general problem in many Western European countries in the second half of the century, and as the value of a currency fell, it usually led to its devaluation against other currencies. The Fourth French Republic and Italy suffered severe inflation and repeated devaluations. The most stable Western currency was that of West Germany. The *command economies* of Eastern Europe, which did not rely on market forces but were content to use planning backed if necessary by subsidies and rationing, were not as open to inflationary pressures. When the Soviet-dominated bloc disintegrated in the early 1990s, all the states there faced rampant inflation as they sought to adapt to market economics.

INF Treaty (Intermediate-range Nuclear Forces Treaty): a 1987 agreement between the Soviet Union and the USA aiming to eliminate all intermediate-range nuclear weapons.

Inönü, Ismet: president of Turkey, 1938–50, prime minister, 1923–37 and 1961–65. He had a distinguished military career in the First World War and against the Greeks from 1919 to 1922. He was initially appointed as first prime minister of the new Republic of Turkey by Atatürk, and in 1938 was unanimously elected president on the latter's death. He led the Turkish negotiators at the successful Treaty of *Lausanne* in 1923. From 1950 to 1961, he was leader of the parliamentary opposition and became prime minister again in 1961, surviving an army coup and several assassination attempts. He died in 1973.

International Brigades: international groups of volunteer troops fighting for the republic against Franco's nationalists in the *Spanish Civil War*. Many were communists, usually drawn from the working class, but there were also some intellectuals, who then and since have attracted much attention. The volunteers numbered 20,000 at most, and their impact on the war should be kept in proportion.

International Court of Justice: the principal court of justice of the UN, sitting in The Hague, Holland. It has limited powers, only handling cases referred to it as breaches of UN covenants, for example on human rights, and cases can only be enforced if a nation has agreed to accept the decision in advance. There is a seldom-used right of appeal from the court to the Security Council.

International Development Association: founded in 1960 as a specialized agency of the UN to assist "least-developed countries" with loans.

International Labor Organization: an agency of the League of Nations established in 1919 by the Treaty of Versailles to improve working and living conditions worldwide.

International Monetary Fund (IMF): a UN agency set up in 1946 to stabilize international trade by creating a fund from which member nations could obtain temporary financial assistance in times of economic crisis. It arose from the *Bretton Woods Agreement* of 1944. The fund:

- advises members on their economic and financial policies
- acts as an international forum for the discussion of economic issues
- supports long-term efforts at economic reform, as in helping to create market-led economies in the formerly communist command economies of Eastern Europe.

The IMF's importance can be gauged from the fact that in 1998 there were 182 member states.

inter-war: a shorthand term for the period between the First and Second World Wars, usually taken as 1919 to 1939.

IRA (Irish Republican Army): a group committed to the cause of uniting the British province of Ulster and the Republic of Ireland in one independent state. They carried out a terrorist campaign from 1969 until 1997, when their ceasefire paved the way for *Sinn Féin* to participate in peace talks with the British and Irish governments. They are also known as the Provisionals to distinguish them from the, now largely obsolescent, Official IRA, from which they broke away.

Ireland: a republic formally founded in 1937. In that year, *de Valera* introduced a new constitution which ended the powers of the British crown in what had been the Irish Free State, set up in 1921 as a dominion within the British Empire. In 1938, an agreement to stop the British use of naval bases on Irish territory ended the last British presence in the republic.

- In the Second World War, Eire, as the republic was officially known, remained neutral
- Full recognition of Eire's independent republican status came only in 1949.
- In 1973, the republic joined the European Community.

The 1921 arrangements excluded the province of *Ulster* (Northern Ireland) from the new state, and as troubles developed there from nationalist desires to reunite the two parts of Ireland, the republic, by the 1985 Anglo–Irish Accord, was given a consultative role in Ulster. In 1998, the electorates of both Ireland and Ulster voted to approve the Northern Ireland Accord, the culmination of the lengthy peace talks between the governments of Britain and Ireland, and the political parties of Northern Ireland. The Accord recognized that change in the status of Northern Ireland can only come about with the consent of its population. The Irish electorate also voted to amend the 1937 constitution which declared the national territory of the republic to be all of the island of Ireland.

Irish Free State: the state set up in 1921 by agreement between Britain and the leaders of *Sinn Féin* with dominion status within the British Empire. It survived until 1937, when it was replaced by the republic of *Ireland*.

Iron Curtain: the term used by Churchill to describe the line dividing Europe between the Soviet bloc and the West as the Cold War developed. He used it in a speech in 1946 in the USA, and it caught the popular imagination. Churchill was no geographer, and his description of the line "From Stettin ... to Trieste" placed East Germany on the wrong side of the real divide, but the impact of his speech helped to develop the US commitment to the protection of Western Europe from the perceived expansionism of the Soviet Union.

Iron Guard: the Romanian fascist party of the 1930s.

Irredentism: an Italian nationalist movement which sought to incorporate Italian-speaking lands on its northern frontier into Italy proper. It provided the main motive for Italy's entry on the Allied side in the First World War. After the war, most of the areas had been incorporated but with the exception of the most important, the port of *Fiume*.

Iskra: the Russian Marxist newspaper produced from 1900 by Lenin, living in exile in Western Europe.

isolationism: the policy of avoiding alliances and international commitments. The most important example was that of the USA, which broke with a strong isolationist tradition when it entered the First World War in 1917. The revival of isolationist feeling after the war prevented the USA from becoming a member of the League of Nations, which greatly weakened the organization in its efforts to prevent aggression in the 1930s.

Italian Campaign: the military campaign of the Second World War, from July 1943 to 1945. It followed the successful Allied campaign in North Africa, with landings first in Sicily and then in mainland Italy. The Allied invasion brought about the deposition of Mussolini who was, however, rescued by German paratroopers. In October 1943, Italy declared war on its old ally, Germany.

Stubborn German resistance and the mountainous terrain meant that the Allied advance was both slow and costly.

- The advance was halted for weeks at the battle for the monastery of *Monte Cassino*
- The daring Allied *amphibious* landing behind the German lines at *Anzio* did not produce the expected breakthrough
- Rome was taken in June 1944 when the Germans chose not to defend it
- Not until the very end of the war in Europe did the Allies break through into the North Italian Plain
- Milan fell only six days before the end of the war
- The German armies in northern Italy surrendered on 2 May 1945.

The Italian campaign had tied down German troops who, in the late stages of the war, were desperately needed in northern Europe. However, it did not provide the easy route into Nazi-occupied Europe which the Allied leaders had hoped.

Italo–Ethiopian War: the 1935–36 invasion and conquest by fascist Italy of the independent African kingdom of *Ethiopia*. Mussolini, Italy's dictator, sought glory in foreign conquest and wished to follow other European countries in building a colonial empire. Neighboring areas, Eritrea and Italian Somaliland, were already Italian territory, but in 1896, the attempt by Italian troops to conquer Ethiopia had been humiliatingly repulsed. Mussolini now sought both imperial glory and revenge.

- Border incidents, notably at *Wal Wal*, provided the excuse
- The Italians invaded in October 1935, using modern weapons and poison gas against primitive tribesmen
- By April 1936, they had captured the capital, Addis Ababa
- Guerrilla fighting continued, but the country was controlled by Italy, which created a network of roads and forts and pursued a policy of savage repression, including public executions, against any opposition.

The efforts of the League of Nations to prevent or to end this aggression against a member state were of little value.

- Economic sanctions against Italy were ineffective because they were systematically evaded and, crucially, were never applied to supplies of oil, coal and steel
- The *Suez Canal* was never closed to Italian shipping
- An emotional speech by the Ethiopian emperor, *Haile Selassie*, failed to provoke the League into taking effective steps to defend his country.

This failure of the League and that of its two most important members, Britain and France, to take any worthwhile action in defense of Ethiopia undermined the reputation of the League as a protector against aggression. The Franco–British attempt to mediate between aggressor and victim, via the *Hoare–Laval Pact*, was widely regarded as being particularly cowardly and had to be disowned by the two governments. Britain and France did far too little to save Ethiopia but did enough to alienate Mussolini and turn him towards the prospect of alliance with Hitler's Germany. In this respect, the Italo–Ethiopian war was an important turning point in international affairs in the 1930s. Ethiopia was liberated from Italian occupation in 1941 by a British Commonwealth army, and Haile Selassie was then restored as emperor.

Italy: a country which became a unified kingdom, with Rome as its capital, in 1870.

Events to 1945

Italy fought on the Allied side in the First World War but was bitterly disappointed with its reward at the Paris Peace Conference. This, and political weakness at home, led to the establishment of *Mussolini*'s fascist dictatorship, from 1922 to 1943, which founded the *corporate state* and, after fighting the *Italo–Ethiopian War*, established an Italian Empire in East Africa. In the Second World War, Italy remained neutral in 1939, but fought on the German side from 1940. When, in 1943, the *Italian Campaign* swung towards the Allies, Mussolini was deposed and Italy switched sides. In 1946, a referendum ended the monarchy and Italy became a republic.

Since 1945

Italy's post-war history has been a mixture of economic growth and increasing prosperity alongside corruption and continuing political instability, with 50 governments in all between 1947 and 1995. Coalition governments were usually short-lived. In the 1950s and 1960s, the communists under *Togliatti* were a significant presence, but worked within the democratic framework rather than trying to take over the state. The considerable political influence of the Catholic Church had usually been exercised through the conservative Christian Democratic Party, but this came under pressure in the 1990s with the emergence of regional and populist parties like the Northern League and the Forza Italia, led by the media tycoon *Berlusconi*. In 1958, Italy was a founder member of what became the European Union, and has been an enthusiastic supporter of it since then.

Izmir: a city in western Turkey: see *Smyrna*.

J

Jajce Congress: the meeting of partisans convened by *Tito* in November 1943 which resolved to establish a Federal Republic of Yugoslavia.

Jaruzelski, Wojciech: prime minister of Poland, 1981–85 and president, 1985–90. He had a distinguished military career but, as prime minister, had to cope with a worsening economy and the rising political influence of *Solidarity*. He imposed martial law from 1981 to 1983, and until 1989 made Solidarity an illegal organization, imprisoning its leaders. As president from 1985, he remained a dominant political influence in the country but adopted more reforming policies. It was he who, as head of state, saw through the relatively peaceful transition from communist rule to the creation of a multi-party democracy in 1989.

Jenkins, Roy: a British politician and historian. He was an ardent supporter of closer ties between Britain and the European Community, and served as president of the European Commission from 1976 to 1981.

jingoism: fanatical patriotism. The term was coined in a British music-hall song of 1878 to focus strong anti-Russian feeling. It was in common use in the period of fevered nationalism prior to 1914.

Joffre, Joseph: a French general. Prior to the First World War, he had devised the plan which, put into practice at the first Battle of the Marne in September 1914, prevented the German invasion, based on the *Schlieffen Plan*, from becoming a swift total victory. As commander-in-chief of the French forces, he was blamed for military failures at *Verdun* and the *Somme*, and resigned in 1916.

John XXIII: pope, 1958–63. He attempted to liberalize Roman Catholic policy on social questions and urged the need for international peace. In 1962, he summoned the Second *Vatican Council* to revitalize the life of the Church.

John Paul II: pope, 1978– . Of Polish origin, he was the first non-Italian to be elected pope since the sixteenth century. He had previously been a symbol of Catholic identity and resistance to the communist government of Poland. Unlike his predecessors, he traveled widely, particularly to nations of the Third World and back to his native Poland. On moral issues, he firmly asserted conservative values, being opposed to abortion, birth control, euthanasia and homosexual acts.

Juan Carlos: king of Spain from 1975. The grandson of King *Alfonso XIII*, he was nominated as king by the dictator Franco, succeeding on the latter's death. He has ruled as a constitutional monarch above the disputes of party politics, and succeeded, despite continued separatist feelings among the Basques, in bringing about remarkable political stability in Spain.

July Days: an ill-organized uprising in Petrograd in July 1917 against the Russian Provisional Government. It was led by Russian sailors angry at the continuation of the war. The Bolsheviks at first encouraged it but then failed to lead it. The government did enough to cause the demonstrators to disperse after having achieved nothing but some street violence. The episode enabled the government to crack down on the Bolsheviks, portraying them as German agents. Lenin feared he was to be arrested and fled to Finland. The plot led by *Kornilov* in August 1917 allowed the Bolsheviks to recover from this setback.

July Plot: a plot in July 1944 to assassinate Hitler. It was organized by discontented German army officers in order to bring an end to Nazi rule so that peace negotiations could be opened with the Allies. A bomb was planted by Colonel von *Stauffenberg* in Hitler's headquarters which killed four people, but not Hitler. Stauffenberg, however, believed that he had succeeded, and his co-conspirators, advised to this effect, came into the open in order to set up an alternative government. Hitler used his remarkable survival not only to wreak terrible revenge on the plotters, but also as an excuse to purge the army and to rid himself of high-ranking government officials whose loyalty he doubted. One hundred and fifty alleged plotters were killed in various ways, many involving great cruelty. In the aftermath of the plot, others, including Field Marshal *Rommel*, who had not been involved were forced, by threats to their families, to commit suicide.

Jung, Carl: a Swiss psychiatrist, and in the early years of the century, with *Freud*, a founder of psychoanalysis. He later introduced the concept of "introvert" and "extrovert" personalities and became critical of Freud's insistence on the psychosexual origins of neuroses. He died in 1961.

Jutland: the only great sea battle of the *First World War*. It:

- took place in the North Sea on 31 May 1916
- involved heavy battleships and battle-cruisers of the British and German navies, which had been so important a part of the pre-war arms race between the two countries
- led to both sides claiming victory after two brief, long-range gun duels and subsequent accidental collisions when sections of the two fleets sailed into each other in the dark
- resulted in heavier British losses – 14 ships and 6,000 men – than those of the German navy – 11 ships and 2,500 men.

The strategic importance of the battle was that the German navy withdrew again to the safety of the Baltic Sea, from which it did not again emerge in force. The British navy retained its control of the North Sea, so vital both to the defense of the country and for its ability to continue to supply the army on the Western Front.

K

Kádár, János: prime minister of Hungary, 1956–58, 1961–65. He had been imprisoned from 1951 to 1954, but in October 1956 he was appointed general secretary of the Communist Party at the opening of the *Hungarian Revolution*. At first, he supported *Nagy*'s liberalization policies, but when the latter announced that Hungary was to leave the Warsaw Pact, he changed sides and led Soviet tanks into Budapest to crush the rising, thereby giving the Soviet action some appearance of legitimacy. He then became prime minister and ruthlessly pursued those who had supported the rising. Later, he carried out modest policies of liberalization and decentralized the economy. In 1988, he took the office of president and died in 1989, just before the communist regime collapsed.

Kadets: a Russian political party; see *Cadets*.

kaiser: the title of the emperor of the *German Second Empire* from 1870 to 1918.

Kalinin, Mikhail: head of state of the Soviet Union, 1919–46. He was a Bolshevik from 1903, took part in the 1905 Revolution, was one of the founders of *Pravda* and played an important part, as mayor of Petrograd, in the October Revolution of 1917. He was head of state of the Soviet Union for over 30 years, becoming one of the few politically prominent survivors of the Stalinist purges of the 1930s, aided in this by his unswerving loyalty to Stalin himself.

Kamenev, Lev: a Soviet politician. An early Bolshevik who rose to prominence during the Lenin period. After Lenin's death, he combined with Stalin and Zinoviev to prevent Trotsky from taking power. He later opposed Stalin and was sentenced to death for his alleged part in the murder of Kirov in 1935. This was in the first of Stalin's great *show trials* which marked the beginning of the Soviet Great Purge of the late 1930s.

Kapp Putsch: a right-wing rising in 1920 to overthrow the *Weimar Republic* and restore the monarchy. The rebels, mainly *Freikorps* members led by Wolfgang Kapp, seized control of government buildings in Berlin and forced the government to flee the city. Ominously, it both had the approval of the eminent soldier *Ludendorff* and, until the *Ebert–Groener Pact*, looked likely to benefit from the stance of the German army. Kapp lost his nerve because:

- Berlin was paralyzed by a general strike
- civil servants and local government officials refused to carry out the instructions of the rebels.

This working-class solidarity in support of Weimar is one important reason why the republic, in its early years, survived the hostility of so many right-wing enemies. The Weimar authorities were so wary of alienating the right wing in general that the leaders of the putsch, like *Ehrhardt* and *Lüttwitz*, received minimal punishment, though this did not stop random right-wing violence, as the murder of *Rathenau* showed.

Kapp, Wolfgang: the instigator of the *Kapp Putsch*. When it failed he was arrested, and he died in prison in 1922.

Karadžić, Radovan: the 1990s leader of the Bosnian Serbs. He led their military resistance to the creation of a multi-ethnic Bosnian republic and sought to bring Bosnia into a greater Serbia. The ensuing civil war was particularly bitter and marked by many atrocities. From 1996, following the discovery of mass graves of Muslim and Croat men and boys, there were UN and other demands that Karadžić be tried as a war criminal. However, he retained the support of the Bosnian Serbs, and it seemed unlikely that he would be easily surrendered.

Karamanlis, Constantine: prime minister of Greece, 1955–63, 1974–80, president 1980–85. He was a right-wing politician who, at the time of the *Greek Civil War*, worked closely with the leader of the royalist forces, *Papagos*, whom he succeeded as prime minister. He used US *Marshall Aid* to rebuild the Greek economy. He was an exile during the rule of the "*Greek Colonels*" but returned in 1974 and was prime minister at the time of the referendum which confirmed Greece as a republic.

Katyn Massacre: the massacre of 15,000 Polish-officer prisoners of war in the early stages of the Second World War. After the Germans discovered the bodies in 1943, both they and the Soviets accused each other of carrying out the massacre. Only in 1990 was it clearly established that Soviet troops had been responsible, presumably in an effort to wipe out possible opponents of any future Soviet occupation of Poland.

Kellogg–Briand Pact: a 1928 international pact renouncing war. It was named after its originators:

- the French statesman, Briand, who proposed such a pact between France and the USA
- the American government official, Kellogg, who suggested that it should embrace many countries.

Eventually, 61 nations ratified the pact, and it was one hopeful indicator in the late 1920s that a new stability was entering international relations. Unfortunately, the pact included no machinery for enforcing its resolutions, and it had little or no relevance in the crises of the 1930s.

Kemal, Mustafa: president of Turkey – see *Atatürk*.

Kennedy, John: president of the USA, 1961–63. He resisted demands from Khrushchev that West Germany leave NATO and that the West recognize East Germany, and later paid a much-publicized, morale-boosting visit to West Berlin when the building of the Berlin Wall was raising great anxieties there. He also forced Khrushchev to back down in the 1962 Cuban Missile Crisis. In general, he overplayed the role of Cold War warrior, but the consequences were felt mainly in US policy towards Asia rather than towards Europe. Kennedy was assassinated in 1963.

Kerensky, Alexander: prime minister in the Russian Provisional Government, July to October 1917. He was, from 1912 to 1917, a moderate, middle-class, Social Democrat member of the fourth Duma. After the tsar's abdication in February, he was, until July, minister of justice and then minister for war in the Provisional Government led by Prince Lvov. He:

- insisted on continuing the war against Germany
- was unable to deal with the deteriorating economy

- could not carry out the agrarian reforms for which the peasants were pressing
- failed to gain the trust of the Petrograd working class and found difficulty in working with the Petrograd Soviet which assisted the Bolshevik's growing power in the city.

It was widely believed in August 1917 that he had initially encouraged General *Kornilov*'s movement of troops to Petrograd to restore "order," and this lost him further popularity with the working class of the city, handing the political initiative to the Bolsheviks, who claimed that they had prevented Kornilov's coup. Kerensky's government was overthrown by the Bolsheviks in the *October Revolution* of 1917, and he proved incapable of organizing a counter-coup.

He then lived in exile until his death in 1970, writing his memoirs, in which he blamed the failure of the Provisional Government on those, like Kornilov, who had betrayed it into the hands of the Bolsheviks. A less partisan verdict on why the Provisional Government collapsed would also have acknowledged his own indecisiveness and a willingness, faced with the obstruction of the Petrograd Soviet and the growing power of the Bolsheviks on that body, to let things drift.

Kesselring, Albrecht: a German field marshal and airman. He commanded the stunningly effective *blitzkrieg* bombing attacks of 1939 and 1940 against Poland, Holland, Belgium and France. His failure, in the *Battle of Britain*, to gain air supremacy over southern England denied the Germans the opportunity of invading Britain, but this has since been blamed on the interference of Goering and Hitler. In 1943–44, he commanded the fierce German resistance in the *Italian Campaign* and was, at its conclusion, tried and imprisoned for atrocities against Italian partisans. He was released in 1952 and died in 1960.

Keynes, John Maynard: a British economist. He criticized the reparations levied on the Germans at the Paris Peace Conference as being likely to damage the flow of international trade. He believed that even democratic governments had a duty to manage the economy, and his ideas had some influence on Roosevelt's New Deal in the USA. His views came too late and were insufficiently regarded for them to have any real impact in ending the Great Depression. After 1945, however, they had wide currency, particularly with British governments – until they fell out of favor with the post-1979 Thatcher government.

KGB: a Soviet intelligence-gathering agency set up in 1954 after the downfall of *Beria*. Under its formal title, the Soviet Committee for State Security, it also supervised the secret police and maintained security within the Soviet state. Its operations were questioned after 1985 under Gorbachev's policy of *glasnost.*

Khrushchev, Nikita: a Soviet statesman

His career

He fought in the Red Army in the Russian Civil War, rose through the ranks of the Communist Party and was prime minister in the Ukraine from 1943 to 1947, coping with the problems of post-war devastation and carrying out a massive reorganization of agriculture. He became first secretary of the USSR Communist Party on the death of *Stalin* in 1953, a post he held until 1964. He was also chairman of the council of ministers from 1958 to 1964. His denunciation of Stalin, at the *Twentieth Congress* in 1956, was one of the most dramatic moments in the history of the Soviet state and led to hopes of liberalization there and in Soviet-dominated Eastern Europe. Khrushchev was then, and until 1964, the most important political figure in the Soviet Union.

His political position

From 1956 to 1958, he was victorious in a power struggle with *Malenkov, Molotov* and *Bulganin,* and then himself achieved something approaching a Stalinist personality-cult status. The worst days of Stalinist terror, however, were over, and Khrushchev's defeated enemies were disgraced rather than killed.

Economic policy (see also the entry *Soviet economy after 1945*)

Khrushchev retained in full the apparatus of Soviet economic planning but wished to make it work more efficiently. His main policies with regard to the Soviet economy were:

- to extend grain production to the *Virgin Lands* of Soviet Central Asia
- to improve agricultural output generally by decentralizing planning and giving more powers to regional economic councils
- to concentrate farming development in large-scale units but accepting that the peasants' private plots had to be retained
- to switch the emphasis in industrial investment from heavy to light industry in order to provide more consumer goods.

The results in agriculture were disappointing: production in the traditional areas increased only slowly, and the abolition of tractor stations – so that the cooperative farms (*kolkhoz*) could buy their own capital equipment – was a mistake, for many farms were unable to afford to do so. The Virgin Lands scheme, started in 1954, went well for the first few years, but poor soil and a marginal climate could be compensated for by the overuse of fertilizers for only so long. The 1963 grain harvest failed on both the Virgin Lands and in the traditional Ukraine grain-growing area, and the need to import US wheat contributed to Khrushchev's downfall. Progress in switching industrial investment from heavy to light industry was slow, for in this new field the Soviet *command economy* did not function as efficiently as it had with heavy industry. The bureaucratic complexity of *Gosplan* prevented innovation and economic flexibility, and the size of the country imposed heavy transport costs on industry. The burden of high military spending continued to weigh on all sections of the economy.

Social policy

There was some liberalization of society under Khrushchev:

- police procedures were tightened up and were more closely supervised by the newly established KGB
- many prison camps were closed and their inhabitants sent home
- trial processes were made more just.

The worst excesses of Stalinist terror were ended but, on the other hand, official attacks on religion increased and, as crime increased, further death-penalty offenses were introduced. Above all, direct attacks on the Soviet system and the role of the Communist Party were not tolerated. In the arts, the same process of limited liberalization also took place: *Solzhenitsyn* was published, *Pasternak* was not. Secondary and higher education both expanded.

Foreign policy

Khrushchev's record in foreign policy was as erratic as was his behavior on some well-publicized occasions. He:

- encouraged liberal reforms and appointments in the Eastern European satellite states
- then crushed the 1956 *Hungarian Rising*
- met Kennedy in a peace-seeking summit in 1961
- then caused the most serious confrontation of the Cold War in the 1962 *Cuban Missile Crisis*
- subsequently climbed down and ordered the withdrawal of Soviet missiles from Cuba in an episode which became one reason for his removal from power
- brought Soviet relations with China close to war in this period, thanks in part to his personal feud with *Mao Zedong*, and this became another reason for his colleagues' removing him from office in 1964.

Despite occasional outbursts, and excepting the Cuban crisis, relations between the power blocs improved significantly during his years in power. That he was able, after dismissal, to live quietly in obscure retirement, rather than in prison or worse, suggested that the Soviet Union had become a more civilized place during his years in power.

Kiel Canal: a ship canal opened in 1895 connecting the North Sea and the Baltic. The German Navy Law of 1906 arranged for its widening to allow *dreadnought*-class battleships to pass through, and this was done between 1909 and 1914. The secure base it provided for the German fleet increased British concerns about the German naval build-up during the early twentieth century, and was an important feature of the *Naval Race* of the period.

Kiel Mutiny: an October 1918 mutiny by German sailors when ordered to mount a cruiser raid in the English Channel. It followed years of naval inactivity since the Battle of *Jutland*. It was ended by the socialist defense expert *Noske*, but not before it had spread to other ports. The mutiny, and the collapse of public order as workers' and sailors' councils took over local government, was one element in the collapse of the German Second Empire, and it encouraged its successors to sue for an armistice.

Kiesinger, Kurt: chancellor of West Germany, 1966–69. A founder member of the Christian Democratic Party (CDU) who had briefly flirted with the Nazis in the 1930s, he replaced Erhard as chancellor in a coalition government with the CDU's main rivals, *Brandt*'s Social Democrats. Despite his strongly pro-Western views, he tried to move away from *Adenauer*'s hard line on relations with the East, if only to accommodate his coalition partners. However, he lost first their support and then the 1969 election, and was succeeded as chancellor by Brandt. He died in 1988.

Kirov, Sergei: a leading Soviet politician. He organized the communist victory in the Russian Civil War in the Caucasus region. In the late 1920s and early 1930s, he worked closely with Stalin, but at the 1934 Communist Party Congress he attacked Stalin's arbitrary personal rule. He was assassinated in December 1934, and hundreds were executed in revenge. Stalin used the murder to launch the *Yezhovshchina* (or *Great Purge*) of any suspected rivals, which was to dominate Soviet life for the next three years. It seems probable that Stalin himself had ordered Kirov's assassination.

Kitchener, Earl: a British general. He saw service in the Boer War and was made secretary for war – a political, not a military, post – in 1914. He realized, contrary to popular opinion, that the First World War would be a long one. A muddle over supplies, especially artillery shells, on the Western Front damaged his reputation. He was drowned in 1916 while on his way to Russia on board a British warship.

Kohl, Helmut: chancellor of West Germany (from 1990 the reunified Germany) from 1982-1998. As leader of the *Christian Democrats* (the CDU), he re-established the traditional alliance with the *Free Democrats* in 1982, and after victory in the 1983 election, he swung German politics back to the right after years of *Social Democratic* (SPD) government. He was a remote and unpopular figure but played a decisive role in the reunification of Germany as the East German regime crumbled.

- In July 1990, he offered to unify the currencies of East and West Germany on a one-for-one basis
- He negotiated with *Gorbachev* that the reunited Germany would continue to be a member of NATO.

In September 1990, his initiative bore fruit in the *Treaty on the Final Settlement with Respect to Germany* agreed between East Germany, West Germany and the four former occupying powers, Britain, France, the Soviet Union and the USA. The treaty reunified Germany as a single state, incorporating the territory of the two Germanys and Berlin. Kohl's CDU formed the government of the newly unified state in coalition with the Free Democrats after nation-wide elections in 1991, a result confirmed in the 1994 election. He worked closely with French political leaders, especially Mitterrand, to promote the development of the *European Union*.

Kolchak, Alexander: a Russian admiral. He led the *White Russian* forces in Siberia during the *Russian Civil War*, successfully clearing the vast region of Bolshevik troops. Later, many of his men deserted, and in 1920 he was betrayed to the Red Army and shot.

kolkhoz: a large-scale Soviet cooperative farm. They were introduced as part of Stalin's radical restructuring and *collectivization* of agriculture in the late 1920s and 1930s, and almost a quarter of a million of them existed by 1941. Peasants:

- lived rent-free on state land
- pooled their resources and shared the profits from selling produce to the state.

The kolkhoz were distinct from and more important than the *sovkhoz*, state-owned farms, of which there were only some 2,000.

Koniev, Ivan: a tsarist army officer who joined the Bolshevik Party and the *Red Army*. Unlike many of his fellow officers, he avoided suspicion in Stalin's 1930s purge of the Red Army and held major commands in the fighting during the

Second World War, ending with an important role in the capture of Berlin.

Korean War: the war in the Korean peninsula in Asia, 1950–53. European troops formed part of the UN force defending South Korea. The war confirmed the spread of the Cold War, now in hotter form, from Europe to Asia. It also imposed severe financial burdens on the European countries involved, particularly Britain.

Kornilov, Lavrenti: a Russian general. He organized a military coup in August 1917 to restore order in Petrograd and to end the growing influence of left-wing agitators. Many assumed that he was about to set up a military dictatorship. He had negotiated with *Kerensky*, but the latter then ordered him to surrender. The railway workers, on orders from the Petrograd Soviet, refused to transport his troops, and agitators undermined their morale. The attempted coup then fizzled out. It undermined the authority of the *Provisional Government* and strengthened that of both the Petrograd Soviet and the Bolsheviks, and so marked a significant stage in the government's collapse.

Kosygin, Alexei: Soviet prime minister, 1964–80. During his period in office, he was in the shadow of *Brezhnev* and concentrated mainly on economic and administrative matters. He was unsuccessful in his efforts to make the Soviet economic system more flexible and to give managers more freedom because:

- of Brezhnev's anxiety not to allow economic changes to lead to political turmoil
- he was obstructed by the inertia of Soviet bureaucracy centered on *Gosplan*
- he was frustrated in his efforts to restrict military expenditure by the influence of the Soviet military
- like so many members of the Soviet leadership of the period, his efforts were restricted by bouts of poor health.

Kosygin achieved international acclaim when his diplomacy ended the Indo–Pakistan war of 1966. He also attended a summit meeting with US President Johnson in 1967, failing to bring an end to the Vietnam War but achieving some agreement on the need for arms control. He died, aged 76, in 1980.

Kreisky, Bruno: chancellor of Austria, 1970–83. A strong Social Democrat, he sought better relations with neighboring communist states, particularly Czechoslovakia and Yugoslavia, and continued to build up the welfare state at home.

Kremlin: strictly the site of the former Imperial Palace in Moscow, but regularly used as a shorthand term for the government of the Soviet Union.

Kristallnacht: or "Crystal Night," from the glass of Jewish homes and shops broken by organized Nazi mobs in March 1938.

- The murder of a German diplomat by a Jewish student in Paris was the excuse for the organized violence which marked the beginning of a more savage persecution of German Jews by the Nazi state
- As well as countless acts of violence and intimidation, some 100 Jews were murdered and 7,000 Jewish businesses ransacked, with General *Heydrich* playing a key role in organizing the assault

- In November 1938, Jews were prevented by law from working in many occupations, including the sales and service industries.

Kronstadt Mutiny: a mutiny by Russian sailors in March 1921. They had formerly been zealous communists but, weary of the civil war and of the hardships of *war communism,* they mutinied under the slogan "Soviets without communists." It needed 10 days of vicious fighting before they were defeated by detachments of the Red Army. War communism was, by this time, generally unpopular, but it was the mutiny which made Lenin decide that changes had to be brought about to prevent a general uprising against the communist state, and he then introduced the *New Economic Policy.*

Krupp: based in Essen in the Ruhr, it was by far the most important German armaments manufacturer.

- Before the First World War, it supplied steel for the German naval-building program and had a monopoly on the supply of heavy artillery to the army
- In the 1930s, the head of the Krupp family, Gustav Krupp, became a keen supporter of Hitler at a late date, having in 1933 urged Hindenburg not to appoint him as chancellor. His firm benefited greatly from his rapid conversion and played a big part in carrying out the Nazi rearmament program
- During the Second World War, the firm used forced concentration-camp labor, and Gustav's son Alfred was imprisoned as a war criminal but was released after only five years of his twelve-year sentence
- After 1945, the firm avoided restrictions imposed upon it by the Allies, diversified and survived as one of the largest firms in the European Community, playing a full part in the *German economic miracle* of the 1950s. In 1959, it made token payments to Jewish, but not other, victims of forced labor.

kulak: a term used to describe the better-off Russian peasants. They had benefited from the agrarian reforms of *Stolypin,* becoming small landowners employing labor, and were the main beneficiaries of Lenin's *New Economic Policy* in the early 1920s. Their existence and their prosperity challenged communist ideas of equality and of economic organization. They:

- were held responsible for the grain shortages of 1927 which endangered urban food supplies
- were brutally treated from 1928 as Stalin developed his agrarian *collectivization* policies
- had their lands and capital seized and handed over to the collective farms
- slaughtered many of their cattle to prevent them being seized by the state.

By 1934, Stalin's ruthless collectivization of agriculture had the desired effect, and the kulaks, as a class, had been eliminated.

Kun, Béla: a Hungarian communist leader. In 1919, he set up a communist state which was, within months, overthrown by *Horthy.* He went into exile in the Soviet Union, was a victim of Stalin's purges in 1938, and was shot as a Trotskyist.

Kurds: an ethnic minority in Turkey, many of whom want to set up an independent Kurdish state. A terrorist campaign and guerrilla activity from 1958 were a source of considerable embarrassment to Turkey, whose repressive measures jeopardized its prospects of joining the European Union. Many Kurds live in bordering areas of Iraq, and despite incursions across the border by the Turkish army, this made their repression more difficult.

Kursk: a Second World War battle on the *Eastern Front*. With over 5,000 tanks involved, it was the largest ever tank battle, and it came in July 1943 from a German counter-attack which was intended to stop the Soviets exploiting their victory at *Stalingrad*. The German defeat, with the loss of over 70,000 men and 1,500 tanks, gave the initiative on the Eastern Front to the Soviets, and the *Red Army*'s long march to the ruins of Berlin had begun.

L

Lansbury, George: a British politician. Leader of the Labour Party, 1931–35, he was a convinced pacifist who even rejected the imposition of sanctions against Italy at the time of its war with Ethiopia. He nicely illustrates the public mood of horror at the prospect of another war, which influenced British foreign policy in the 1930s and which made *appeasement* so acceptable.

Lansdowne, Lord: British foreign secretary, 1900–05. He negotiated the 1902 *Anglo–Japanese Treaty* and the 1904 *entente cordiale* with France, thereby opening up a new phase in British foreign policy involving international obligations which led in 1914 to Britain's involvement in the First World War.

Lateran Treaties: 1929 agreements between Pope Pius XII and Mussolini. They brought to an end the quarrel between the Italian state and the Vatican which had festered since 1870 when the unification of Italy had included the incorporation of extensive Church lands. The treaties, sometimes also called the Lateran Accords because of the *concordat* attached to them:

- paid compensation for the lost lands to the Church
- recognized Roman Catholicism as the only religion of the Italian state
- recognized the *Vatican City* as an independent state ruled by the pope.

In 1924, the pope had given considerable help to the Italian fascists when he withdrew support from the Catholic Popular Party, democratic rivals of the fascists. Fascist rule seemed to provide the Catholic Church with the best available protection against the godless Communist Party, and the toleration extended by the Church towards the fascist regime greatly assisted it in extending its support and control over all of Italy. The treaties are generally regarded as being Mussolini's most significant political achievement.

Latvia: one of the three *Baltic Republics* which, until 1917, formed part of tsarist Russia.

- In 1918, following the Bolshevik Revolution in Russia, it was proclaimed independent and, after the Russian Civil War, gained international recognition as an independent republic
- In 1934, a neo-fascist government took over
- In 1939, under the terms of the *Nazi–Soviet Pact* of 1939, the country was occupied by the Red Army
- In 1941, there was widespread welcome for the German invasion which formed part of Hitler's *Operation Barbarossa.*
- In 1944, the Red Army reoccupied the country and Latvia then became a republic within the Soviet Union.

Latvian nationalism remained a powerful, if underground, movement, and in 1988 the Popular Front of Latvia was formed to demand independence. When it won the 1989 elections, the Latvian Supreme Soviet declared Latvia to be independent. There were clashes in 1990 and 1991 with ethnic Russians and with the Soviet army, but in a 1991 referendum 73 percent voted for independence, which was then declared. The Soviet Union formally accepted this verdict on 10 September 1991, and the independent state of Latvia was reborn.

Lausanne, Treaty of: an international treaty of 1923, replacing the 1920 Treaty of *Sèvres*. Following the military success of Mustafa Kemal (*Atatürk*) against the Greeks, the main terms were:

- the city of Smyrna and areas of western Turkey and European Turkey reverted from Greek to Turkish rule
- the Sèvres arrangements making Palestine and Syria British and French mandates were confirmed
- Italian control of the Dodecanese islands was also confirmed
- as at the Treaty of Sèvres, the Dardanelles strait was demilitarized and to be open to all shipping under League of Nations supervision.

Laval, Pierre: French prime minister in the *Vichy* government from 1942 to 1944. Originally a socialist, he moved steadily to the extreme right politically. He had previously been prime minister for two short periods in the 1930s. In 1935, he combined with the British politician Hoare to produce the *Hoare–Laval Pact* to divide Ethiopia between Italy and the legitimate Ethiopian government. He resigned when the cynicism of the arrangement led to public outcry but continued to urge closer ties with Germany and Italy. After France surrendered in 1940, he became deputy prime minister to *Pétain* and, at this stage, followed a neutral line in relation to the war. He was then dismissed by Pétain but was, in 1942, reinstated on German insistence. By then, he was virtually dictator and pursued a policy of active cooperation with the German forces. He:

- accepted a policy of sending French forced labor to work in Germany
- set up a fascist militia
- instituted savage anti-Semitic measures
- pursued a policy of terror against suspected members of the French Resistance.

In 1944, he was arrested by the Germans but escaped and fled to Spain. On his return to France in 1945, he was tried by the French and shot.

League of Nations: founded after the First World War as an organization for international cooperation. It was proposed by President Woodrow *Wilson* at the 1919 *Paris Peace Conference*, and arose from the *Fourteen Points* for the conduct of peace which he had issued in 1918. It was originally accepted by 27 nations at the conference, and the *covenant* (or constitution) of the League was included in the terms of the Treaty of *Versailles* and the Treaty of *Saint Germain*. The League's headquarters were set up in Geneva. The chief principles included in the covenant were:

- collective security
- arbitration in international disputes
- armaments reduction
- open diplomacy.

The League also established a number of specialist committees, including the International Labor Organization, which did much to improve working conditions, and others on world health and on education, as well as on post-war economic reconstruction. The work of these committees represents the most successful side of the League's achievements, and one that is often neglected. One of the first political tasks carried out by the League was the creation of *mandates* for the government of the colonies and other territories of two of the powers defeated in the war, Germany and the Ottoman Empire.

An early and major setback for the League was the refusal of the US Senate to ratify the Versailles Treaty, which meant that the USA never joined the League. Early defiance of the League came in 1919 with D'Annunzio's seizure of Fiume. The League was apparently much strengthened by the admission of Germany in 1926 and the Soviet Union in 1934, but this proved illusory. In the late 1920s, the League's unspectacular work still seemed one part of a new and promising stability in international relations. However, the League commanded little money and no military forces with which to enforce its decisions. The 1924 attempt in the *Geneva Protocol* to help meet this weakness having failed, it was entirely dependent on the separate efforts of its member nations to carry out its will.

In the 1930s, the members too often put their own national interests before the needs of international cooperation. The League could only propose moral arguments or ineffective economic sanctions at best when faced with Japanese aggression in *Manchuria*, Italian aggression in *Ethiopia*, or German expansionism in the *Rhineland*, Austria or Czechoslovakia. Increasingly, the two major League powers, Britain and France, conducted their diplomacy quite apart from the League. Germany and Japan left the League in 1933, Italy in 1937, the latter two in response to the ineffective rebukes administered by the League at their acts of aggression, and Germany in order to pursue a policy of rearmament and reversal of the Versailles Treaty. Long before the Second World War began, it was clear that the League had failed in its political purpose, and in 1945 it was replaced by the United Nations.

In summary, the main reasons for the political failure of the League were:

- the absence from its ranks, for all or part of its existence, of major nations
- that it lacked any effective mechanism for enforcing its decisions on reluctant nations
- that its use of economic sanctions and moral arguments were, in any serious crisis, ineffective
- that its two leading members, Britain and France, increasingly took account of their own national interests and conducted their foreign policy outside the League.

lebensraum: German for "living space." It became the slogan of the Nazi Party in the 1920s and 1930s to justify its cry that Germany needed to expand eastwards. It assumed that Germany was overpopulated and that only more territory would restore the true balance between urban and rural populations. Expansion would also ensure the nation's food supplies and restore the lands that had been taken from the German race by the *Versailles* Treaty. It was used in 1938 and 1939 to justify expansion at the expense of Czechoslovakia and Poland. Hitler's 1941 attack on the Soviet Union suggested that he, at least, had a wider vision than just that of regaining lost lands and saw lebensraum as the need for a great, German-dominated empire across Eastern Europe.

left, or left wing: political shorthand for progressive parties, socialists and communists, and their sympathizers.

Left Communists: a political group in the early days of the Soviet Union. They opposed the peace made with Germany and the employment of ex-tsarist officers in the Red Army.

Left Opposition: a group of Soviet politicians which, from 1925, wanted to end the *New Economic Policy* (NEP). It was led by *Trotsky*, who was joined by Kamenev and Zinoviev, and wanted a policy of rapid industrialization to be financed by a squeeze on those peasants who had become wealthy under the NEP. This program was at first opposed by Stalin as part of his battle with Trotsky for the leadership of the Communist Party, but in 1928 the policy of rapid industrialization became the basis of the first five-year plan. By then, Trotsky was in exile and Stalin's position was unchallengeable.

legislature: a law-making body, like the British Parliament. It should not be confused with the executive, i.e. the government.

Lend-Lease: US aid to Britain in the Second World War. It enabled Britain to obtain war supplies for which it could not pay, under the fiction that these supplies would be returned or paid for after the war.

Lenin, Vladimir Ilyich: founder of the *Soviet Union.*

Pre-1917

In youth, Lenin became a convinced Marxist and engaged in working-class politics. From 1895, he was a revolutionary leader committed to the overthrow of tsardom. He was exiled to Siberia, and in 1900 left Russia to live in the West. In 1903, he took a leading part in the London debate within the Russian Social Democrat Party, at which the split into *Bolshevik* and Menshevik factions occurred. He then became leader of the Bolsheviks. His book WHAT IS TO BE DONE? was influential among socialist activists, and he also edited the socialist newspaper ISKRA ("The Spark"). He took part in the 1905 Revolution, but on its collapse he had to flee once more. In exile he then founded the newspaper *Pravda* and controlled revolutionary movements in Russia from Switzerland.

1917

- In March, the German army, hoping to foment trouble in Russia, allowed Lenin to return there by traveling across Germany in a sealed train
- In April, he issued his *April Theses*, which committed the party to seizing power as quickly as possible rather than waiting, as pure Marxist theory suggested they should, until the bourgeois February Revolution had worked itself out. The theses set the agenda for the *October Revolution*
- The *Provisional Government* expelled him in July at the time of the *July Days*, and he went to Finland
- He returned in October to lead the Bolshevik overthrow of the Provisional Government, making the decision to launch Trotsky on the Bolshevik coup on the eve of the meeting of the *All-Russian Congress of Soviets.*

In these few months in 1917, Lenin played a crucial part in building and maintaining the momentum of revolution. This was one of his great contributions to Soviet history.

1917–24

After the October Revolution, he became chairman of the Council of People's Commissars, and took dictatorial powers in the state. In these years, he:

- closed down the *Constituent Assembly* by force when the Bolsheviks found themselves in a minority there
- became virtual dictator of the new Soviet state and emphasized the need for strong central government
- ruthlessly put down opponents of the Bolsheviks in the crucial period of the state's existence during the *Russian Civil War* by use of the *Cheka*
- took Russia out of the unpopular war with Germany at the Treaty of *Brest-Litovsk*, at the cost of huge losses of territory on Russia's western border
- devoted considerable energy and organizing ability to saving the Bolshevik state in the 1918–21 Russian Civil War, assisted by the work of Trotsky as leader of the Red Army
- was responsible for introducing the civil-war economic policy of *war communism*, enforcing state ownership of industries and banks, and control of agriculture via the forcible confiscation of rural food supplies in order to feed the urban workers and the army
- in 1921, he abandoned war communism in favor of the *New Economic Policy* (NEP), which allowed private production and the trade of agricultural products. He did this when it became clear that war communism had aroused such opposition, notably at the *Kronstadt Mutiny*, that it had become a threat to the position of the Bolsheviks. It was then argued that war communism had been a purely temporary policy to fit wartime conditions, but it can also be claimed that, with the NEP, Lenin showed the flexibility needed to abandon Marxist principles in order to save the communist regime.

Lenin proposed that the Bolshevik Party be known as the Communist Party, and was its chairman until his death in 1924. The Party was structured around the political principle of *democratic centralism*, which was one of Lenin's major contributions to Marxist theory and practice. He also founded the *Comintern*. In 1922, he suffered a stroke but struggled on to meet the many demands of the highly centralized system that he had created. Lenin has been much criticized for failing to make clear decisions on who was to succeed him as leader of the Soviet state. This matter, indeed, led to an acrimonious scramble for power and the eventual emergence of *Stalin* as leader.

Leningrad, Siege of: a military action of the Second World War. The 1941 German northern thrust into the Soviet Union, as part of Operation *Barbarossa*, had met such fierce resistance that, when winter came, it had failed to take Leningrad. The German army then besieged the city for 900 days, reducing the inhabitants and garrison to absolute starvation. The Soviet government would not evacuate the inhabitants, over a million of whom died as the city was subject to aerial bombardment and shelling. The Soviet counter-attack took almost a year to complete the relief of the city, in January 1944.

Leopold III: king of Belgium, 1934–51. He led the Belgian forces at the time of the 1940 German invasion. His surrender to the Germans was denounced by Belgian politicians, who set up a government in exile in London. Leopold was imprisoned by the Germans and freed in 1945 by the Allies. His wartime actions had made his continuation as king the cause of much civil disturbance, and he abdicated in 1951.

liberalism: political philosophy favoring moderate political and social reform. It emphasizes parliamentary government, liberty and human rights and also usually endorses capitalism. In all this, it falls politically between the extremes of left and right.

Libya: a North African state. It was part of the Ottoman Empire until 1911, when it was conquered by Italy. As a colony it proved a drain on Italian resources, and very few Italians were prepared to settle there. It was the scene of fierce fighting during the North Africa Campaign of the Second World War and was conquered by the Allies. After the war, Italy renounced its claim to the territory, and in 1951 the UN declared it to be an independent state. From 1969, when Colonel Gadafy emerged as its military leader, it had stormy relations with a number of European states over its provision of refuge or aid for terrorist groups.

Lidice: a mining village in Czechoslovakia. It was destroyed by the Germans in 1942 as an act of revenge for the assassination in Prague of *Heydrich*, the ruthless Nazi ruler of Bohemia. The men were killed and the women and children sent to concentration camps. It became a symbol both of resistance heroism and of the depths to which Nazi depravity could sink.

Lie, Trygve: the first secretary-general of the UN, 1946–53. He arranged the UN intervention in the Korean War and was accused by the Soviet Union of exceeding his authority. Their consequent obstruction of his work prompted his early retirement back to Norwegian politics.

Liebknecht, Karl: the leader, with Rosa *Luxemburg*, of the *Spartacist* uprising. In 1918, he had helped to found the German Communist Party. When the uprising occurred, he was arrested and shot.

Lithuania: one of the three *Baltic Republics* which, until 1917, were part of tsarist Russia.

- In 1918, a German-appointed king reigned briefly before an independent republic was proclaimed, and an attempt by Bolshevik troops to reconquer the country failed
- In 1920, the Soviet Union recognized its independence
- In 1926, democratic government gave way to a neo-fascist regime
- In 1941, as the Germans advanced eastwards in Hitler's Operation *Barbarossa*, the Lithuanian parliament voted to be incorporated into the Soviet Union
- From 1941 to 1945, the country was occupied by the German army, with disastrous consequences for its Jewish population as the full horrors of the Holocaust were unleashed
- In 1944, the Red Army reconquered the country and it became a republic within the Soviet Union, remaining so until 1991.

A strong nationalist movement survived in Lithuania, and in 1989 public pressure forced the Lithuanian communists to accept multi-party elections which, in 1990, were won by supporters of an independent Lithuania, who declared independence after the election. Violence between the people and the Soviet military followed this, but in 1991, 93 percent of the voters in a referendum voted for independence, and this was recognized by the Soviet Union on 10 September 1991. Lithuania then became an independent state once more.

Little Entente: a system of alliances among the smaller nations of eastern Europe.

- Czechoslovakia and Yugoslavia allied in 1920
- Czechoslovakia and Romania allied in 1921
- Romania and Yugoslavia allied in 1921.

It was intended as a common front against any revival of Austrian or Hungarian territorial ambitions in the region. However, it had little power or cohesion and was unable to influence events in the crises of the 1930s, collapsing at that time.

Litvinov, Maxim: Soviet foreign minister, 1930–39. He was strongly in favor of collective international security against the Axis powers but, because of reluctance in Britain and France, was unable to achieve this. Stalin dismissed him just before Soviet policy did a U-turn and signed the *Nazi–Soviet Pact* in August 1939. He was reinstated after Hitler's 1941 invasion, serving as ambassador to the USA during the critical 1943–46 period. He died in 1951.

Lloyd George, David: British prime minister, 1916–22. Prior to 1914, he had been a leading member of the reforming Liberal government, and from 1908 chancellor of the exchequer. He gained a reputation as a dynamic and efficient war leader when he was made minister of munitions in 1915, with the task of dealing quickly with the scandal of the shell shortage afflicting the British army on the *Western Front*. In 1916, he replaced Asquith as prime minister, leading a powerful wartime coalition government. He:

- reorganized the war effort, creating a small inner war cabinet to direct it
- forced the reluctant admiralty to accept the *convoy* system for merchant shipping crossing the Atlantic, and so safeguarded crucial war supplies
- failed, however, to impose his ideas on the army generals in terms of rethinking the stalemate on the Western Front.

In 1919, he represented Britain at the *Paris Peace Conference* where, in private, he urged moderation in the demands made against Germany but had, in public, both to reflect popular determination that Germany must pay for the havoc of the war and also to recognize French insistence on full compensation for the war damage inflicted on it. In 1921, he made an agreement with *Sinn Féin* over the government of Ireland, and in 1922 he was prepared to fight the Turks in the *Chanak Crisis*. His rivalry with Asquith was in part responsible for the disintegration of the British Liberal Party after the First World War, and after 1922, he never held office again. He died in 1945.

Locarno Pact: an international pact of 1925 guaranteeing Western European borders. The main signatories were Belgium, Britain, France, Germany and Italy.

- The main agreement was that confirming the border of Germany with France and Belgium
- Germany renounced any claim to Alsace-Lorraine
- France renounced any ambition to create an independent Rhineland state between it and Germany.

The pact was one of the boldest initiatives of the Weimar statesman, *Stresemann*, in his search for post-war international rehabilitation for Germany. However, it left certain problems in its wake:

- even Stresemann was not prepared to recognize Germany's frontiers in the east with Czechoslovakia and Poland as being permanent, though he agreed that any revision should be negotiated peacefully
- in order to meet anxieties caused by the pact in Eastern Europe, France signed protection treaties with Czechoslovakia and Poland, and thus entered into ill-defined commitments which would be difficult to honor when a crisis arose involving Germany
- in 1936, Hitler denounced the pact when he put German troops into the demilitarized Rhineland.

London, Treaty of: imposed in 1913 by the European powers in order to end the First *Balkan War*. The Turks lost almost all their European lands except Constantinople. Serbia was not satisfied and fighting resumed in the Second Balkan War, which was ended by the Treaty of *Bucharest*.

London Treaties: separate treaties made in 1915 to extend the war effort against Germany and its allies.

- In the first treaty, Britain promised that, after the war, Russia should control the key Turkish city of Istanbul and so have naval access to the Mediterranean. The Soviet government later published these dramatic proposals, which totally contradicted much that British foreign policy had stood for in the nineteenth century, and greatly embarrassed Britain
- In the second treaty, Britain and France made promises of land to Italy if it declared war on Austria-Hungary. Italy did enter the war, but at the Paris Peace Conference not all the promises were kept and this was a major post-war Italian grievance, leading to D'Annunzio's seizure of Fiume. Italy's treatment was later exploited by Mussolini to defend his expansionist foreign policy.

Loos: a First World War battle on the *Western Front*, a British offensive in 1915 which cost 60,000 British dead but achieved nothing.

- It illustrated the futility of infantry attacks against well-organized trench fortifications
- It also indicated the stubbornness and casual disregard for life of the leading British generals in the war, in that it was ordered by the commander-in-chief, Sir John French, against the advice of less senior officers who actually knew the conditions
- The British use of chlorine gas in the attack failed dramatically when this blew back into their own trenches.

Low Countries: a term used to indicate Belgium, Holland and Luxembourg.

Lubbe, Martinus van der: a young Dutchman who burned down the German *Reichstag* building in February 1933. He acted alone, but his action enabled Hitler, in his first days in power, to persecute the communists to his great advantage in the election then taking place. Lubbe was tried and put to death.

Ludendorff, Erich von: an able First World War German general. He organized the victory at *Tannenberg*, and from 1916 to 1918 worked in Germany to build up military supplies, combining with Hindenburg to remove the civilian chancellor Bethmann-Hollweg and to establish a new government dominated by the military. He had planned the German advance of spring 1918, but as the scale of the Allied counter-attack became clear, in August he urged the kaiser to make peace. He was linked to the 1920 *Kapp Putsch* and to Hitler's *Munich Putsch* but did not play a central part in either. He was a Nazi member of the Reichstag from 1924 to 1928, but in the 1930s was an isolated right-wing figure with no influence on the Nazi state. He died in 1937.

Luftwaffe: the German air force.

Lusitania: a British liner sunk by a German *U-boat* attack in 1915. The loss of 1,200 lives, including over 100 Americans, inflamed US opinion against Germany, though it was two years later before the German resumption of unrestricted *submarine warfare* against Atlantic shipping played a crucial role in bringing the USA into the war.

Lüttwitz, Walter von: commanding general of the Berlin army garrison in 1920. He was one of the originators of the *Kapp Putsch* to overthrow the Weimar government. The army under *Seeckt* refused to act against him, and when the coup collapsed because of working-class resistance, his only punishment was that he was made to retire from the army. His actions and fate indicate how fragile the loyalty of the army was to the Weimar Republic.

Luxembourg: a grand duchy, independent since 1815. It was invaded by Germany in both 1914 and 1940. It became part of Germany from 1942 to 1945, when all aspects of life down to the level of street names and the language used in schools were Germanized. Men conscripted into the German army were invariably sent to the Eastern Front and, in terms of percentages of population killed, Luxembourg came second only to Poland in its losses. Luxembourg joined what became the European Union as a founder member in 1958, and is the home of the European Court and the Secretariat (administration) of the European Parliament.

Luxemburg, Rosa: a German revolutionary. In 1915, she founded the *Spartacist* group, and in 1918 the German Communist Party. She attacked Lenin's centralization policies in Bolshevik Russia as being dictatorial. During the Berlin Spartacist uprising of 1919, she was captured and shot by right-wing Freikorps members.

Lvov, Prince: the first head of the Russian *Provisional Government*. It was set up in March 1917 by members of the Duma at the time of the February Revolution. In July, he was succeeded by *Kerensky*, and then lived in exile until his death in 1925.

M

Maastricht, Treaty of: the 1991 treaty which formally established the *European Union* (EU). It had many implications for economic union among its members, including:

- the introduction of a single European currency
- the development of common foreign and defense policies
- increased powers for the European Parliament and the Council of Ministers, apparently at the expense of rights retained within the nations making up the EU.

The treaty's ratification and its implications for national sovereignty produced great acrimony in some member states.

MacDonald, Ramsay: British prime minister, 1924, 1929–35. A strong supporter of the League of Nations and promoter of international disarmament, he was one of the generation of British politicians who failed to discern the Nazi threat to international peace.

Macedonia: once part of the Ottoman Empire. In 1913, after the *Balkan Wars*, it was partitioned between Greece and Serbia. During the First World War, there was fierce fighting there in the *Salonika Campaign*, and in 1919 the territory was again divided between Greece and Yugoslavia at the Treaty of *Neuilly*. It was occupied by Bulgaria during the Second World War, but the 1919 division was confirmed again in the 1947 Treaties of Paris. The south of the region became a federal republic within Yugoslavia, while almost half a million Macedonians continued to live in Bulgaria.

The hope of a united and independent Macedonia remained alive on the back of cultural and language revivals, and was further boosted when, with the disintegration of Yugoslavia, an independent Macedonian republic was set up in the former Yugoslavian part of the region. The alleged territorial ambitions of the new state so alarmed the Greek authorities that, in 1994, they closed the frontier between the two countries and enforced a trade embargo. Within the new Republic of Macedonia, founded in 1992, ethnic tensions between Macedonians and Albanians remained acute, and a UN peacekeeping force was deployed on the state's borders in 1995 to prevent these from spreading. In 1998, the situation both within the country and in relations with its immediate neighbors remained volatile.

Macmillan, Harold: prime minister of Britain, 1957–63. He took office from Eden soon after the *Suez Crisis*. He:

- rebuilt Anglo–US friendship following the estrangement over Suez
- saw the need for decolonization in Africa, where his *"wind of change"* speech had a great impact
- attempted to take Britain into the European Economic Community but was prevented from doing so by the veto of de Gaulle in 1963.

Madrid: the capital of Spain. It suffered two lengthy sieges by Franco's nationalist forces during the Spanish Civil War. Its capture in March 1939 marked the end of the war.

Mafia: an international criminal society. It originated in nineteenth-century Italy and then spread to the USA, especially in the inter-war period when the Italian fascist government cracked down on its activities. Since 1945, it has become a world-wide organization, dealing especially in illegal drugs. Rumors persist that, late in the Second World War, the Allies did a deal allowing the Mafia to rebuild its empire in Italy in return for its support in the conquest of Italy. Post-war campaigns against the Mafia in Italy, and especially in Sicily, have attracted much publicity but have done little to limit its activities.

Maginot Line: a line of French fortifications stretching along the border with Germany from Belgium to Switzerland. It was built between 1929 and 1934, and reflected deep French pessimism about future German military intentions and their own ability to counter them. It was not continued along the border with Belgium lest it should seem that France was willing to abandon that country. Instead, it was assumed that no attacking German army would be able to come through the mountainous Ardennes forest of Belgium. This was a serious military miscalculation for which the French paid in 1940 when the German *blitzkrieg* offensive swept through Belgium and outflanked the Maginot Line. The Germans in fact approached the line from its rear, and little fighting took place along its length. After the war, parts of it became France's most surprising tourist attraction.

Magnitogorsk: a Soviet industrial town of the 1930s set around a vast ironworks complex. It was in the newly developed Urals industrial area, and is the best-known example of the massive expansion of heavy industry undertaken during the 1930s under Stalin's Five-Year Plans.

Magyars: the dominant race in the Hungarian part of the Austro-Hungarian Empire. Their language had a privileged status in both education and public life. They dominated the Hungarian parliament and official positions in the country. All this caused great resentment among the other racial groups, particularly the Croats.

Major, John: prime minister of Britain, 1990–97. He inherited a mood of skepticism about developments towards greater European integration which caused deepening divisions in the Conservative Party. He defied the pundits to win the 1992 election, but suffered a substantial defeat in the subsequent election, in May 1997, in which the Labour Party came to power, electing Tony Blair as the new prime minister.

Makarios III, Archbishop: president of *Cyprus*, 1960–77, also head of the Greek Orthodox Church in Cyprus. He:

- supported *enosis* in the 1950s
- was for this reason exiled by the British
- negotiated with the British for the establishment of an independent Cypriot state
- served as its first president from 1960
- was, in 1974, ousted for a few months by the revolt of Greek officers of

the Cyprus National Guard, who attacked the presidential palace and proclaimed enosis.

Makarios returned to Cyprus on the collapse of the coup and remained in office until his death. The 1974 coup had, however, totally changed the situation in Cyprus, since the Turkish army had invaded in order to protect the Turkish Cypriots. They partitioned the island, setting up an independent Turkish Cypriot state of North Cyprus. Makarios was unable to reassert his authority over the Turkish areas, and thereafter was in practice just president of Greek Cyprus until his death in 1977.

Malenkov, Georgi: Soviet prime minister, 1953–55. He had been closely linked to Stalin during the 1930s, both in the purges and in collectivizing agriculture. He had held senior posts during the war and had become the favorite to succeed Stalin. After Stalin's death in 1953, he became prime minister, working in partnership with *Khrushchev*, the Communist Party secretary. He:

- planned to switch economic capacity from arms production to consumer goods to improve living standards and
- linked this to the need to relax international tensions.

He was opposed by many die-hard communists and military men, and Khrushchev took advantage of this to attack Malenkov as a "revisionist." In 1955, Malenkov was forced to resign and confess his errors. He then lived quietly in retirement, a sign that the Stalinist terror was at an end. His downfall meant:

- that government by a cooperative of leaders was nearing an end
- that Khrushchev was emerging as the new, strong leader, a sign of which was that Malenkov was succeeded as prime minister by *Bulganin*, a close associate of Khrushchev.

Malta: a British island colony in the Mediterranean from 1814 to 1964. The island played a key role as a British naval base in the Second World War with regard both to control of the Mediterranean and to the *North Africa Campaign*. It was subjected to severe bombing from bases in Italy. In the 1950s there was agitation for independence, and this was conceded in 1964, with Malta staying in the Commonwealth. Negotiations for it to join the European Union began in 1997.

Manchuria: a province of China occupied by the Japanese in 1931. The failure of the *League of Nations* to take effective action to protect a member was the first serious blow to the organization's credibility and acted as a precedent for the 1935 failure to help Ethiopia. The Japanese aggression marked the opening of a new period in international relations. It brought to an end the period of apparent stability of the late 1920s, and marked the first of a series of crises which culminated in the Second World War.

mandates: trusteeships given by the League of Nations. They were granted, to France and Britain in particular, at the end of the First World War to administer former territories of defeated Germany and the Ottoman Empire.

Ottoman lands in the Middle East were mandated to:

- Britain: Jordan, Iraq and Palestine
- France: Lebanon and Syria.

In each case, the mandates included a remit to prepare the countries for independence.

The German colonies in Africa were mandated to:

- Belgium: Rwanda and Burundi
- Britain: East Africa (Tanganyika)
- Britain and France: the divided Cameroons
- South Africa: South West Africa

These German colonies in Africa were viewed as permanent mandates.

The mandates resulted in:

- a considerable extension of the imperial role for both Britain and France
- an innovation in international law, as the mandated territories were to be supervised by the League of Nations.

Mannerheim, Carl: president of Finland, 1944–46. In the 1930s, he had planned defensive fortifications, the Mannerheim Line, against Soviet attack, and these were used to good effect by the Finns in the *Finnish–Russian War* of 1939–40. After Hitler launched Operation *Barbarossa*, Mannerheim allowed the Germans to use Finland as a base from which to attack Leningrad, but in 1944, as the Red Army turned the fortunes of the war, he signed an armistice with the Soviet Union. In March 1945, he brought Finland into the war against Germany.

Mao Zedong (Mao Tse Tung): leader of communist China from 1949 to 1976. An admirer of Stalin, he bitterly opposed Khrushchev's attempts to change Stalinist domestic and foreign policy.

Maquis: the French resistance movement of the Second World War.

Marchais, Georges: leader of the French Communist Party during the Fifth Republic. He encouraged its independence from the Soviet Communist Party and so made it more electable. Under him, the party briefly held office from 1981 to 1983 in a left-wing coalition government. He then took a less reforming line in party matters. Largely because of him, the French communists retained a strong presence in the large towns and cities. He was an unsuccessful candidate in the 1981 presidential election.

March on Rome: a fascist myth about *Mussolini*'s coming to power in Italy in 1922. He put pressure on *Facta*'s government and King *Victor Emmanuel* by threatening a mass march of his followers on Rome. The king invited Mussolini to form a government, and he traveled to Rome by train. The "march" did not in fact occur, for the 30,000 fascists who gathered near Rome had also traveled by train. However, it had a great propaganda impact, and may well have influenced the king not to back Facta's government in taking a strong line against the fascists. After the end of fascist rule, the king excused his conduct by saying he had believed that the fascists had 100,000 men about to enter the city, and that he was afraid the army would be overwhelmed and civil war would follow.

Marne: a river in northern France, the scene of *Western Front* battles in the First World War in both 1914 and 1918. In 1914, the repulse of the German army stopped their initial onslaught when they were only 25 miles from Paris and so frustrated the German *Schlieffen Plan*. It led on to the four-year stalemate of *trench warfare*. In 1918, Ludendorff led a further offensive close to Paris which was met with an Allied counter-attack, marked by the first totally successful use of tanks, under Foch. This led to the Allied break through the German lines which brought about the armistice of November 1918.

Marshall, George: the US secretary of state who, in 1948, initiated the European recovery program, or *Marshall Plan*. He was an important *Cold War* political figure who also helped to create NATO and stiffened Western resolve at the time of the Berlin Airlift. He received the Nobel Peace Prize in 1953 and died in 1959.

Marshall Aid: financial aid provided to Western Europe by the USA from 1948 to 1952 under the *Marshall Plan*.

Marshall Plan: an economic aid program for Europe, agreed by the USA in 1948, developed from 1947 proposals by US Secretary of State Marshall. Recipients had to submit a plan for economic recovery, and the Soviet Union refused to take part, claiming that the Marshall Plan was an attempt to secure American capitalist domination of the European economy. It also prevented its East European satellite states from participating. This helped to cement the divide in Europe between the capitalist nations and the communist bloc and so heightened the tensions of the Cold War. The plan was a great success in the West, restoring agriculture and industry and promoting international trade. The $17,000 billion provided between 1948 and 1951 contributed greatly to the economic recovery of the states of Western Europe so recently totally devastated by war.

martial law: military government by which ordinary law is suspended, for example with the rule of the "*Greek Colonels*" from 1967 to 1974.

Martov, Julius: a Russian *Menshevik* leader who, in the Russian Civil War, supported Lenin against the White forces. He left Russia in 1920 and died in 1923.

Marxism: the political and economic theory of Karl Marx. Marx, a German in origin, lived much of his life in exile in London where, in extensive writings, he developed the ideological basis for communism and state socialism. Marxism:

- is an historical explanation of the evolution of human societies moving from feudalism to capitalism
- predicts the collapse of capitalism from its own internal contradictions, which in turn will lead to the rule of the *proletariat*
- has led to the formation of schools of historical interpretation which stress the importance of economic factors in explanations of the past.

Marxism had great influence over nineteenth- and early-twentieth-century revolutionary groups. In the first half of the twentieth century, there were many revisions, most interestingly in the Soviet Union where Marxism-Leninism combined Marx's analysis of capitalism with Lenin's theories of government to produce the idea of *democratic centralism*.

Marxism-Leninism: an extension of Marxist theory proposed by *Lenin*. Its main features are:

- that imperialism was an extension of capitalism which continued to survive because imperialism had provided it with new markets and raw materials

- that the profits from imperialism had kept the working class quiet and non-revolutionary
- that the working class would never reach socialism without help from the (Communist) Party
- that the Party would provide the élite who would lead the Marxist proletarian revolution and then go on to run the new communist state.

These ideas, placing the Communist Party at the head of the Marxist revolution, are closely linked with Lenin's concept of *democratic centralism*, which became the fundamental idea in developing the government of the Soviet Union.

Masaryk, Jan: a Czechoslovak politician, son of Tómaš *Masaryk*, who served his country as a diplomat between the wars. In 1945, on the liberation of *Czechoslovakia*, he became foreign minister in the coalition government. He opposed the Soviet refusal to let his country accept *Marshall Aid*. President *Beneš* asked him to stay in office after the communist coup in 1948, but a few days later his body was found beneath an open window at the foreign ministry. Speculation has continued since as to whether he committed suicide because of the advance of communist domination of his country, or whether he was murdered.

Masaryk, Tómaš: president of Czechoslovakia, 1918–35. He campaigned in exile for an independent Czechoslovakia, and in 1918 was elected its first president. He resigned just before the full pressure of Nazi expansionism was felt in Eastern Europe, and died in 1937.

master race: a lunatic concept dear to Nazi hearts. It arose from the writings of such men as *Gobineau* and Houston *Chamberlain*, who argued that the Aryan race, and in particular the Germans among them, constituted a master race with the duty of saving civilization and the right to dominate the lesser races such as the Slavs.

- It was essential in this philosophy that the purity of the master race be preserved from contamination by "lesser" races
- This provided the basis for identifying both the "Jewish Problem" and its *"Final Solution"* in the *Holocaust.*

Masurian Lakes: the setting of a First World War battle on the *Eastern Front* in 1914. It followed the Russian defeat on the same part of the Eastern Front at *Tannenberg.* A lack of coordination between the Russian armies led to this second defeat, with the capture of 100,000 prisoners. A further Russian defeat in the region of the lakes early in 1915 checked the Russian advance into East Prussia and put them on the defensive against the German army for the rest of the war.

Matteotti, Giacomo: an Italian socialist politician. One of the very few Italian political leaders prepared openly to oppose Mussolini gaining totalitarian power; he wrote a book, THE FASCISTS EXPOSED, giving details of their many illegal actions. He publicly denounced the fascist victory in the 1924 parliamentary elections as being based on fraud and the use of force. Within days, he was found murdered. The consequences of the murder included:

- rioting following the discovery of the body
- the walk-out of some politicians from Parliament, in protest at the murder, in the *Aventine Secession*

- Mussolini accepting technical responsibility for the murder and ordering some arrests
- Mussolini in fact using the murder to tighten up on the press
- the fascists using terror to browbeat their opponents
- the king again refusing to act against the fascists
- Mussolini's clever use of the dangerous aftermath of the murder, with the Aventine Secession, to destroy the opposition to the fascists.

The episode indicates the political skill shown by Mussolini in a potentially very dangerous situation as he moved towards securing absolute power in the state.

Max, Prince of Baden: chancellor of the German Second Empire for a few desperate days in October 1918. It was he who persuaded the kaiser to abdicate and so opened the way for the creation of the Weimar Republic.

medical advances: the twentieth century saw many advances in medicine, for example:

- the mass production of penicillin during and after the Second World War
- the total eradication of smallpox in the 1970s.

Other diseases, like malaria and cancer, remained immune to the developments in medicine, and new diseases, like *AIDS*, posed terrible threats. Much of the new medicine was available only in the rich, developed world. Elsewhere, death through famine and associated diseases remained an everyday reality. For the mass of humanity, improvements in public health, pure food, pure water and efficient sewage provided the best hope of improved mortality. The impressive advances in medical technology, heart surgery, hip replacements and the like remained available only to the privileged few of the developed world.

Mein Kampf: a book written by Hitler when in prison following the failure of the *Munich Putsch*. The title translates as "My Struggle," and it is a mixture of auto-biography, racist, authoritarian philosophy and general assertions about the future direction of Nazi policy. Hitler wrote of:

- the need for racial purity within Germany
- the need for the German people to be prepared to fight for living space, *lebensraum*, in Eastern Europe.

In the light of what happened later, it was seen by Churchill and others as giving a clear indication that Hitler had at an early stage drawn up a radical plan for domination of Europe which, once in power, he proceeded to carry out quite systematically. This view has been challenged, notably, among British historians, by A. J. P. *Taylor*, who:

- saw MEIN KAMPF simply as the daydreaming of a failed revolutionary
- argued that Hitler's foreign-policy ambitions were only a restatement of traditional German aims, as realized, for instance, at the Treaty of *Brest-Litovsk*
- claimed that, while Hitler in MEIN KAMPF had stressed the need for *Anschluss*, i.e. union with Austria, in practice he had no master plan to bring this about but was pressured into action by the activities of the Austrian Nazis and by the tumultuous reception he received when he visited Vienna in 1938.

Other historians, notably E. H. Carr and E. Wiskemann, took MEIN KAMPF more seriously as a systematic statement of a plan for national expansion and racial superiority. These contrasting analyses of the status of MEIN KAMPF are then reflected in the historians' differing interpretations of the causes of the Second World War.

Memel: a Baltic port in East Prussia until 1919 when, at the Treaty of Versailles, it was made a free city under the supervision of the League of Nations. It was seized by Lithuania in 1923. A Nazi movement in the city, demanding its return to East Prussia, found widespread support among the largely German population in the 1930s. In March 1939, Hitler occupied the city and reintegrated it into East Prussia in one of a number of territorial aggressions carried out between the Munich Agreement of September 1938 and the outbreak of the Second World War in September 1939. In the later stages of the war, Memel was reconquered by the Red Army and taken back into Lithuania, by then itself reincorporated into the Soviet Union.

Menderes, Adnan: prime minister of Turkey, 1950–60. He:

- brought Turkey into NATO
- accepted the British decision to create an independent Cyprus.

He was deposed by the army and, in 1961, was executed for treason for having taken dictatorial powers in order to quell unrest brought on by economic problems.

Mendès-France, Pierre: prime minister of France, 1954–55. He had been a member of de Gaulle's wartime government in exile in London. He was the most dynamic and most innovative of the many politicians who led France during the *Fourth French Republic*. He had been a critic of French colonial policy in Indo-China and, becoming prime minister in the wake of the Dien Bien Phu disaster, he resolved to end the French presence there, and did so in the *Geneva Agreements* of 1954. He began to prepare Tunisia for independence, but strengthened the French garrison in Algeria, despite his own personal convictions regarding the need for eventual Algerian independence and to the fury of his left-wing supporters. At home, his government's austerity program to meet France's economic problems made him unpopular, and he had to resign. He later opposed both de Gaulle's proposals for strong presidential powers in the constitution of the Fifth Republic and also his increasingly autocratic use of power, but he never again commanded the support to form a government himself. He died in 1982.

Mensheviks: the Russian revolutionary party. They were part of the Social Democrat Party and, at the party's 1903 convention held in London, they argued that it should aim to become a socialist party with a mass membership. The Bolsheviks, however, argued against this in favor of a small party of dedicated activists. The term Menshevik translates as "minority men," reflecting the fact that they lost the vote to the Bolsheviks or "majority men." They continued in existence until the October Revolution of 1917, but as a group played no part in the establishment of the subsequent communist state. *Trotsky* was the most famous Menshevik, but before 1917 he had come to support Lenin and the Bolsheviks.

merchant shipping: ships carrying commercial goods, as distinct from fighting ships. In the Second World War, however, many merchant ships were armed for defensive purposes, as for example in the Battle of the *Atlantic*.

metropolitan: usually an adjective from "metropolis," meaning "the chief city." It was also used in French politics until 1962 to indicate that Algeria was a full part of "Metropolitan France" and not a colony.

Metaxas, Ioannis: dictator of Greece, 1936–41. In 1940, he led the successful defense of the country against the Italian invasion, but died early in 1941 before the German occupation occurred.

Mihailovich, Draza: the Yugoslav *chetnik* leader in the Second World War. He led the royalist partisans fighting the German invaders, but his relations with Tito's communist partisans were strained, and as the war progressed, the Allies preferred to support the latter's more effective opposition to the occupation. The communists accused him of working with the Germans, and after Tito had gained power, he was shot for collaboration and war crimes.

Mikoyan, Anastas: a Soviet politician. He supported Stalin in the power struggle with Trotsky from 1924 to 1927 and was then an effective trade minister. His policies included:

- adopting Western techniques in food manufacture, developing the Soviet canning industry
- working to improve living standards.

He survived the 1930s purges, and in 1956 associated himself with Khrushchev's denunciation of Stalin, favoring a collective leadership for the Soviet Union. In the 1950s and early 1960s, he acted as Khrushchev's diplomatic link with the Soviet satellite states of Eastern Europe at a time when relations with Hungary and Poland were particularly difficult. He served as president of the Presidium of the Supreme Soviet in 1964–65, and then retired, to be succeeded by *Podgorny*. He died in 1978.

Military Revolutionary Committee: set up by the Congress of Northern Soviets and dominated by the Petrograd Soviet. It:

- was set up to organize those committed to defending the gains of the February Revolution
- was dominated by the Bolsheviks
- was used by *Trotsky* to organize the takeover of power in the 1917 *October Revolution.*

Members of the committee first took over command of the Petrograd army garrison, and a week later, on the night of 24–25 October, its members personally took control of the key points in the city and brought about the almost bloodless coup which transformed Russian history.

Milošević, Slobodan: president of *Serbia* from December 1992. He prevented attempts at provincial breakaway within Serbia and so maintained the integrity of the republic. He supported the Serbs in Bosnia until UN trade sanctions in 1994 forced him to end his support. He then urged them to compromise over the issue of joining a greater Serbia, and thus opened up the prospect of a UN-brokered peace deal in Bosnia. His subsequent rule in Serbia became increasingly authoritarian.

Milyukov, Paul: a Russian liberal politician. He had helped to coordinate groups demanding reform in 1905, and in the same year founded the *Cadet Party*. In 1916, he delivered a sharply eloquent attack in the Duma on the tsarist government's incompetence in fighting the war. He was foreign minister in Prince Lvov's Provisional Government from March to May 1917 when his support for continuing the war, from which he still believed territorial gains were possible, led to his enforced resignation. He joined the White Russian forces in the south during the Russian Civil War, and on their defeat fled into exile. He died in 1943.

Mindszenty, Cardinal József: Roman Catholic archbishop of Hungary, 1945–48. In 1948, he was tried for treason and imprisoned, later commuted to house arrest, by the communist government. This caused great resentment among Hungary's large Catholic population, and at the time of the 1956 *Hungarian Revolution,* he was released by the *Nagy* government. When the revolution collapsed, he took refuge in the US embassy in Budapest, where his presence became a thorn in the side of US–Hungarian relations. Kádár's post-1956 government worked hard to improve relations with the Vatican and with the Catholic community in Hungary, but Mindszenty was reluctant to go along with this, and it was not until 1971 that he was persuaded to leave the US embassy. He then went to live in the Vatican, where he died in 1975.

mir: a Russian peasant commune. After the abolition of serfdom in 1861, the peasants had to make redemption payments to the landowners through the government in order to gain ownership of the land. These payments were charged to the mir. The mir was an obstacle to agrarian progress because:

- it resisted reorganization of the scattered strips of peasant land
- it prevented peasants from leaving the mir lest the redemption payments fall more heavily on those left behind
- it was dominated by the less ambitious peasants.

Stolypin, in his efforts to transform Russian agriculture, worked with some success to break the power of the mir and so set the more ambitious peasants free.

Mitterrand, François: president of France, 1981–95. In the Second World War, he had a distinguished military and resistance record and after it, a convinced socialist, he served in 11 of the *Fourth French Republic*'s short-lived governments. He distrusted de Gaulle as a danger to the democratic traditions of the republic and opposed the creation of the *Fifth French Republic,* seeking, in the 1960s, to build a coalition of left-wing parties to oppose Gaullism. In 1965 and 1971, he stood unsuccessfully in presidential elections, but defeated *Giscard d'Estaing* in 1981. In his first presidency, he pursued radical economic and social policies, but an economic crisis caused a shift in direction, and after socialist election losses in 1986, he had to work with the right-wing government of *Chirac,* whom he easily outmaneuvered and then beat in the 1988 presidential election. His foreign policies included:

- support for both an active French foreign policy and retention of the French nuclear deterrent
- a commitment to furthering the political integration of the European Community, in this clashing frequently with Margaret Thatcher
- a concern that the West should respond positively to the changes in Eastern Europe.

In the last months of his second presidency, he suffered from deteriorating health, but continued his public duties until the end of his term of office. He died in 1996.

mobilization: to assemble troops for service. Mobilization is usually an indicator of a serious international crisis. The Russian decision to mobilize in July 1914 was one of the crucial steps leading to the outbreak of the First World War.

modernism: a term in art history used to describe developments in the early twentieth century following on from impressionism. It was also used to describe developments in literature and music.

Mollet, Guy: prime minister of France, 1956–57. A socialist, he served in several *Fourth French Republic* governments. As prime minister, he was deeply involved in the *Suez Crisis* of 1956, entering into secret negotiations with Britain and Israel to attack Egypt. He survived French left-wing and international hostility to this adventurism, and its failure, to become the longest serving French prime minister since the creation of the Fourth Republic. He was a leading anti-Gaullist in the first years of the Fifth Republic, and died in 1975.

Molotov, Vyacheslav: a Soviet politician best known for conducting Soviet foreign policy in the late 1930s and 1940s. In 1906, he was exiled from tsarist Russia, and in 1917 he supported Lenin's opposition to the Provisional Government. After the Bolshevik takeover of the state, he was a prominent member of the party, working with Lenin and later Stalin, in 1926 helping Stalin to defeat Zinoviev. From 1928, he played an important part in implementing the First Five-year Plan and in May 1939, apparently effortlessly surviving the Great Purge, was placed in charge of foreign affairs.

From 1939 to 1945, he:

- was the Soviet signatory of the remarkable U-turn in Soviet policy, the *Nazi–Soviet Pact* of August 1939, which led into the opening of the Second World War
- also signed the Anglo–Soviet Treaty of 1942, following Hitler's invasion of the Soviet Union
- was Stalin's closest adviser at wartime conferences at *Yalta* and *Potsdam.*

After the war, he was at the center of Soviet foreign policy as the wartime alliances against Germany broke up and the Cold War began. He supported the Soviet rejection of Marshall Aid and the decision to blockade Berlin, and he had a reputation in the West as a hard-line communist and a tough, even belligerent, negotiator. After Stalin's death, he was demoted by Khrushchev and later expelled from the Communist Party, all as part of the de-Stalinization policy. He died in 1986, two years after being allowed back into the party.

Moltke, Helmuth von: chief of staff of the German army from 1906. He was firmly in favor of the strategy, embodied in the *Schlieffen Plan*, of a swift victory in the west against France. In 1914, he was in command when the plan was put into effect. Russian successes on the *Eastern Front* and the effectiveness of the Franco–British response to the German invasion, at the battle of the *Marne*, caused him to modify the plan. He was concerned that, by following the plan, the German army would be split in two in the sweep south around Paris. The swift knock-out blow never arrived, and before the end of 1914, he was dismissed.

monetarism: an economic theory which became fashionable, particularly in Britain in the 1980s, where the Thatcher government followed its proposals, in part at least. Its followers argue that:

- the supply of money is at the center of economic activity
- it is the government's responsibility to control its supply with care, in particular to avoid inflation through printing too much money
- governments should keep out of other areas of economic activity which are better regulated by market forces.

Monnet, Jean: a French economist and administrator. After the Second World War, at the request of *de Gaulle*, he prepared a plan for the economic recovery of France which became known as the *Monnet Plan*. He then became commissioner-general of the plan. He was a strong supporter of steps towards European union, working closely with *Schuman*, and was, from 1952 to 1955, president of the *ECSC*.

Monnet Plan: a plan for the economic recovery of France after the Second World War. It took its name from the economist *Monnet*, who produced it in 1946 at the request of de Gaulle. In the five-year period covered by the plan, 1947 to 1952, its proposals for investment and growth were so successful that French gross annual production came to exceed that of the pre-war period. Concentration on the political ills of the *Fourth French Republic* has led historians to undervalue this and other economic achievements.

Monte Cassino: a rocky outcrop in central Italy topped by a monastery which was the scene of some of the fiercest fighting of the *Italian Campaign* in the Second World War. In early 1944, the Allies were held up there for many weeks by fierce German resistance, despite having reduced the monastery buildings to rubble.

Montenegro: with the break-up of *Yugoslavia* in the early 1990s, Montenegro linked with *Serbia* in the rump Federal Republic of Yugoslavia. The small mountainous province, lying between Serbia and the Adriatic Sea, had become independent of Turkish rule in the nineteenth century and a kingdom in 1911. It fought alongside Serbia in the *Balkan Wars* and, after the First World War, was absorbed into the new kingdom of Yugoslavia. After the Second World War, it became the smallest of the republics making up the Socialist Federal Republic of Yugoslavia founded by Tito.

Montgomery, Bernard: a British field marshal. He was commander in North Africa during the Second World War, where his victory at *El Alamein* marked a crucial turning point in British fortunes, and later was also commander in Italy. He then commanded British Commonwealth forces on the *Second Front*, playing an important part in defeating the German *Ardennes* offensive.

Montreux Convention: the 1936 agreement that Turkey could revise the *Lausanne* Treaty in order to fortify the Dardanelles. Turkey had claimed that Mussolini intended to attack its western coastline, and wished to protect itself.

Moro, Aldo: Italian prime minister, 1963–68, 1974–76. A *Christian Democrat*, he also served in several other short-lived governments of the period. In 1978, he was kidnapped and then murdered by *Red Brigade* terrorists.

Morocco: a state in North Africa. In the early twentieth century, France and Spain established *protectorates* there. In 1906, it was the occasion of a quarrel between France and Germany when the kaiser, William II, visited Tangier and spoke out in favor of Morocco's right to be independent. The international *Algeciras Conference* followed, and the French position was confirmed. In 1911, as the French tightened their control, the kaiser again intervened, sending the warship PANTHER to *Agadir* in protest. This produced a crisis which rumbled on for several months until, in 1911, the Germans backed down. These episodes are important because they show:

- the deep suspicions between France and Germany
- the belligerent conduct of foreign policy by the German kaiser
- how Britain and France, faced by German belligerence, began to work more closely together following the signing of the *entente cordiale.*

Moscow: became the capital of the Soviet Union in 1918, replacing Petrograd.

Moscow Coup: a coup in August 1991 by hard-line communists against *Gorbachev.* It was blocked by:

- street demonstrations
- the refusal of the Red Army to join it
- the televized street defiance of *Yeltsin* in central Moscow.

The coup, however, did permanent damage to Gorbachev's power and reputation and, by giving the political initiative to Yeltsin and the leaders of the other Soviet republics, had the opposite effect to that which the plotters intended, leading by the end of 1991 to the disintegration of the Soviet Union.

Mosley, Oswald: the British fascist leader in the 1930s. He failed to persuade the voters to desert their allegiance to the traditional democratic parties.

Müller, Hermann: chancellor of the Weimar Republic, 1928–30. His coalition government of center and left-wing parties was fatally divided over how to deal with the growing economic crisis in the aftermath of the Wall Street Crash, with the socialists opposing a retrenchment policy agreed by the other parties. Müller was forced to resign, and it has been claimed that proper parliamentary government came to an end in Germany at that point. His successor, *Brüning*, increasingly governed the country through the emergency powers available in the constitution to President Hindenburg.

Munich Agreement: a 1938 international agreement on the future of *Czechoslovakia*. It came in response to Hitler's pressure on that country with regard to the protection of the large German minority in its *Sudetenland* region. To avoid war, the British prime minister Neville *Chamberlain*, in what became the classic move in his policy of *appeasement*, three times traveled to meet Hitler, only for the latter to extend his demands. The third meeting, at Munich, was set up by Mussolini at Chamberlain's request, with Mussolini, Hitler, Chamberlain and the French prime minister *Daladier* as the principal players. No Czech leaders were invited to attend. Britain and France agreed to most of Hitler's demands and then pressured the Czechs to accept, making it clear that, despite the alliance they had with France, if they refused they would have to resist alone.

The consequences were that:

- Hitler gained the Czech Sudetenland without having to fire a shot

- Hungary and Poland took advantage of the occasion to make small gains of territory at Czechoslovakia's expense
- in the following March, despite the pledges he had made at Munich, Hitler took over the rest of Czechoslovakia.

The agreement has come to represent the shortsightedness and naïvety of Britain and France. Chamberlain waving Hitler's empty pledge to work for better relations, when he stepped from the plane on his return from Munich, has often been seen as the most potent token of the futility of appeasement. The Western Allies' most serious error had been to ignore the Soviet Union, and from this rebuff and their Munich surrender to Hitler, Stalin began to consider other foreign-policy options, a move which ended in the momentous *Nazi–Soviet Pact*.

Munich Olympic killings: the killing of 11 Israeli athletes during the 1972 Olympic Games by Palestinian terrorists. It was a particularly dramatic episode in the pattern of growing terrorism of the period. Nine of the eleven dead were killed as attempts were made to secure their release by the use of force.

Munich Putsch: a 1923 attempt by Hitler to organize a coup against the Weimar Republic, intending to install *Ludendorff* as a military dictator. When 3,000 supporters marched into central Munich, the police opened fire on them and 16 of their number were killed. Hitler was tried and sentenced to five years' imprisonment but was released after nine months. He used his trial to secure publicity and support for the Nazi cause from right-wing elements in the state. The drastic police action in support of Weimar was, however, one of the reasons why it survived in the 1920s, despite its many enemies.

Mussolini, Benito: the creator of *fascist Italy* and dictator of *Italy*, 1922–43. Originally a socialist and a newspaper editor, he enlisted and was wounded in the First World War. After the war, he moved politically to the right, now attacking socialism and pacifism. In 1919, he organized right-wing fasci (groups) into the Fascist Party and formed links with *D'Annunzio*. His new position won middle-class support, and the party won 30 seats in the 1921 parliamentary elections.

Italy was in turmoil, with high unemployment, strikes and dissatisfaction at the outcome of the war. Mussolini organized his supporters to take to the streets to oppose the communists in the cities. He convinced many anti-communists that he was better able to halt the communist threat than were the ineffective coalition governments of the democratic parties. In 1922, he organized the so-called *March on Rome* and was invited by the king, *Victor Emmanuel*, to form a government. He still had to establish total power, and this took until 1926. He succeeded in this because:

- he appeared to provide stable and vigorous government, saving the country from the dangers of socialism and giving Italians pride in their country
- from 1922 to 1925, economic conditions improved, and with unemployment falling from half a million to just over 100,000, and with small businessmen and the professional classes sharing in the boom, fascism seemed to be bringing solid benefits
- his supporters, like *Farinacci*, worked to build up the party and state administration, anonymously carrying out the mundane tasks for which Mussolini had little aptitude

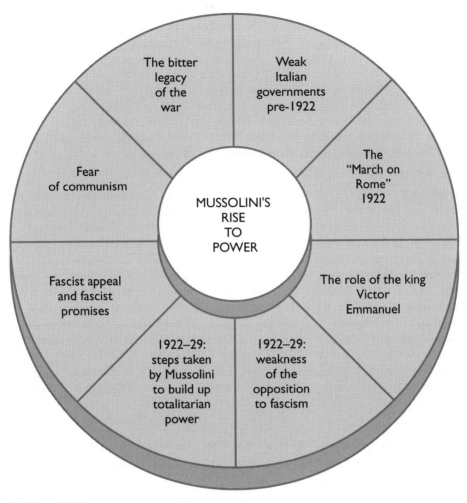

11 *Mussolini's rise to power*

- his opponents were divided and more suspicious of each other than of Mussolini. A number of liberal politicians, like *Salandra*, linked themselves to the fascists while others, like *Nitti*, went into exile
- many Catholics favored the fascists as firm opponents of godless communism, and their trust appeared to be rewarded when, in the 1929 *Lateran Treaties*, Mussolini made peace between the state and the Catholic Church
- he pushed through the *Acerbo Law* and also used violence and intimidation, particularly in the 1924 elections, to cow potential opposition
- in 1924, the *Matteotti* affair enabled him, after the opposition had made the mistake of withdrawing from Parliament in the *Aventine Secession*, to

silence his opponents and alter the constitution so that only candidates nominated by the fascist Grand Council could stand in elections

- in 1925, the Legge Fascistissime placed controls on the press and local government under the control of fascist nominees; the prime minister was to be responsible only to the king and not to Parliament
- in 1926, Mussolini was authorized to rule by decree
- in 1928, voting rights were restricted to those paying taxes so that the electorate fell from 10 to 3 million and parliamentary candidates had also to be approved by the fascist Grand Council, which would select a short list among them for submission to the electorate.

The economy under Mussolini

From 1922 to 1925, the Italian economy developed steadily, with falling unemployment and government finances stabilized. In the late 1920s, however, Mussolini, who was too inclined to listen to the pleas of important businessmen, switched to a policy of protecting inefficient Italian industries and agriculture, and in 1926 revalued the currency (the lira) at the very high rate of 90 to the pound. This was excellent initial propaganda for the strength of fascism but it crippled the export and tourist trades and led Italy into serious economic problems, even before the Great Depression hit Europe generally. In the 1930s, the Italian state was reorganized economically and politically as a *corporate state*, and a series of public-works programs began. Propaganda featuring Mussolini made the most of these achievements, as in the *Battle for Grain*, the *Battle for Births* and the *Battle for Land*, only the first of which achieved even limited success. On the other hand, the electric-power and car-manufacturing industries grew rapidly behind protective tariff barriers.

Foreign policy

Mussolini's early foreign policy, other than the *Corfu Incident*, was cautious:

- notably, in 1934, he checked Nazi German expansionism into Austria and
- in 1935, he joined the *Stresa Front*.

From 1935, his foreign policy became more expansionist. He sought an empire in Africa, and in 1935, in the *Italo–Ethiopian War*, he invaded Ethiopia. The ineffective resistance of the League of Nations led by Britain and France drove him towards a more friendly relationship with Hitler:

- creating the *Axis* with Germany in 1936
- following Germany out of the League in 1937
- accepting the *Anschluss* in 1938
- signing the *Pact of Steel* in 1939.

Much of Mussolini's conduct of foreign policy was impulsive, and the unnecessary 1939 invasion of *Albania*, which Italy already controlled, and the Pact of Steel are examples of his seeking propaganda victories rather than following a consistent strategy.

Second World War

Italy was not prepared for war in 1939 but attacked France in 1940 after its invasion by the Germans. Italian forces did not do well in the campaigns in Greece or North

Africa and had to be reinforced by German troops in both theaters. After the Allied invasion of Italy, Mussolini was deposed in 1943, but after a dramatic rescue by German paratroops, he was restored as head of a German puppet government in north Italy. In 1945, he was captured close to the Swiss border by Italian partisans and was summarily shot. His body was taken to Milan and put on public display, strung by its feet from a lamp post.

Nagy, Imre: prime minister of Hungary, 1953–55 and 1956. In his first term in office, he introduced social and economic reforms easing state control but was then accused of *Titoism*, removed and replaced by the more orthodox communist, *Rákosi*. When the 1956 *Hungarian Revolution* began, he

- was recalled to office
- inaugurated a program to reform the communist regime
- announced that Hungary would leave the *Warsaw Pact*.

This last step alienated his coalition partner, *Kádár*, and provoked Soviet military intervention. Nagy made emotional appeals to the West for help, but when this did not materialize, he surrendered to the Soviets in return for guarantees of safety but was handed over to the restored Hungarian communists and, in 1958, secretly shot. His reputation was rehabilitated when the communist regime collapsed in 1989.

napalm: jellied petrol made from naphthalene and oil and used during and after the Second World War as the basis for firebombs and flamethrowers.

nationalize: to convert to public ownership. The British Labour government of 1945 to 1951, for example, nationalized major heavy industries and most forms of public transportation.

nationalism: a devotion to one's nation; a desire for national independence. A nationalist is a person who advocates national rights. Nationalism was strong among the many peoples of the pre-1918 *Austro-Hungarian Empire*, and the 1919 *Paris Peace Conference* tried to accommodate this by creating separate nation states from the empire. Throughout the long, post-1945 Soviet domination of the states of Eastern Europe, and perhaps because of it, nationalism remained a potent, if hidden, force. When the Soviet empire disintegrated, nationalist groups emerged in many countries, and many problems ensued.

- The disintegration of *Yugoslavia* was brought about by the desire of its various peoples to recover their separate national identities
- The independence of the *Baltic Republics*, leaving the Soviet Union, prefaced its wider collapse into the much looser *Commonwealth of Independent States* as the separate "nations" even within the Soviet Union sought their own national status
- From 1992 and continuing in 1998, the people of tiny *Chechenia*, totally surrounded by the Russian Republic, continued a struggle against apparently overwhelming odds for separate nationhood
- The separation at the beginning of 1993 of the *Czech Republic* and the Republic of *Slovakia*, which had together made up the state of Czechoslovakia, was a more peaceful instance of the same tendency further west.

Nationalism was not always, however, a force for disintegration, and in 1990 it brought together once more East and West Germany which had been separate since 1945.

nationalists: in the Spanish Civil War, the forces loyal to Franco and opposed to the republic.

National People's Party: the right-wing political party in Weimar Germany. The willingness of its leader, *Hugenberg*, to work with Hitler played a significant part in letting the Nazis form the government in January 1933. In June 1933, after the Nazi takeover, its offices were taken over by the police and Hugenberg resigned from the coalition government and then "voluntarily" dissolved the party.

National Socialist Party: the fuller title of the German Nazi Party. To be totally, and perhaps unnecessarily, accurate, it was entitled the National Socialist German Workers Party (NSDAP). It was founded in 1919 as the German Workers Party, assumed its new name in 1920 and came under Hitler's control in 1921. A decree of July 1933 declared it to be the only political party in Germany.

NATO (North Atlantic Treaty Organization): an association of European and North American states formed, at the height of the *Cold War* in 1949, for defense against any Soviet attack. (See map on p. 172.) It committed the nations involved to the common defense of all the members, and was an unprecedented step for the USA to take in peacetime, ensuring a permanent US military presence in Western Europe. The USA was always the dominant member, in terms of both policy decisions and actual military contribution. The collapse of the Soviet bloc from 1989 left NATO with an uncertain future, though in 1995 it was drawn into a peacekeeping role amid the chaos created in Bosnia after the collapse of Yugoslavia.

Naval Agreement: a 1935 agreement between Britain and Nazi Germany on the size of navies. Britain's action helped to undermine the already vulnerable *Stresa Front* and illustrated the inability of the European powers to follow a consistent and united policy with regard to Hitler.

Naval Race: the build-up of rival navies by Britain and Germany from around 1900. It centered on the building of heavy battleships, *dreadnoughts*, but also involved battle-cruisers and submarines, and contributed greatly to the mistrust between the two countries in the years before the First World War. For Britain, it was one aspect of the awareness that her power, industrial, imperial and now naval, was being challenged by the relatively recently united state of Germany. *Tirpitz*, for Germany, and *Fisher*, for Britain, were the two chief protagonists, but the race also engendered much popular patriotic fervor in both countries, contributing in turn to the heightened tensions of the period.

Navy Laws: German laws of 1897, 1900 and 1906 developing a program of warship building, particularly heavy battleships and cruisers, but also arranging for the widening of the *Kiel Canal* to allow them passage. The program, the brainchild of Admiral *Tirpitz*, was intended to provide Germany with a navy worthy of its world-power status and capable of sustaining its imperial ambitions. The laws aroused great anxiety in Britain, causing it to start reviewing its international situation and to embark on a naval building program of its own, thus inaugurating the *Naval Race*.

Navy League: a German pressure group at the beginning of the century. It had over a million members, and existed, much under the influence of Tirpitz, to promote the development of the German imperial navy. Its popular support is an

12 NATO, 1949 and later

indication of the increasingly belligerent mood of German public opinion in the years leading up to the First World War.

Nazi: a popular shortening of "National Socialist" that was used to describe both the National Socialist German Workers Party and individual members of the party. During the Second World War, it became, on the Allied side, a term of disparagement used and pronounced particularly effectively in public speeches by Churchill.

Nazi Party: the right-wing, authoritarian German political party led from 1921 to 1945 by *Hitler*. It opposed the Weimar Republic, and indeed democracy in general, and, having developed a philosophy of the superiority of the Aryan race and the need for racial purity, was marked by virulent anti-Semitism. It had appeal to:

- traditional German supporters of authority, who looked back to the Second Empire
- sections of the working and lower-middle classes, to whom it offered the Jews and the Treaty of Versailles as scapegoats for their own and Germany's problems.

Party members shared many of the ideas of Italian fascism, and the party also copied Mussolini's love of uniforms, salutes, marches, military music and mass rallies. Following the failure of the *Munich Putsch*, it followed a constitutional route to power. Its electoral progress was slow in the 1920s as Weimar Germany seemed to find a new stability, so that the Nazis gained only 12 seats in the 1928 *Reichstag* elections. The Great Depression of the early 1930s transformed its prospects as the economic crisis swamped the democratic politicians.

- In September 1930, the Nazis captured 107 Reichstag seats
- In July 1932, they held 230 seats
- The loss of 34 seats in the November 1932 election did not stop the momentum of their advance to power. Their electoral base had made them indispensable to other right-wing politicians, like *Hugenberg* and von *Papen*, who believed that they could easily manipulate Hitler and the Nazis
- In January 1933, President Hindenburg offered Hitler the post of chancellor, the head of government. The Nazis had achieved power by legal means. Their skillful use of mass propaganda, the physical presence on the streets of the paramilitary *SA* and Hitler's own powers as a public speaker had done much to bring this about
- Once in power, they were able to use the powers of the state to cow their opponents and consolidate their own position so that in the March 1933 election, aided now by their control of the state administration, they won 288 seats.

They used the *Reichstag Fire* to outlaw the communists and crude intimidation to force through the *Enabling Act* which became the basis of Hitler's personal dictatorship. The violence of the *Night of the Long Knives* purged their own ranks of undesirables. In 1934, all other political parties were closed down. After 1933, Nazi parties were founded, copying the German model, in many other countries, and during the Second World War, they were imposed on German-occupied states.

Nazi–Soviet Pact: the military agreement of 23 August 1939 between the Soviet Union and Nazi Germany. The two states agreed not to go to war with each other and also to remain neutral if either were attacked by a third country. Secret clauses, which did not become public until long after the end of the Second World War, arranged both for them to divide up Poland and for the Soviet Union to take what action it wished against the Baltic Republics and Finland. The pact may well have been encouraged by the slow pace of British and French approaches to the Soviet Union and by their policies and actions in the *Munich Agreement*. It marked a revolution in international diplomacy and allowed Hitler within days to attack Poland and

RENDEZ-VOUS

13 The British reaction to the division of Poland by Nazi Germany and the Soviet Union

thus inaugurate the Second World War. In June 1941, Hitler broke the pact when he launched Operation *Barbarossa* against the Soviet Union.

nepmen: private entrepreneurs operating in the Soviet Union under Lenin's *New Economic Policy* (NEP). They controlled three-quarters of the retail trade and were generally unpopular as profiteers from shortages. Their existence offended true communists as a concession to capitalism, and the penalties and extra taxation imposed on them in Stalin's early years was generally welcomed. They disappeared under Stalin's reorganization of the economy in the early 1930s.

Netherlands, The: an independent kingdom generally referred to simply as *Holland* – as in the other entries in this handbook. It remained neutral in the First World War but was occupied by Germany after a blitzkrieg attack in the second. A large Dutch *fifth column* had welcomed the invasion, but once the country was occupied, its Jewish population suffered the full rigors of the *Holocaust*. A resistance movement grew up and the country was liberated by the Allies in late 1944, at which point a massive aid program had to be mounted to get food to its starving inhabitants.

The Netherlands was an important colonial power, particularly in the Dutch East

Indies, and almost all of this latter area was occupied by the Japanese from 1941. After the Second World War, the Dutch were unable to regain control of these imperial possessions, and after four years of war the East Indies in 1949 became independent as Indonesia. Since the Second World War, The Netherlands has been enthusiastically in favor of European unity. It joined, in all cases as a founder member:

- the *Benelux Union* in 1947
- NATO in 1949
- the European Coal and Steel Community in 1951
- the European Community in 1958.

In the 1980s and 1990s, The Netherlands found itself out of step with other members of the EU over its liberal policy towards both hard and soft drugs. Its capital, Amsterdam, was seen in some quarters as the undesirable source of drugs throughout Western Europe.

Neuilly, Treaty of: the treaty imposed on Bulgaria, Germany's ally, in November 1919 as part of the *Paris Peace Conference*. Bulgaria lost land to both Romania and Greece, and in the process lost its access to the Mediterranean.

neutrality: not helping or supporting either of two opposing sides.

Neuve Chapelle: a 1915 battle on the Western Front in the First World War.

New Economic Policy (NEP): introduced in Russia by *Lenin* in 1921. The Bolsheviks were fighting for survival in the Russian Civil War, it was a time of severe famine and the pressures of *war communism* were creating much unrest, notably the *Kronstadt Mutiny*. The Bolshevik government could not afford to risk its position by making political concessions, but the NEP eased the economic rigors of war communism in order to win it support. It restored a range of capitalist practices:

- some private trading was allowed
- small firms were restored to private ownership
- financial incentives and bonuses were introduced.

The restoration was limited, since large industrial firms, foreign trade and banking were still state-owned and the trade unions remained under the control of the Communist Party. The major changes were in agriculture, where peasants were allowed to sell their surplus crops on the open market. The NEP led to the re-emergence of a class of small capitalist businessmen, the *nepmen,* and to the restoration of a class of wealthier peasants or *kulaks*. The changes pacified the peasantry and restored economic stability so that, by 1926, Soviet economic production had recovered from the years of war, revolution and civil war to reach once more the levels of 1913. The NEP was reversed in the late 1920s by Stalin's introduction of *Five-Year Plans* and the *collectivization* of agriculture.

Nicholas II: tsar of Russia, 1894–1917. He was a believer in the principles of *autocracy*, which he sought to maintain against democratic or revolutionary tendencies.

Before 1914

- In Europe: prior to his becoming tsar, Russia had moved from alliance with Germany to closer relations with France. This culminated in the

Franco–Russian Alliance of 1893 which became the cornerstone of Russian foreign policy with regard to Europe and led on both to the 1907 entente with Britain and to alliance in war with France and Britain from 1914

- In the Far East: Nicholas wished to expand Russia's empire into Manchuria and Korea, but this led to clashes with the developing power of Japan and ended in defeat and the destruction of the Russian fleet in the *Russo–Japanese War* of 1904–05.

Defeat, and the unnecessarily brutal repression of a peaceful demonstration on *Bloody Sunday*, helped to provoke the *Revolution of 1905*, after which Nicholas agreed to set up an elected *Duma*, whose powers he then worked to limit by passing the *Fundamental Law*. It was at this point that he abruptly dismissed *Witte*, arguably the most competent minister of his reign, replacing him with the reactionary *Goremykin*. In 1911 too, he appeared to have been about to dismiss a reforming minister, *Stolypin*, just prior to the latter's assassination.

In the First World War

In 1914, Nicholas declared war on Germany, and this, though popular at first, ended in disaster for the monarchy when, in September 1915, he took personal command of the army and was then blamed for any defeats or inefficiencies which occurred. He had from the start believed that waging the war was a matter for the tsarist autocracy alone, and refused to compromise on this, preferring to dismiss first the Duma and then any government ministers who raised awkward issues. Equally serious was the fact that in his absence his wife, the tsarina *Alexandra*, and her adviser, *Rasputin*, undermined effective government at home, repeatedly dismissing and replacing key ministers. Amid growing government chaos during the *February Revolution* of 1917, Nicholas felt unable to compromise the tsarist autocracy by agreeing to constitutional reforms, but accepted the advice of the leaders of the Duma and abdicated. He and his family were murdered by the Bolsheviks in July 1918.

Niemöller, Martin: a Protestant Christian opponent of the Nazi regime. He fearlessly preached against the evils of the Nazi state and, from 1937 to 1945, was held in concentration camps. After the war, he led the acknowledgment of the German churches that they had not done enough to resist Hitler. He also challenged the abuses of the de-Nazification courts and was a fierce opponent of both German rearmament and the nuclear arms race.

Nietzsche, Friedrich: a German philosopher who died in 1900. His detestation of democracy and his expression of the cult of the superman who can create and impose his own law became popular in German Nazi circles as apparently providing a philosophical basis for National Socialism.

Night of the Long Knives: the murder in June 1934 of the leading members of the *SA* and others by the SS under orders from Hitler. Both Hitler and the German army feared the SA's power and political radicalism. It is likely that Hitler carried out the murders in return for the Reichswehr promising to support his becoming president on the death of Hindenburg; certainly, General *Blomberg* congratulated him on the action taken.

- Hitler, Goering and Himmler personally organized the event, using the SS and the Gestapo and with weapons provided by the army.
- Several hundreds died both on the night of 30 June and during the next three days, summarily shot down; they included *Röhm* and all the other SA leaders
- The opportunity was also taken to dispose of unreliable elements among German right-wing politicians, including *Schleicher* and his wife, together with close associates of von *Papen*, who was himself lucky to survive.

Nitti, Francesco: Italian prime minister, 1919–20. His government failed to act against *D'Annunzio*'s occupation of Fiume, and this:

- was a good example of Italian democratic governments surrendering to right-wing violence
- illustrated the general weakness of Italian democracy
- encouraged Mussolini's political adventurism in 1922.

When Mussolini gained power, Nitti went into exile in Paris.

Nivelle, Robert: a French soldier. He was commander-in-chief of French forces on the *Western Front* in early 1917, but when his offensive plan of that year failed to break the German lines, and this at enormous cost in lives, he was replaced by *Pétain.*

NKVD: the Soviet secret police. It took over the functions of *OGPU* in the 1930s and became the chief instrument in the Stalinist purges, using arbitrary powers ruthlessly. It came under the control of *Beria,* and on his fall in 1953, it was replaced by the *KGB.*

Nobel Peace Prize: awarded annually, along with prizes in physics, chemistry, medicine and literature, since 1901. The money comes from the fortune of the Swedish scientist Alfred Nobel. The Peace Prize has been awarded to a variety of organizations and individuals, including:

- in 1953, to the US statesman George *Marshall*
- in 1954, to the UN High Commissioner for Refugees
- in 1965, to *UNICEF*
- in 1983, to Lech *Walesa* of the *Solidarity* movement in Poland.

non-aggression pact: a formal agreement between two or more nations that they will not attack each other. The public terms of the *Nazi–Soviet Pact* of August 1939 constituted a non-aggression pact, though secret clauses went beyond this to provide for joint military action against Poland.

non-alignment: not linked to either of the two world power blocs of the USA or the Soviet Union. In the 1950s, Tito of Yugoslavia was an important influence in the foundation of a non-aligned movement, which held its first international meeting in Bandung, Indonesia in 1955. The movement came to be dominated by non-European countries, and its impact on the course of international events, especially in Europe, was never great.

non-interventionist: a policy of avoiding involvement in wars and civil wars. The term describes Britain and France's policy with regard to the Spanish Civil War as opposed to that of Germany, Italy and the Soviet Union, all of which aided one side or the other.

Non-Proliferation Treaty: an international treaty in 1968 to stop the spread of nuclear weapons. Britain, the Soviet Union and the USA agreed not to assist any other countries in acquiring nuclear weapons, but this, and the support of 59 other nations, failed to stop their spread.

Nordic Council: founded in 1952 to provide annual meetings of the government representatives of the Scandinavian countries to consider issues of mutual concern. In 1971, it developed a council of ministers able to make recommendations for action which can become binding on the member states. Its importance is limited by the facts both that it cannot consider defense and foreign affairs and that many of the other decisions it makes have to be ratified by the individual state parliaments. In 1995, Finland and Sweden joined Denmark in the European Union, and the council's importance seemed likely to decline.

Normandy Campaign: in 1944, the opening campaign of the *Second Front* during the Second World War. From the *D day* landings on the Normandy beaches, Allied troops captured the vital port of Cherbourg and the key communications centers of Caen and St Lô, before breaking out into northern France. The invasion had involved the largest single fleet of vessels ever assembled and followed years of preparation on the south coast of England. An artificial harbor, code-named Mulberry, and a pipeline under the English Channel, code-named Pluto, illustrate the careful planning and the technical expertise which backed the campaign.

North Africa Campaigns: campaigns from 1940 to 1943 during the Second World War.

The Axis offensive, 1940–42

The opening campaign was an Italian invasion of Egypt from Libya in June 1940 which was repulsed by British Commonwealth troops under Wavell who counter-attacked and, capturing Tobruk, overran most of Libya. In a separate campaign early in 1941, the British conquered Ethiopia and the Italian colonies in the Red Sea region, opening up a valuable supply line to Egypt. In March 1941, German troops under Rommel reinforced the Italians in Libya and the British were pushed back, leaving Tobruk under siege. Tobruk was temporarily relieved by forces under Auchlineck but finally fell in June 1942, and the British took up position to defend Egypt and the Suez Canal at El Alamein.

The German retreat, 1942–43

By September 1942, the Allied defensive line was sufficiently stabilized for British Commonwealth forces, now commanded by Montgomery, to counter-attack. Rommel's supply lines were dangerously long and under air attack from Malta, and he had to retreat westwards, closely pursued by fast-moving Commonwealth troops advancing out of Egypt through Libya into Tunisia. A feature of all the campaigns to this point had been the importance in desert conditions of tanks and tank battles.

In November 1942, massive amphibious landings in Morocco and Algeria, commanded by *Eisenhower*, opened up a second North African front to the west, behind the German and Italian armies. In the spring of 1943, the Axis forces were squeezed between the Allied armies, and it is a tribute to Rommel's military skill in adverse circumstances that, although he lost 250,000 men taken prisoner, he still managed to get the nucleus of his army's strength back to Sicily to fight again, in the *Italian Campaign.*

North Atlantic Treaty Organization: see *NATO*

Northern Ireland: a self-governing province of the United Kingdom set up in 1920.

- It consists of the six northeastern counties of the island of Ireland which formed part of the ancient region of *Ulster*
- Its creation reflected the determination of its Protestant majority not to allow the British government to incorporate it into a united independent Ireland where it would be heavily outnumbered by the Catholics.

A provincial parliament was established in Stormont Castle (subsequently abolished in 1972), but Northern Ireland also continued to send MPs to the Westminster Parliament. Since 1969, the province has been troubled by pressure, peaceful and violent, from republicans, who wish to see it incorporated into a united Ireland free from British rule.

The Northern Ireland Accord, agreed in April 1998, provided for the creation of three interconnected bodies of government within Northern Ireland, between the north and the rest of Ireland, and between the Irish Republic and the United Kingdom as a whole.

Norway: a country which gained its independence from Sweden in 1905, with Haakon VII as king. Neutral in the First World War, it was in 1940 invaded and swiftly conquered by Germany during the Second World War. A Nazi puppet government under *Quisling* was set up, and ruled the country until 1945. After Norway recovered its independence it was happy, especially in view of its common frontier with the Soviet Union, to become a founder member of NATO. With the discovery of oil under the North Sea, the country enjoyed great prosperity. In 1992, the Norwegian Parliament voted to apply for membership of the European Union and this was successfully negotiated, but the people, in a referendum held in November 1994, voted against entry by a 5 percent majority.

Noske, Gustav: a German defense expert and socialist defense minister in the early days of the Weimar Republic.

- In the last days of the First World War, he persuaded the German sailors to end the *Kiel Mutiny*
- In 1919, he created the *Freikorps* to break the *Spartacist* revolution in Berlin
- In 1920, he was dismissed by Ebert after the Freikorps had been involved in the unsuccessful *Kapp Putsch.*

Novotný, Anton: president of Czechoslovakia, 1957–68. He:

- played a leading part in the 1948 communist takeover of the state
- was a hard-line Stalinist who opposed Khrushchev's attempts at liberal reform
- mismanaged the economy, placing too much emphasis on heavy industry, which led to recession and unrest in the 1960s.

He then attempted to introduce social and economic reforms in order to placate the growing opposition, but these did not work. In the *Prague Spring* of 1968, the army refused to obey his orders to occupy Prague, and he retired, dying in 1975.

nuclear deterrent: the idea that possession of nuclear weapons, the *atomic bomb* or the *hydrogen bomb*, would deter any attacker. It led, in the second half of the twentieth century, to powers with such weapons building up huge stockpiles, and to their building more and more sophisticated systems, including submarines capable of staying underwater for months, for their delivery in the event of war.

nuclear energy: the peaceful development of the power in atomic nuclei. During the 1950s, this provided a new source of power and created a vast new industry. The capital costs were great, and this, together with the development expertise needed, meant that the industry was first located in the USA, Western Europe and the Soviet Union. By the 1990s, however, many relatively undeveloped countries had built nuclear power stations. There was great concern that such states could exploit the peaceful uses of nuclear energy to acquire nuclear weapons. The disaster at the Soviet nuclear plant at *Chernobyl* in 1986 underlined the potential dangers of the use of nuclear power and increased the nervousness felt at its spread.

Nuremberg Laws: Nazi legislation reducing the Jewish population to second-class status. They were announced by Goebbels at the 1935 Nuremberg rally of the Nazi Party. They:

- took away German nationality from the Jews by decreeing that only *Aryan* blood entitled one to be a member of the German nation
- closed the professions to Jews
- forbade either marriage or sexual intercourse between Jew and non-Jew.

All this was in the name of racial purity.

Nuremberg rallies: annual mass rallies of the Nazi Party held in Nuremberg in September. They were carefully orchestrated to stir up the faithful.

- Uniforms, banners, military music and mass marching dominated the highly emotional proceedings
- Nazi orators, led by Goebbels but culminating with Hitler himself, poured out the Nazi message by loudspeaker.

In 1938, the rally was used to provide a highly effective message to Europe, and particularly the people of Czechoslovakia, as Hitler created the impression that he was about to seize the Sudetenland. The messages from the rallies were carried across Germany and beyond by the relatively recently arrived medium of radio. The 1939 rally was canceled in mid-August, and Germany invaded Poland on 1 September.

Nuremberg Trials: trials of leading German and Austrian Nazis after the end of the Second World War. These individuals were charged with:

- crimes against humanity
- violation of the rules of war
- crimes against peace.

Twenty-five of the 177 accused were sentenced to death; 35 were acquitted. The appalling crimes committed by the Nazis in occupied Europe were held to justify this action, but doubts remained about the morality of the victors acting as judges against the defeated. The trials were notable for rejecting defense pleas that many of the accused were acting under orders which they had no choice but to obey.

OAS (Organisation de l'Armée Secrète): a secret terrorist organization committed to keeping *Algeria* part of *Metropolitan* France. It was formed, in the early days of the Fifth French Republic, by elements in the French army, notably General *Salan*, and die-hard French settlers in Algeria who were dissatisfied with de Gaulle's conduct of the *Algerian War* and distrustful of his commitment to France retaining the country. A revolt in Algiers, led by Salan in 1961, was unsuccessful. The OAS responded to news of the *Évian Agreements* with bomb attacks in Paris and several assassination attempts on de Gaulle. After Salan's capture in 1962, the movement disintegrated.

October Manifesto: issued in 1905 by Tsar Nicholas II. Strikes were spreading across Russia in unrest that had originally been triggered off by the *Bloody Sunday* massacre. The manifesto was a series of political concessions intended to restore order and end the *Revolution of 1905*. Nicholas promised:

- to summon a parliament (*Duma*), with a wide electorate and powers to pass laws and protect civil liberties
- to end the *redemption payments* required from the peasants in order to release their land from the control of the village communities (*mirs*).

The manifesto was issued on the advice of his leading minister, *Witte*, and seemed to set Russia on a new constitutional path. It succeeded in splitting the tsar's political opponents, since the Cadet Party were prepared to cooperate in the new arrangements while the Social Revolutionaries and Social Democrats were not. The immediate disturbances were brought under control by the army but underground plotting against tsardom went on. Nicholas soon backed away from his manifesto promises: just days before the first Duma met, he reasserted his autocratic rights in the *Fundamental Law*, and the first Duma lasted less than three months.

October Revolution: the 1917 *Bolshevik* coup which overthrew Kerensky's *Provisional Government*. By the Gregorian calendar, in universal use in Western Europe, the revolution actually occurred in November. Key elements in the revolution were:

- the Petrograd Soviet, which had fallen under Bolshevik control
- the role of *Trotsky*, who had become chairman of the *Military Revolutionary Committee* set up by the Congress of Northern Soviets.

Lenin had been pressing the other leaders of the Bolsheviks since September that the time was ripe to mount a coup, but they had been slow to be convinced. Bolshevik power in Petrograd was not repeated across Russia, and the *All-Russian Congress of Soviets* was due to meet in the capital on 25 October. It seemed likely that the Bolsheviks would not be in a majority at the meeting. Lenin, wishing to demonstrate Bolshevik strength in Petrograd and to give the initiative to the Bolsheviks before the meeting, ordered a coup against the government.

Trotsky and the Military Revolutionary Committee:

- seized key points, railway stations, telegraph offices, banks and post offices in Petrograd
- stormed the Winter Palace, where Kerensky's government was meeting, though Kerensky managed to escape.

At next day's meeting of the Congress of Soviets, *Lenin* could report that the Petrograd Soviet controlled the city. The 400 Bolshevik delegates were delighted to endorse the action taken, and their opponents, Mensheviks and Social Revolutionaries, had no choice but to accept it.

When the Congress of Soviets agreed to form a ruling council, it was dominated by the Bolsheviks. Kerensky had escaped from the Winter Palace but could not raise enough troops to make a serious attempt to recapture the city. The other political parties made no move to resist the course of events but took part in the elections already arranged for a Constituent Assembly. This met in January 1918, and when the Bolsheviks did not have a majority, it was simply closed down.

The October Revolution:

- had been almost bloodless and, from first to last, had taken from 2 am to 11 am
- is usually regarded as being a tightly organized conspiracy conducted almost entirely within the capital Petrograd
- was not the result of a mass uprising or mass support, and this despite the sharp rise in membership of the Bolshevik Party during 1917.

The coup's success reflected the lack of enthusiasm for the Provisional Government, but the failure of other political groups to oppose or reverse it was still remarkable.

Octobrists: conservative Russian politicians favoring limited political reforms but who were prepared to work with tsardom within the framework of the 1905 *October Manifesto*. They were to the right of the Cadets. In the fourth Duma by 1915, even prominent Octobrists like *Guchkov* and *Rodzianko* had become critical of Nicholas II's conduct of the war, and in 1917 were prepared to join the Provisional Government.

Oder–Neisse Line: the boundary line along the river Oder and its tributary, the Neisse. After the *Second World War*, the line was established as the border between Poland and East Germany, handing to Poland great areas of territory that had formerly belonged to Germany:

- At the 1945 *Potsdam Conference*, the Allied powers accepted the line as a temporary measure
- Between 1950 and 1955, East Germany and Poland both accepted the line as a permanent frontier, but West Germany, the USA and Britain did not
- In 1972, Brandt, the West German chancellor, pursuing his *Ostpolitik*, made a treaty with Poland in which both countries accepted existing frontiers.

OECD (Organization for Economic Cooperation and Development): an organization for international cooperation among industrialized countries founded in 1961. Its aims included:

- helping member governments achieve high, sustained economic growth and financial stability
- promoting international trade
- encouraging member states to provide aid to developing countries.

The member states originally came from the Western capitalist world, but after the disintegration of the Soviet bloc, several Eastern European states applied to join.

OGPU: the Soviet secret police. In 1921, it replaced the *Cheka* and, by the time of the late-1930s Great Purge, had in turn been absorbed by the *NKVD*.

Okhrana: the Russian tsarist political police. It was a large and sinister organization with wide powers of arrest and relying heavily on informers planted in positions throughout Russian life, as well as on the use of bribery and blackmail. Because all citizens had to carry internal passports and, when traveling, had to report to the police, a close eye could be kept on any possible dissidents. It was common for members of the Okhrana to be employed to eavesdrop on the conversations of ordinary Russians, and little attention was paid to any notion of civil rights.

OKW (Oberkommando der Wehrmacht): the high command of the armed forces of Nazi Germany. It was created by Hitler, separate from the old army hierarchy, to act as his personal staff as part of a general tightening of Nazi control carried out in 1938. During the war, there was constant rivalry between it and the army general staff. The *Abwehr*, under Canaris, was founded as the intelligence unit of the OKW.

Olympic Games: international games held every four years since 1896. In the early years, the games were mainly athletics, but this has greatly widened to include, since 1924, a series of Winter Games. The entrants were originally strictly amateurs, but this changed after the Second World War, with state sponsorship in the East and payment of sportsmen and women in the West.

Politics have occasionally intruded on the games:

- in 1936, when Hitler used them for Nazi propaganda purposes
- in 1972, with the tragic terrorist attack on Israeli athletes at the *Munich Olympic* Games
- in 1980, when the USA and many Western nations boycotted the Moscow Games in protest at the Soviet invasion of Afghanistan.

open diplomacy: the public conduct of international relations and negotiations. After the First World War, it was felt that secret treaties had contributed greatly to the war's outbreak. If, for example, Britain's commitments to France had been public, then Germany might have made different decisions than it did, in the weeks before the war began, on backing Austria-Hungary or invading Belgium. In practice, even after the war, there was a limit to how open the conduct of international affairs could be, and references to its importance were often empty gestures.

Operation Barbarossa: a code name for the German June 1941 invasion of the Soviet Union.

Organization for Security and Cooperation: see *Conference on Security and Cooperation in Europe*

origins of the First World War: see separate entry, *First World War, the debate on its origins*

Orlando, Vittorio: prime minister of Italy, 1917–19. He failed to secure more concessions of territory to Italy at the *Paris Peace Conference*, and so resigned. At first, alarmed by the unrest in the country, he supported Mussolini's appointment as prime minister, but resigned from Parliament and left the country in protest at the *Matteotti* murder, returning only after the fall of Mussolini in 1943.

Orthodox Church: the Eastern or Greek Church, separated from the Catholic Church since medieval times. It was formed of national churches, with common beliefs and practices, in countries such as Russia, Romania and Greece. The leaders of the church in Russia had, under the tsars, considerable political importance and were usually firm supporters of tsarist autocracy, opposing all types of reform.

Ostpolitik: a policy towards Eastern Europe developed in West Germany by *Kiesinger* and *Brandt* to normalize relations with the communist countries of the region. It:

- reversed the policy of *Adenauer* which, in the 1957 *Hallstein Doctrine*, had refused to have diplomatic relations with any country, other than the Soviet Union, that had recognized the independence of East Germany
- succeeded in 1972 in establishing normal diplomatic relations between East and West Germany, and led to non-aggression pacts between West Germany and both Poland and the Soviet Union
- led to West German recognition of the *Oder–Neisse Line* as the Polish–German frontier.

Ottoman Empire: an Islamic empire which controlled many areas in the Middle East and in the Balkans. It had, in the nineteenth century, become a byword for inefficiency and corrupt brutality in administration. Its Christian subjects were often savagely persecuted. A revolt in 1908 by the *Young Turks* produced more efficient government and some promise of reforms. In 1913, following the *Balkan Wars*, the empire lost much of its European territory to Bulgaria, Greece, Romania, Serbia and the new state of Albania, retaining only Istanbul and the lands around it. This foothold meant, however, that it continued to command the strategically important Dardanelles strait through from the Mediterranean to the Black Sea.

The empire fought alongside Germany and Austria-Hungary in the First World War, when its lands in the Middle East were occupied by British and French forces. After the war, these became League of Nations *mandates* controlled by their conquerors. The Treaty of *Sèvres* gave much of western Turkey to Greece, but the revival under Mustafa Kemal (*Atatürk*) reversed this decision and led to the Treaty of *Lausanne*. In 1923, Turkey was declared a secular republic, and the ramshackle Ottoman Empire was at an end.

P

pacifism: the rejection of war and violence, and the belief that disputes should be settled by peaceful means. It has been linked with various religious groups, notably the Society of Friends. The term was coined in the early twentieth century and was then applied to those *conscientious objectors* who refused to be conscripted for military service during the First World War. The horror of that war made pacifism popular during the 1930s and encouraged the policy of *appeasement* to avoid war.

Pact of Steel: between Germany and Italy in May 1939. It came a month after the Italian invasion of Albania and committed both parties to aid the other in the event of war, however caused. When Hitler, in August, called on Mussolini to honor the pact, Mussolini had to declare that Italy was not ready for war and then demand so many German supplies that Hitler preferred to go it alone. The existence of the pact, an impulsive move by Mussolini, illustrated how far Italy had moved into the German orbit since the *Stresa Front* alliance with Britain and France in 1935. It also indicated how close Mussolini had become to believing his own propaganda about Italy's military might.

Palach, Jan: a Czech student who committed suicide by setting fire to himself in January 1969. This was as a protest against the brutal suppression of the *Prague Spring* uprising. Each January, opponents of the communist regime staged a public commemoration of his death. The attempts by the authorities to suppress the 1989 commemoration led directly into the marches, riots and formation of opposition groups which, by November, had overthrown the regime.

Palestine: the region of the Ottoman Empire which became a British League of Nations mandate in 1920. Since early in the twentieth century, Zionists had urged the creation of a Jewish national home there, and this was accepted by the Allies when they endorsed the *Balfour Declaration*. The British now had the impossible task of meeting Zionist aspirations and honoring promises given to the Arabs when their wartime help had been needed to defeat the Turks. Anti-Semitism in Europe in the 1930s led many Jews, particularly from Germany and Poland, to emigrate to Palestine, and this led to civil disorder between the racial groups, with the British administration struggling to maintain order. In 1948, the British mandate was ended and the modern history of Israel and its neighbors began.

Palme, Olof: prime minister of Sweden, 1969–76 and 1982–86. He carried out major constitutional reforms but failed to solve the problem of financing Sweden's welfare state. He played an important part in several international issues:

- as a member of the Brandt Commission
- conducting investigations in South Africa
- pressing for a nuclear-free zone in Europe.

He was murdered in 1986, and the failure to find the killers became a political scandal in Sweden. Rumors persisted that it had been the work of the South African security forces.

Panther Incident: in 1911 at *Agadir*. The German gunboat PANTHER was sent to protect German interests in Morocco, an area of French influence. This bullying of France provoked a tense international situation until Germany backed down, accepting small parcels of French land in the Congo to add to its colony in the Cameroons. It brought Britain and France into closer contact in terms of military planning in case the crisis got worse. The incident was therefore another stage on the way to Britain being committed to helping France when war came in 1914, and so amounted to a diplomatic blunder by Germany.

panzer: armored motorized columns of the German army (panzer meaning "tank" in German). They were used to devastating effect in the *blitzkrieg* offensives of 1939 in Poland and 1940 in Belgium and France.

Papadopoulus, Georgios: the leader of the 1967 military coup in Greece which led to the rule of the *"Greek Colonels."* In 1973, when a republic was declared, he was president for a year. With the restoration of democratic government in Greece in 1974, he was tried for treason, but the death sentence then passed on him was later commuted.

Papagos, Alexander: prime minister of Greece, 1952–55. A brilliant soldier before the Second World War, he was a German prisoner from 1941 to 1945 but was then made commander-in-chief of the royalist forces in the *Greek Civil War*, working closely for eventual victory with US advisers. The right-wing Greek Rally Party won the 1951 election and he became prime minister.

Papandreou, Andreas: prime minister of Greece, 1981–89 and 1993–96, the son of George Papandreou. He founded the Pan-Hellenic Socialist Movement (*PASOK*), and in 1981 became the leader of Greece's first truly socialist government. His great achievement, after years of extremist right-wing rule, was to make the socialists electable as an alternative government. In this, he was arguably the savior of democracy in Greece. Out of office, he had advanced radical left-wing views, being opposed both to the European Union and to NATO, but once he became prime minister these softened and he embraced both institutions. Ill-health and scandals in his private life dogged both his ministries, but in the second, he proved remarkably determined to hold on to power, resigning only weeks before his death in June 1996. With the scandals forgotten, his funeral produced remarkable scenes of mass public grief, bringing Athens to a standstill for hours.

Papandreou, George: prime minister of Greece, 1944, 1963 and 1964–65. His socialism made him suspect to the army and ended his 1944 ministry, and later on, arguments with King Constantine II brought an end to his ministry of 1964–65. He was held under house arrest by the "Greek Colonels" from 1967 until his death in 1968. He was the father of *Andreas Papandreou*, later also prime minister.

Papen, Franz von: chancellor of the Weimar Republic, 1932. A right-wing politician with aristocratic connections, and a member of the Catholic Center Party. When appointed chancellor, he opposed the Nazis, but in the course of 1932 came to support them and urged industrialist and financier friends to back them. He persuaded President *Hindenburg* to appoint Hitler chancellor, mistakenly believing that, as vice-chancellor, he would be able to control and manipulate him. His power base was destroyed in the *Night of the Long Knives* but he survived throughout the Nazi period in minor ambassadorial roles and was acquitted in 1946 at the Nuremberg Trials on charges of war crimes. He died in 1969.

paramilitary: organized like a military force but not part of the state's armed services.

Paris: the capital of France. The German army threatened to reach it in 1914 but was held at the Battle of the *Marne*. In 1919, it was the setting for the *Paris Peace Conference*. In the Second World War it was, in 1940, saved from destruction by the French surrender. When, in 1944, Allied troops closed in to liberate the city, Hitler ordered it to be set ablaze, but his commanders ignored the order. The Allied liberating forces then entered without opposition, led by the *Free French* with de Gaulle at their head.

Paris Peace Conference: the international conference held in 1919–20 to make arrangements following the end of the First World War, and from which a series of peace treaties emerged:

- Treaty of *Versailles*
- Treaty of *Saint Germain*
- Treaty of *Trianon*
- Treaty of *Sèvres*
- Treaty of *Neuilly*.

The detail of the arrangements made is given under the heading for each separate treaty.

Among important matters agreed at the conference were the establishment of the *League of Nations* and the introduction of the concept of the *mandate* to provide for the government of territories previously controlled by the defeated powers. The representatives of the great Allied powers dominated the conference, in particular:

- *Clemenceau* of France
- Woodrow *Wilson* of the USA
- *Lloyd George* of Britain.

Orlando of Italy was in theory one of their number, but was in practice an isolated figure who fought vainly for full recognition of Italy's claims to territory. No representatives of the defeated powers were allowed to attend the sessions of the conference, since the terms were not negotiated between victor and vanquished but were instead handed down to be accepted by the latter. The most serious disagreements arose over how harshly Germany should be punished, with France pressing for the most severe treatment, and the final arrangements left many problems for the future. There was great bitterness among the defeated nations, especially Germany, at the way in which they were treated, and many of the territorial arrangements were to provide flashpoints for future trouble. (See map on p. 188.)

Paris Peace Treaties, 1947: treaties between the Allied powers and the allies of Germany in the Second World War, i.e. Bulgaria, Hungary, Finland, Italy and Romania. The main provisions included:

- Italy lost Fiume to Yugoslavia and the Dodecanese islands to Greece
- Romania regained Transylvania from Hungary but had to cede eastern provinces to the Soviet Union

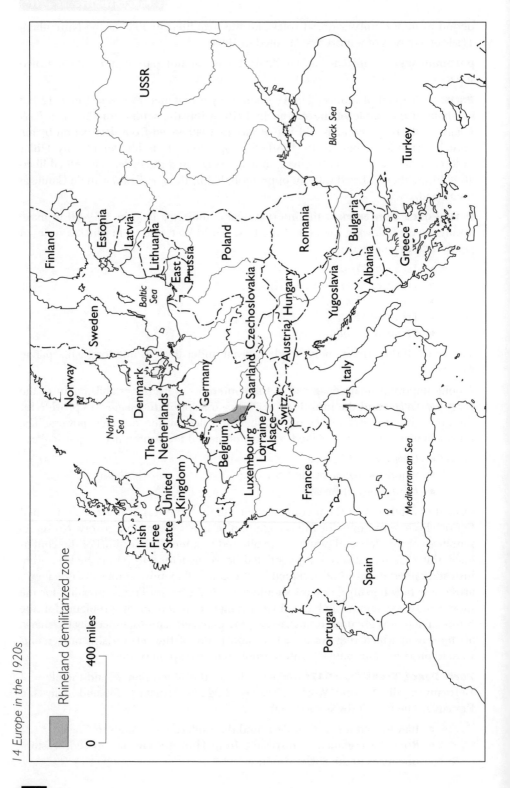

14 *Europe in the 1920s*

Rhineland demilitarized zone

0   400 miles

- Finland had to cede land to the Soviet Union
- Trieste became a free city, which it remained until it was divided between Italy and Yugoslavia in 1954.

The pressures of the Cold War ensured that almost all of these arrangements became permanent.

Parliament: the law-making, or legislative, assembly of a country – in Germany, for example, the *Reichstag*. It should not be confused in use with "*government*," meaning those who run the state.

partisans: a term generally used to describe guerrilla groups who operate behind enemy lines. During the Second World War, partisans were active in many of the countries occupied by the German army, perhaps achieving their greatest successes in Yugoslavia, where the communist partisans were led by Tito. They were often referred to as the *resistance*.

Pašić, Nikola: a Serb politician, prime minister of Serbia for many years, from 1891 to 1918. In 1914, he knew that *Dimitrievitch*, the head of Serbian intelligence, had an assassination plot in hand but did not know the details. He sent a carefully veiled warning to Vienna, but this never reached the proper authorities, and the fateful journey of the heir to the Austrian throne, *Franz Ferdinand*, to *Sarajevo* proceeded as planned. After 1918, he helped to create the union of peoples who went on to form *Yugoslavia*, and was prime minister from 1921 to 1924, and from late 1924 until his death in 1926.

PASOK (Pan-Hellenic Socialist Movement): a Greek left-wing political movement founded by Andreas *Papandreou* in 1974. After a long period in which Greek politics had been dominated by the right wing, it formed Greece's first socialist government in 1981 and won further elections in 1985, 1989 and 1993.

Passchendaele: a First World War battle on the *Western Front*. It was fought from July to November 1917. *Haig*, commander of the British forces, launched an attack on the German lines, despite the fact that persistent rain and the heavy opening bombardment had produced a sea of mud across which no one could advance but in which many who were wounded drowned. Nothing was gained, though the Commonwealth troops suffered 300,000 casualties, and the battle became the symbol of all the horrors of *trench warfare* and the indifference of First World War generals to appalling casualty rates.

Pasternak, Boris: a Soviet poet and translator of foreign literature. His most famous work was DOCTOR ZHIVAGO, described as possibly the greatest Russian novel of the twentieth century, which was published abroad in 1957 after being banned by the Soviet state censors. It was not anti-Marxist, but reflected the disappointments of a convinced communist at the way in which things had worked out. Pasternak was awarded the international Nobel Prize for Literature but was not allowed to go abroad to receive it. His treatment aroused international condemnation and illustrated the limited nature of the intellectual liberalization introduced by *Khrushchev*. He died, still not acknowledged in the Soviet Union, in 1960.

Paul VI: pope, 1963–78. He reconvened John XXIII's Second Vatican Council and pressed on with reforming Catholic Church practices, notably in the use of modern languages in church services. On moral issues, and on the questions of church authority, he remained a traditionalist. He also introduced the practice of the pope traveling outside Italy.

Paulus, Friedrich von: a German field marshal who planned the 1941 German invasion of the Soviet Union. In 1942, his forces failed to capture *Stalingrad* and were surrounded, surrendering in February 1943. This marked the crucial turning point of the war on the Russian front.

Pavelić, Ante: a Croatian fascist leader. He formed a brutal German puppet government in occupied Croatia from 1941 to 1945. On the German defeat, he escaped from Europe to Argentina and died in Madrid in 1959.

peace dividend: the expected reduction in defense spending because of the end of the Cold War with the collapse of the Soviet bloc from 1989. This money would then be available for peaceful social and economic development. It soon became apparent, from tensions in the former Soviet Union and Yugoslavia and the continuation of urban terrorism, that the high hopes of a peaceful world would not be easily realized. This, and pressure from vested military and defense-industry interests, made the "dividend" seem a little uncertain.

peasants: agricultural workers, usually small-scale farmers. Peasants often created important political pressure groups, as in France, usually conservative on matters of social and economic reform, as opposed to the more politically radical urban workers. In Russia, however, their discontent was an element in the instability of the tsarist regime, as demonstrated in the Revolution of 1905; and in 1917, their unfulfilled desire for land reform also contributed to the unpopularity of the Provisional Government. Under communism, the better-off Soviet peasants, the *kulaks*, benefited in the 1920s from Lenin's *New Economic Policy* but, in the 1930s, suffered greatly and were finally eliminated as a class under Stalin's *collectivization* program.

permanent revolution: the post-1917 view that the Marxist proletarian revolution should be exported on a worldwide basis from the Soviet Union. It was associated particularly with *Trotsky* and opposed by Stalin's development of the idea of *socialism in one country.*

Pétain, Henri: a French military hero of the First World War and head of state of *Vichy* France, 1940–44. In 1916, he halted the German advance at Verdun and in 1917 commanded the French forces on the *Western Front.* After the war, he became a right-wing political figure, and when France was defeated in 1940, he was recalled, aged 84, from his post as ambassador in Spain to become prime minister and negotiate a peace deal with the victorious Germans. Under this:

- the French forces were disbanded
- three-fifths of France, including all the Atlantic coastline and Paris, was occupied by the Germans
- a government was set up for the remaining two-fifths of the country; it was based in Vichy, which gave its name to the right-wing regime.

Pétain appointed *Laval* as deputy prime minister but later dismissed him, only to be required to reinstate him as prime minister when the Germans occupied the rest of the country. Pétain became a prisoner of the Germans but, in the bitterness against collaborators which marked the end of the war in France, he was tried for treason and sentenced to death. The sentence, however, was commuted to life imprisonment, and he died, still a prisoner, in 1951.

Peter II: king of Yugoslavia, 1934–45. The country was run during his childhood, until 1941, by his uncle Paul, acting as regent and following pro-German policies, which Peter in 1941 repudiated. When the German army invaded in 1941, and after only three weeks on the throne, he went into exile in Britain, from where he supported the *chetnik* partisans. After the war, Tito's communists abolished the monarchy and deprived Peter of his estates and his Yugoslav nationality. He died in exile in 1970.

Petrograd: the Slav name given to St. Petersburg at the outset of the First World War; the earlier form was considered too Germanic. In 1924, the name was changed again to Leningrad.

Petrograd Soviet: the organizing council of the working class of Petrograd. The deputies began to meet regularly during the period of the Provisional Government, and in August 1917, it was this *soviet* which frustrated the attempted coup by Kornilov. It was by then in the control of the Bolsheviks, and *Trotsky*, as president of the Petrograd Soviet, used its domination of the *Military Revolutionary Committee* to plan and carry out the *October Revolution*.

Petrov Affair: an Australian 1954 spy scandal caused by the allegations of defected Soviet diplomat Vladimir Petrov and his wife. The charges acted as Cold War propaganda on the worldwide nature of Soviet international espionage, but in fact amounted to very little.

Pflimlin, Pierre: in 1958, the last prime minister of the *Fourth French Republic*. It seemed possible that the French army in Algeria might intervene in France rather than allow Algeria to be granted independence. Pflimlin agreed with President Coty that this could not be risked. They turned to de Gaulle as the one man with the prestige to control the army and so avert a civil war, and de Gaulle's conditions for returning to public life were such that the Fourth Republic came to an end.

phony war: the period of the Second World War from the German conquest of Poland in September 1939 to the launch of their attacks in the west on Denmark and Norway in April 1940. In the intervening months, there was little military action, and the period thus became known as the "phony war."

Picasso, Pablo: a Spanish artist. He was the most inventive and most influential artist of the twentieth century. In 1937, in homage to those killed in the bombing of the city in the Spanish Civil War, he painted *Guernica*, and lived in exile until his death in 1973 rather than return to Spain while Franco ruled.

Pilsudski, Joseph: Polish dictator, 1926–35. He fought on the Austro-Hungarian and German side in the First World War in order to secure an independent Poland, but lost faith in German intentions and was then interned by them. After Polish independence was declared, he was, from 1918 to 1922, the first head of state. He led the successful defense of Poland against the Bolsheviks in 1919–20, and established the frontier with the Soviet Union far to the east, gaining much territory for his country.

Following a military revolt in 1926, in which he personally led the rebel troops into Warsaw, he established a dictatorship until his death in 1935. He pursued authoritarian policies in both social and political matters, but himself avoided taking the top political posts. In 1928, the left-wing parties made election gains and so he ordered new elections and ensured himself a submissive Parliament. His foreign minister, *Beck*, signed defense agreements with both Poland's large neighbors, Nazi Germany and the Soviet Union, in 1934. The right-wing regime which he had established continued to rule Poland after his death.

Pius XII: pope, 1939–58. He followed a strictly neutral line in the Second World War and, although involved in efforts to organize war relief, failed to speak out about the *Holocaust.*

plebiscite: a direct vote of all the electors in a state in order to establish opinion on an important issue.

Plehve, Vyacheslav: Russian minister of the interior, 1902–04. He was in favor of the Russo–Japanese War, thinking that victory would rally patriots to the tsar. As minister, he enforced repressive policies, including *pogroms* against the Jews. His assassination in 1904, by terrorists linked to the Socialist Revolutionary Party, was widely acclaimed by opponents of tsarism.

Plekhanov, Georgi: a Russian revolutionary. In 1903, when the Russian Social Democrat Party split, he supported the Mensheviks. From 1883, he lived in exile until 1917, when he returned to Russia but was unable to stop the Bolsheviks seizing power and withdrew to Finland. He died in 1918.

Podgorny, Nikolai: chairman of the Supreme Soviet, 1965–77. With *Brezhnev* and Kosygin, he was part of a collective government of Communist-Party veterans who controlled the Soviet Union after the downfall of Khrushchev. As Brezhnev's power grew, Podgorny's declined, and in 1977 he was ousted and replaced by Brezhnev.

pogrom: a tsarist-approved attack on Jewish communities. The term, in Russian meaning "destruction," was also used to describe such attacks in other Eastern European countries, and later for attacks ordered by Hitler on Jewish communities in Germany.

Poincaré, Raymond: president of France, 1913–20 and prime minister, 1922–24 and 1926–29. He argued for strong measures against Germany after the First World War, and in 1923, when Germany failed to meet its reparations payments, he ordered the French army to occupy the Ruhr, provoking a major crisis in relations with the Weimar Republic.

poison gas: a form of *chemical warfare* employed in the First World War and in the Italian attack on Ethiopia in 1935. Its military use was banned by the League of Nations.

Poland: a country that was part of Russia from the eighteenth century until 1918. In the First World War, many Poles, like Pilsudski, fought for independence on the Austro-Hungarian side. In 1918, following the Bolshevik takeover in Russia, an independent Poland was declared.

- In the Treaty of Versailles, Poland obtained access to the Baltic Sea via the Polish Corridor and Danzig

15 Poland, 1921–39

- By victory in the *Russo–Polish War*, it extended its frontier far to the east.

The most important of its inter-war political leaders were the dictator, *Pilsudski*, and the foreign minister, *Beck*, whose inconsistent foreign policy left Poland without effective allies in 1939.

At the outbreak of the Second World War, Poland was swiftly defeated and divided, after conquest, between Germany and the Soviet Union. In 1941, it was all overrun by German forces in their attack on the Soviet Union. In 1944, it was liberated by the Red Army but only after the tragedy of the *Warsaw Rising*. In the aftermath of the war:

- Poland's frontiers, as agreed by the Allied leaders at the Yalta Conference, moved far to the west, with the Soviet frontier based on the *Curzon Line* and the German frontier on the *Oder–Neisse Line*. Land lost to the Soviet Union was in effect compensated for at the expense of Germany
- vast forcible movements of population followed both of these frontier changes
- a communist government was set up, and Poland was firmly set in the Soviet bloc.

Internal dissent against the communist regime was never entirely silenced:

- In 1956, there were workers' strikes to protest about food shortages, which were suppressed by the army
- After *Gomulka* became prime minister, there was some relaxation of the oppressive laws against personal liberty
- The 1978 election of a Polish pope, John Paul II, gave a boost to the Catholic Church, which had never been silenced, but now became an outspoken critic of the government
- In 1980, the trade union *Solidarity* organized large-scale prolonged strikes in the *Gdansk* shipyard and, although military repression was again the government's answer, economic problems and social unrest forced the government to allow reform
- In 1989, the banned Solidarity union was made legal, and other political parties apart from just the Communist Party were allowed to form.

After elections in June 1989, a coalition government led by members of Solidarity was set up, and in 1990 the leader of Solidarity, Lech *Walesa*, was elected president. Relations between him and the still-powerful ex-communist parties in Parliament, particularly over the scale and pace of economic reform, remained troubled. In 1992, however, the respective powers of president and Parliament were defined in a constitutional review.

Polish Corridor: the corridor of land created between Germany and East Prussia at the 1919 Paris Peace Conference. It was given to *Poland* by the Treaty of Versailles to provide the newly independent state with access to the Baltic Sea. *Danzig*, at the seaward end of the corridor, became a free city under League of Nations control. The corridor and Danzig had many German inhabitants, and its creation caused great bitterness in Germany. In 1939, Hitler's demands for Danzig and much of the corridor to be returned to Germany led to the outbreak of the Second World War.

Politburo: in full, "The Political Bureau of the Communist Party." It was the highest policy-making body in communist countries. The Soviet Politburo was set up in 1917 by the Bolsheviks to lead the revolution. Until 1921, it shared this role with the Council of People's Commissars (the *Sovnarkom*), but then went on to control all aspects of life in the Soviet Union until its abolition in 1952.

Pompidou, Georges: president of France, 1969–74. He was:

- a Gaullist politician who was the key negotiator at the *Évian Agreements*

which ended the Algerian War
- involved in 1958 in drawing up the constitution of the *Fifth French Republic*
- prime minister from 1962 to 1968.

In 1968, he succeeded in containing student and working-class demonstrations short of revolution, but was then dismissed by the increasingly isolated President de Gaulle. When the latter suddenly retired, Pompidou easily won the presidential election. He continued most of de Gaulle's domestic policies, but took more decisive action to improve the economy, including a sharp devaluation of the currency and the introduction of a price freeze and other austerity measures. In foreign affairs, he remained as concerned as his predecessor to maintain the prestige of France, but ended the French veto on Britain joining the European Community. He died in 1974.

Pontine Marshes: unproductive land in central Italy which the fascist regime drained and turned to grain production as part of its much-publicized *Battle for Grain*. It was the main single economic achievement of Mussolini's government and was exploited by the regime for its propaganda value. Neglect of the recovered land in the later stages of the Second World War meant that much of it had to be recovered again after 1945.

popular front: a 1930s term to describe left-wing political alliances which included communists and were set up to resist the advance of fascism.

- A popular-front government gained power in Spain in 1936, and this caused the military uprising which led to the Spanish Civil War
- A popular-front government under *Blum* governed France in 1936, but collapsed because of differences within it on how to react to the Spanish Civil War.

populist: a political term used to describe a policy or person seeking to please the people. Use of the term often involves the idea of pandering to popular prejudices.

Port Arthur: a Pacific port, control of which was desired by both Russia and Japan. It was taken from China by the Japanese in 1895, but pressure from the European powers forced them to relinquish it. In 1898, the Chinese leased Port Arthur to Russia. In 1904, after Russia had proved slow to discuss the problem of zones of influence in Manchuria and Korea, Japan started the *Russo–Japanese War* by launching a surprise attack on the port which, after a long siege, was forced to surrender. At the Treaty of *Portsmouth* (USA) which concluded the war, Port Arthur was handed over to Japan.

Portsmouth (USA), Treaty of: a treaty of 1905 between Japan and Russia. It was arbitrated by the USA and ended the *Russo–Japanese War* of 1904–05, with the Russians forced to concede territory including *Port Arthur*, effectively ending their dream of dominating Korea and Manchuria.

Portugal: a republic since 1910. A military coup in 1926 led to General Carmona becoming first prime minister and then president. Real power rested with the finance minister, Antonio *Salazar*, who became prime minister in 1932. Salazar ruled as a dictator until 1968, favoring right-wing policies and supported by the conservative elements in the state, particularly the Catholic Church. Portugal supported the Allies in the First World War and remained neutral in the second. Until the 1970s, Portugal was an imperial power with colonies in Africa, India and China, and devoted much of its resources to retaining its imperial possessions. In 1961, however, a brief military action by India enabled it to seize Goa, and in 1974, this time after prolonged guerrilla warfare, Portugal had to grant independence to its southern African colonies of Angola and Mozambique. Its one remaining imperial possession, Macao, reverts to China in 1999.

Potemkin Mutiny: a mutiny in 1905 on board the Russian Black Sea battleship POTEMKIN. Excited by the rash of protests and public disorder which made up the *Revolution of 1905*, the sailors, protesting against appalling conditions aboard ship, seized control and, after killing some of their officers, shelled the port of Odessa. Tsardom was very dependent on the loyalty of the armed forces, and this mutiny was potentially a most serious development. However, mutinies on other ships were quickly suppressed and the army stayed loyal when the tsar promised improved pay and conditions. The Potemkin mutineers had to flee to Romania. Later, the film BATTLESHIP POTEMKIN, directed by the Soviet film-maker Eisenstein, occupied as important a place in the history of the cinema as the original mutiny had done in the build-up of opposition to tsardom.

Potsdam Conference: a conference of the Allies held outside Berlin in July–August 1945 after the defeat of Germany in the Second World War. It followed on from the *Yalta Conference* and was called both to decide on future Allied policies and to arrange peace settlements ending the war. Stalin represented the Soviet Union, President Truman the USA, and Churchill Britain – until after the British general election, when he was replaced by the Labour prime minister, Attlee. The conference agreed:

- to Polish and Soviet administration of German territory in the east
- to the forcible transfer of the German population out of these areas
- to confirm the agreement reached at *Yalta* that free elections would be held to provide a government for Poland
- to set up a council of ministers to arrange a peace treaty with, and to set up and supervise the future government of, Germany.

In practice:

- the German lands to the east were absorbed into Poland, an outcome not accepted by West Germany until Brandt came to an agreement with the Poles in 1972
- Soviet influence in Poland ensured that a communist government took over there
- the future government of Germany became based on the four separate *zones of occupation* by the Allied military forces
- the final arrangements for Eastern Europe had to reflect the overwhelming power of the Soviet Union in the region, following on from its liberation by the Red Army.

Many issues had not been fully resolved at Potsdam, and disputes later arose over the future of Poland and Germany. Within two years, these differences had led to the onset of the Cold War.

Poujade, Pierre: the 1950s organizer of the French Poujadist movement. This was largely an alliance of small businessmen who resented the taxation policies of the *Fourth French Republic.* The Poujadists, who held far-right-wing views, won 52 National Assembly seats in the 1956 election but then faded away quite rapidly. They were an indication of the political instabilities which afflicted the Fourth Republic's short-lived governments.

Prague: the capital of the republic of Czechoslovakia. It was occupied by Nazi Germany in March 1939, and at the end of the Second World War, was the last city in Europe to be freed from Nazi occupation.

Prague Spring: a brief period of liberal reform in communist *Czechoslovakia* in 1968. It followed intellectual criticism of the regime of *Novotný* and student protests against it. *Dubček* formed a reforming government which promised to introduce personal freedoms and multi-party politics but, despite his assurances that Czechoslovakia would remain in the Warsaw Pact, troops from the Soviet Union and other pact countries occupied Prague and ousted the reform government. The episode led to the Soviet Union promulgating the *Brezhnev Doctrine.*

Pravda: a Bolshevik newspaper founded in 1912. First Molotov and then Stalin were its editors after the February Revolution of 1917. It became the official paper of the central committee of the Communist Party of the Soviet Union.

Presidium of the Supreme Soviet: elected by the Supreme Soviet of the USSR, and representing it when that body was not in session. Its chairman acted as the president of the Soviet Union, but in practice had little real power.

Primo de Rivera, Miguel: Spanish dictator, 1923–30. After the end of the First World War, there was much civil unrest in Spain, fomented by an active communist party. In 1923, Primo de Rivera carried out a coup and, backed by the king, Alfonso XIII, the army, the Catholic Church and the landowners, he established an authoritarian right-wing government under which:

- many opponents of his regime were imprisoned
- the conservative nature of his support prevented him from carrying out urgently needed reforms, especially in agriculture
- he had limited success in relieving the considerable distress brought about by the Great Depression
- as unrest increased, he lost the support of the army.

Having survived three attempted coups, ill health forced him to resign in 1930 and he died in the same year. The Spanish monarchy outlived him by only a few months. In 1933, his son founded the *Falange Party.*

Princip, Gavrilo: assassin of Archduke *Franz Ferdinand,* heir to the throne of Austria-Hungary, and his wife in *Sarajevo* on 28 June 1914. He was a Bosnian member of a murder squad trained in Serbia by Colonel *Dimitrievitch,* the organizer of a Serbian secret terrorist society "The Black Hand," though not himself a member of the society. These connections led to the Austrian demands against Serbia to curb terrorism which led to the outbreak of the *First World War.*

prison camps (Russian): set up in Siberia by both the tsarist and the Bolshevik regimes to remove the threat from potential dissidents. Under Lenin, they were operated by the *Cheka*. Under *Stalin*, they housed millions and were often linked to forced labor. Conditions were almost invariably brutal and degrading.

prisoners of war (Second World War): the early German victories made the Germans the main holders of prisoners of war. Despite conventions negotiated by the Red Cross, many were treated very badly. The worst treatment was that of Soviet prisoners, of whom there were some 5 million, only 1 million of whom were found alive by the liberating Allied armies in 1945. Some of these 5 million became collaborators, others simply disappeared, and perhaps 2 million died in the camps from disease and starvation. A deliberate policy of exterminating these prisoners was clearly practiced and was based on Nazi notions of racial inferiority. The policy also represented a colossal waste of potential labor, and is an example of how inefficient the Nazi state could be, even under crucial wartime pressures. Except in relatively few cases of individual sadism, the treatment of British and US prisoners, whose numbers were far fewer, was comparatively mild and, coming more under the eye of Red Cross visitors to the prisoner-of-war camps, was more in accord with the *Geneva Conventions* on the treatment of prisoners.

privatization: the policy of denationalizing state-owned concerns, usually by selling shares in them on the stock market. Its main proponents were the post-1979 Thatcher governments in Britain, but it was then also widely copied by other Western countries. In Eastern Europe, the collapse of the communist economies led to a similar process. Privatization met the political feeling that the management of economic enterprises was not a legitimate state function, and it also provided large sums of money for the governments which undertook it.

proletariat: the working class. A common term in *Marxism*, where it is contrasted with the *bourgeoisie*, or middle class.

propaganda: publicity intended to spread ideas or information. It is often used dismissively to imply that the publicity has shown scant regard for the truth. In the 1930s, the term "propaganda machine" was used to describe the efforts in Nazi Germany and Stalin's Soviet Union to win public support, regardless of the truth. The efforts of *Goebbels* in Germany were particularly notorious. A common technique was to identify an enemy, for example "Jew" or "Bolshevik," and arouse group loyalty by accusations against, and verbal abuse of, these outsiders. The need for propaganda grew as it became important to win the support of the masses for political ends. The effectiveness and scale of propaganda was much extended in the early twentieth century as radio and film grew in importance, and particularly so when these media were under the control of totalitarian states. A negative form of propaganda also arose from censorship of unacceptable views.

proportional representation: an electoral system in which each party is allocated parliamentary seats in proportion to the total number of votes received by its candidates. The constitution of the *Weimar Republic* provided a system of proportional representation for *Reichstag* elections, thus ensuring fair representation of smaller parties, but also necessitating coalition governments when no one party could obtain a majority of the seats. Most Continental parliaments are elected by some system of proportional representation, which can accommodate the representation of minority parties more fairly than the British "first past the post" system. The results of elections under proportional representation often lead, in the absence of a clear one-party victory, to the formation of coalition governments, and have been cited as a major cause of government instability in, for example:

- Italy prior to Mussolini's seizure of power in 1922, and again after 1945
- Weimar Germany from 1930 to 1933
- the Fourth French Republic from 1946 to 1958.

protectionism: a system of tariffs to protect home industries or agriculture. In the late nineteenth century, Britain pursued a *free trade* policy, with open markets, but Continental European countries and the USA imposed tariffs to protect infant industries in their own home markets. Britain abandoned total free trade in favor of *imperial preference,* a form of protectionism, after the First World War. By 1939, international trade was dominated by protectionism which, it was later argued, slowed down the recovery from the Great Depression. The setting up of the UN agency *GATT* in 1948 was in an attempt to lower tariff barriers and other obstacles to trade. Protectionist tendencies, however, survived, causing tension between the European Community and the USA, and also with Japan, in the late 1980s and 1990s.

protectorate: protectorship of a weak state by a stronger one. So, for example, the republic of Slovakia became a protectorate of Nazi Germany in 1939.

Provisional Government: the government of Russia after the abdication of the tsar in March 1917 (the *February Revolution*) until the coup by the Bolsheviks in November 1917. At first, Prince *Lvov* led the government and saw its main task as running the country until a new constitution could be agreed (hence its "provisional" nature). Its existence was from the start precarious because:

TIMELINE: RUSSIA 1917

The February Revolution (old-style calendar)

March 8–10 Riots and strikes in Petrograd supported by troops

March 12 *Duma* formed *Provisional Government* under Prince *Lvov*

March 15 Tsar *Nicholas II* abdicated. His brother refused the throne, abdicating in favor of the Provisional Government

April *Lenin* and other *Bolsheviks* returned from exile abroad to Petrograd

June–July Military offensive defeated after initial success. Russians driven back

July Bolshevik attempt to seize power in Petrograd failed
Lenin fled to Finland
Kerensky replaced Lvov as prime minister

September *Kornilov* right-wing coup defeated. This weakened the Provisional Government but restored Bolshevik fortunes

October Bolsheviks gained control of the Petrograd Soviet

The October Revolution (old-style calendar)

November 6 Bolshevik revolution, ordered by Lenin and executed by *Trotsky,* seized control of key points in Petrograd

November 7 All-Russian Congress of Soviets met for first time and approved the Bolshevik seizure of power

---

- its power was limited by the existence of the *Petrograd Soviet*, formed by workers and soldiers, whose control of the rail, telegraph and postal services meant that the Provisional Government was powerless without its cooperation. From May 1917, six members of the Soviet became government ministers, and this increased its influence
- it faced growing disorder in the countryside as peasants seized the property of the landowning class. The government had recognized their right to the land but could not set up an official land-redistribution scheme without provoking mass desertions from the army by conscripted peasants anxious for their share
- it felt committed to continuing the war, and indeed hoped for victory and land annexations in Eastern Europe. In July 1917, the army suffered major defeats, and as war shortages increased, the war became more unpopular with the working class, the latter increasingly organized into *soviets* and also open to Bolshevik propaganda.

Kerensky replaced Lvov in July 1917, but the policies and problems remained the same. His government:

- put down a poorly organized Bolshevik coup in the *July Days*, when Lenin had to flee into exile in Finland
- at first seemed to encourage a right-wing coup, led in August by General *Kornilov*, which intended to restore order in Petrograd but which would also have checked the power of the Petrograd Soviet
- then relied on the Petrograd Soviet to organize the resistance to Kornilov by the working class and the common soldiers, the latter having crucially refused to obey Kornilov's orders.

This second coup undermined the reputation of the government and increased the support for the Bolsheviks which had been at a low ebb after the July Days. In a well-organized conspiracy carried out by a relatively small group of plotters, they seized control of Petrograd in November (the *October Revolution*). The Provisional Government in the end collapsed without a struggle, with Kerensky unable to rally support to reverse the Bolshevik seizure of power.

Provisional IRA: an *urban guerrilla* group committed, particularly after 1970, to the use of force to secure the union of Northern Ireland (*Ulster*) with the Republic of Ireland in an independent state free of any British presence. *Sinn Féin* is its political wing. The IRA ceasefire of July 1997 enabled Sinn Féin to participate in the Northern Ireland peace talks.

Prussia: the kingdom of Prussia, under its chancellor, Bismarck, was the key state in the creation of the Second German Empire in 1871. Its king became the first kaiser. In 1918, it simply became one state within the Weimar Republic. At the Treaty of Versailles, East and West Prussia were divided from each other in order to create the Polish Corridor. After the Second World War, much territory which had formed part of Prussia was incorporated into Poland and the German population was expelled.

Pugwash Manifesto: issued in 1955. It was a protest, by eminent scientists including *Einstein*, at the dangers for humanity of the developing nuclear arms race.

puppet government: see *puppet state*

puppet state: a state allowed to retain a pretence of independence, but which is in practice controlled by an outside power. The term is also used of governments: the French *Vichy* regime, or *Quisling*'s regime in Norway, retaining a façade of power, were puppet governments of Nazi Germany.

Putilov Works: a vast steelworks built up in St. Petersburg in the late nineteenth century. It was the backbone of the Russian armaments industry. The thousands of workers, who labored and lived in appalling conditions, were an obvious target for left-wing revolutionary propaganda and provided recruits for anti-tsarist agitations, culminating in the 1917 *February Revolution* which overthrew Tsar Nicholas II.

putsch: an attempt at a political revolution. It is a German term equivalent to the French "coup d'état."

Q

Quisling, Vidkun: prime minister of German-occupied Norway, 1942–45. In 1933, he founded the Norwegian Fascist Party. He visited Hitler only months before the German invasion of Norway in April 1940 and assisted him in the planning. After the invasion, he served as head of a German puppet government and, when Norway was liberated by the Allies, was charged with treason and executed. His name has passed into general use as the term used to describe someone who gives support to an enemy occupying his country.

R

R101 Disaster: the crash of the British airship in northern France in 1930. It brought to an end British interest in developing this type of craft.

radar: a system by which radio instruments can detect distant objects in the air. It was the invention in 1935 of a British scientist, *Watson-Watt*, and it eventually confounded all the pessimists and airforce authorities who had accepted the fashionable 1930s view that the bomber would always get through. By 1940 and the *Battle of Britain*, a radar chain scanned the approaches across the English Channel and was an invaluable asset to Britain in winning the battle.

radical: a political term for someone advocating far-reaching reforms or revolutionary changes.

Radek, Karl: a Soviet communist leader. He:

- accompanied Lenin across Germany to Russia after the 1917 *February Revolution*
- assisted at the Treaty of *Brest-Litovsk*
- took part in the 1919 *Spartacist* rising in Berlin
- returned to Moscow and was a leading member of the *Comintern*
- was exiled to Siberia in 1928 for supporting Trotsky and was reinstated after apologizing for his errors.

In 1936, Radek and Bukharin drafted the new constitution of the Soviet Union shortly before they were arrested at the beginning of the Great Purge. Radek was, in 1937, one of the accused in the second Stalinist *show trial*, and was sent to a prison camp, where he disappeared, probably dying in 1939. His later career neatly illustrates the fate of those who were seen by Stalin as potential enemies.

radio: a popular medium of light entertainment in the 1920s and 1930s. It also provided a useful avenue of propaganda for dictators like Hitler and Mussolini. It was an invaluable medium for the transmission of news and for maintaining morale in Britain during the Second World War, when services to Nazi-occupied Europe were also set up.

Rákosi, Mátyás: prime minister of Hungary, 1952–53. He:

- helped, after the Second World War, to establish the hard-line communist government in Hungary
- remained the strong man of the regime even after he resigned as prime minister.

Soviet pressure, because of growing opposition to him in Hungary, led him to step down just months before the 1956 *Hungarian Revolution*, which his political rigidity and fierce suppression of any sign of dissent had done so much to provoke. He died in 1971.

Rapacki Plan: a 1957 proposal by the Polish foreign minister, Adam Rapacki, to the UN General Assembly. It was to create a nuclear-free zone by banning nuclear weapons from East and West Germany, Czechoslovakia and Poland. Khrushchev welcomed the plan, but the Western powers rejected it in 1958, arguing that it would leave the Soviet Union still commanding a vastly superior amount of conventional forces in the region.

Rapallo: a treaty of 1922 between Weimar Germany and the Soviet Union. Each party:

- agreed not to pursue financial or territorial claims against the other arising from the First World War
- agreed to cooperate economically
- through secret clauses, arranged for the training of German troops in the Soviet Union in defiance of the Treaty of Versailles.

The treaty marked an end to the diplomatic isolation of the Soviet Union following the Bolshevik takeover of 1917, and was a first step out of post-war diplomatic isolation for the Weimar Republic. Its secret terms also indicate how even democratic Germans resented, and were determined to evade, the humiliating terms of the Versailles Treaty. In 1926, relations between the two countries were further strengthened by the *Berlin Treaty*.

rapprochement: a resumption of friendly relations between previously hostile states.

Rasputin, Grigori: a Russian holy man with great influence over Tsarina *Alexandra* in the last years of tsardom in Russia. His influence over her came from his ability to alleviate the heir to the throne's hemophilia. After the tsar left the court to lead the army, Rasputin's closeness to the tsarina created a public scandal. Together, they dominated the government and dismissed reforming ministers. Their influence on the war effort was disastrous, denying the army desperately needed supplies and destroying civilian morale. Rasputin's drunkenness and the sexual scandals with which he was associated led to his being murdered by court nobles in 1916.

Rathenau, Walther: a German-Jewish industrialist and politician. From 1914, he took the first steps towards planning Germany's war economy, reorganizing its industries and ensuring the supply of raw materials for the war effort, and he has been described as "one of the great men of the war." As foreign minister in the Weimar Republic in 1922, he negotiated the Treaty of *Rapallo* with the Soviet Union. He was assassinated by right-wing extremists later in the same year in one of many such episodes to plague the early years of the Weimar Republic.

rationing: a system permitting an official allowance of food etc. in times of shortage. It was introduced in Britain during the course of the First World War as *U-boat* attacks on merchant shipping created food shortages. It was considered important for wartime morale that people were seen to be treated equally, and so rationing was again in place in Britain from the outset of the Second World War.

reactionary: a political term for someone opposed to progress or reform, or backward-looking.

Red Army: the army of the Soviet Union. It was formed by Trotsky in 1917 and under his command defeated the White Russian forces in the *Russian Civil War*. Trotsky employed ex-tsarist officers to command his untrained peasant troops, and attached Bolshevik political commissars to units to ensure loyalty to the revolution. Many of the Red Army's officers were removed in Stalin's 1930s purges, and it did badly in the war of 1939–40 against the Finns. However, it was much reorganized and better equipped prior to the German invasion, and in 1942 the political commissars were removed to provide a clearer command structure. Nevertheless, it was forced to retreat on all its fronts in the first months of the Second World War campaign on the *Eastern Front*. Lines were stabilized outside Leningrad, Moscow and *Stalingrad*, though with tremendous loss of men. The victory at Stalingrad at the end of 1942 marked the beginning of the Red Army's long and bitter, but victorious, reconquest of Eastern Europe through to the ruins of Berlin.

After the end of the war, units of the Red Army remained as garrisons in the Soviet Union's satellite states in Eastern Europe, most visibly in the divided city of Berlin. From 1979, it fought in *Afghanistan*, on behalf of the communist government in Kabul, against native Islamic forces but, despite superior fire power and air-force superiority, it was unable to defeat the guerrilla forces. The army withdrew, none of its objectives achieved, in 1989. Its experience in Afghanistan, alongside that of the USA in Vietnam, indicated that there was a limit to what the military power of even the greatest nations could achieve in political terms.

Red Army Faction: an alternative name for the *Baader-Meinhof Gang*.

Red Brigade: an Italian left-wing terrorist group. They were a loosely organized gang of assassins, bombers and kidnappers, who abducted and killed the ex-prime minister, *Moro*, in 1978.

Red Cross: founded in 1859 to help wounded soldiers. It set up its headquarters in traditionally neutral Switzerland.

- In 1906, its work was extended, under the *Geneva Convention*, to take in war at sea and to protect the victims of shipwrecks
- In 1929, its work was further extended to include the welfare of prisoners of war
- In 1949, it took responsibility for the welfare of civilians caught up in war.

Many Allied prisoners in the Second World War owed their well-being to the aid from, and the inspections carried out by, the Red Cross. After the Second World War, the Red Cross became involved on an increasing scale in general relief work, usually outside Europe. However, it also had an important presence in the various conflicts which erupted from 1990 as Yugoslavia disintegrated.

redemption payments: payments by Russian peasants for the land they had obtained after the end of serfdom in 1861. Such payments were often a charge on the village community (the *mir*), and peasants were often prevented from leaving for the towns lest a heavier burden of payment fall on those remaining. Despite later easing of the burden, the payments remained a serious grievance and caused peasant unrest as late as 1905. The payments were brought to an end in 1907 as part of *Stolypin*'s attempts to promote economic reform and social stability by creating a class of prosperous landowning peasants.

referendum: the referring of a particular issue to the entire electorate for decision by a direct vote. It is commonly used to decide issues in Switzerland, but only in special circumstances in most parliamentary democracies. In a referendum in 1935, the inhabitants of the Saar region voted for its restoration to Germany, a process which was repeated in 1955. The president's right to consult the people via a referendum was an important feature built into the constitution of the *Fifth French Republic* by de Gaulle.

refugees: people fleeing from political or religious oppression or danger. There have been many mass movements of refugees in the twentieth century:

- thousands of Belgian refugees fled to Britain when in 1914 the Germans invaded their country
- tens of thousands of Russians fled from Bolshevik rule
- Armenians and Greeks fled from the Turkish advance in the 1920s
- Spanish opponents of Franco fled to France in the last stages of the Civil War
- Jewish refugees fled from anti-Semitism in Germany and Austria in the 1930s.

All of these were dwarfed by the mass movements of civilian populations across Europe that resulted from the campaigns of the Second World War. The redrawing of frontiers in post-war Eastern Europe resulted in the forced expulsion of native populations, including:

- nearly 2 million Ukrainians and inhabitants of the three Baltic Republics, who tried to flee westwards before 1944–45 to escape from the path of the advancing Red Army; an unknown number did not succeed
- Poles who were moved from what had been eastern Poland across into what had been eastern Germany
- the entire German population of Danzig, which was expelled when the town became the Polish port of Gdansk
- the 3 million German refugees who were forcibly removed from areas taken into Poland
- the German population of what had been the Sudetenland, which was forcibly expelled when that area was taken back into the re-formed state of Czechoslovakia
- the 3 million German refugees who settled in the one-time Danish provinces of Schleswig-Holstein, and who were able to swamp a referendum there and ensure that the two provinces voted to rejoin Germany.

In total, between 7 and 10 million Germans were forced out or simply fled westwards from lands annexed by the Czechs, Poles and Russians. It was well into the 1950s before these European population movements ended, as political stability and economic prosperity returned. The refugee problem then became a largely non-European problem involving countries of the Third World, until the collapse of Yugoslavia into ethnic violence in the 1990s made the plight of refugees once more a European issue.

regent: a person administering a state during the childhood/youth of a monarch. In an extreme example, the mother of Alfonso XIII of Spain ruled on his behalf as regent from 1886 to 1918.

regime: the system of government, as in "the Nazi regime" or "the tsarist regime."

Reich: a term used to describe the German Empire.

- The First Reich was the medieval Holy Roman Empire
- The Second Reich ran from 1870 to 1918 (see *German Second Empire*)
- The Third Reich is the common reference to the Nazi regime from 1933 to 1945, though the Nazis stopped using the term in the early 1930s (see *German Third Empire*).

Reichsrat: the upper house of the Weimar Republic Parliament. Its members represented the various German states, such as Bavaria and Prussia.

Reichstag: the lower, but more influential, house of the German Parliament under the German Second Empire and the Weimar Republic. Under the Weimar Republic, it was elected on a wide franchise, with membership allocated by proportional representation. After the initial meeting in Weimar, it met in Berlin.

Reichstag Fire: on 27 February 1933, the German Parliament building was burnt down. Hitler, who had been chancellor for a month, blamed the fire on the communists, and used it to order the arrest of communist members of the Parliament. Some suspected that the fire was the work of the Nazis themselves, but it was in fact started by a young Dutchman, Martinus van der *Lubbe*, acting alone. Nazi propaganda about the fire, however, persuaded most Germans, including non-Nazi members of the Reichstag, to accept that more powers were needed to combat the communist threat, and helped Hitler in March 1933 to push through the *Enabling Act* granting him full legislative and executive powers for four years. This act provided the basis for the imposition of the Nazi dictatorship, and was retained until 1945.

Reichswehr: the Weimar Republic army. Hitler changed its name to the *Wehrmacht* in 1935.

relief agencies: the development, since the Second World War, of organized charitable activity on behalf of the victims of war, oppression and natural disaster. A notable example is the Oxford Committee for Famine Relief (Oxfam), founded in 1942.

reparations: payments imposed on states defeated in war by the victors in order to compensate them for the cost of the war and to make amends for the damage done by fighting the war. The best known example is the imposition of reparations on Germany by the Treaty of *Versailles* which cast a shadow over the stability of the Weimar Republic. Reparations:

- were based on the principle, enshrined in the *war-guilt clause*, that Germany had been responsible for starting the war
- were fixed, not as part of the treaty but by a Reparations Committee in 1921, at £6,600 million
- were reduced by both the *Dawes Plan* and the *Young Plan*
- were abandoned in 1932 in the aftermath of the economic dislocation caused by the Great Depression
- were denounced by Hitler in 1933 when he made it clear that no further payments would be made.

Rentenmark: a special Weimar German currency. It:

- was introduced in 1923 by *Schacht* to combat the *hyperinflation* hitting the economy
- had its value guaranteed by a mortgage on all land and industry
- succeeded in restoring public confidence in the value of money
- was the basis of Weimar Germany's economic recovery in the late 1920s.

resistance, the: the popular term during the Second World War for opposition groups to the Nazi regime. They existed:

- in Germany itself from the mid-1930s; during the war, Admiral *Canaris* led the most important group
- in France, where the resistance, or *Maquis*, was often organized and supplied from London; in 1943, it liberated Corsica, and in 1944 did much to hamper German resistance to the Allied invasion
- in Greece, as the *ELAS* fighters
- in Yugoslavia, as communist partisans led by *Tito* and *chetniks* who supported the monarchy
- in Poland, which had probably the largest resistance movement in Europe. It was distrustful of the advancing Red Army, and its efforts ended in the tragedy of the *Warsaw Rising*
- in most other occupied countries, including Belgium, Holland, Denmark and Norway.

The French resistance, like that in other countries, particularly Greece and Yugoslavia, was often deeply divided between communist and non-communist groups, though until Hitler attacked the Soviet Union in 1941, the communists had often stood aloof from the struggle. Resistance groups, often referred to as *partisans*, everywhere practiced sabotage of military and other installations. They acted as spies, sending strategic information by radio to the Allies, and helped escaping prisoners of war. The resistance in Western Europe was coordinated by the British Special Operations Executive (the SOE), though after the war the effectiveness of its role was questioned.

results of the First World War: see *First World War*, results of the war

results of the Second World War: see *Second World War*, results of the war

revisionist: a charge often brought against dissidents in communist countries. It indicated that the accused had deviated from the true Marxist path.

Revolution of 1905: unrest and uprisings in Russia triggered by the events of *Bloody Sunday* and following defeat in the Russo–Japanese War. Strikes, street disorders and peasant uprisings spread across Russia after the *Bloody Sunday* massacre in January 1905, and included the *Potemkin Mutiny*. Calm seemed to have been restored by the summer, but the strikes resumed in the autumn, starting with a printers' strike in Moscow, until Nicholas II's *October Manifesto* brought renewed calm by the end of the year. The tsar's government re-established control because:

- the army remained loyal
- the agitators found it impossible to arouse the peasants to fight the army
- once the revolution was over, the government savagely repressed those who had opposed it.

The setting up of *soviets* by industrial workers in many towns and cities had at the time provided only weak leadership for the protests, but was to be very important in the future. Even in 1905, it had required an artillery bombardment to break the resistance of the Moscow soviets. Russia's revolutionary leaders were slow to appreciate the significance of the events of 1905; even Lenin and Trotsky returned from exile too late in the day to influence events. In this sense, there was no revolution but simply a series of outbursts of discontent which never found the leadership needed to be effective against the tsar's government and army. The new soviets pointed the way forward for the tsar's opponents.

Reynaud, Paul: prime minister of France for three months in 1940. He had to announce the French defeat, and then handed over power to *Pétain*. He was imprisoned by the Germans during the war. Having held office briefly during the Fourth French Republic, he supported de Gaulle at the inauguration of the fifth. He died in 1966.

Rhine: a river flowing from Switzerland to the North Sea. For an important part of its length, it runs between France and Germany, and the control of lands on each side has frequently raised difficult political issues.

- On the west bank of the river, *Alsace-Lorraine* was part of France until 1870, and was then, after the French military defeat, taken by Germany, only to be restored to France in 1919. During the Second World War, it was again occupied by Germany, but in 1945 reverted once more to being part of France
- On the east bank of the river was the German *Rhineland* which, in 1919, the Allies at the Versailles Treaty insisted should be demilitarized as a condition of its being allowed to stay within Weimar Germany.

During the Second World War, the river did not, in 1945, provide as serious an obstacle to the Allied advance as had been feared, but the symbolism of its crossing, marking the invasion of Germany, was much stressed.

Rhineland: a German province on the east bank of the Rhine bordering France. At the *Versailles* Treaty, it was demilitarized under the direction of the League of Nations, but, in 1936, German troops were sent back into the province by Hitler without any serious attempt by France or the League to stop them. This was cited, by critics of *appeasement*, including *Churchill*, as a classic case of the Western powers feeding Hitler's ambitions by failing to stand up to his demands, and as an early example of the policy of appeasement. Supporters of appeasement saw it at the time as a case of the Germans "moving into their own backyard," an act which could be justified as a rejection of the unfairly harsh terms of the Versailles Treaty.

Ribbentrop, Joachim von: a German Nazi politician. He was a close friend of Hitler, and served as ambassador to Britain from 1936 to 1938, and as foreign minister from 1938 to 1945. His greatest triumph was the negotiation of the 1939 *Nazi–Soviet Pact*. He was condemned at the Nuremberg Trials and executed.

Riefenstahl, Leni: the most famous German film director of the inter-war years. Her major works reflected the Nazi period in which she did her best work.

- TRIUMPH OF THE WILL, in 1936, was a powerful account of the Nazi rally at

Nuremberg, giving one of the most compelling insights into Hitler's public appeal as an orator

- OLYMPIA, in 1938, was her outstanding record of the Berlin Olympics, and its first showing was the highlight of Hitler's birthday celebrations.

Her close links to the Nazi regime caused her to be blacklisted by the Allies until 1952. Her later films never reached the same standard or achieved the same notoriety as her epic work of the Nazi period.

Riga, Treaty of: a 1921 treaty between the Soviet Union and Poland. It ended the *Russo–Polish War*, with Poland gaining much land to the east. These gains were reversed in 1939, when the Soviet Union reoccupied the area in military action following the *Nazi–Soviet Pact*, only for it to be overrun in 1941 by the German army in Operation *Barbarossa*. The victories of the Red Army against the German army in the later stages of the Second World War ensured that the territory lost at the Riga Treaty was then restored to the Soviet Union.

right, or right wing: a term used politically to describe individuals and parties in favor of tradition, order, continuity and authority. Its precise meaning depends on the political context within which it is used. Right-wing in a parliamentary democracy could indicate very different views from those indicated by its use in a communist state or a dictatorship.

Rocco Law: Italian legislation of 1926. The law arranged to set up fascist syndicates to organize workers and employers, and for corporations to negotiate between the two. It was 1934 before the corporations came into existence, when they came to represent many branches of Italian economic life and, by 1939, were the basis of the *corporate state.*

Rodzianko, Mikhail: a Russian politician. He was a landowner, and a member of the conservative *Octobrists*, who became president of both the third and fourth *Dumas*. In February 1917, he telegraphed to Nicholas II that there was chaos in Petrograd and that a new government should be formed. Nicholas instead dismissed the Duma, and the slide into anarchy accelerated. Rodzianko did not fully accept this dismissal, but kept a provisional committee in being, and from this emerged the Provisional Government. Rodzianko next urged Nicholas to abdicate. These actions, by a right-wing politician, illustrate the extent to which, at the end, the tsarist government had lost the confidence of even its traditional supporters, and were crucial in the transfer of power from the tsar to the Provisional Government.

Röhm, Ernst: leader of the German *SA*. He was an early friend of Hitler, and his support had been vital to Hitler's rise to power, giving the Nazis control of the streets. Once in power, he and his followers wished to see a social and economic revolution to complement the political one. He and the SA were distrusted by the army, whose support Hitler now needed, and on 30 June 1934 Röhm and hundreds more members of the SA were killed on Hitler's orders in the *Night of the Long Knives.*

Rokossovsky, Konstantin: a respected Soviet Second World War general. He defended Moscow, surrounded the German armies at Stalingrad and played an important part in the victory at *Kursk.* In 1944, he failed to respond to appeals from the *Warsaw Rising*, allowing the Germans to put it down and so remove possible opposition to the imposition of Soviet-dominated communism in Poland. After the war, he returned to Poland, his birthplace, becoming minister of defense, and in 1956 brutally crushed unrest among the workers. He was made to resign when *Gomulka* became prime minister, and was then recalled to Moscow and worked in the Soviet ministry of defense. He died in 1968.

Romania: from 1947 to 1989, a communist-dominated republic. It had been an independent kingdom since 1878, carved out of the Ottoman Empire. Romania traditionally pursued a pro-German foreign policy, but in 1916, it joined the Allied attack on Austria-Hungary and in consequence doubled its territory at the *Paris Peace Conference.* King *Carol II* imposed a right-wing regime in the 1930s but abdicated when Romania had to surrender land to both Hungary and the Soviet Union following the 1939 *Nazi–Soviet Pact.* Romania joined Hitler's 1941 attack on the Soviet Union but paid a high price when the Red Army rolled back the Germans, losing land to both the Soviet Union and Bulgaria, but then regaining Transylvania from Hungary when it switched sides to support the Soviet advance.

After 1945

A communist government took office, and for the next 40 years Romania was a Soviet satellite, but one following a distinctly independent role, thanks particularly to its long-serving president, *Ceauşescu*, 1967–89. His regime:

- often attracted favorable comment in the West for its independence from the Soviet Union
- was the only member of the Soviet bloc to join the International Monetary Fund
- grew increasingly tyrannical and isolated from the people
- came to reflect its president's ego, from the absurdly monumental architecture of its public buildings to such ruthless decisions as the destruction of all the country's villages, so that the inhabitants were forced into barrack-like communal housing
- had an average standard of living among the lowest in Europe
- had one of Europe's largest secret-police forces, the *Securitate*, which showed scant regard for civil or personal rights.

As the Soviet bloc came under pressure to reform, Romania alone seemed able to resist, but in December 1989 the *Romanian Revolution* occurred, when the military suppression of demonstrations in the east of the country led to strikes and riots in the capital, Bucharest. At first these were brutally suppressed, with hundreds shot, but then the loyalty of the army wavered and finally turned against Ceauşescu, who was captured and shot. A non-communist party, the National Salvation Front, was formed to provide an alternative government, and it won the 1990 election. Many ex-communists were still active in Romanian politics, and the pace of reform, particularly economic reform, was much slower than in other ex-communist states.

Romanian Revolution: the events, at the end of 1989, in the provincial town of Timişoara, the capital, Bucharest, and other towns, when thousands were killed and wounded in popular uprisings against the communist regime of President *Ceauşescu*. He and his wife were captured as they tried to flee the capital at the height of the fighting, and after summary military trial, both were shot.

Romanov: the dynasty ruling Russia from 1613 to February 1917.

Rome: since 1870, the capital of Italy. It was not defended by the Germans in the Second World War and so avoided damage in the bitter fighting of the *Italian Campaign*.

Rome Treaties: two international treaties in 1957 establishing the *European Economic Community* (EEC) and the European Atomic Energy Community (*Euratom*). Signatory countries were Belgium, France, Italy, Luxembourg, The Netherlands and West Germany.

Rommel, Erwin: a German field marshal.

- He commanded troops in the 1940 *blitzkrieg* attack into France
- In 1941, he led the German Afrika Korps in Libya, losing the battle of *El Alamein* when his supply lines became too extended and he had to retreat
- In early 1943, having fought a determined series of defensive battles in the *North Africa Campaign*, he conducted a masterly withdrawal of the bulk of his forces to Italy
- In 1944, he was placed in command of the German defense of Western Europe against the Allied invasion. In this, he was handicapped by interference in strategy by Hitler, who cared little for the notions of strategic retreat and defense in depth.

Rommel was wounded and returned to Germany, where the Gestapo, believing him to have been involved in the *July Plot*, forced him to commit suicide by threatening his family. He is generally regarded as one of the most effective of the Second World War military commanders.

Roosevelt, Franklin Delano: president of the USA, 1933–45. He was personally opposed to the European fascist dictatorships but had to move cautiously in resisting them because of strong isolationist feelings in his country. After the Second World War broke out in 1939, the USA remained neutral, but he gradually increased aid and assistance to Britain, particularly after the defeat of France in 1940. This aid reached the point where the US navy seemed to be deliberately trying to provoke an attack by German submarines in order to provide an excuse for US military action. It was the Japanese attack on the US Pearl Harbor naval base in December 1941 which actually brought the USA into the war, when its declaration of war on Japan was followed by German and Italian declarations of war on the USA. Roosevelt then played a full part in developing and maintaining the artificial anti-Nazi alliance of Britain, the Soviet Union and the USA. His committed view that it was first necessary to defeat Hitler and only then Japan dictated the course of the Allied war effort. He had already met Churchill at sea and issued the *Atlantic Charter*, and he now went on to summit meetings with Churchill at Casablanca, and with Churchill and Stalin at *Tehran* and *Yalta*. He died in 1945, just weeks before the final victory over Germany.

Rosenberg, Alfred: a Nazi administrator of territories occupied in the Second World War. In this role, he became an effective plunderer of art and other treasures. He had earlier earned a reputation for developing a so-called philosophy of Nazism based on crude racial analysis and nostalgia for Germanic folk myths.

He was hanged after trial at Nuremberg.

Ruhr: the heavy industrial region of Germany. It developed rapidly after unification of the country in 1871. The vast defense firm of *Krupp* of Essen was at its heart. It symbolized how the united, industrialized Germany was capable, in the late nineteenth century, of undermining the political balance in Europe. Even after 1918, France remained fearful of the military potential it represented, and in 1923 the French and Belgians occupied the Ruhr when Germany failed to meet its reparations payments. This was met by strikes by the German workforce, and in 1925, under the *Dawes Plan*, the occupation ended. From 1933, Nazi Germany defied the disarmament terms imposed at Versailles and built up its Ruhr armaments industry once more. For this reason, it was the target for very heavy Allied bombing in the later years of the Second World War.

Rundstedt, Gerd von: a German field marshal, regarded by Eisenhower as the most able of the German generals in the Second World War.

- In 1939 and 1940, he commanded troops in the invasions of Poland and France
- In 1941, he led the forces making the southern thrust into the Soviet Union as part of Operation *Barbarossa*. When that offensive stalled, he was dismissed for defying Hitler's orders not to retreat when he wished to regroup his forces to resist a Soviet counter-attack
- From 1942 to 1945, he was commander of German forces in France and was responsible for the *Ardennes* offensive.

Russell, Bertrand: a British philosopher. He was a prominent anti-nuclear activist in the 1950s and 1960s.

Russia: by 1900, a vast empire, autocratically ruled from 1894 by *Nicholas II* of the Romanov dynasty, and stretching from the Baltic Sea to the Pacific.

Events to October 1917

The economy remained backward, despite the reforms of *Witte* and *Stolypin*, and communications poor, despite the completion of the Trans-Siberian Railway in 1904. Ambitions in the Far East were thwarted by defeat in the *Russo–Japanese War*, 1904–05, and Russian support for *Slavs* in Eastern Europe was a source of tension culminating in the outbreak of war in 1914. In the *First World War*, and contrary to later perception, the army did well, though perhaps being too ambitious in moving on to the offensive in order to assist its hard-pressed Western allies. It lost the early battles of Tannenberg and the Masurian Lakes, but defeated the Austrians in 1916. Supply difficulties and government inefficiency undermined the morale of the army in the period leading into the 1917 *February Revolution* and the end of the monarchy. The country was ruled by the *Provisional Government* from the February Revolution onwards until the *October Revolution* established a communist state, the *Soviet Union*.

From 1917

Russia, now geographically more narrowly defined to exclude other regions more properly seen as previously parts of the Russian Empire, became by far the largest of the constituent republics of the Soviet Union. At the end of 1991, with the collapse of the Soviet Union, Russia became an independent state and the most important member of the *Commonwealth of Independent States.*

Russian Civil War: the war from 1918 to 1921 between the forces of the newly installed *Bolsheviks* and the *White Russian* counter-revolutionary forces. The war led to a series of foreign interventions opposing the Bolshevik takeover, including:

- an international force at Murmansk in the north
- French and British forces around the Black Sea and in the Caucasus in the south
- Americans and Japanese at Vladivostock in the Far East.

Nationalist uprisings in European Russia led to the *Baltic Republics* and Finland gaining their independence, and to Poland greatly extending its borders to the east. In Siberia, the counter-revolutionary *Kolchak* used released Czech prisoners to seize control of stretches of the Trans-Siberian Railway, and after his murder these forces were led by *Denikin,* who fought on in the south until 1920. The Bolsheviks, despite at times being hard pressed to survive, gained the initiative and were eventually victorious because:

- they used the *Cheka* in the areas they controlled for the ruthless persecution of any possible traitors
- they harnessed the total resources of the areas they commanded through the policy of *war communism*
- of the creation and the organization of the *Red Army* by *Trotsky*
- of the ruthless suppression of the 1921 *Kronstadt Mutiny*
- of the total inability of their enemies to combine effectively together
- of the failure of the White Russians to attract the support of the mass of the people through any proposals for economic and social reform.

The foreign powers, disappointed in their hopes of a quick victory, withdrew, and the Bolshevik state was secured.

Russian economy, pre-1914: by Western European standards, the Russian economy was backward and heavily dependent on agriculture. It was not, however, stagnant. It is worthwhile to set out a few sample statistics on Russia to illustrate both these points. Between 1870 and 1910:

- its population more than doubled, from 80 to 170 million
- its rail track increased from 8,000 to 47,000 miles
- its coal output rose from less than 1 million tons to 25 million tons
- its pig-iron production rose from 0.3 to 3.5 million tons, and its steel production from 0.2 to 3.3 million tons.

Much of this increase in industrial production came about after 1890 behind heavy tariff barriers on foreign imports introduced in the 1890s by *Witte,* with the textile industry dominant and accounting for 40 percent of industrial output. Foreign investment was important to industrial growth, and its importance increased after Witte, in 1897, put the currency on the *gold standard.* By 1914, foreign investors owned one-third of Russia's industrial capacity.

The production figures need to be set in an international context:

- the 1910 production figures above can be set against those of Germany's production in the same year, which amounted to 222 million tons of coal,

RUSSIAN ECONOMIC GROWTH PRE-1914

	Coal	Petroleum	Iron ore	Steel
		In thousands of tons		
1890	6,010	3,864	1,736	378
1895	9,100	6,935	2,851	879
1900	16,160	10,684	6,001	2,216
1905	18,670	8,310	4,976	2,266
1910	25,430	11,283	5,742	3,314

15 million tons of pig iron and 13 million tons of steel
- in 1910, only 30 percent of Russian production was industrial, compared to 75 percent of Britain's and 70 percent of Germany's.

Industry and transport

Russian heavy industries were often centered on vast factories like the *Putilov Works* in St. Petersburg, and, with primitive technology, were very labor-intensive. The main industrial areas were around St. Petersburg, in and around Moscow, in Poland and in the Donbas region in the south. The country was so vast that transport inefficiencies were always a drag on economic growth.

Rail growth slowed before 1914, but the *Trans-Siberian Railway*, instigated by Witte, stood as one of the world's great engineering feats. Russia in 1914 had the world's second-largest rail network, with 38,000 miles of track, dwarfed of course by the USA's 248,000 miles. Roads between towns were generally bad, and most of Russia's international trade was carried in foreign ships.

Trade and finance

Foreign trade also grew dramatically in the early twentieth century. Exports were largely of agricultural produce, often on such a scale that grain shortages were a frequent occurrence at home, and imports were largely of industrial goods. Germany was Russia's main trading partner. Much of the capital which financed industry and trade came from abroad, one-third of it from France, for it was not just the tsarist government that was in debt to Western financiers, and so much of the profit arising from economic activity was also siphoned off abroad. Russian reformers, like Witte, were concerned that Russia might simply become a market for goods from the Western industrial powers and that this would inevitably affect its political power and status.

Agriculture

Agriculture, the dominant economic activity, was by Western standards desperately backward. Population growth kept the Russian peasants poor, and landholdings, despite *Stolypin's* ambitious reforms, were often too small to be economic, or to allow for improved techniques. Nevertheless, farm yields improved steadily in the years to 1914, with 1913 providing a bumper harvest.

In summary:

- the internal social and political problems related to industrial and urban growth were of great concern to the tsarist government, providing fertile ground for opposition to the inflexible and autocratic regime. Even without a war, it seems probable that they would have resulted in some sort of crisis for the regime

- the economic growth and development of the previous decades was interrupted by the outbreak of war in 1914, and it is idle, if intriguing, to speculate on what might have happened to the economy if that had not occurred
- the 1917 *October Revolution* and the establishment of the communist state meant that capitalist economic development was at an end, and Russia embarked on a quite different route to developing its vast resources and feeding its population.

(On the development of the Russian economy pre-1914, see also the entries on *Witte* and *Stolypin*.)

Russian revolutions: of 1917. The Russians still operated the "old-style" calendar, so that their so-called *February Revolution* took place in early March in terms of the Gregorian calendar in general use elsewhere. This revolution occurred when strikes in Petrograd were supported by troops, and it led to the abdication of Tsar Nicholas II. The Provisional Government under Lvov and then Kerensky ruled until November 1917, when the *October Revolution* brought the Bolsheviks to power.

Russo–Japanese War: a war fought in the Far East in 1904–05. The war occurred because:

- of Russian dreams of expansion into Manchuria, which had been given a new reality by the building of the Trans-Siberian railway, completed in 1904
- Russian troops had moved into Korea, and in 1900 Russia had occupied all of Manchuria, taking advantage of the weakness of the Chinese Empire
- Japan also had ambitions in Korea, and was emboldened to pursue these by its 1902 defensive alliance with Britain
- Nicholas II ignored Japanese requests for the Russians to leave Korea and was slow to enter into negotiations with them.

In 1904, the Japanese attacked the Russian *Port Arthur* and drove the Russian forces back in both Korea and Manchuria, as well as destroying their Pacific fleet. Port Arthur surrendered in January 1905, and in March the Japanese won their biggest victory to date in the battle of Mukden. The biggest humiliation for Russia came when its Baltic fleet, after an eight-month voyage around Africa and across the Indian Ocean, arrived off Korea to be sunk within hours, losing 30 battleships. The tsar accepted US mediation and then the onerous terms of the Treaty of *Portsmouth* (USA). Russian ambitions to gain territory in the Far East were ended. Its defeat in the war helped to spark off the *Revolution of 1905*.

Russo–Polish War, 1919–21: a war started by the Poles to gain land at the expense of the Bolshevik state which was involved in the Russian Civil War. Early Polish successes were met by a Red Army counter-attack which almost captured Warsaw. The *Curzon Line* was proposed as the frontier between the two states in 1920, but this was never ratified. The Poles recovered and, after an armistice, the 1921 Treaty of *Riga* gave them considerable Russian territory which the Soviet

Union only recovered in 1939 as a consequence of the *Nazi–Soviet Pact* and the subsequent invasions.

Rykov, Alexei: a Soviet politician. He was disgraced in 1928 for opposing Stalin's drive against the wealthier peasants and the beginning of the collectivization of agriculture. In 1938, he was accused of treason, in one of the big *show trials* which marked the Great Purge, and, with Bukharin and Yagoda, was executed.

SA: the paramilitary wing of the Nazi Party. The initials are the common abbreviation of Sturmabteilung. From their uniform, the members were also often referred to as the "brownshirts." The SA was established in the early 1920s, and their physical presence played a vital part in Hitler's coming to power, winning the Nazis control of the streets and so turning them into a mass movement. Led by *Röhm*, they were among the most radical and most anti-capitalist members of the Nazi Party, wanting a social and an economic revolution as well as a political one. In 1933, they expected their reward for services rendered but were quickly disillusioned for, in order to consolidate his power, Hitler now needed the support of the army and of the social and political establishment. In June 1934, amid rumors that the monarchy might be restored, the army leaders made it clear to Hitler that unless the unrest in Germany was brought under control they might have to take power. At the same time there were, almost certainly unfounded, fears that the SA were themselves going to carry out a coup. On June 30, Hitler acted in the *Night of the Long Knives*, and the power of the SA was broken in one bloodbath. The organization survived, but it was now firmly within the power structure of the Nazi Party.

Saar, the: a river, on the borders of France and Germany, which gave its name to an industrial region. It was part of Germany from 1871 to 1919 and was then placed under the League of Nations by the Versailles Treaty. Its extensive coalfields went to France as part of the First World War reparations. A 1935 *referendum* led to it again becoming part of Germany. After the Second World War, it was again under French military occupation, but in 1955 a further referendum returned it once more to Germany.

Saint Germain, Treaty of: drawn up at the 1919 *Paris Peace Conference* to deal with matters between the Allies and Austria. The Austro-Hungarian Empire had ended with the abdication of Charles I, so the treaty was with the new republic of Austria.

- Its frontiers were defined to confine it within the Germanic lands of the old empire
- *Anschluss* (union) with Germany was forbidden
- Its army was limited in size to 30,000 men, and reparations were imposed.

St. Petersburg: the capital of tsarist Russia. Its name was changed to Petrograd at the outset of the First World War in 1914, because the original name sounded too Germanic.

Sakharov, Andrei: a Soviet nuclear scientist, peace campaigner and *dissident*. In the early 1950s, he was largely responsible for developing the Soviet hydrogen bomb but, in the 1960s, became critical of the Soviet state. He:

- supported the *Prague Spring* of 1968
- called for democracy in the Soviet Union
- attacked the 1979 Soviet invasion of *Afghanistan*.

He was awarded the Nobel Peace Prize but was put under house arrest by the Soviet authorities. Following the liberalization of Soviet society under Gorbachev, he was elected to the Soviet Congress of People's Deputies in 1989 and there attacked the government of the country, but died suddenly at the end of that year.

Salan, Raoul: a French general. He fought in the unsuccessful war in Indo-China in the early 1950s and was then a ruthless commander of French forces trying to suppress the Algerian nationalists, with equal lack of success. When he realized that de Gaulle was preparing to do a deal granting Algeria independence, he organized the *OAS* to resist this by force. His 1961 Algiers revolt failed, and he was in prison for six years.

Salandra, Antonio: Italian prime minister, 1914–16. He led Italy into the First World War but in 1922 was one of the democratic politicians who, though opposed to Mussolini, totally failed to face up to the threat that he represented. In 1928 he abandoned that opposition and became a senator in the fascist regime, thus helping to legitimize Mussolini's seizure of totalitarian power.

Salazar, Antonio: prime minister of Portugal, 1932–68. In 1933, he turned Portugal into a one-party state on fascist lines. Relying on army support, he then ruled as a virtual dictator.

- His efforts at social and economic reform, copying some of the corporate state ideas of Mussolini, had limited impact, and after the Second World War the Portuguese had the lowest standard of living in non-communist Europe
- His reactionary regime protected the privileges of his supporters, namely the army, the great landowners and the Catholic Church
- His rule was authoritarian, paying scant attention to civil rights. It involved a growing personality cult, with monumental statues to himself and his naming the great bridge across the Tagus the Salazar Bridge
- He kept Portugal neutral in both the Spanish Civil War and the Second World War
- He was strongly committed to maintaining Portugal as an imperial power, involving it in heavy military expenditure in resisting the nationalists in the African colonies of Angola and Mozambique in the 1950s and 1960s.

His illness in 1968 and death in 1970 opened the way for Portugal to begin to shed its increasingly burdensome colonial obligations in Africa, and for the country to move towards a democratic constitution.

Salonika Campaign: a battle front in northern Greece during the First World War. It was opened in 1915 with French aid to the Greeks and to try to help the Serbs against Austria-Hungary. Later, other Allied forces were sent, and the main enemy became Bulgaria. There was, in fact, little fighting until, in 1918, the enemy forces began to crumble for internal reasons. The Allied forces then made an unopposed spectacular advance northwards and eastwards so that in under three months they had reached both the Danube and Istanbul.

SALT (Strategic Arms Limitation Talks): talks between the USA and the Soviet Union to eliminate nuclear competition between them and to reduce stockpiles of nuclear arms. They started in Helsinki in 1969, and by 1972 there was agreement on anti-ballistic missiles and on strategic offensive arms (SALT I). The second stage

(SALT II) began in 1974, and reached agreement in 1979 in a pact to limit the strategic arms race, a pact that was never ratified by the US Senate.

sanctions: penalties or restrictions imposed on nations to put pressure on them, usually short of military action, so that they cease committing acts not acceptable to the international community. Sanctions were a device included in the covenant of the *League of Nations*. Economic sanctions were imposed by the League in 1935 against Italy, when it invaded Ethiopia. Full international cooperation could not be achieved, and sanctions were, for example, never imposed on vital oil and steel supplies, so that they failed to prevent the Italian occupation of the country.

San Francisco Conference: a 1945 international conference which set up the *United Nations Organization.*

Sarajevo: the main city in *Bosnia.*

Pre-1914

It was from 1908 within Austria-Hungary, and the place where, in 1914, the Bosnian student *Princip*, trained and armed by the head of Serbian intelligence, Colonel *Dimitrievitch*, assassinated the heir to the Austrian throne, *Franz Ferdinand*, and his wife. This started the chain of events which led, via Austrian pressure on *Serbia*, to the outbreak of the First World War.

In the 1990s

From 1992 to 1995, it was the scene of savage fighting and atrocities as the Yugoslav Republic disintegrated and Muslim and Croat forces wishing to set up an independent Bosnia were besieged in the city by Serb forces wanting it to be part of a Greater Serbia. A UN-brokered deal in favor of the Bosnians, but with safeguards for the Serb inhabitants, created little confidence among the latter, who withdrew from their suburbs and left the city only after destroying as much of it as they could. In 1998, NATO peacekeeping troops were still stationed in Sarajevo to observe the ceasefire arrangements.

satellite state: a small country controlled by or dependent on another and following its lead. After 1945, countries such as East Germany and Hungary were satellites of the Soviet Union.

Schacht, Hjalmar: a German politician and financier. In the 1920s, as a member of the Democratic Party, he was largely responsible for stabilizing the Weimar currency, and so for the new economic stability enjoyed by the state in the late 1920s. He had been appointed currency commissioner by *Stresemann* to bring the runaway inflation to an end.

- He introduced new notes, *Rentenmark*, their value backed by mortgages on all industrial and agricultural land. These notes, whose value could be relied on, squeezed the other currency issues out of the economy
- He refused to print more Rentenmark, imposing instead severe deflationary policies, cutting salaries, sacking state employees and increasing taxation.

In 1930, Schacht joined the Nazis and was, from 1934 to 1939, minister of economics with responsibility for unemployment and rearmament programs. He was forced to resign in 1939 after urging Hitler to cut spending on arms. In 1944, he was put in a concentration camp for alleged involvement in the *July Plot*. He was tried at Nuremberg but found not guilty. He died in 1970.

Scheer, Reinhard: a German admiral. From 1910, he commanded the German high-seas fleet, and in 1916 his skill saved it in the indecisive battle of *Jutland*.

Schengen Agreement: an agreement of 1985 among some European Union countries to abolish internal border controls between members. In March 1995, seven member states enforced its provisions, which included:

- international police cooperation against criminals
- tougher external frontier controls against illegal immigrants and drugs.

It was anticipated that the agreement would be implemented by most member states – but not Britain, which was anxious to preserve the integrity of its Channel frontier – by the end of 1996. In that year, France, becoming concerned both about its implication for a spate of terrorist attacks in France and about the ease with which illegal drugs could be brought into France from Holland, withdrew from full participation. The agreement illustrated the increased pace of European integration in the 1990s and also some of the tensions which this threw up in member states.

Schindler, Oskar: a German industrialist who, during the Nazi regime, protected his Jewish employees from persecution. Long after the Second World War, his feats achieved international recognition and publicity through a novel and a film. He was honored by the state of Israel and, on his death in 1974, was buried with great honors in Jerusalem and mourned across the world by those he had saved.

Schirach, Baldur von: founder and leader of the *Hitler Youth*. From 1940, as governor of Vienna, he vigorously pursued the policy of shipping Austrian Jews to concentration camps, where they became victims of the *Holocaust*. He was sentenced to 20 years' imprisonment at Nuremberg and died in 1974.

Schleicher, Kurt von: briefly chancellor of the Weimar Republic from December 1932 to January 1933 following von *Papen*'s resignation and prior to Hitler's succession.

- He was a resolute opponent of Nazi illegal activities, but President *Hindenburg* failed to support him, and he resigned
- He had earlier wrecked *Brüning*'s government by withdrawing his support
- His own government was in turn undermined by von Papen's intrigues and willingness to do deals with Hitler.

These twists in Schleicher's career throw into sharp focus the inability of the other right-wing parties to perceive the nature of the Nazi threat and to combine together to block Hitler's rise to power. Schleicher was murdered by the Nazis in 1934 in the *Night of the Long Knives*.

Schlieffen Plan: a military plan, devised by the German field marshal von Schlieffen in 1895. The plan:

- was intended to deal France a swift knock-out blow if a European war

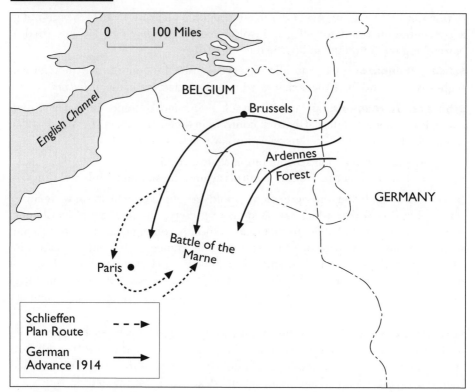

0   100 Miles

BELGIUM

Brussels

English Channel

Ardennes
Forest

GERMANY

Battle of the
Marne

Paris •

Schlieffen
Plan Route   - - - ➤

German
Advance 1914   ———➤

In 1914, the German army was slowed down by Allied resistance in Belgium and on the Marne, and became afraid that its forces would become separated. The western thrust of the plan was therefore changed from an encirclement of Paris to a direct attack from the north. When this became bogged down, the four years of trench warfare on the Western Front began.

16 The Schlieffen Plan

occurred, so that German forces could be concentrated against France's ally, Russia

- proposed an attack through Belgium, which would then enter France and sweep around to the west of Paris, cutting the city off from the sea and splitting the French army in two.

Early success in applying the plan in 1914 was halted by French and British forces at the Battle of the *Marne*, and German troops had to be withdrawn in order to counter Russian attacks on the *Eastern Front*. However, in 1940, in the Second World War, the principles of the plan were successfully applied, with the aid of motorized transport and aerial support, in the dramatic and totally successful invasion of France.

Schmidt, Helmut: chancellor of West Germany, 1974–82. He was a Social

Democrat and friend of *Brandt*, whom he succeeded as chancellor. In foreign policy:

- he continued Brandt's *Ostpolitik* in order to improve relations with East Germany and the Soviet Union
- he worked energetically and in close cooperation with Giscard d'Estaing, president of France, to promote European cooperation.

He headed an uneasy coalition government with the Free Democrats which was troubled by the economic recession of the late 1970s and by the emergence of the Green Party. He won the 1980 election, but resigned in 1982 when the Free Democrats switched back to their more traditional alliance with the Christian Democrats, led by Kohl.

Schumacher, Kurt: a German politician. An outspokenly courageous opponent of National Socialism, he spent from 1933 to 1945 in a Nazi concentration camp and after 1945 worked to rebuild the *Social Democratic Party* (SDP). He led the opposition to Adenauer's Christian Democrats until his death in 1952, but was less skilful than his opponent in doing deals with the smaller parties in the Bundestag. His Marxist sympathies, his distrust of NATO and his opposition to West German rearmament made him an object of suspicion to many middle-of-the-road German voters as the Cold War developed.

Schuman Plan: a plan promulgated by Schuman in 1950 for pooling the coal and steel resources of Western Europe. It led to the formation, in 1951, of the *European Coal and Steel Community.*

Schuman, Robert: prime minister of France, 1947 and 1948. He strongly supported the need for close Franco–German relations and, in 1950, promoted the *Schuman Plan* as well as assisting the work of *Monnet* in forming the European Coal and Steel Community and helping in setting up NATO. He was, from 1958 to 1960, the first president of the European Assembly in Strasbourg. He was one of the key figures in developing the momentum towards European unity.

Schuschnigg, Kurt von: chancellor of Austria, 1934–38, immediately before the *Anschluss.* He tried both to resist the Austrian Nazis' efforts to create anarchy in the country and to prevent the absorption of Austria by Germany by developing an authoritarian-style government. In 1936, he considered restoring the Habsburg monarchy but this led to an international outcry led by Britain. In 1938, he was browbeaten by Hitler into accepting Austrian Nazis into his government. He was prevented from rallying support through a referendum and, the day before German troops moved into Austria, had to resign. He spent the war a German prisoner and then emigrated to the USA, dying in 1977.

Scotland: a distinctive part of the United Kingdom with its own legal system, education system and church, but for international purposes governed by the United Kingdom's Parliament at Westminster. From the 1960s, there was growing support in Scotland for some form of home rule or total independence within the framework of the European Union, and following the May 1997 general election and installation of the Labour government the Scottish people voted in a referendum overwhelmingly in favor of a Scottish parliament within the UK.

sea warfare:

In the First World War

- The great battle fleets, so costly to build, met only once, and that briefly, in the Battle of *Jutland*
- *Submarine warfare*, however, developed remarkably during the war, especially in the Atlantic, as German *U-boats* attacked supply ships to Britain with considerable success until the introduction of the *convoy* system limited British losses
- The German decision to resume attacks without warning on unarmed merchant ships helped President Woodrow Wilson to bring the USA into the war, this following two years after the much-publicized sinking of the liner LUSITANIA with US citizens on board.

In the Second World War

- The Battle of the *Atlantic* concerning supply routes was one of the critical conflicts of the war. The U-boats came close to denying Britain crucial war supplies and food, but the convoy system, first adopted in the First World War, denied them victory, though at great cost
- The invasion fleet launching the *Normandy Campaign* and the Second Front on *D day* in 1944 represented the greatest fleet of ships ever assembled
- Fleets became increasingly vulnerable to attacks from the air, as illustrated by the events at Pearl Harbor and the fate of the British battleships REPULSE and PRINCE OF WALES in 1941. In the final stages of the war against Japan, they existed mainly to support aircraft carriers.

During the Cold War period, the USA in particular maintained fleets in many of the world's seas as a deterrent against aggression. The aircraft carried by these fleets saw occasional action in support of land operations, but not in European waters until

NATIONAL INCOME AND MILITARY EXPENDITURE 1937		
	National income (billions of US dollars)	Percentage on defense
USA	68	1.5
British Empire	22	5.7
France	10	9.1
Germany	17	23.5
Italy	6	14.5
Soviet Union	19	26.4
Japan	4	28.2

Note:
- the much heavier percentage expenditure on defense by all the totalitarian powers than that by the democracies
- the economic reality behind Hitler's colossal Second World War gamble in first attacking the Soviet Union and then declaring war on the USA.

the 1990s crises in Yugoslavia. A new development was that of nuclear armed submarines, allegedly undetectable, as part of the deterrent strategy. The Soviet Union, the USA and, on a much smaller scale, Britain, all built such fleets.

Second Front: a military front established in Western Europe during the Second World War. The Western Allies landed in Normandy on *D day* in June 1944. The Soviet Union, wanting relief from the German invasion, had been pressing for this since 1942, but Britain in particular hesitated to act until plans had been fully prepared and resources built up – a cautious attitude resulting from the disastrous experience of the *Dieppe Raid*. The Second Front then became the Allied line of advance eastwards across France and Belgium into Holland and Germany. (See map, p. 63.)

Second World War: the war of 1939–45 between the Axis powers, principally Germany, Italy and Japan, and the Allied powers, principally Britain, the Soviet Union and the USA.

The European war, 1939–41

The Second World War started in September 1939 with the German invasion of Poland and the consequent declarations of war on Germany by Britain and France. Germany, aided by the Soviet Union, was swiftly victorious against Poland in the east and, after some months of *phony war*, in 1940 gained devastating victories in the west, overrunning Denmark and Norway before sweeping through Belgium and Holland to invade France and forcing it to surrender. Prior to this, British forces had been evacuated across the English Channel from *Dunkirk*. German plans to invade Britain were thwarted when they failed, in the Battle of *Britain*, to win control of the air. However, Germany, from 1940 to 1944, controlled the European Continental coast from the North Cape of Norway to the Spanish border. Italy entered the war in 1940, at the height of German successes against France. Its invasion of Greece spread the war into the Balkans and out from Europe into the Mediterranean and to the French and Italian colonies in North Africa. Italian failures both after invading Greece and in North Africa drew German forces into these regions in what was to become a costly diversion of resources away from the main European battlefields.

War in the Atlantic

Sea warfare had at the same time spread in the Battle of the *Atlantic* as German U-boats sought to cut British supply lines, and this led to the gradual involvement of the USA. Despite continued American isolationist feeling, President *Roosevelt* at least was aware that the German success in dominating Europe posed a growing threat to American interests, and he sought, particularly by the *Lend-Lease* agreement, to provide essential supplies to Britain. The US navy took up an increasingly active, if still technically neutral, role in the Atlantic, but often appeared to be willing to provoke incidents between US destroyers and U-boats, until, in 1941, US destroyers began to escort and protect British supply convoys.

The Eastern Front

In June 1941, Hitler created an entirely new war front when, in Operation *Barbarossa*, he ordered the invasion of the Soviet Union and so opened up an *Eastern Front*. The three-pronged invasion thrust proved remarkably successful:

TIMELINE: MAJOR EVENTS OF THE SECOND WORLD WAR

1939 Sept   Germany invaded Poland
Britain and France declared war on Germany
Poland overrun

1939 Oct–Apr 1940 *Phony war* in the west

1940 April   Germany conquered Denmark and Norway
      May   Germany invaded Belgium, Holland and Luxembourg, and broke through into France
British army evacuated from Dunkirk
      June   Italy entered the war
      June   France surrendered
      Aug–Sept   *Battle of Britain*
      Sept   Italian attack on Egypt, opening of *North Africa Campaign*
      Oct   Italian invasion of Greece
1940–43   *Battle of the Atlantic* at its height

1941 June   German invasion of the Soviet Union (Operation *Barbarossa*)
      Dec   Japanese attacked US fleet at Pearl Harbor
Germany and Italy declared war on the USA

European war now a world war

1942   Sweeping Japanese victories in Asia and across the Pacific
1942 May   Germans drove British back to Egypt (El Alamein)
      Sept   German forces reached Stalingrad
      Highpoint of Axis fortunes
      Oct   British victory at El Alamein turned the war in North Africa
      Nov   Americans invaded North Africa by sea

1943 Jan   German forces at Stalingrad surrounded and forced to surrender; beginning of Soviet advance on the *Eastern Front*
      July   Allied invasion of Sicily
      Sept   Allied invasion of Italy
1943   Start of systematic heavy bombing of Germany

1944 Apr   *Red Army* entered Romania
      June   Allies entered Rome
      June   *D day* landings opened the *Normandy Campaign* and the *Second Front*
      Aug   Paris liberated
      Dec   German counter-attack in the *Ardennes Campaign* defeated in Jan 1945

1945 Jan   Red Army took Warsaw and reached the German border
      Feb   Allied armies in the west reached the Rhine
      Apr   Red Army reached Berlin
Hitler committed suicide
      May   Germany surrendered
      End of the war in Europe
      Aug   Atomic bombs dropped on Japan; Japanese surrendered
      End of the Second World War

- in the north, Leningrad was besieged
- in the center, German troops were within 50 miles of Moscow
- in the south, the capture of the key city of Kiev opened up the rich resources, including oil, of the Ukraine.

Losses of men on both sides were enormous, and the German army, still just short of its objectives, became bogged down in the Russian winter.

World War, 1941

The most dramatic extension of the war occurred on 5 December 1941, when a Japanese air attack on the American Pacific naval base at Pearl Harbor destroyed much of the US fleet based there.

- The USA immediately declared war on Japan
- Germany and Italy followed with declarations of war against the USA
- These events turned what had been a basically European war into a world war, with Britain, less than a year earlier fighting alone, now joined by the world's two largest powers and increasingly a junior partner among the Allies.

The USA and the Soviet Union were now actively committed on the same side, and this made the eventual outcome of the war quite predictable. It was largely Roosevelt's decision that the Allies should first defeat Hitler that decided the war's future pattern, with the build-up in Britain of a vast Commonwealth and American force preparing to invade the Nazi-dominated European Continent.

German domination of Europe

In Europe, German domination lasted for four years, from 1940 to 1944.

- It was always oppressive and, for the Jews in particular, often fatal, with the establishment of over 30 *concentration camps* and *death camps*
- The material resources of the occupied countries were plundered and their inhabitants forced into labor for the occupying power
- In all the occupied countries, there were those, like *Laval* in France, who collaborated with the occupying power and those, like the *Maquis*, also in France, who actively resisted.

The North Africa and Italian campaigns, 1942–43

In 1942 and early 1943, British and American troops drove the Axis forces out of North Africa. In July 1943, they invaded and captured Sicily, and in September invaded mainland Italy. The Italians had forced the dictator *Mussolini* from office, and it was German, not Italian, forces which now provided stubborn resistance to every Allied advance northwards through Italy.

Soviet victories in the east, 1943–45

The bulk of the German forces, however, were committed on their *Eastern Front* against the Soviet Union. The 1943 campaigns were fought deep inside the Soviet Union, but with the *Red Army* increasingly wresting the initiative from the Germans, as at the Battle of *Stalingrad*. By July 1944, the Red Army had crossed into Poland, and before the end of the year, all of the Soviet Union was cleared of German troops. The Soviet forces were poised to attack Germany itself.

The Second Front, 1944–45

In June 1944, western Allied forces, largely American and British, invaded Continental Europe, with amphibious landings in Normandy, and created a *Second Front* in the west. Despite fierce resistance, the bridgeheads were consolidated and the Allied forces broke out into France. In August 1944, they liberated Paris and, after a major German counter-attack was repulsed in the *Ardennes Campaign,* crossed the Rhine into Germany in March 1945. The Allied advance was accompanied by saturation day-and-night bombing of targets within Germany, including the later controversial bombing of *Dresden.* The Red Army had meanwhile pushed far into Germany, bypassing Berlin, to make the first link-up with American troops advancing from the west in April 1945. German resistance, resolute for so long, now collapsed totally. The new *V1* and *V2* rockets had come too late to save Germany, and Hitler's Third Reich collapsed with his suicide on 30 April in the ruins of Berlin, and with Soviet troops only streets away. Hitler's successor, Admiral Doenitz, surrendered unconditionally on 7 May, and the war in Europe was over.

War in the Pacific, 1941–45

In the Pacific theater of war, early Japanese success had rivaled those of the Germans in Europe. Japan's military and naval forces:

- had been at war with China since 1937, and controlled large areas of that country
- conquered the British colony of Hong Kong in December 1941
- swept south early in 1942 to occupy Burma, the Dutch East Indies, British Malaya, Singapore and the American Philippine Islands, threatening Australia and New Zealand
- occupied many of the tiny island groups across the Pacific.

Their spectacular advance was checked in June 1942, when US planes inflicted heavy losses on the Japanese fleet at the Battle of Midway Island. From late 1942, the American fleet counter-attacked, eliminating the Japanese navy, and the costly business of recapturing occupied islands could begin. In 1944, the mainland of Japan was subjected to heavy bombing.

By August 1945, Japan was much on the defensive but, with its defensive capability intact, it still constituted a formidable enemy when the dropping of *atomic bombs* on Hiroshima and Nagasaki forced it to surrender.

THE MILITARY DEAD IN THE SECOND WORLD WAR			
Allies	**Millions**	**Axis powers**	**Millions**
Soviet Union	20.0	Germany	4.2
Poland	4.3	Japan	1.2
China	2.2	Romania	0.5
Yugoslavia	1.7	Hungary	0.4
France	0.6	Italy	0.4
USA	0.4	Austria	0.3
Britain	0.4		
		Total dead: 36.6 million	

Results of the war

The war:

- caused some 50 million deaths
- divided Europe between the areas liberated from the Nazis by the Soviet Red Army and those liberated by the Western Allies, and so created the basis for the *Cold War*
- led both to the redrawing of many Eastern European frontiers, notably those of the Soviet Union, Poland and Germany, and, by 1949, to the division of Germany into two separate states
- led to the re-creation of the republics of *Czechoslovakia* and *Poland* which had disappeared in 1939
- saw the *Baltic Republics* reabsorbed back into the Soviet Union
- created a serious post-war *refugee* problem arising both from voluntary flight and, far more importantly, from forcible relocation, usually from east to west
- established the USA and the Soviet Union as *superpowers*
- destroyed the economies of many European countries
- hastened the end of *European empires* through the process of post-war decolonization.

On the Second World War, see also the following general headings: *Atlantic, Battle of*; *blitzkrieg*; *Eastern Front*; *Holocaust*; *Italian Campaign*; *North Africa Campaign*; *partisans*; *phony war*; *prisoners of war*; *resistance*; *sea warfare*; *Second Front*; *tank warfare*; *Western Front*.

secession: a separation or breaking away (from the verb "to secede"). The Baltic Republics of Estonia, Latvia and Lithuania, for example, seceded from Russia at the end of the First World War and again, from the Soviet Union, in 1991.

secularization: a term describing the end of any official position in the state for religion. Turkey, for example, became a secular state in the 1920s. The term often also describes the declining importance of religious belief and practice in society.

secular state: a state free from the political influence of religion, as with Atatürk's republic of Turkey.

Securitate: the secret police of communist *Romania*. They were a large and sinister body, with no regard for individual civil rights, employed in the service of the dictator *Ceauşescu*.

Security Council: the executive arm of the *United Nations Organization*. Its chief features were:

- its responsibility for maintaining world peace and security
- its design to provide for swift action in international emergencies and to balance the interests of the great powers against the very democratic *General Assembly*
- its membership of 15 states; five permanent members, i.e. China, France, Russia, the UK and the USA, who each have a right of veto on any action; and 10 non-permanent members elected for two years by the General Assembly
- its dependence in any action on forces provided by the member states, until, in 1992, planning began on creating a UN army

- its ineffectiveness during the Cold War period because of superpower rivalry, as demonstrated by the use of the veto by the permanent members, particularly the Soviet Union, which regularly found itself in a minority of one.

Seeckt, Hans von: commander-in-chief of the German army, 1920–26. He was not prepared in 1920 to defend the *Weimar Republic* by using the army to put down the *Kapp Putsch,* informing President *Ebert* that "troops do not fire on troops." He built up the Weimar Republic army, the *Reichswehr,* in the 1920s, training them to be the nucleus of a much larger force, to be created when the restrictions imposed at the Versailles Treaty could be ignored or defied. Secret clauses of the *Rapallo* Treaty enabled him to train soldiers in the Soviet Union and so avoid the Versailles terms. His work created an excellent basis for Hitler's 1930s rearmament program.

self-determination: a nation or part of a nation determining its own course of action, government or allegiance. This is sometimes done in a referendum of the inhabitants, as in the Saar in 1935 and 1955.

Serbia: in 1900, an independent kingdom to the south of Austria-Hungary, part of Yugoslavia from 1919. Its *Slav* inhabitants had long wished to unite all the Slav peoples of the Balkans into one state. This made them a menace to the multi-national Austria-Hungary, and the latter in 1908 took full control of its separate province of Bosnia in order to thwart any prospect of Serbian expansion. In 1914, Austrian pressure on Serbia following the assassination at *Sarajevo* led Russia to support a fellow Slav state, and so to the outbreak of the First World War.

In the Second World War, Serb partisans fought ruthlessly against the German army occupying their region, and after the war Serbia became part of the communist republic of *Yugoslavia* created by the partisan leader Tito.

When Yugoslavia disintegrated in the 1990s, Serbia:

- took over the rump of the republic based on Belgrade
- tried to prevent Croatia and later Bosnia from gaining independence.

Pressure from the UN, including economic sanctions, forced Serbia to abandon its claims on Croatia and its military help to the Serbs in Bosnia. By 1998, the republic of Serbia, with its capital, Belgrade, and the republic of Montenegro together constituted the rump of the old Federal Republic of Yugoslavia, which lived in an uneasy peace, NATO-monitored, with its neighbors but lacked international recognition as the successor state to Tito's Yugoslavia.

serfdom: a system of tying farm laborers to their lord's land. The laborers' movements were restricted and they could not dispose of their property. In Western Europe, serfdom had disappeared by the nineteenth century, but was only abolished in Russia in 1861. The burden of the *redemption payments* that the Russian peasants then had to make to obtain their land was still a serious grievance in the early twentieth century.

Sèvres, Treaty of: agreed in 1920 between the Allies and the Ottoman Empire as part of the Paris Peace Settlement. It reflected the total collapse of the empire at the end of the First World War and involved it in considerable loss of lands.

- In the Middle East, Jordan, Iraq and Palestine became League of

Nations *mandates* administered by Britain, with Lebanon and Syria to be administered by France

- More serious for the future of the state was the loss to Greece of land close to Istanbul, including Adrianople
- The Bosphorus and Dardanelles were to be international and demilitarized waterways
- Smyrna (Izmir) in western Turkey, and much land around it, was also awarded to Greece.

The treaty was not accepted by Mustafa Kemal (*Atatürk*), and a war with Greece followed. Turkish military successes provoked the *Chanak Crisis*, but then led to revision of the terms at Sèvres in the 1923 Treaty of *Lausanne*.

Seyss-Inquart, Arthur: the Austrian Nazi leader. Pressure from Nazi Germany in 1938 forced the Austrian chancellor *Schuschnigg* to take him into government as interior minister responsible for security. After Schuschnigg had been forced to resign, Seyss-Inquart became chancellor and invited German troops into Austria to keep order, and this gave an appearance of legality to the German takeover of the state. Having organized the *Anschluss*, and with Austria incorporated into Germany, he served Hitler as governor of Vienna. During the Second World War, he administered occupied lands, first Poland and then Holland, cooperating enthusiastically in the deportations of both suspected opponents of the occupying power and all Jews to concentration camps. He was executed after trial at Nuremberg.

show trials: public trials in the Soviet Union for propaganda purposes in the late 1930s. They formed part of Stalin's *Great Purge* or *Yezhovshchina* and were reserved for previously powerful figures whom Stalin wished to portray as enemies of the state.

Siberia: a vast region of the former Soviet Union in northern Asia with an extreme winter climate. It lies to the east of the Ural mountains and was used by both the tsarist and Soviet authorities as a place of exile for offenders and the politically suspect. It was opened up by the building, from the 1890s, of the *Trans-Siberian Railway*. *Stolypin* had some success in persuading peasants from European Russia to emigrate there, but its real development came during the 1930s and the Second World War, when the mineral resources of the Urals area became the basis of a new industrial region, including the great iron-making town of *Magnitogorsk*.

Siegfried Line: a German fortified defense line on Germany's western frontier. It was built following the Nazi remilitarization of the *Rhineland* in 1936, but first the *phony war* and then the devastating German advance of 1940 meant that it never served its defensive purpose, except that its existence might, in the first two months of the war, have deterred an Allied attack on Germany which could possibly have helped the Poles. It was an irrelevance in the Allied 1944–45 advance into Germany.

Sikorski, Wladyslaw: a Polish politician and general. He:

- was involved against the Bolsheviks in the Russo–Polish War of 1919–21, including the defense of Warsaw in 1920
- was, in 1922, prime minister of Poland until he was dismissed as too liberal by *Pilsudski* in 1926

- led, after the defeat of Poland in 1939, an army of Polish exiles based in Britain and set up a Polish government in exile in London.

His attempts, after Hitler launched Operation *Barbarossa*, to establish links with the Soviet Union and Polish exiles there were wrecked when the Germans revealed details of the *Katyn Massacre*. Sikorski died in an air crash in 1943.

Silesia: a region in Eastern Europe important for coal mining and steel production.

- From 1815, much of it was in Prussia (from 1871, Germany) and the rest in Austria
- In 1918, it was divided, after plebiscites had tried to establish the wishes of the inhabitants, between Czechoslovakia, Poland and Weimar Germany. In the inter-war years, there were many disputes in the region between the different nationalities
- In 1939, after the German invasion, Polish Silesia became part of Nazi Germany
- Since 1945, all parts of the region have formed part of Poland.

Silesia illustrates well how, in the first half of the twentieth century, national borders in Eastern Europe were drawn and redrawn so as to reflect the ebb and flow of military success.

Single European Act: 1986 *European Union* legislation to promote trade between member states, most, but not all, of which came into effect as intended in 1993. It:

- removed obstacles to trade by such devices as eliminating frontier controls
- provided for opening tenders for public contracts on equal terms to firms from all member states
- allowed the free movement of capital
- arranged for the future standardizing of VAT (value-added tax) and excise duties
- changed the arrangements for law-making by introducing majority voting in the Council of Ministers and the European Parliament so that the veto rights of individual nations over many matters were ended
- extended the responsibilities of the EU into new areas, including monetary policy, environmental issues and external policy.

Many of these matters remained controversial, and full implementation of the act, though not several of its commercial clauses, looked unlikely to be achieved before the end of the century.

Single Market: a concept of the *European Union* (EU). It emerged as a response to the slow economic growth of the early 1980s, with the purpose of sweeping away barriers to trade within the EU (then known as the European Community). The main step towards the single market was the *Single European Act* of 1986.

Sinn Féin: a political party, founded in 1902, committed to the cause of an independent Ireland. It supported the 1916 *Easter Rising* and won the vast majority of Irish seats in the British general election of 1919. Those elected refused to go to Westminster but met in Dublin and declared Irish independence. Many members of Sinn Féin deeply resented the 1921 division of Ireland negotiated between the

British government and their own leaders, a division which set up the *Irish Free State* but excluded Ulster, and conducted a civil war against it which lasted until 1924. Sinn Féin was declared an illegal organization in the Irish Free State in 1926, but since 1945 it has operated openly in the Republic of Ireland but does not contest elections there. Since the 1960s, it has been best known as the political wing of the *Provisional IRA*, continuing to press for the integration of Ulster into the Republic of Ireland. Its support was seen as critical to the 1990s' Peace Process.

Six, the: the common collective name for the original states which created the 1952 *European Coal and Steel Community* and the 1958 *European Economic Community* and *Euratom*. They were Belgium, France, Holland, Italy, Luxembourg and West Germany.

Skoda works: large Czechoslovak armaments and engineering works in Prague. They fell under German control in March 1939, when Hitler occupied what was left of Czechoslovakia following the earlier annexation of the Sudetenland, and were invaluable to the Nazi war effort in the Second World War. Churchill argued, then and later, that the works and the efficient Czech army had provided compelling reasons for not appeasing Hitler at the time of the 1938 *Munich Agreement*.

Slansky Trial: the 1952 communist Czechoslovak trial of Rudolf Slansky, deputy prime minister of the country, and 13 other Jews for "Titoism" and as bourgeois traitors. The evidence was blatantly rigged, but 10 of the defendants were hanged. It is claimed that Stalin, obsessively anti-Semitic in his last years, was personally responsible for ordering the trial, an interesting indication of how tightly he controlled the Soviet bloc.

Slavs: people of Eastern and Central Europe. The greatest Slav nation was *Russia*, and in the early twentieth century, this country felt a need to show regard for the interests of other Slav nations, notably *Serbia*. This was one element in the crisis of 1914, when Russia felt it had to back Serbia in the face of Austrian threats.

Slovakia: an independent republic, formerly part of Czechoslovakia, which separated from the Czech Republic at the beginning of 1993. In 1994, the privatization reforms of the communist economy were halted indefinitely, and the future direction of the state was placed in doubt.

Slovenia: an independent state, formerly one of the republics making up Yugoslavia. Its independence was proclaimed in 1991. There was a 10-day war as the Yugoslav army tried to prevent this secession, but it then withdrew and allowed the new state to be set up.

slump: a severe or prolonged fall in the demand for goods. This is often accompanied by a decline in prices and quickly leads to a collapse in business activity and large-scale unemployment. The most famous slump was the Great Depression of the early 1930s (see *Depression, the Great*).

Smyrna: (Izmir) a city on the west coast of Turkey. It was ceded to the Greeks by the Allies at the 1920 Treaty of *Sèvres*, but was taken by the Turks in the revival stimulated by Atatürk and was returned to them by the 1923 Treaty of *Lausanne*.

social Darwinism: the adaptation of Darwin's mid-nineteenth-century theories on the origin of species to explain the functioning of human societies. It:

- argued that societies (nations) compete against each other, and that, like all species, the strong survive and prosper
- was used to justify policies aimed at building up the strength of society in order for it to be better able to compete internationally
- was, in the twentieth century, used to justify racist theories such as that concerning the essential superiority of the Aryan race which underlay much of Nazi philosophy.

social democracy: non-doctrinaire socialism, combining the wish for greater equality with acceptance of a largely capitalist economy.

Social Democratic parties: a term used to describe left-wing democratic political parties in many countries, notably Germany. The German SDP was the largest political party in Weimar Germany and was banned by the Nazis in 1933. In West Germany after 1945, the Social Democrats (SDP) were the party of *Schumacher* and *Brandt*. They should be distinguished from the more right-wing Christian Democrat parties. In France, Italy and Spain, Social Democratic parties became known as socialist parties. The title was used only briefly in Britain to describe a breakaway group from the British Labour Party, which survived from 1981 to 1988.

Social Revolutionaries: a Russian subversive political party formally established in 1907; some members were Marxists, others anarchists. They were associated with acts of violence, including assassinations like that of *Plehve* in 1904. They were far more loosely organized than the Bolsheviks, but supported a series of peasant uprisings and so built up considerable support in the countryside. In the 1917 national election for the Constituent Assembly, they and their allies gained a majority of the votes, hence the Bolshevik forcible closure of the Assembly.

socialism: a political philosophy. It:

- advocates community or state ownership of much of the economy, often referred to as nationalization
- seeks the redistribution of wealth by political action, for example through taxation policy
- wishes to eliminate poverty and to improve welfare, for example education and health
- seeks a more egalitarian society.

Socialism developed in late-nineteenth-century Europe, owing a great debt to the writings of Karl Marx. It had much in common philosophically with communism, but was generally seen as less revolutionary. In Western societies, socialists strove to develop their program by parliamentary democratic means, often by proposals to nationalize the major economic assets of the state.

- In the 1980s, the tide turned against socialist ideas.
- The communist command economies of Eastern Europe, including the Soviet Union, proved less and less efficient, and began as a result to disintegrate politically
- In the West, a new right-wing mood, best exemplified by the post-1979 Thatcher government in Britain, increasingly questioned the basic philosophy of the socialist welfare state and its nationalized economy.

The reversal of the nationalization process, under the title of *privatization*, took on what seemed an unstoppable momentum in Britain, and was widely copied in other countries of both Western and post-communist Eastern Europe.

socialism in one country: a doctrine promoted by *Stalin* in the early 1920s in opposition to Trotsky's idea of permanent revolution. It was clear that the infant Soviet Union was in no position to promote successful communist revolution in other European states, so Stalin urged that the main task was to create a communist society within the Soviet Union. His support for this helped him to achieve power after the death of Lenin.

Solidarity: a Polish trade-union movement, led by Lech *Walesa*, which emerged from strikes in *Gdansk* in 1980. It demanded the liberalization of the communist regime, but the threat of a Soviet invasion led the Polish army to act against it. It was declared illegal in 1982, and survived only as an underground movement until 1989. In that year, as communist rule crumbled, it was made legal once more, and its leaders joined the first non-communist government of Poland since the 1930s.

Solzhenitsyn, Alexander: a Soviet writer and leading *dissident*. He was imprisoned in a Soviet prison camp for eight years and based his most famous novel, A DAY IN THE LIFE OF IVAN DENISOVICH, on that experience. Its publication in 1962 suited *Khrushchev* in his efforts to expose the errors and horrors of Stalinism, and so was permitted. In 1974, however, with *Brezhnev* in control, his work exposing the corruption of the Soviet system, THE GULAG ARCHIPELAGO, led to his being exiled.

Somme: a river in Northern France which gave its name to a First World War battle on the *Western Front*. This was fought from 1 July to November 1916, with the loss to the British and French forces of some 600,000 men in a futile attempt to break the German lines. The British and French commanders, Haig and Joffre, mounted the offensive because they wanted to ease German pressure on the French defenders of *Verdun*.

- Twenty thousand British and Commonwealth troops, ordered to walk, not run, towards the German machine guns, were killed on the first morning of the battle
- Despite days of advance bombardment, German machine gunners were able to mow down the attackers as they came over the top of their trenches and across the sea of mud created by their own shells
- Tanks were first used in this battle but, like the wounded, they became bogged down in the mud.

Eventually, the Germans fell back a few miles to previously prepared positions, and nothing worthwhile had been gained by the Allies. At the 80th anniversary of the battle in 1996, the handful of survivors, mainly centenarians, revisiting the battlefield repeated the charge that the British troops had been lions led by donkeys, adding "We were too young to ask any questions." One commentator claimed that, for Britain, the twentieth century and the age of cynicism both began on 1 July 1916.

sovereignty: a political term meaning supreme power or authority. When applied to a country, it means that it exists as a fully independent state. If a state claims sovereignty over territory, it means that it is claiming supreme power there.

soviet: meaning, in Russian, an elected governing council. After 1905, when a soviet of workers' deputies was formed in St. Petersburg to coordinate strikes and anti-government activity, the term was commonly associated with revolutionary purposes. During the First World War, workers' soviets were set up in many Russian towns and provinces. Control of the *Petrograd Soviet* was, in November 1917, crucial to the Bolshevik overthrow of the Russian Provisional Government. In the Soviet Union, a hierarchy of soviets became the basis of both local and national political organization.

Soviet constitution: formal constitutional proposals were adopted in 1918, 1924, 1936 and 1977.

- The 1918 constitution was a purely temporary affair
- That of 1924 formalized the establishment of the federal USSR (Union of Soviet Socialist Republics), with the power in Moscow rather than in the republics
- The 1936 constitution was the work of men who were soon to die in the Yezhovshchina (Great Purge), *Bukharin* and *Radek*. Stalin took the credit for it and trumpeted its democratic virtues which, in practice, did not exist because the Communist Party and the secret police could sweep aside any legal obstacles. The constitution did not acknowledge that the Communist Party was the only one with a legal existence
- The 1977 constitution followed that of 1936, but specifically asserted the central role of the Communist Party and the process of *democratic centralism*, and the 1936 reference to merging the various nationalities into one great Soviet nation was dropped.

Soviet economy to 1941: once in power, the Bolsheviks set up a Supreme Council of National Economy which set out to create a planned economy. The demands of the civil war caused the government to introduce *war communism*, taking control, for purposes of national survival, of even small economic units.

- Agriculture was instructed what to produce by a vast, newly formed bureaucracy
- Surplus peasant crops were requisitioned.

The policy was brutally enforced and led to such great resentment that, in 1921, Lenin had to step back and let the economy take a new direction with the *New Economic Policy* (NEP), a strategic retreat towards capitalism, but with the larger industrial undertakings remaining under state control. This new, mixed economy survived until the late 1920s, by which time total Russian production had again reached the levels of 1913.

Under Stalin

The next economic phase began in 1928 with Stalin's abandonment of the NEP and his introduction of the first of a number of *Five-Year Plans*. The central aims were:

- the *collectivization* of agriculture, as originally envisaged at the time of the Bolshevik takeover
- the development of heavy industry.

Peasant farming was inefficient and the activities of the NEP private traders, or *nepmen*, frequently corrupt so that, by 1927, food supplies were again in peril. Through large-scale economies and mechanization, collectivization could, it was held, solve these problems and also provide grain for export and thus foreign currency for importing machinery to develop Soviet industry. The Stalinist reforms reintroduced the concept of a *command economy* with a central planning authority, *Gosplan*. Targets were set for industry, which was to concentrate on the production of capital goods and on prestige power projects like hydroelectricity schemes. In both industry and agriculture, the emphasis was on meeting targets, and these were enforced by rewards of titles like *Stakhanovite*, and by savage punishments.

Industrial production increased so sharply that by 1939 the Soviet Union came second only to the USA. Between 1928 and 1937:

- electricity capacity increased sevenfold
- coal production increased fourfold
- steel more than fourfold
- oil almost threefold.

Consumer-goods production was allowed to lag in the first two Five-Year Plans, and when it was given more prominence in the third plan, it was only for this to be sabotaged by rearmament demands. The standard of living enjoyed by Soviet industrial workers therefore remained miserably low by Western European standards.

In agriculture, the 25 million peasant proprietors of 1928, until then protected by the NEP, were the real victims of the Stalinist economic revolution. The peasants, who worked over 95 percent of the country's productive land, resisted collectivization fiercely, especially the wealthier peasants, the *kulaks*; they wanted to retain their own plots of land and to work for their own profit. To achieve his ends, Stalin, between 1928 and 1930, destroyed the kulaks, forcing through collectivization by the most brutal physical means, and by 1934 almost all of Soviet agriculture was collectivized. Peasants might keep a scrap of private land, but the *kolkhoz* dominated, selling almost all its produce to the state at a fixed price and obtaining its machinery from the state.

Despite heavy capital investment in machinery and fertilizers, agricultural production remained low, almost certainly because of peasant resentment up to the point where the peasants would slaughter livestock rather than hand it over to the collectives, in what became a war with the bureaucrats enforcing the policy. Only at the end of the 1930s did farming production recover and rise again above 1913 levels. The rural economy and rural society had by then been totally transformed, dominated by a quarter of a million collective farms and a few thousand state farms. The peasants as a landowning class had vanished, many dead from famine and persecution, others directed by the planners into the towns. In 1928, only 18 percent of Soviet citizens had lived in towns; at the outbreak of war with Germany in 1941, 33 percent did so.

Soviet economy after 1945: the economy of the European areas of the Soviet Union was devastated by the Second World War.

- 100,000 collective farms and 40,000 miles of rail track had been destroyed

- Industry had been built up east of the Urals, but it was entirely geared to war production
- Some 20 million people had died; and millions more had fled eastwards, voluntarily or forcibly.

The Stalinist period

The Fourth *Five-Year Plan*, introduced in 1946, concentrated on restoring the infrastructure and heavy industry. Forced labor and prisoners of war contributed, as did capital equipment seized as reparations from Germany, so that by 1950 the plan was largely fulfilled, with industrial production back to pre-war levels. Progress in agriculture was less satisfactory, and despite the work of Khrushchev from 1949 to increase the size of collective farms (*kolkhoz*), output on Stalin's death in 1953 was still not back to the levels of the late 1930s.

Under Khrushchev (see also the main *Khrushchev* entry)

From the late 1950s, as the post-war reconstruction was completed, the very high annual growth rate in the gross national product declined from 10 percent to 7 percent, still much higher, however, than in Western countries. Malenkov and then Khrushchev, from 1953 to 1964, placed greater emphasis on light industry and consumer goods, but the continuing needs of military spending and heavy industry, together with inflexibility in planning the direction of the *command economy*, meant that living standards rose only slowly. The reforms in agriculture and in economic planning introduced by Khrushchev were only partly successful.

Under Brezhnev (see also the main *Brezhnev* entry)

In the Brezhnev years, from 1964 to 1982, grain production fluctuated wildly, and in years of shortage, grain had to be imported, as in 1975, when a contract was signed for annual imports from the USA. The peasants' private plots were retained, and the inefficiency of the collective farms was illustrated by the much higher production obtained from them. The Soviet Union under Brezhnev continued to develop its vast natural resources, but by the 1970s it was clear that:

- the expansion of agricultural production on the scale envisaged by Khrushchev was not going to happen
- industrial rates of growth were slowing
- the Soviet economy was having difficulty in adapting to changing needs, notably to the need to produce more and better consumer goods
- the planning of the *command economy* through *Gosplan* was inflexible and increasingly inefficient
- military demands were blocking industrial expansion in other fields.

In this period, it became clear that the Soviet economy was lagging behind the West, especially with regard to quality and cost of production. In the 1950s, informed Western observers had seriously assumed that the Soviet planned economy could outstrip the West, but by the 1970s it was clear that this was not the case.

Under Gorbachev (see also the main *Gorbachev* entry)

This was the situation inherited by Brezhnev's successors, notably Gorbachev, who wanted to introduce ideas and techniques from the West, including a return to private enterprise and self-employment. The Soviet Union was, for example, making little use of the revolutionary advances in computing; indeed, in terms of information technology, even its telephone and mail services were notoriously inefficient. Gorbachev introduced the policies of perestroika and glasnost to overcome the well-established economic stagnation, but this led to fierce opposition from the many who had managed to survive within the confines of the communist system but who could not easily adapt to a new capitalist model, the introduction of which inevitably led to great economic dislocation. The failure to solve the problems of the economy played a large part in the disintegration of the Soviet Union from 1989, and left serious problems for its successor states.

Soviet history, 1917–41: topics and issues which interest historians include:

- accounting for the end of tsardom in the *February Revolution*
- explaining the failure of the *Provisional Government*
- the events and the reasons for the success of the *October Revolution*
- the events and outcome of the *Russian Civil War*
- how did the *Bolsheviks* establish and consolidate their power 1917–21?
- assessing *Lenin*'s contribution to Soviet history
- the struggle for power on Lenin's death
- the economic revolution of the 1930s in agriculture and industry
- the Stalinist purges of the 1930s
- everyday social and economic life in *Stalin*'s totalitarian state
- Stalin and Nazi Germany, 1939–41.

Soviet Union (Union of Soviet Socialist Republics): a state formed in Russia following the 1917 seizure of power by the *Bolsheviks*, which survived until 26

TIMELINE: THE SOVIET UNION 1945–91

1945	End of Second World War
1945–53	**Restoration of Stalinist repression**
1953	Death of *Stalin*
1954	*Malenkov* and *Khrushchev* the two main successors
1955	Malenkov forced to resign. *Bulganin* and *Zhukov*, supporters of Khrushchev, promoted
1956	Khrushchev denounced Stalin at Twentieth Congress of the Communist Party
1956–64	**Khrushchev dominated Soviet political life**
1964	Khrushchev removed from office
1964–82	**The Brezhnev years**
	Podgorny (to 1977), *Kosygin* (to 1980) and *Brezhnev* (to 1982) were the leading political figures, but Brezhnev dominated
1982	Death of Brezhnev
1982–84	*Andropov* the leading politician
1984–85	*Chernenko* the leading politician
1985–91	***Gorbachev* in power**
1991	Independence of the *Baltic Republics* recognized by the Soviet Union
1991	*Yeltsin* came to prominence in opposing the failed communist coup
1991	End of the Soviet Union, replaced by the separate republics loosely linked in the *Commonwealth of Independent States*

December 1991. Formally established in 1922 under a constitution drawn up by *Lenin*, it then consisted of four republics: Russia, the Ukraine, Belorussia and Transcaucasia. It eventually had 15 constituent republics. The Soviet Union was a one-party state, and the supreme law-making body, the Supreme Soviet of the Union, was largely controlled by the *Politburo* of the Communist Party.

In the Second World War

It gained much territory in eastern Poland as a result of the Nazi–Soviet Pact of August 1939, but in the Second World War it was invaded by Germany, in June 1941, and lost some 20 million people as war casualties. The Soviet Union played a full part in the wartime alliance against Nazi Germany and in the international conferences at Tehran, Yalta and Potsdam which held the alliance together. By 1945, the Soviet Red Army was deep into German territory, and after the war it took steps to ensure that this military position was used to create a buffer of sympathetically governed, i.e. communist, states which could act as some protection against any future invaders.

In the Cold War

Distrust of Soviet actions, on the part of Britain and the USA, led to the rapid breakdown of the wartime alliance and to the onset, from 1945 to 1949, of the Cold War.

The Soviet Union:

- in 1948, forced the Western powers to mount the *Berlin Airlift*, producing one of the most critical episodes of the Cold War, and masterminded the communist takeover of Czechoslovakia
- in 1949, exploded its first atomic bomb
- in 1955, founded the *Warsaw Pact* military alliance with its satellite states
- in 1956, intervened militarily to prevent Hungary from breaking away from the bloc
- in 1962, provoked the *Cuban Missile Crisis*
- in 1968, with its Warsaw Pact partners, intervened militarily in Czechoslovakia to protect the communist estate from being dismantled.

Even after the death of *Stalin* in 1953, under *Khrushchev* and *Brezhnev*, the apparatus of a police state controlling people's lives remained largely intact, as did the command economy, suffering many inefficiencies and creaking under the great burden of the defense budget.

In 1985, *Gorbachev* became general secretary of the Communist Party, and a new era opened. He was committed to:

- modernizing the economy
- reducing the corruption and the interference in private lives by the state bureaucracy
- securing an end to the escalating defense budget through international arms control.

He introduced the policies of perestroika (restructuring) and glasnost (openness):

- private enterprise was allowed
- political prisoners were released

- the leading role of the Communist Party was abolished.

A 1991 coup to reimpose communist control was defeated, in large part through the personal energy and courage of *Yeltsin*. The coup, however, had weakened Gorbachev, and let the initiative slip to the leaders of the separate republics within the Soviet Union, especially the Russian leader, Yeltsin. Gorbachev resigned at the end of 1991, and a day later the Soviet Union officially ceased to exist and was succeeded by its constituent republics which became independent states.

sovkhoz: Soviet state farms. They were formed as a result of Stalin's agrarian *collectivization* policies in the 1930s but were outnumbered almost 50 to 1 by the peasant collective farms or *kolkhoz*.

Sovnarkom: the Council of People's Commissars set up by Lenin in the Soviet Union in 1918. It played a key role in establishing Bolshevik power and the communist state in the years of the Russian Civil War, 1919–21, but was later overtaken in importance by the *Politburo* of the Communist Party.

Spaak, Paul-Henri: prime minister of Belgium, 1938–39 and 1947–49. He was a strong advocate of European unity who also played an important part in founding the UN. He helped to found the *Benelux Union,* was president of the Assembly of the *Council of Europe* and secretary-general of NATO. His ideas and his career make him one of the important figures in the early days of the foundation of the *European Union.* He died in 1972.

Spain: until 1931, an independent kingdom. It was then a republic until 1975, when the monarchy was restored. Its political and social life were, prior to the *Spanish Civil War*, deeply divided between left and right.

- From 1924 to 1930, *Primo de Rivera* ruled as a dictator
- From 1931 to 1936, the left-wing republic was torn by the demands for autonomy from the regions, particularly from the Basques and Catalonia
- By 1936, increased violence against the conservative Catholic Church and many communist-inspired strikes created a situation in which, in the eyes of conservative Spaniards, the country was on the brink of anarchy or disintegration.

In 1936, the army acted to prevent the threat they saw hanging over the country, and the Spanish Civil War began. The nationalist victory in the civil war created the dictatorship of General *Franco*, which lasted until his death in 1975, when Spain reverted to being a monarchy under *Juan Carlos II.* Internal peace after 1975 was disrupted by the activities of the Basque terrorist group *ETA* and by two attempted military coups. Spain granted independence to its last African colonies in the 1980s and joined the European Union in 1986. This, combined with growing prosperity from tourism and acceptance by the other Western nations, gave the at-first fragile democracy a new stability, allowing socialist governments to be elected and to take power peacefully in a state once split into civil war by the rift between left and right and then dominated for decades by dictatorial right-wing governments.

Spanish Civil War: a civil war from 1936 to 1939. It arose from deep divisions in Spanish society which became acute following the end of the monarchy in 1931. On the political right were:

- the Catholic Church
- landowners
- most of the professional classes
- the military.

On the left were:

- the republicans
- the Basque and Catalan separatists
- socialists, communists and anarchists
- the mass of the urban working class.

In July 1936, the army, with *Franco* a key figure, mounted a coup against the left-wing *Popular Front* government formed in the previous February, and this action led to civil war. The main strongholds of the republic's supporters were Barcelona and Madrid. The latter city was besieged by the nationalist, pro-Franco forces for two and a half years. In 1937, the nationalists began to gain the initiative, overrunning the Basque region and dividing the republican forces.

- The nationalists received military aid both from fascist Italy, which sent 70,000 volunteer troops, and from Nazi Germany, which most crucially provided over 100 planes of the *Condor Legion*. These helped to bring Franco's own regiments from garrison duty in Morocco to join the fighting in Spain, and they also bombed republican military lines and republican-held towns, most notoriously *Guernica*. Foreign intervention gave the nationalists air superiority.
- Soviet aid to the republicans was on a much smaller scale, and was withdrawn totally in 1938
- The British and French governments followed a policy of non-intervention and failed to support the democratically elected republican government, though many volunteers from both countries went to Spain to do so.

The republicans themselves found it difficult to work together against their common enemy, and after the failure of a counter-offensive at the Battle of the *Ebro* in November 1938, Barcelona fell to the nationalists in January 1939. After bitter quarrels among different factions within the defenders, the nationalists entered Madrid in March 1939. The civil war was at this point over, Franco became the head of state and the *Falange* the only legal political party.

Results of the war

- About 500,000 people had been killed, and there was vast urban destruction from bombing and shelling attacks
- The events of the war are often seen as a rehearsal for military action in the Second World War, and the nationalist success as emboldening Hitler and Mussolini on the road to further aggression
- The cinema pictures of the bombing of towns, shown across Europe, had a powerful impact on public opinion, and promoted the idea that any future war would be so utterly destructive that reasonable people must do all possible to prevent its happening.

The debate on the outcome of the war

An issue for historians has been the extent to which the nationalist victory was brought about both by German and Italian help and by the failure of the Soviet Union and the Western democracies to help the official government against the right-wing coup. However, there were other, perhaps more important, reasons for Franco's success, including:

- the greater unity of the nationalists, based upon military discipline and centered around Franco, who emerged as a strict and authoritarian leader
- the unswerving support of the Catholic Church's hierarchy for the nationalists
- the greater military expertise of Franco's professional troops against the "citizen" army supporting the republic. The troops Franco brought from Morocco were the élite of the Spanish army
- the numerous divisions among the republic's supporters between communists, anarchists, socialists and liberal republicans. They were all capable of acts of heroism but found it difficult to coordinate their efforts
- acts of political extremism on the republican side, like the confiscation of property in some of the areas they controlled, which drove potential supporters from the agrarian and middle classes to support the nationalists
- that nationalists controlled the main agricultural areas and so could deny food supplies to the republican-held cities. They also found it easier to obtain supplies from abroad, notably oil supplies from American oil companies.

Spartacist: a left-wing German socialist movement led by Rosa *Luxemburg*. It was founded in 1915, and in 1918 it helped to found the German Communist Party. In 1919, inspired by the communist takeover in Russia and taking advantage of Imperial Germany's defeat in the First World War, it staged a rising in Berlin which briefly threatened the survival of the *Weimar Republic*, but which failed because:

- the *Ebert–Groener Pact* between the Weimar president and the German army leader gave the government the support of the army in the crisis
- after a week of street violence, it was crushed by the paramilitary *Freikorps*, thanks to the benevolent neutrality of the army towards their action.

Speer, Albert: the Nazi architect and politician. In the 1930s, he was involved in designing the grandiose buildings which were seen as appropriate for the glories of the Nazi state, the most famous of which was the Nuremberg Stadium which was the annual setting for the Nazi rallies. In the Second World War, he was minister for armaments from 1942 and had a key role in planning the wartime economy. His administrative skills led to greatly improved industrial performance and helped, despite the Allied bombing campaign, to prolong German resistance. The role involved knowledge of the use of forced and slave labor, and at the Nuremberg Trials, despite having opposed Hitler openly in the last months of the war, he was sent to prison for 20 years. He was released in 1966 and wrote a revealing history, INSIDE THE THIRD REICH. He died in 1981.

Spiegel Affair: a 1962 political scandal in West Germany. *Strauss*, the defense minister, ordered the arrest, on a charge of treason, of the editor of the magazine

DER SPIEGEL, after the latter had criticized the performance of the German army in recent NATO exercises. This caused a major political storm and was portrayed as the type of action taken by the Nazi government during the Third Reich. Strauss was forced to resign, but the episode added greatly to the growing unpopularity of the aged chancellor, *Adenauer*, and led to his partners in the coalition government insisting that he stand down in the course of the next year, which he did.

Squadristi: a paramilitary organization backing the Italian fascists. It was made up of large numbers of ex-servicemen who, wearing black shirts as a uniform, indulged in acts of violence against opponents and fought the communists for control of the streets. They were commonly called *blackshirts*. Liberal politicians, fearful of communism, turned a blind eye to their illegal activities. In 1922, the Squadristi were given official status as the Militia for National Security, and were then regularly employed in the 1920s to intimidate voters and other political parties in elections. The Squadristi were an important element in Mussolini becoming prime minister in 1922 and then achieving totalitarian power in the state.

SS (Schutzstaffel): the Nazi secret and security police. It was formed in 1925 as Hitler's personal bodyguard, and from 1929 was led by *Himmler*. In 1934, it helped to carry out the murders of the *Night of the Long Knives*, eliminating the leadership of the rival *SA*. The *Gestapo*, a subdivision of the SS, and the Waffen SS, an élite independent army group, ran the German *concentration camps*.

Stakhanovite: a title awarded in the 1930s to Soviet workers who performed particularly remarkable production feats. It was named after a Soviet miner Stakhanov who, it was claimed, produced more than 100 tons of coal in a single shift. Eventually, the title became devalued, and over half the industrial workforce had it awarded to them.

Stalin, Joseph: dictator of the Soviet Union.

- Prior to the First World War, he worked secretly in Russia for the *Bolsheviks*
- After 1917, he became *Lenin*'s right-hand man
- After Lenin's death, he won the struggle for the leadership with *Trotsky*.

He developed his policy of "*socialism in one country*" as opposed to the idea of promoting worldwide revolution. From 1928, he carried through a series of *Five-Year Plans* which transformed Soviet agriculture and heavy industry but at great human cost. In agriculture, this involved abandoning Lenin's *New Economic Policy* in favor of massive, state-owned collective farms. He became increasingly intolerant, not only of opposition but even of dissent, and in the mid and late 1930s carried out a series of ruthless persecutions, the Great Purge or *Yezhovshchina*, of suspected rivals and opponents in a process which spun out of control and led to the imprisonment of millions of ordinary citizens.

Most Soviet foreign-policy initiatives came from Stalin personally. These included the *Nazi–Soviet Pact* of August 1939. After the 1941 German invasion, Stalin was presented to Soviet citizens as the savior of his country, in what became known as the *Great Patriotic War*.

- He attended Allied wartime conferences, holding the anti-German alliance together, and accepted both British and American aid

- At the *Yalta* and *Potsdam* conferences, he won agreements from the other Allies which led to the post-war Soviet domination of Eastern Europe
- After the war, he rejected American aid and led his country into Cold War opposition to the West.

At home, his regime remained as oppressive as ever, and returning prisoners of war, perhaps corrupted by what they had seen abroad, were treated particularly brutally, many spending considerable further periods of time in concentration camps. His suspicions of alleged rivals and of plots against him took on an anti-Semitic tinge, and many of those whom he came to distrust paid with their lives, as in the alleged *Doctors Plot* of 1953. Only some years after his death in 1953 were the Soviet people made aware of many of the excesses of the Stalinist years, a process begun in 1956 by Khrushchev in a historic speech to the Twentieth Congress of the Communist Party.

Stalingrad: a Soviet city on the river Volga. It was the scene of a savage *Second World War* battle in 1942–43. The *Red Army* stopped the German invasion of the Soviet Union in the south on the banks of the river Volga at Stalingrad, and a Soviet counter-attack then surrounded much of the German army under von *Paulus* which lost in total 300,000 men – killed or captured. The battle marked the end of German successes on the *Eastern Front* and was the crucial turning point in the war there. After 1956, as part of the process of de-Stalinization, the city was renamed Volgograd.

START (Strategic Arms Reduction Talks): international talks in the 1980s to reduce both the danger and the cost of the continuing arms race. They were overtaken both by US reluctance to abandon the *Strategic Defense Initiative* (SDI) and by the disintegration of the Soviet Union.

status quo: from Latin, it means the state of affairs as it is, or as it was before a recent change. So, for example, statesmen making a peace treaty may seek to restore the status quo which existed before the war.

Stauffenberg, Claus von: the German officer who, in 1944, planted the bomb in the unsuccessful *July Plot* attempt to kill Hitler.

Stolypin, Piotr: the chief minister of Tsar *Nicholas II* from 1907 to 1911. He ruthlessly repressed all signs of unrest and discontent after the disturbances of the *Revolution of 1905*.

- Summary courts carried out hundreds of trials and executions
- Workers' unions were closed down, as were over 1,000 newspapers
- Minorities, Jews and other non-Russians were resolutely persecuted.

By 1908, this repression ensured that the assassinations of state officials and other terrorist activity had been brought under control and reasonable order restored. Stolypin tried to stage-manage the elections to the second *Duma* to make it more acceptable to the tsarist authorities than the short-lived first Duma had been. When he failed, he altered the electoral law, drastically reducing the number of voters, so that the third Duma at least was suitably subservient.

Stolypin realized that if long-term stability was to be achieved, he also had to tackle Russia's economic and social problems. Unlike *Witte*, he saw the key to improvement as lying with the condition of agriculture and the peasantry. He aimed to create a prosperous peasantry that would want political and social stability, and to achieve this he freed the individual peasant from the control of the village community (*mir*).

- In 1906, peasants were given the right to withdraw themselves and their land from the control of the mir
- In 1907, the *redemption payments* by the peasants were ended
- The peasants were offered loans from the Peasants' Land Bank to help them acquire and develop their own farms
- In 1910, all mirs where no land had been redistributed since the abolition of serfdom in 1861 were abolished, and the lands given to the peasants.

At the outset of these reforms, only 20 percent of peasant households owned their own land, but by 1914 some 50 percent did so. It was a massive social reform carried out by a reactionary government but at the expense of the mirs rather than the land-owning nobility or the state, which together owned over 50 percent of the land. Stolypin also tried to reorganize the holdings of land so that typically scattered strips of land were consolidated into economically run farms, but this process was in its early stages when war began in 1914. On the other hand, half a million peasants had been persuaded to emigrate to Siberia and to open up new farming land there.

Stolypin was assassinated in 1911, when he was already distrusted by the nobility and was losing the support of the tsar. What might have happened in Russia if his reforms had been given time to come to fruition remains one of the tantalizingly unanswerable questions of Russian history. The rise in farm yields prior to 1914 suggests that the reforms might have done much to improve Russian agriculture, but also that the political stability for which Stolypin aimed would have been much more difficult to achieve within the tsarist autocratic state. (See also the entry on the *Russian economy, pre-1914*.)

Strasser, Gregor: a left-wing German Nazi. He wished to use the Nazi revolution to overthrow capitalism. Hitler did not share this vision for Germany's future, and Strasser was one of those murdered in the *Night of the Long Knives* in 1934.

strategy: the planning of large-scale troop movements in war, or in preparation for war. It should be distinguished from *tactics*, which are the more detailed maneuvers of troops during the course of a battle. The pre-1914 German *Schlieffen Plan* for the swift defeat of France in the event of a European war is a famous example of strategic planning.

Strategic Defense Initiative (SDI): a US 1980s project to establish a defense system in space which could make existing nuclear weapons ineffective. Commonly referred to as "Star Wars," it was much favored by President Reagan, but its practical possibilities were never established. The project's existence undermined the US willingness to bring the *START* talks to a successful conclusion, but arguably made Soviet leaders realize that they could never match US spending on defense projects, and so made *Gorbachev* more willing to reach an accommodation over Cold War issues.

Strauss, Franz-Josef: a West German politician. He held office in *Adenauer's* Christian Democrat coalition government with the Free Democrats from 1955 to 1962, and was the man chiefly responsible for bringing about German rearmament.

He was forced to resign over his autocratic actions in the *Spiegel Affair*.

Streicher, Julius: a leading Nazi. He was notorious, even in Nazi circles, for the violence of his anti-Semitic views and his zeal in persecuting the Jews, whipping up popular feeling against them in the columns of the newspaper DIE STÜRMER which he had founded. He was sentenced to death at the Nuremberg Trials.

Stresa Front: this was set up at a conference between Italy, Britain and France held in August 1935. The three powers:

- issued a protest at German rearmament contrary to the Versailles Treaty
- pledged themselves to resist any such unilateral repudiation of treaties which might endanger the peace of Europe.

This agreement looked imposing, but in practice none of the signatories was prepared to back up the pledge with action. Each power hoped that the very existence of the front would make any further action by them unnecessary. Mussolini in particular wanted the agreement in order to be safe in Europe so that he could pursue his imperial ambitions in Ethiopia. However, the front quickly collapsed when Britain signed a separate *Naval Agreement* with Germany and Italy began the *Italo–Ethiopian War*. The reaction of Britain and France to the Italian invasion drove Mussolini to join Hitler in the Rome–Berlin *Axis*. The failure of this, the only attempt by the other powers of Europe to combine to check Nazi German expansionism, is often cited as clear evidence of both the shortsightedness and the weakness of the foreign policies pursued by the powers in the 1930s.

Stresemann, Gustav: a leading politician in the *Weimar Republic*. More than anyone else, he re-established Germany's international diplomatic position following its defeat in the First World War. He was briefly chancellor in 1923 and then foreign minister from 1923 to 1929. He argued that Weimar Germany should honor the commitments it had entered into at Versailles, and by this won the confidence of the Allies.

- He ended the passive resistance with which the French and Belgian occupation of the *Ruhr* had been met, and then negotiated withdrawal of the occupying troops
- To end the hyperinflation which plagued the economy, he appointed *Schacht* as currency commissioner
- He secured as advantageous terms as he could on reparations when, in 1924, he negotiated the *Dawes Plan*, seeing it as a means both of removing foreign troops from Germany and of securing foreign loans to aid economic recovery
- He welcomed the 1929 *Young Plan* to rationalize further the payment of reparations
- He played a central part in the negotiations leading to the *Locarno Pact* and Germany's entry into the League of Nations in 1926
- In 1928, he signed the *Kellogg–Briand Pact*.

Stresemann continued to argue that Weimar Germany's eastern frontier had to be renegotiated and that *Danzig*, the *Polish Corridor* and parts of *Silesia* should return to Germany. He struck up personal friendships with other European statesmen, and the progress made internationally by Germany while he was in charge of its foreign affairs was part of a new stability in European relations in the late 1920s. That even he was not prepared to accept Weimar's frontier with Poland indicates what a bitter issue it was for Germans in general.

student revolts: demonstrations, peaceful and violent, by university students against state authorities or policies, which have marked key moments in the history of several European states. Many were left-wing in origin and ideas.

- In 1968, French students combined with workers to pose a formidable but eventually unsuccessful challenge to the Fifth French Republic. Unrest spread from Paris to universities across Western Europe, but never achieved the intensity or the revolutionary commitment of the French students
- Students in Eastern Europe often led the protests against communist authorities, notably in Hungary in 1956 and Czechoslovakia in 1968, in each case providing the spark which led to a wider challenge to the state authorities
- Students across Eastern Europe were again at the forefront of the 1989 demonstrations which swept away the region's communist regimes.

The success of student revolts seemed to depend crucially on whether the students could win the support, or at least the neutrality, of the army.

submarine warfare: an important feature of *sea warfare* in both world wars. In the First World War, German *U-boat* attacks on merchant ships helped to bring the USA into the war. In the Second World War, their attacks on supply routes in the Battle of the *Atlantic* were a serious threat to the Allied war effort. After the war, nuclear-powered submarines capable of staying underwater for months became a part of the *nuclear deterrent.*

Sudetenland: until 1918, part of Austria-Hungary. At the Paris Peace Conference, this geographically fragmented area was added to the provinces which went to make up the newly created Republic of *Czechoslovakia.* It was a heavily industrialized area, with 3 million Germans forming a large minority among its inhabitants. There were few problems until after 1935, when the Nazi, *Henlein,* formed a political party pledged to seek union of the Sudetenland with Germany. He stirred up public disorder, and this led to the pressure on Czechoslovakia from Nazi Germany that brought about the 1938 *Munich Agreement.* Under these, Hitler took the Sudetenland into Germany without opposition. The region was returned to Czechoslovakia in 1945, when the German inhabitants were expelled.

Suez Canal: this canal joins the Mediterranean and the Red Sea, and so provides a route to the Indian Ocean. It was opened in 1869 and fell under British control, with British troops stationed along it. In both world wars, the British, despite its having been guaranteed as being open to all in peace and in war, closed the canal to enemy ships. In 1935, however, it was not closed to Italian shipping engaged in the invasion of Ethiopia. British troops withdrew from the Canal Zone in 1956, and the canal was then nationalized by the Egyptian government. This led to the *Suez Crisis* of the same year.

Suez Canal Zone: land adjoining the *Suez Canal* which was controlled until 1956 by British troops.

Suez Crisis: the crisis arising from the attack by Israel on Egypt in 1956. It provided an excuse for the intervention of Britain and France, who had advance notice of Israeli intentions. The Western forces set out to occupy the *Suez Canal Zone* in order to protect the canal, which the Egyptians had just nationalized. Military progress was slow, and international outrage, particularly in the Third World and including condemnation in the UN General Assembly, became a factor in continuing the operation. More crucial was the opposition of the USA and the likely strains on the fragile economies of Britain and France if the USA applied financial sanctions. The British and French forces had to withdraw, with little hope of saving face. The episode marked an important stage in the ending of European imperial pretensions, and demonstrated the worldwide power of the USA.

suffrage: the right to vote in political elections.

superpower: a state having a dominant position in world politics, one having worldwide interests and able to act decisively around the world. It came into use after the Second World War, and particularly during the period of the Cold War, to describe the status of the USA and the Soviet Union. It was sometimes less accurately used with regard to communist China.

Svoboda, Ludovik: president of Czechoslovakia, 1968–75. He had been out of favor in the post-war Stalinist period, but with Khrushchev's help, he was rehabili-tated in the 1960s. In 1968, he succeeded the hard-line Novotný as president and tried, in the *Prague Spring*, to support the reforms introduced by Dubček. After the reform movement was crushed, he played an honorable and dangerous role in seeking the relaxation of the repressive measures imposed on the country by the Soviets. He died in 1975, a much-respected survivor of the disappointments of 1968.

swastika: a symbol, in the shape of a hooked cross, adopted by extreme right-wing groups in the *Weimar Republic*. It became the symbol of National Socialism and, from 1935, the national emblem of Nazi Germany.

Sweden: an independent kingdom from which Norway separated in 1905. It remained neutral in both world wars. Since the Second World War, it has been one of the more active members of the UN, it was a founder member of EFTA, and in 1995 it became a member of the European Community.

Switzerland: a multilingual republic which remained neutral in both world wars. It provided a home both for the headquarters of the Red Cross, which reversed the colors of the national flag to provide its own international emblem, and later for the League of Nations and its many agencies. To protect its traditional neutrality, it has declined to participate in the post-1945 development of European institutions.

syndicalism: a political theory which advocated the ownership and running of industry by workers through the medium of trade-union organization. Syndicalists saw the power of the trade unions, by direct action such as the *general strike*, as providing the structure for political life and as acting as an agent for major social and political change. The term comes from the French "syndicat," a trade union, and the movement was particularly strong in early twentieth-century France. Syndicalism was less influential after 1918, when many syndicalists joined communist, or occasionally fascist, organizations.

tactics: the art of maneuvering troops in the course of a battle. It needs to be distinguished from *strategy*.

Tangier: a North African port which was the landing point of the German kaiser in 1905 while cruising. The kaiser then created a crisis with France with some outspoken views on Moroccan independence. The issue was resolved at the *Algeciras Conference*.

tank warfare: tanks were first deployed, by the British army, in the Battle of the *Somme* in 1916, but became bogged down in the battlefield mud. They did, however, play an important part in the final 1918 advance of the Allied forces.

In the Second World War, tanks:

- were of primary importance in the German *blitzkrieg* advances of 1939 and 1940
- were employed in great numbers in the desert warfare of the *North Africa Campaign*
- were engaged in the largest tank battle in history, at *Kursk* on the Russian front in 1943
- played a central part in the movements of both the Red Army and the Western Allies on the Second Front in their separate advances into Germany.

Tannenberg: a First World War battle fought on the *Eastern Front* in August 1914. Soon after the outbreak of war, the Russian army invaded East Prussia and scored initial victories. The Germans then drafted *Hindenburg* and *Ludendorff*, two generals who were to make their reputations during the war, to the Eastern Front. The Russians had moved too quickly, and their generals did not cooperate with each other. One Russian army was surrounded at Tannenberg and lost 100,000 men taken prisoner. In September, a second Russian force was defeated at the Battle of the *Masurian Lakes*. A second battle in the region of the lakes early in 1915 brought the Russian attack to a halt and ended the danger of a Russian occupation of East Prussia. However, the initial speed of the Russian attack had compelled the Germans to pull troops from the *Western Front*, and so had contributed to the failure of the *Schlieffen Plan*.

tariffs: customs duties charged on imports to a country.

Taylor, A. J. P.: a British historian who challenged the general view, first argued by Churchill, that Hitler had, from an early stage, a master plan for dominating Europe through war. He argued that Hitler pursued traditional German foreign-policy aims, as had been achieved, for example, with the territorial gains at *Brest-Litovsk*, and was not alone among German politicians in wishing to see the terms of the *Versailles* Treaty overturned. He also claimed that Hitler, far from having a long-term plan, was a gifted opportunist who took advantage of circumstances which arose. Taylor argued that the views in *Mein Kampf* were no more than the idle dreams of a disappointed revolutionary, and that the *Hossbach Memorandum* was not the plan of conquest that had been alleged, and he cited the *Anschluss* and the *Munich Agreement* as the classic examples of Hitler taking advantage of circumstances that he had never foreseen.

Tehran Conference: an Allied wartime conference attended by Churchill, Roosevelt and Stalin in November 1943. The main business discussed was the pursuit of the war against Germany, including the opening of a *Second Front* in Western Europe. The prospect of setting up a United Nations organization after the war was also considered.

television: this replaced cinema in the 1950s as the mass-entertainment medium. The immediacy of its news coverage placed national and international crises right before the public. Its political impact has been difficult to establish.

- In Italy, a television-station proprietor, *Berlusconi*, used his control of the media to win political power in 1994, but this did not help him solve Italy's acute financial problems, and he lost the 1996 election
- In times of internal crisis, control of the television stations became important, as in Romania in 1989, and with the use of television pictures to influence events in the 1991 attempted coup in the Soviet Union, where the pictures of Yeltsin standing on a tank, ready to defy the army if necessary, did much to rally people to support the government
- It was claimed that, outside Europe, the intense 1960s television coverage in the USA of the Vietnam War was crucial in turning US opinion against the war and in forcing the US withdrawal.

terrorism: the deliberate use of assassination, bombing and kidnapping to create a climate of fear from which the terrorists hope to gain some political end. The use of terror for political ends has a long history. Anarchist terrorists used bombs to destabilize tsarist Russia, and both Mussolini and Hitler employed crude intimidation and violence against people as steps to power. Such tactics by *urban-guerrilla* groups became much more widespread in the second half of the twentieth century, particularly in acts of terrorism against the state. The German *Baader-Meinhof Gang*, the Italian *Red Brigade* and the *Provisional IRA* all employed terrorist tactics.

Teschen: a part of Silesia that was the subject of dispute from 1919 to 1938 between Poland and Czechoslovakia, and was divided between them in 1920. The 1938 *Munich Agreement* and Hitler's seizure of the Sudetenland encouraged the Poles to take control of all of it. Its fate illustrates how disputes between the smaller nations of Eastern Europe prevented them working together for their mutual protection, even when faced by the growing ambitions and power of Nazi Germany.

Thatcher, Margaret: British prime minister, 1979–90. Her governments vigorously pursued a policy of *privatization* and took pride in "rolling back the frontiers of the state" in economic matters. She was largely responsible in 1982 for regaining the Falkland Islands, after their conquest by Argentina, by launching the risky Falklands War. In foreign affairs, she was most noteworthy because of her opposition to many policies of the *European Union* (EU), particularly with regard to issues which she held touched on national sovereignty. This was largely responsible for a 1990 challenge to her leadership and her subsequent resignation.

Thatcherism: a British political term of the 1980s and 1990s. It did not identify any specific ideology which the Thatcher administrations espoused. It was used, mainly by opponents, to refer to whatever policies the Thatcher government was pursuing at any one time. These could include:

- privatization
- cutting public spending
- strengthening central at the expense of local government
- taking a strongly patriotic line on international issues
- resisting any moves that seemed likely to draw Britain into further commitments within the European Union.

Third French Republic: established in 1870 in the aftermath of military defeat by Prussia. It faced many crises, and one of the most divisive was the *Dreyfus Affair*, which revealed the depth of anti-Semitism in French society and also the sharp political divisions between the left and right in both society and political life. Until 1914, the Third Republic existed under the shadow of the military defeat of 1870, and the consequent loss of the two provinces of Alsace and Lorraine. Political instability, an apparently declining population and certainly a declining birth rate, together with Germany's ever-expanding industrial might, added to French feelings of inferiority. The alliance with Russia in 1893 and the 1904 *entente cordiale* with Britain were both made to meet these feelings of insecurity.

The republic suffered greatly during the *First World War*, when much of the fighting on the Western Front was conducted across northern France, and in 1917 French front-line troops were close to mutiny.

The dominant French leader of the war years and of the ensuing Paris Peace Conference was *Clemenceau*. After the war, unfortunately, no politician of his stature emerged. Between the two world wars, France was governed by a succession of either right-wing or left-wing coalition governments. In these 20 years of political instability, there were 20 different prime ministers serving in no less than 44 separate governments. This instability goes a long way to explaining the ineffectiveness of French foreign policy in the dangerous 1930s. The deep split in French political life between the left and the right prevented continuity in the conduct of policy, but even parties closer to each other in political sympathy found difficulty in reaching a common stance, as is illustrated by the disintegration of *Blum*'s popular front government when faced with how to respond to the Spanish Civil War.

The Third Republic was replaced in 1946 by the Fourth, but for all practical purposes it had ceased to exist six years earlier, with the surrender to Nazi Germany and the imposition of the puppet *Vichy* government.

Third International: also known as the Communist International, or *Comintern*. It was founded by Lenin in 1919 to organize and control the separate national communist parties. It was suspected in the non-communist world of being an agency promoting revolution, and was closed down by Stalin in 1943 in a gesture of wartime solidarity with the other Allied powers.

Third Reich: the common term used to describe Nazi Germany, 1933–45. See *German Third Empire*.

Third World: a term which became common after the Second World War to describe the nonaligned countries outside the Western (First World) and Soviet (Second World) blocs. It was later more loosely used to describe underdeveloped countries with a low gross national product (GNP). It fell into disuse with the collapse of the Second World in the late 1980s.

Thorez, Maurice: a French communist politician. He served in parliament throughout the Fourth Republic, and as party leader in the elections of 1945 and 1946. After 1956, he persuaded the French Communist Party to accept the need for the process of de-Stalinization.

Thousand-Year Reich: a common Nazi reference to the *Third Reich* (1933–45). It figured prominently in the rhetoric of *Nuremberg Rally* speeches.

Thyssen, Fritz: a German industrialist. He was, in the 1920s, the head of a vast steel combine and, before the Nazis came to power in 1933, became one of the first industrialists to provide Hitler with money, an action which he later came to regret.

Tirpitz, Alfred von: a German admiral. He was put in charge of the naval ministry in 1897 and then organized the German naval rearmament program which led to the *Naval Race* with Britain. Particularly significant were:

- his 1907 decision to build a new class of heavy battleships commonly referred to as *dreadnoughts*
- his work in arranging for the deepening of the Kiel Canal to accommodate the new class of battleships and so provide them with totally safe anchorage in the Baltic Sea.

In the First World War, he commanded the German submarine war in the Atlantic until, with the sinking of the LUSITANIA in 1915, the kaiser ordered this to be restricted. Tirpitz then resigned.

Tiso, Josef: a Slovak politician. In the 1930s, he wanted a separate Slovak state to be cut out from Czechoslovakia. He was made president of the Nazi German puppet republic of *Slovakia* from 1939 to 1945. His career shows how Hitler was able to use nationalist politicians in other countries to promote his expansionist foreign policy. After the war, he was hanged.

Tito, Josip: founder of the communist Federal Republic of *Yugoslavia* at the end of the Second World War. He was then its prime minister, 1945–53, and president 1953–80. He had served in the Soviet Red Army in the Russian Civil War and then returned to Yugoslavia to found its Communist Party. After the German occupation of the country in 1941, he became the leader of communist *partisans* fighting the occupying power from bases in the mountains. Despite bitter divisions with other partisan groups, notably the *chetniks*, his forces had liberated large areas of the country from the Germans even before the arrival of the Red Army. In 1943, he already had the standing to convene the *Jajce Conference*, which agreed to set up a Yugoslav republic with himself as leader. After the war, he stressed his country's independence from the Soviet Union and followed a *nonaligned* policy in the Cold War. The importance of his personal contribution to holding together his disparate state was indicated when, after his death in 1980, the presidency was replaced by a collective government of the leaders of the six republics which made up Yugoslavia.

The failure of this structure led to the anarchy and disintegration of the early 1990s.

Titoism: a charge brought against Eastern European communist dissidents. It was in use after Stalin's quarrel with Tito and Yugoslavia's expulsion from the *Cominform* in 1948. Major political figures who were accused of Titoism included:

- *Slansky* of Czechoslovakia, in 1951
- *Nagy* of Hungary, in 1955.

It was an all-purpose charge based on the idea that the accused was breaking away from the true path of socialism.

Tobruk: a port in Libya. It was the setting, during the *North Africa Campaign* of 1941–42, of two extended sieges of British Commonwealth troops, mainly Australian and South African, by German and Italian forces.

Togliatti, Palmiro: an Italian communist politician. After Mussolini banned the Communist Party in 1926, he lived in exile, working for a time for the Spanish Republic during the Spanish Civil War. He returned to Italy in 1944 and had a long career as leader of the most successful communist party in Western Europe. He:

- controlled the local government of many towns and won 135 parliamentary seats in 1948
- advocated a separate Italian road to communism, based for example on recognition of the Roman Catholic Church
- is regarded as the inspiration for the *Eurocommunist* movement promoting a more liberal and varied version of communist rule than that in the Soviet bloc.

However, his dream that the communists could achieve power in Italy via the ballot box was never realized. He died in 1964.

totalitarian: involving total control of institutions by the state authorities and permitting no rival political parties. It involves a group having absolute power in the state and seeking to control the lives of its citizens; an example of totalitarianism in practice in Nazi Germany is given in the *Hitler Youth* entry. States can be more or less totalitarian depending on the degree of control they exercise. It is a term often used to condemn states which are seen as undemocratic, as with Nazi Germany or the Soviet Union under Stalin.

total war: the mobilization of all of a country's resources to achieve victory in war, as with Britain, Germany or Russia in the Second World War.

Trans-Siberian Railway: connected Moscow with Vladivostock on the Pacific. It was started in 1891 and completed as a single track by 1904 and as a double track in the 1930s. It was promoted by *Witte* and was part of the Russian thrust to the Far East which was rebuffed by defeat in the *Russo–Japanese War* of 1904–05.

transformismo: an early twentieth-century Italian political term. It described the practice of creating large political coalitions to back particular governments. They lacked any unity and denied Italy effective government as they rested not on agreed political programs but on the bribery of coalition supporters to back individual political leaders such as *Giolitti*. This led to disillusionment with democratic politics, and so helped the rise of *Mussolini* and the fascists.

Treaty on the Final Settlement with Respect to Germany: a 1990 treaty between West and East Germany and the four post-1945 occupying powers, Britain, France, the Soviet Union and the USA. It followed the collapse of East Germany, and unified Germany as a sovereign state occupying the territory of the two former German states. Its creation marked the end of the Cold War in Central Europe and owed much to Chancellor *Kohl* of West Germany.

Treblinka: a Nazi extermination camp in Poland. It was probably the most infamous after the much larger Auschwitz.

trench warfare: best exemplified on the *Western Front* in the First World War. This was static warfare in which both sides dug long lines of defensive trenches topped by sandbags and fronted by barbed wire. These were backed by complex lines of communication trenches and defended by men armed with rifles and machine guns. They proved remarkably difficult and costly to penetrate, even when attacks were supported by artillery barrages, poison gas or tanks. Attacking forces going "over the top" of the trenches into no-man's land to attack the enemy lines were mowed down mercilessly and rarely made significant territorial gains at such battles as the *Somme, Passchendaele* and *Ypres*.

Trentino: a territory on the borders of northern Italy and Austria. It was ceded to Italy at the Treaty of *Saint Germain* at the end of the First World War.

Trianon, Treaty of: a peace treaty imposed on Hungary in 1920. It was a delayed part of the *Paris Peace Conference* settlement. It:

- replaced the kingdom of Hungary, part of the *Austro-Hungarian Empire*, with a republic
- took two-thirds of the land of the old kingdom away from its successor in order to create the new states of Czechoslovakia and Yugoslavia and to greatly enlarge Romania.

These arrangements were justified as meeting the national aspirations of the inhabitants of the vast region, but they meant that many Hungarians (Magyars) would be living in exile from their former homeland. In the *Vienna Awards* of 1938 and 1940, Hungary regained some territory from Romania in return for supporting Germany. This was again lost at the end of the Second World War.

Trieste: a port situated at the head of the Adriatic Sea. Until the First World War, it was the main port of the Austro-Hungarian Empire. It was given to Italy at the Paris Peace Conference of 1919. At the Treaties of Paris in 1947, it was declared to be a free city, but in 1954 Italy and Yugoslavia reached agreement on division of the territory between them.

Triple Alliance: an 1882 alliance of Germany, Austria-Hungary and Italy formed by *Bismarck*. Its existence persuaded France and Russia to ally in 1893, but in practice the Triple Alliance never functioned because Italy at first remained neutral in the First World War and then joined the *Allies*.

Triple Entente: an international understanding reached in 1907 between Britain, France and Russia. It arose from:

- the Franco–Russian Alliance of 1893
- the *entente cordiale* between Britain and France in 1904
- the *Anglo–Russian Entente* of 1907.

The three powers were motivated by the perceived threat from Germany, and by the existence of the *Triple Alliance.*

Trotsky, Leon: a Russian revolutionary leader and communist theorist. He was with *Lenin* in exile in London in 1902, but after the 1903 split between the Bolsheviks and the Mensheviks, he favored the latter. In the Revolution of 1905, he set up the first workers' soviet in St. Petersburg, but when the spontaneous revolution collapsed, he was exiled to Siberia and later again went abroad. He returned in May 1917 a committed Bolshevik. His major contribution to the creation of the Bolshevik state included:

- his work in establishing Bolshevik control of the *Petrograd Soviet,* of which he became chairman in November 1917
- his use of this political base to play a key role in the events of the *October Revolution*
- acting through the *Military Revolutionary Committee* of the Petrograd Soviet during the October Revolution to organize Bolshevik supporters to seize the buildings occupied by the Provisional Government and other key points in the city
- from 1917 to 1924, serving as Lenin's closest adviser and support
- taking responsibility in the new Bolshevik state for foreign affairs, including negotiating the Treaty of *Brest-Litovsk* with Germany and so securing breathing space for the new regime, as well as meeting the aspirations of many Russians that the war be ended
- the creation, as commissar for war during the *Russian Civil War* (and until 1924), of the largely peasant *Red Army.* He organized its recruitment based on conscription, established its discipline and employed ex-tsarist officers, accompanied by reliable political commissars, to give it professional competence
- organizing the strategy for victory against the White Russians. He was left to do this by Lenin, who concentrated on political and economic problems. In pursuit of victory, he traveled repeatedly across the country in a specially armored train.

His work to this point had saved the Bolshevik revolution, but when Lenin died in 1924 Trotsky lost the leadership succession to *Stalin.* He had failed to establish a power base within the Communist Party and was outmaneuvered by Stalin. After 1924, he quickly lost influence. His support for the idea of permanent revolution leading to world communism did not fit the early 1920 reality of the Soviet Union's capabilities, and Stalin's policy of *socialism in one country,* which Trotsky bitterly opposed, seemed the safer approach. In 1927, Stalin intrigued to have him expelled from the party and, in 1929, deported from the country. In exile, he remained an influential communist thinker and a persistent thorn in Stalin's side until, in 1940, Stalin arranged for his assassination.

Trotskyist: a term loosely used to describe someone who supported the ideas associated with Trotsky. In the Soviet Union, this could simply be someone who opposed the authoritarian rule of Stalin, but internationally it often described a supporter of Trotsky's notion of worldwide revolution and one who rejected Stalin's excessive Russian nationalism. It has often been used simply as a convenient insult in factional fighting among left-wing politicians.

Truman, Harry S: president of the USA, 1945–53 and responsible for the *Truman Doctrine.* He succeeded *Roosevelt* on the latter's death early in 1945, having had no experience of international affairs. It has been argued that the tough US stance against the Soviet Union in the early days of the Cold War owed much to this change at the top of the US government, but it should be remembered that there were important issues at stake and that the situation in Europe, as it moved from war to peace, was changing rapidly. Roosevelt, for all his commitment to the anti-Nazi alliance, might not have easily been able to smooth away the causes of conflict between the Soviet Union and its ex-partners once Germany was defeated.

Truman Doctrine: this was promulgated by US president Truman in March 1947. He:

- asked the US Congress for aid to Greece and Turkey
- stressed his disquiet about the coercion practiced by the Soviet Union in Poland, Romania and Bulgaria
- expressed his concern for the outcome of the Greek Civil War and for the continued independence of Turkey
- pledged, in the central message of the "Doctrine," that the USA would "support free peoples who are resisting attempted subjugation by armed minorities and outside pressures."

Truman was successful in obtaining large sums of money for military and financial aid. This episode was the key moment in the continued US commitment to Western Europe in the aftermath of the Second World War, and the opposite response to the isolationist decisions taken after the First World War. It had led, by 1949, to US membership of *NATO* and so to a binding commitment to the military defense of Western Europe.

tsar: the title of the Romanov rulers of the Russian Empire until February 1917.

Tunisia: a North African country, once part of the Ottoman Empire, which became a French protectorate in 1881. In the 1920s and 1930s, agitation for national independence grew, and there were disturbances and repression. In the Second World War, it was occupied by the Germans in 1942 and liberated by the Allies in 1943. After the war, France tried to reimpose its control but encountered a strong movement for Tunisian national independence to add to its other commitments in Algeria. In 1956, France conceded independence to the country, but continued to hold military bases from which it fought its *Algerian War.*

Turkey: a republic established after the overthrow of the *Ottoman Empire.* It came from the determined resistance of the Turks to the Treaty of *Sèvres* in 1920. Under Mustafa Kemal (*Atatürk*), the Turks:

- drove the Greeks out of western Turkey
- reoccupied the independent republic of Armenia
- forced the Allies to agree to revised terms at the 1923 Treaty of *Lausanne.*

Atatürk became president and undertook the modernization of the state as a secular republic. The powers of Islam were severely curtailed, and a Western way of life was enforced by law. Many old customs, for example women covering their faces or men wearing the fez, were banned.

Post-1945

Until 1950, Turkey was a one-party state run on strictly authoritarian lines. It remained neutral during the Second World War but, conscious of its long border with the Soviet Union, joined NATO in 1952. The invasion of Cyprus in 1974, and its protection of the North Cyprus Republic since then, increased the tension between Turkey and Greece. Kurdish and Armenian violence to achieve some form of autonomy has been met with harsh repression from the military which, in 1995, involved entry into Iraq, where large-scale military action was taken to destroy Kurdish bases. Almost 200,000 Turkish troops have been deployed against the Kurds, some 2 million of whom have been driven from their homes. An Islamic revival in the early 1990s also threatened Atatürk's vision of a Westernized state. After a period of martial law and military government from 1980, party politics resumed in 1988, when the military leaders handed power back to the politicians. Turkey then applied for membership of the European Union, but its record on civil liberties and the hostility of Greece suggested that this would not be easily achieved.

Twentieth Congress: the February 1956 Congress of the Soviet Communist Party notable for *Khrushchev*'s denunciation, in a secret session, of Stalin. It led to *de-Stalinization* in the Soviet Union and in many of the other communist countries of Eastern Europe, and was the cause of unsuccessful uprisings intended to overthrow the communist regimes in Hungary and Poland.

Tyrol: a region in the southern Alps. Until the First World War, it was part of the Austro-Hungarian Empire, but at the Paris Peace Conference was given to Italy.

U

U-boat: a German submarine of the First and Second World Wars.

U2 Incident: a US high-altitude U2 reconnaissance plane was shot down in 1960 over the center of the Soviet Union while on a photography mission. It led the Soviets to cancel a summit meeting with US president Eisenhower to have been held two weeks later.

UK: the abbreviation for *United Kingdom.*

Ukraine: an independent republic which was part of the *Soviet Union* until 1991. It is an agriculturally rich region which, until 1917, formed part of tsarist Russia. It was then the scene of fighting in the *Russian Civil War* until, in 1922, it came under Soviet rule after the attempt to establish an independent state was defeated by the successes of the Red Army. Stalin's *collectivization* of agriculture hit the region particularly harshly, and the German invasion of 1941 was welcomed by many Ukrainian nationalists. It saw very heavy fighting and much destruction during the Second World War but, with the victories of the Red Army, again became part of the Soviet Union. After 1945, its economy was rebuilt, and large-scale industry was developed.

In 1991, after the failure of the *Moscow Coup*, the Ukraine declared itself independent, and this was confirmed in a referendum, when 90 percent of the electorate voted in favor. However, power remained with the former communists, and this limited the scale of change. The Crimea, with an ethnic-Russian majority among its population, sought independence from the Ukraine, causing tension there from 1992 until, in 1994, limited Ukrainian military intervention reduced the Crimea to a region within the Ukraine.

Ulbricht, Walter: an East German political leader, 1950–71. He:

- spent the Second World War in exile in the Soviet Union
- returned in 1945 as a Soviet tool in the creation of a communist state in what had been the Soviet *zone of occupation*
- survived popular disturbances in 1953, thanks to the use of Soviet troops
- was noted for his hard-line, repressive policies.

He will probably remain best known for the 1961 decision to build the *Berlin Wall.* He retired as Communist Party secretary in 1971 and died in 1973.

Ulster: the historical name for *Northern Ireland,* which remained part of the United Kingdom in the 1921 treaty which divided Ireland and allowed the setting up of the Irish Free State. It was the scene of an Irish nationalist terrorist campaign from 1969 and also of a counter terror campaign by Protestant extremists determined to keep Ulster part of the United Kingdom. An uncertain peace was established in 1995, and the governments of Britain and the Republic of Ireland began to construct political arrangements which would have a chance of making this permanent, culminating in the 1998 Northern Ireland Accord.

ultimatum: a final statement of terms presented by one state to another which, if not agreed to, will lead to the breaking of diplomatic relations or even war. Notable examples were the British and French ultimatums of 1 September 1939 to Germany that if it did not give an assurance within 48 hours that it would cease its attack on Poland, then a state of war would exist between them and Germany.

UNESCO (United Nations Educational, Scientific and Cultural Organization): a specialized agency of the UN founded in 1946, with its title indicating the range of its interests. Allegations of undue left-wing bias in UNESCO led Britain and the USA to withdraw their membership and funding in 1985. Britain rejoined in 1997.

UNICEF (The United Nations Children's Fund): established in 1947 as a specialized agency of the UN. Its work has been mainly conducted in the world's developing countries.

unilateral: something done by, or affecting, one side only. Pressure in Britain from the 1950s for unilateral nuclear disarmament demanded that nuclear weapons be dispensed with, regardless of what other states intended to do in the matter.

UNO: the *United Nations Organization*, founded in 1945.

United Kingdom: in the nineteenth century and until 1921, the official title of the British islands was The United Kingdom of Great Britain and Ireland. Irish independence in 1921 altered the title to The United Kingdom of Great Britain and Northern Ireland. The UK consists of England, Scotland, Wales and Northern Ireland.

United Nations Organization (UN): the successor to the *League of Nations*. It:

- was a product of the wartime conferences between the leaders of the Allies
- was formally established at a conference in San Francisco in 1945 that drew up the UN charter which was then signed by representatives of the 51 nations present
- had 185 members in 1998.

Its main debating forum is the *General Assembly,* and its executive arm is provided through the *Security Council.* It also acts as the umbrella for a large number of international specialized agencies, which have often achieved greater success in their fields than the parent body; these include the *World Health Organization,* the *Food and Agriculture Organization,* the *International Labor Organization, UNICEF* and *UNESCO.* In Europe, the UN:

- succeeded in separating the warring parties in Cyprus in 1964
- maintained a peacekeeping force of 3,000 men in Cyprus whose main task, after the Turkish invasion of 1974, was to patrol the new frontier between Turkish North Cyprus and the Greek south
- failed to prevent Soviet intervention in Hungary in 1956
- failed to prevent Warsaw Pact intervention in Czechoslovakia in 1968.

This pattern indicated the UN's usefulness in disputes not involving the direct interests of the major powers, but also its limited effectiveness when such powers were involved.

The UN peacekeeping missions in the former Yugoslavian republics of Bosnia-

Herzegovina, Croatia and Macedonia from 1992 to 1995 had their operations plagued, and their effectiveness greatly reduced, by the unwillingness of the warring factions to agree to a ceasefire. International support for UN operations had never been such that it could, in any crisis, actually impose a peace by military force.

United States of America: the world's most powerful nation. In the early twentieth century, it was the destination for many millions of European emigrants, notably Jews from Eastern Europe, Italians and Irish, until, in the 1920s, the USA curbed the inflow. At many critical moments of European history in the twentieth century, the role of the USA was crucially important.

1917–39

In 1917, the USA entered the First World War on the Allied side in response to the German unrestricted submarine campaign in the Atlantic. President Woodrow *Wilson* played an important part in the *Paris Peace Conference* but failed to persuade his country to join, and so gravely weakened, his cherished League of Nations. Despite this, the USA did not follow a policy of total isolationism towards Europe in the 1920s, as the *Dawes Plan* and the *Young Plan* testify. In the 1930s, however, the USA faced serious internal economic problems and was reluctant to become involved in maintaining peace in Europe, and this undoubtedly influenced Chamberlain and others to follow a policy of appeasement towards Hitler.

The Second World War

From 1939, the USA gave considerable material assistance to Britain in the Second World War, and in December 1941, following the Japanese attack on the US fleet at Pearl Harbor, Hitler and Mussolini declared war on the USA. The US role in the war was then crucial to the Allied victory, for American resources were on such a scale that Britain became the junior partner in the alliance.

After 1945

After the war, the USA:

- maintained its military presence in Western Europe
- provided economic aid to assist the reconstruction of Western European national economies – the *Marshall Plan* and the *Truman Doctrine* were central to this.

The American presence remained important in the crises of the *Cold War*:

- its *nuclear deterrent* provided a shield for the capitalist West
- its military might formed the backbone of *NATO*
- it intervened in specific European crises, notably with the 1948 *Berlin Airlift.*

Relations between Western European nations and the USA sometimes contained hidden tensions:

- Britain tried to assure itself that it had a special relationship with the USA, but this could not easily be quantified and it took a sharp knock at the time of the *Suez Crisis* in 1956
- France under *de Gaulle* came to resent American dominance and sought to develop an independent European identity in the Cold War

- after the Second World War, US dislike of colonialism was one factor leading to the decline of the European empires
- US domination of world trade was a fact of life for all the capitalist countries of the West until, in the 1980s, the full economic impact of the emerging European Union introduced some balance into international economic relations.

On the other hand, the USA provided the major part of Western Europe's protection against the communist threat. Eventually, indeed, US military and economic resources proved too great for the Soviet Union to match in terms of defense spending, and the strain of trying to do so did much to undermine the Soviet economy in the 1970s and 1980s. If the West "won" the Cold War, it was for these reasons.

urbanization: the degree of urbanization relates to the percentage of the population living in urban areas or towns, as opposed to rural areas or the countryside. It is usually used to refer to the increased rate of town growth in a region or across a period of time. Medieval and early modern Europe was largely a continent of villages. Population and industrial growth in the nineteenth century led to significant urbanization, especially in Western Europe. By 1900, there were large urban industrial areas in Britain, northern France and parts of Germany, such as the Ruhr. By 1945, 70 percent of Germany's population lived in towns, as did 55 percent of the French, 80 percent of the British and 47 percent of Soviet citizens. Urbanization produced the rise of the industrial *proletariat* from whom Marxists expected so much in terms of revolutionary fervor. The emergence of a mass industrial working class which gradually gained some form of political recognition transformed the practice of politics in both democratic and totalitarian states through:

- the development of mass political parties
- the use of *propaganda*
- the use of new media such as radio, the cinema and mass-circulation newspapers.

urban guerrillas: groups using military methods and terrorist tactics in towns and cities to achieve political ends. Italy's *Red Brigade* or West Germany's *Baader–Meinhof Gang* are examples.

Uruguay Round: the most recent round of international trade negotiations under *GATT*. It lasted from 1986 to 1994, and the relaxations on trade restrictions which were agreed would only be fully enacted in 2002. The final act of the round was to replace GATT by the *World Trade Organization* (WTO).

USSR (Union of Soviet Socialist Republics): the formal title of the *Soviet Union*. It was formed on 30 December 1922 as a federation of communist republics, and survived until 26 December 1991.

V

V1 and V2 rockets: German Second World War weapons.

- The V1 was strictly an unmanned light aircraft with the range to reach southern England from launching pads in German-occupied Europe. It had significant nuisance and propaganda value
- The V2, a genuine rocket, was more formidable but came too late in the war to affect the outcome. The British authorities were very concerned about its effect on civilian morale, and it was only the capture of the launch sites on the Continent by the advancing Allied armies that ended the menace.

Vatican City: by 1870, all the territories belonging to the pope, as head of the Roman Catholic Church, had been incorporated into the newly unified Italy. In 1929, the *Lateran Treaties* recognized the full independence of the papal lands in the city of the Vatican within Rome. This area, of some 100 acres, has since that date functioned as an independent state.

Vatican Council: the second council of the leadership of the Catholic Church called by Pope John XXIII in 1962. It examined spiritual and organizational matters, and was reconvened in 1963 by Pope Paul VI, sitting until 1965 and attended at its peak by 8,000 bishops. It aroused hopes of reform and renewal which hard reality suggested would be difficult to fulfill.

Venizelos, Eleutherios: prime minister of Greece on several occasions between the world wars. In 1905, he was responsible for the union of Crete with Greece, and later for bringing Greece into the *First World War* on the Allied side. He gained Greece's reward at the Treaty of *Sèvres*, only to see it snatched away by *Atatürk*'s revival of Turkish fortunes.

Verdun: a town in northern France and the setting in 1916 for one of the bloodiest battles of the First World War. It followed from a German offensive against the heavily fortified town pursued by Falkenhayn, regardless of casualties. His aim was to break the morale of the French army and to draw in its reserves in irreplaceable numbers. The French garrison, under Nivelle and Pétain, held out and then regained the fortifications earlier lost. The French troops, however, were at one point close to general mutiny. It is argued that the need to relieve the pressure on Verdun justified the costly British offensive at the Battle of the *Somme*. At Verdun, both the French and the Germans suffered some 400,000 casualties.

Versailles, Treaty of: a treaty of 1919, the most important single part of the settlement at the *Paris Peace Conference* which ended the First World War. The treaty followed the armistice of November 1918 and was between the Allied powers and Germany. It was not negotiated between the ex-combatants but was imposed upon the representatives of the Weimar Republic. The terms imposed on Germany included:

- a *war-guilt clause* in the treaty which required Germany to take responsibility for bringing about the war; on this basis, the Allies proceeded to punish her

- the payment of *reparations* to the Allies, for war damage and the cost of the war; though the amount to be paid was left to the Reparations Committee
- the loss of its colonies, which became League of Nations *mandates*
- the return of *Alsace-Lorraine* to France
- the loss of some border villages to Belgium
- the surrender to Poland of the *Polish Corridor* and parts of *Silesia*
- in the east, the loss of *Danzig* and *Memel*, both of which were to become free cities under the supervision of the League of Nations
- the surrender of parts of Silesia to Czechoslovakia
- the *Saar* coalfield to be occupied by the French for 15 years
- the *Rhineland* to be demilitarized
- *Anschluss* (union) between Germany and Austria was forbidden
- the German army was limited to 100,000 men; and it was not to have tanks or artillery
- Germany was forbidden to have submarines and military aircraft.

At the Allied negotiations, the French had pressed for even sharper punishment of Germany, and for a treaty that would ensure that it would never again be a threat to the peace of Europe. The final terms of the treaty were still seen as too lenient by the French, but their harshness nonetheless caused great bitterness in Weimar Germany, and the sense of grievance was exploited by the Nazis.

The treaty also included a clause setting up the *League of Nations*. The US Senate refused to ratify the treaty, partly as a consequence of domestic political disputes but also because of the open nature of the commitment to the League.

Vichy: a French provincial town. It was the seat of the German puppet government set up to administer the areas of France not directly occupied by the German army from 1940 to July 1944 when, with the Allied invasion of France, the government moved into Germany, collapsing in 1945. The head of state was *Pétain*, but the real leaders were first *Laval* and then *Darlan*. The regime:

- was never recognized by the Allies
- collaborated with the German authorities
- fell more and more under the control of French fascists.

In 1942, the German army occupied all of France, and the Vichy government's freedom of action became very limited. Pétain and Laval had based their policies on the belief that Germany would win the war and that France's interests would be best served by cooperating with the victors. In practice, their collaboration with the Germans gave them little or no bargaining power. The collaboration included the rounding up of some 80,000 Jews in a Paris railway siding by French police and then sending them to their deaths, the majority at Auschwitz. Only in the 1990s were many French people made to accept the reality of this action and of the numbers involved, and only then was a memorial erected to these victims of Vichy collaboration.

Victor Emmanuel III: king of *Italy*, 1900–46. He failed, after the First World War and at a time of growing political disorder, to suppress fascist riots. In 1922, fearing the growing power of town-based communists, and despairing of the strength of purpose of Italy's democratic politicians, he invited Mussolini to form a government, having earlier refused to sign *Facta*'s government decree imposing martial law as a means of blocking the fascist threat. This timidity was crucial in enabling Mussolini to become prime minister. After 1922, he failed to check the growth in Mussolini's power and became an impotent spectator in the fascist state, being installed as emperor of Ethiopia in 1936 and king of Albania in 1939. In 1943, as Italy faced defeat in the Second World War, he dismissed Mussolini and opened negotiations with the Allies. After the war, a referendum turned Italy into a republic, by some 11 million votes to 10 million, and the king went into exile. He died in 1947.

Vienna: capital of the Austrian Empire until 1867, and then joint capital, with Budapest, of the Austro-Hungarian Empire. From 1919, it was the capital of the Republic of Austria. In 1938, its inhabitants gave German troops and Hitler himself such a tumultuous reception that Hitler decided to effect the *Anschluss* immediately. From 1945, it was again the capital of the republic of Austria.

Vienna Awards: land awards in favor of Hungary in 1938 and 1940.

- The first, exploiting Czech weakness shortly after the Munich Agreement, secured it land in Slovakia at the expense of Czechoslovakia
- In the second, under German pressure, Romania was forced to concede most of Transylvania to Hungary.

Hungary then fought on the German side in the Second World War.

Vimy Ridge: a First World War battle in northern France. In 1917, Canadian troops retook the ridge which had been held by the Germans since 1914. It represented one of the few dents made in the opposing front lines on the *Western Front* prior to the final offensives of 1918.

Virgin Lands: the Soviet lands in Central Asia and Siberia which *Khrushchev* determined in the 1950s should be turned into productive, grain-growing land. Massive investment in supplying water and fertilizers produced encouraging early yields, but the poverty of the soil and the marginal climate then led to a rapid decline in productivity.

Vittorio Veneto: an Italian victory against Austria-Hungary right at the end of the First World War. It reversed the Italian defeat at *Caporetto* and led the Austrians to request an armistice.

Voroshilov, Kliment: along with Molotov and Kalinin, a supporter of Stalin in the 1920s power struggle to lead the Soviet Union.

vote of confidence: sometimes a technical term in parliamentary debates. It implies that if the vote is lost, the government of the day will resign. Often used more casually to indicate signs that confidence in some organization or policy is being eroded.

Vladivostock: a Russian port on the Pacific built after 1860. From 1904, it was the Far East terminus of the *Trans-Siberian Railway* and figured prominently in tsarist imperial ambitions in the region.

Vyshinsky, Andrei: a Soviet politician and lawyer. He was:

- notorious as the chief prosecutor in the rigged state trials in Stalin's 1930s *Yezhovshchina* or Great Purge
- the main Soviet delegate at the UN from 1945 to 1949
- Soviet foreign minister from 1949 to 1953.

In both of these later posts, he pursued a hard-line Stalinist Cold War approach to international issues. The Soviet Union usually found itself in a minority of one when controversial issues were considered by the UN *Security Council.* In these circumstances, Vyshinsky became notorious for employing the Soviet veto on actions of which he disapproved.

Waldheim, Kurt: secretary-general of the UN, 1972–81, president of Austria, 1986–92. His election as president was the occasion of charges that, as a Nazi intelligence officer during the Second World War, he had taken part in the transportation of Jews to death camps. This did not prevent his election but it did provoke an outbreak of anti-Semitism in Austria.

Wales: a country which, with England and Scotland, forms Great Britain and, with Northern Ireland added, the United Kingdom. In the second half of the twentieth century, there was a persistent, but never powerful, move for some form of self-government for Wales. In 1997 the Welsh people voted narrowly in favor of a devolved Assembly but continued, for all international purposes, to be ruled by the United Kingdom's Parliament at Westminster.

Walesa, Lech: president of Poland, 1990–95. He:

- was a trade unionist and strike leader at the Gdansk shipyards
- was the key figure in the founding of *Solidarity*, which became the chief opponent of the communist regime
- gained widespread support for his oratory and for his publicly avowed Catholicism.

In the 1980s, he was briefly imprisoned, then awarded the Nobel Peace Prize and received in audience by the pope when on a visit to Poland. In 1989, he secured the legalization of Solidarity and the establishment of a multi-party state. He was elected president in 1990 but had to work with a parliament divided among many small parties, and with a revival of left-wing influence creating political tension over the pace and direction of economic reform. In February 1995, he forced the resignation of the government, which he believed was obstructing reform by threatening to dissolve the Parliament.

Wall Street Crash: the sudden collapse in share prices on the New York Wall Street stock exchange in October 1929. It:

- followed a long boom in share prices which had not taken account of weaknesses in the US economy
- led to panic-selling of shares, so that values fell by 40 percent within days and continued to fall over the next three years
- caused many personal bankruptcies and business closures throughout the USA.

Its impact spread across the capitalist world, first hitting Europe when it led to the closure of the Austrian *Creditanstalt* Bank which in turn had a knock-on effect on other European banks. The crash led directly into the worldwide Great Depression (see *Depression, the Great*) which had catastrophic economic, social and political consequences for many European countries.

Wal Wal: an oasis on the disputed border between *Ethiopia* and the Italian colony of Somaliland. It was the site of a border incident in December 1934 in which some

Italian soldiers were killed. Despite the League of Nations, at Ethiopia's request, setting up an investigation, Mussolini used the incident as an excuse to take military action against Ethiopia, and so launched the conquest of the country in the *Italo–Ethiopian War.*

war communism: an economic policy introduced by *Lenin* in 1918 to enable the Bolshevik regime to survive the Russian Civil War. The Bolsheviks, on coming to power, had started a process of encouraging the peasants to break up the landed estates into separate peasant holdings. By June 1918, this policy was reversed and war communism was instituted.

- There was strict state control in all areas of economic production and trade
- Private trade was banned
- The money economy was destroyed by the simple device of printing vast quantities of notes
- In order to feed the towns, grain was requisitioned on a large scale, which soon came to include forced confiscation by the army, and the peasantry were set against each other by the poor peasants being encouraged to control the *kulaks*
- Food supplies were distributed by the commissariats of food and of agriculture, and were also rationed according to one's job
- Thirty-seven thousand urban enterprises employing 10 people or more were nationalized
- Strikes were banned, and labor was forced to work where directed.

War communism reduced many people, in both town and country, to starvation levels, and there were numerous peasant uprisings against the rigors of the policy. Food became so scarce in the towns that there was mass migration to the country-side on a scale inconceivable in Western Europe. Petrograd's population fell from 2.5 million in 1917 to around half a million in 1920. War communism was an economic disaster. Famines in southern Russia alone caused 5 million deaths, and associated disease perhaps as many again. Industrial production crumbled, with the coal industry at a quarter, steel at one-twentieth and pig-iron production at one-fortieth of their pre-war levels. The rigors of the policy and its economic failings created dangerous political unrest, notably the *Kronstadt Mutiny*, and led to its being replaced in 1921 by the *New Economic Policy.* War communism occurred during years of civil war, when the Bolshevik regime was fighting for its existence. It should not therefore be assumed that all the ills of the time were the result of this policy, since many were caused or aggravated by the war instead.

war criminal: a concept first linked to the cry of "Hang the kaiser!" heard at the end of the First World War. The horrors of the Second World War and its associated genocide led to the concept being formalized and used as the basis of the charges against leading Nazis in the *Nuremberg Trials.* Twenty-five of the 177 so tried were sentenced to death. The term was revived in 1996 when it became clear that massacres of male civilians had taken place during the civil war in *Bosnia.* Alleged Serb war criminals were then put on trial, and there were UN calls for *Karadžić,* the leader of the Bosnian Serbs, to be among their number.

war-guilt clause: a clause inserted into the 1919 Treaty of *Versailles* which required Germany to acknowledge its guilt, both for starting the war and for the subsequent damage that the war had caused. This, strictly Article 231 of the 440 articles in the treaty, then became the basis for punishing Germany. It caused great resentment in the *Weimar Republic* and was exploited by the Nazis to arouse nationalist feeling.

Warsaw Pact: a military grouping of Eastern European communist states formed in 1955. The members were Albania (until 1968), Bulgaria, *Czechoslovakia*, East Germany, *Hungary*, Poland, Romania and the Soviet Union. It:

- was in response to the admission of West Germany into *NATO*
- provided for mutual defense assistance among the members of the pact
- created a unified command structure for their separate armies
- arranged for the maintenance of Soviet troops in the member states.

In 1956, the attempt by Hungary to leave the pact provoked military intervention in its internal affairs by the Soviet army stationed there. In 1968, pact armies invaded Czechoslovakia, after the promulgation of the *Brezhnev Doctrine*, to end the *Prague Spring* uprising against the communist regime. In 1989–90, the pact collapsed as the Soviet communist bloc disintegrated, and by the late 1990s, in the most telling demonstration that the old Cold War divisions in Europe were over, some former Warsaw Pact countries were actually applying to join NATO.

Warsaw Rising: the rising of Polish *partisan* groups which, in late 1944, seized control of the city of Warsaw from its German garrison. They were encouraged in this by the Polish government in exile in London. The advancing Soviet Red Army reached the outskirts of the city but did not help the uprising. The German counter-attack was led by heavy bombing raids and shelling of the city; the inhabitants faced starvation, and the Polish garrison had to surrender. The Germans deported the inhabitants and systematically destroyed the city. The Red Army made no attempt to help the Poles and in fact refused use of their airfields to British and American aircraft wanting to ship arms and food to the Poles. Once the German destruction of the city was completed, the Red Army resumed its advance. The Polish supporters of the London government in exile were thus wiped out, and the imposition of a pro-Soviet government on Poland was more easily achieved. The episode stands, along with the *Katyn Massacre*, as one of the most cynical acts of Soviet power politics during the war.

wartime conferences: meetings of the leaders of the Allied powers, *Churchill*, *Roosevelt* and *Stalin*.

Washington Conference: an international naval-disarmament conference in 1921–22. It:

- established a ratio of large fighting ships (battleships and cruisers) between the USA, Japan, Britain, France and Italy
- suspended all building of new ships for 10 years.

It was one of the very few concrete disarmament proposals of the inter-war years. Japan, Britain and the USA amended and then extended the agreement in 1930, but France and Italy opted out of the agreement at that point.

Watson-Watt, Robert: a British scientist who, in 1935, invented *radar*, one of the decisive innovations of the Second World War, playing a key part in the *Battle of Britain.*

Wavell, Archibald: a British field marshal. In 1939–41, he was commander-in-chief in the Middle East and had victories in 1940 against the Italians in Ethiopia, which he conquered, and in Libya. Having had to send troops from the Libyan campaign to the campaign in Greece, he then had to face the German army under Rommel and was forced to retreat back to Egypt, at which point he was dismissed by Churchill and sent to other duties in India.

Wehrmacht: the army of Nazi Germany. The name was introduced by Hitler in 1935 to replace the *Weimar Republic* name of *Reichswehr.*

Weimar Republic: set up at the moment of defeat in 1918 when the *German Second Empire* collapsed and *Ebert* was left to provide for the future government. An elected assembly met at Weimar and drew up the republic's constitution. This was on very democratic lines.

- The lower house of parliament, the *Reichstag* was to be elected at least every four years
- Voting in the Reichstag elections was by secret ballot based on universal suffrage
- There was a system of *proportional representation* deciding the number of members to which each party was entitled
- Governments would be based on support in the Reichstag, and the head of government, the chancellor, would be answerable to the Reichstag
- The head of state, the president, was to be elected every seven years; in 1920, Ebert became the first president
- A guarantee of basic human rights was included
- The use of *plebiscites* was provided for to find out the will of the people in important matters
- *Article 48* of the constitution provided for the president to have power to suspend the constitution in order to restore public safety and order in times of emergency. This article was to be significant in the early 1930s with the return of authoritarian government to Germany.

The early 1920s

The republic was saddled with the blame for the unpopular Treaty of Versailles, a situation which right-wing groups hostile to it exploited. Its early existence, from 1919 to 1923, was precarious, for it faced:

- the *Spartacist* uprising
- the *Kapp Putsch*
- French occupation of the *Ruhr*
- the destruction of its economy by *hyperinflation*
- a world dominated by its wartime enemies
- Hitler's *Munich Putsch* of 1923.

Ebert's unassuming work as a democratic politician working in this distinctly hostile setting until his death in 1925 has often been seriously underestimated.

The late 1920s

It was *Stresemann* who was the key figure in the development of Weimar towards a new stability and international acceptance. In 1923, he appointed *Schacht* as currency commissioner with orders to end the runaway inflation. Agreement on the US *Dawes Plan* and the withdrawal of the French from the Ruhr were Stresemann's two early diplomatic achievements, and later he also negotiated the *Locarno* Treaty and signed the *Kellogg–Briand Pact*. In the late 1920s, Weimar appeared to enjoy a new stability and prosperity which was undermined by the effects of the Great Depression. The prosperity was not, however, securely based since it:

- arose largely from the progress made by heavy industry only; agriculture and small businesses did not perform well
- relied too heavily on borrowing from abroad
- rested on a generous system of social welfare payments, which would be difficult to sustain in bad economic times.

The late-1920s stability can also be exaggerated, since the republic suffered from serious political weaknesses, with the proportional-representation system allowing too many political parties to survive, so that unstable coalition governments became the norm.

In the early 1930s, economic dislocation, the consequent social misery and the apparent failure of the democratic parties to take effective action made extremist politics seem more attractive to many Germans.

Weimar's political parties

The main democratic parties committed to supporting the Weimar Republic were:

- the Social Democrats (Socialists), the party of *Ebert* and *Müller*
- the Democrats, the weakest of these parties, with no notable leaders and declining electoral support
- the Catholic Center Party, the party of *Brüning* and von *Papen*, though the latter moved to the right
- the People's Party, the party of *Stresemann*.

Then there were the non-democratic parties with no commitment to the survival of the republic. On the extreme left was:

- the Communist Party, which was not prepared, until too late, to consider working with the democratic parties to block the right;

and on the extreme right were:

- the Nationalists, the party of *Hugenberg*
- the Nationalist Socialist NSDAP (Nazis) led by *Hitler*.

With the collapse of the economy, the extremist parties flourished:

- some of the working class turned to the communists as the best protectors of their interests
- many of the middle class and vested-interest groups of businessmen turned to the National Socialists as their best protection against a left-wing coup.

In these circumstances, the Nazis, who had made a poor showing in the 1928 election, did well in the elections of 1930 and 1932, and Hitler became chancellor in 1933. The *Reichstag Fire* gave Hitler the excuse he needed to declare a state of emergency and to give himself extraordinary powers which were to last until 1945. At this point Weimar was effectively dead, but its official demise dates from the death of President *Hindenburg* in August 1934, when Hitler declared himself Führer of the Third Reich. Democratic Weimar had been subverted by largely legal means, and it came to an end because the stability of the republic in the late 1920s had been based on an illusion that was unable to match the economic reality of the early 1930s.

welfare state: a country ensuring the welfare of its citizens by social services operated by the government.

West, the: a post-1945 shorthand term for the Western powers, an alliance of mainly Western European, American and British Commonwealth nations linked to the USA in opposition to the communist bloc dominated by the Soviet Union and China. Most of the countries making up the West were parliamentary democracies and had largely capitalist economies.

West Berlin: this consisted of the former British, French and US *zones of occupation* in the city. It was a Western enclave inside East Germany which, in 1948, acted as a flashpoint in the Cold War with first the Soviet blockade and then the *Berlin Airlift.* West Berlin became self-governing in 1948, but the Western garrisons remained. Its prosperous capitalist economy became a magnet for East German refugees, and in 1961 the East German government built the *Berlin Wall* to separate it from East Germany. Its separate existence ended with the union of East and West Germany in 1990.

Western European Union (WEU): a mutual defense pact entered into in 1955. The members were the Benelux countries, Britain, France, Italy and West Germany. Its functions have always remained rather vague, but it was revived in the 1980s when Spain and Portugal joined it. Some saw it as a possible future military arm of the European Union, though France and especially Britain were unlikely to agree to this.

Western Front, First World War: the line of fighting that stretched across Belgium and northern France during the *First World War.* After the failure of the *Schlieffen Plan* offensive, the war became static, conducted from elaborate lines of *trenches* fronted by barbed wire, dominated by the machine gun and occasionally punctuated by massive artillery barrages. Mud was everywhere, and barbed wire and machine guns ensured that every offensive would result in lengthy casualty lists. Neither the use of poison gas nor the introduction of tank warfare could break the stalemate. The flimsy aircraft of the time were helpless to do much more than observe the conflict. There were numerous costly but inconclusive battles, including:

- the first Battle of the *Marne* and the first Battle of *Ypres* in 1914
- *Neuve Chapelle*, the second Battle of Ypres, and *Loos* in 1915
- the siege of *Verdun* and the Battle of the *Somme* in 1916
- *Passchendaele* and *Cambrai* in 1917.

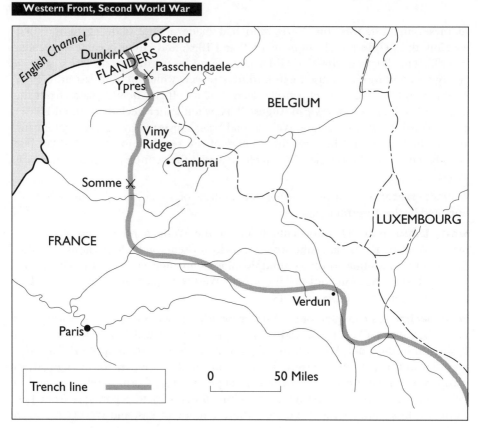

17 The Western Front, 1914–18

From June 1917, US troops were arriving on the Western Front, and this prompted a final German offensive in the spring of 1918. This appeared close to breaking the stalemate, but in fact exhausted both German resources and the German army so that, after four years of static warfare, the first real break in the front came with the Allied counter-offensive in the summer of 1918. In this advance, at last, the tank proved to be decisive, and large gains of land were made in the northern part of the line. Before Germany could be invaded, it had surrendered in November 1918.

Western Front, Second World War: the series of separate campaigns in France, Belgium and Holland from 1939 to 1945. From September 1939 to May 1940, there was the *phony war*, with little fighting. In May–June 1940, the German army's *blitzkrieg* offensive swept the British army back via *Dunkirk* to Britain and forced both Belgium and France to surrender. Until 1944, the Western Front ceased to exist, as Germany controlled all the Continental coastline. In June 1944, the Western Allies opened the *Second Front* and fought their way from Normandy across France into Germany.

Western powers: the term used to describe the USA and its allies, mainly drawn from Western Europe, the Americas and the British Commonwealth. It is normally only used for the period after 1945. If related to an earlier period, it could mean Britain and France as opposed to Nazi Germany. It was often shortened to "the West."

West Germany: a sovereign state founded in 1949 from the territories forming the British, French and US post-Second World War *zones of occupation*, but excluding *West Berlin*. Its official title was the *Federal Republic of Germany* (FRG), and its constitution was drawn up in the *Basic Law* drafted by a committee under *Adenauer*. The principal political parties were the:

- CDU (Christian Democrats), the party of *Adenauer, Erhard, Kiesinger* and *Kohl*
- SPD (Social Democrats), the party of *Schumacher, Brandt* and *Schmidt*
- CSU (Christian Socialists), the party of *Strauss*, which soon formed close links with the CDU
- FDP (Free Democrats)
- KPD (Communists), outlawed from 1956 to 1968.

During the 1950s, the country made such rapid recovery from the devastation of war that this is often referred to as the *German economic miracle*. Early in the Cold War, West Germany became firmly established within the Western bloc. Relations with East Germany were poor under Adenauer, but in the late 1960s, with Brandt as chancellor, they improved notably. In 1990, with the collapse of Soviet control in Eastern Europe, it was largely owing to *Kohl* that international agreements were reached which allowed the state to amalgamate with East Germany and to take in Berlin within a unified Germany. The country's political history is best studied by looking up the entries on individual politicians indicated above.

Westminster: location of the British Parliament. The Statute of Westminster of 1931 gave the British dominions control of their foreign as well as domestic affairs, and this included separate representation in the League of Nations.

White Russians: a term used to describe the counter-revolutionary force which fought the Bolsheviks in the Russian Civil War, 1918–21. They were most active in the south, and among their military leaders were *Denikin, Wrangel* and *Kolchak*. The Whites did not work together effectively, and they lost the support of the masses because of their reluctance to carry out social and economic reforms, particularly land reforms. They were finally defeated by the Red Army, created and led by Trotsky.

Whittle, Frank: the pioneer of jet propulsion who faced total indifference to his work by the British authorities. His engine was used successfully in 1941 and went on to revolutionize air transport. After the war, he lived in the USA, dying in 1996.

WHO: the *World Health Organization*, a specialized agency of the UN.

Wilhelmina: queen of The Netherlands (Holland), 1890–1948. She kept her country neutral in the First World War but, on its invasion by Germany in the Second, set up a government in exile in London. When the German kaiser, William II, fled to Holland at the end of the First World War, she made it clear to the Allies that there was no question of him being extradited to face war-crime charges.

William II (Wilhelm II): German kaiser from 1888 to 1918. In 1890, he dismissed his chancellor, *Bismarck*, the man who, in the period to 1870, had been chiefly responsible for the creation of the *German Second Empire* and who, in the 20 years since then, had built up a system of alliances to protect it. William embarked on a more adventurous foreign policy, for he was anxious for Germany to extend its overseas empire and he wanted Germany to be a naval as well as a military power.

William II:

- wanted friendship with Britain, but his support for *Tirpitz*'s naval building program made this difficult to achieve
- failed to realize that Germany's unification and industrial might made other nations nervous
- remained a resolute friend of Austria-Hungary, but neglected Bismarck's policy of reassuring Russia, and this led to France and Russia becoming allies
- attempted to indicate support for the Boers in their fight against Britain and to browbeat France over Morocco, both of which initiatives backfired and played a part in bringing Britain and France closer together.

The kaiser's adventurous foreign and naval policies played their part in heightening tension in Europe in the period leading up to the First World War, though it should be noted that from 1908 he took a less active interest in politics. He had no part in either the decision to go to war in 1914 or the conduct of the war. He abdicated at the point of defeat in 1918 and ended his life in exile in Holland, dying in 1941.

Wilson, Harold: prime minister of Britain, 1964–70 and 1974–76. He was largely preoccupied with domestic affairs, but his governments did mark the changing nature of Britain's international interests and commitments.

- In 1968, for example, the decision was made to pull back British military forces from east of Suez
- In 1975, he arranged a referendum of the British people on membership of the European Community, and accepted the 2-to-1 decision in favor.

Wilson, Woodrow: president of the USA, 1913 to 1921. He wished the USA to remain neutral in the First World War, but came to favor the Allied side and was drawn into war against Germany in April 1917, after the latter resumed its policy of unrestricted submarine warfare in the Atlantic. His *Fourteen Points* had been an attempt to give the war a moral purpose, and at the end of the war, he went to the *Paris Peace Conference* determined to secure a just and lasting peace. This idealism ran up against the wish of the French to see Germany punished and its military threat ended. In particular, Wilson advocated self-determination for the subject nationalities of Eastern Europe, and a series of *plebiscites* tried to put this into effect, though inconvenient geographic and political facts kept getting in the way of full application of the principle. He also proposed an international peacekeeping organization, which was incorporated in the Versailles Treaty as the *League of Nations.* Traditional isolationism in the USA, and also his own poor handling of the issue and his ill health, meant that the US Senate, on a tide of anti-war feeling and suspicion of British and French imperialism, refused to ratify the treaty and therefore also refused to join the League. In his last months in office, poor health robbed him of all political influence.

wind of change: the phrase of the British prime minister *Macmillan,* used in addressing the South African Parliament in 1960. Its main impact was in Africa, but it also illustrated how even right-wing British politicians were beginning to face up to the emergence of demands from the non-white world for justice and for political rights, which marked the end of the *British Empire*'s domination of so much of the world.

Winter Palace: the tsar's palace in St. Petersburg. It was the scene in 1905 of the *Bloody Sunday* massacre of members of a peaceful crowd gathered to petition Nicholas II.

wireless: the common term for radio in Britain in the first half of the twentieth century.

Witte, Sergei: a Russian politician. He was minister of finance under Alexander II from 1892, and under Nicholas II until 1903. He was largely responsible for the construction of the Trans-Siberian Railway and showed great financial skill in keeping the tsars from bankruptcy, especially by borrowing money from France. He was accused at the time of being extravagant, and of being too subservient to foreign capitalists. Later historians have argued that he failed to appreciate the importance of the need for agricultural reform. He:

- believed that the modernization of Russia depended upon industrialization
- erected tariff barriers against foreign goods in order to encourage the development of Russian industries
- tried to encourage the investment of foreign capital in Russian industry
- in 1897, in order to give foreign investors confidence, placed the Russian currency on the *gold standard.*

In November 1905, he was appointed chief minister, but one week before the first Duma met in the aftermath of the 1905 Revolution, Nicholas II dismissed him in favor of the reactionary *Goremykin.* Witte had been in favor of political and constitutional reform to complement his economic modernization, but he had throughout been dependent on the favor of the tsar. (See also the entry on the *Russian economy, pre-1914.*)

World Bank: a specialized agency of the UN set up in the *Bretton Woods Agreement* of 1944. It uses money from members to finance development loans. In its first years, it was mainly involved in European post-war reconstruction projects, but it subsequently turned to helping less developed countries. By 1998, its membership had grown from the original 44 nations to 180.

World Health Organization (WHO): a specialized agency of the UN set up in 1948. It collaborates with governments to raise health standards and to control diseases. There were 191 member nations in 1998.

World Trade Organization: established on 1 January 1995 to replace *GATT.*

World War I, World War II: see *First World War* and *Second World War.*

Wrangel, Piotr: a capable *White Russian* general defeated in the Russian Civil War. He succeeded Denikin too late to reverse the tide of defeats.

Y

Yagoda, Genrikh: head of the Soviet *NKVD*, the secret police, 1936–38. He became one of the first victims of Stalin's *Yezhovshchina* (Great Purge) immediately after his removal from office.

Yalta Conference: a meeting of the wartime Allied leaders held at Yalta in the Soviet Union in February 1945. It was attended by *Churchill, Roosevelt* and *Stalin.* The war in Europe was going well, and the main topics of discussion related to post-war issues in general, rather than in any detail. The leaders agreed:

- to divide Germany into *zones of occupation*
- that the borders of both the Soviet Union and Poland would move westwards. The Soviet–Polish border would follow the *Curzon Line*, laid down but never implemented in 1920, and would roughly coincide with the border between Nazi and Soviet Poland as agreed in the *Nazi–Soviet Pact* of 1939; the Soviet Union thereby regained the vast areas of land it had lost to Poland in 1920–21
- that Poland was to be compensated for the loss of land in the east by acquiring German lands on its western frontier
- that the Polish government should include both representatives of the government in exile in London and the recently formed communist partisan government in Poland
- that they would establish the *United Nations Organization*
- that Stalin would enter the war against Japan.

The remarkable degree of unity achieved hid the fact that the details of the arrangements in Germany and Poland had still to be hammered out and, as became clear at the *Potsdam Conference* in August 1945, this was not going to be straightforward.

Yeltsin, Boris: president of Russia, 1991– . He came to international attention when, as president of the Russian Soviet Republic in 1991, he led the street resistance to the attempted hard-line communist coup against the president of the Soviet Union, *Gorbachev.* This gave him the initiative in pressing to dissolve the Soviet Union, at which point, in December 1991, Russia became an independent state, with Yeltsin as its president. He faced strong opposition from the communist bureaucracy and the military to his attempts at constitutional and economic reform, and in 1993 there was an attempted armed coup against him. This failed, but the fragmented state of the Federal Assembly, and the existence of both far right and communist parties in it, led to a series of compromises and the end of radical economic reforms. From 1994, Yeltsin's health, and indeed his mental stability, began to be questioned, but in 1996, despite the uncertain political outlook facing both himself and his country, and the civil war raging in *Chechenia*, he was re-elected president, defeating a strong communist challenge.

Yezhovshchina: a term used to describe the Stalinist purges particularly of the late 1930s. The name comes from the man who led the Soviet secret police from 1936 to 1938, N. I. Yezhov, who organized the purges during their bloodiest period. It is often translated into English as the Great Purge. It started after the murder of *Kirov*, and before it was over, 10 million had been arrested and 3 million executed, with perhaps as many dying in concentration camps. There were great *show trials* of leading political figures for propaganda purposes, like that of *Bukharin*, but most of the victims were dealt with swiftly and secretly:

- by a confession gained by torture
- by a brief appearance without representation before a three-man tribunal
- by verdict and sentence following immediately.

Leading Bolsheviks and Red Army officers were among notable groups to be particularly targeted. It is, however, worth noting that the *kulaks* had been eliminated from Soviet society by 1934 and so were not among the victims of the Yezhovshchina.

Young Plan: a US plan of 1929 to regulate German payment of *reparations*. It:

- revised the *Dawes Plan*
- reduced the reparations debt as first set in 1921 by three-quarters
- arranged for the reduced sum to be paid in 59 installments, the last payable in 1988
- made proposals to encourage foreign investment in the German economy.

In return, British and French troops were withdrawn from the Rhineland. The onset of the Great Depression led to the suspension of the revised payments after only the first had been made. When Hitler came to power in 1933, he repudiated Germany's liability to pay reparations.

Young Turks: a reform group which:

- in 1908 staged a revolt against the drift and corruption in the government of the *Ottoman Empire*
- held power from 1913 until the collapse of the empire at the end of the First World War.

The term has passed into wider usage as shorthand for a reforming group who wish to put the state, or some other institution, onto a new path.

Ypres: the location of several important First World War battles on the *Western Front*.

- In their 1914 advance, the Germans failed to take Ypres and so break through to the Channel ports
- In 1915, another German attack also failed, despite the use of poison gas
- In 1917, an Allied advance became part of the ill-fated battle of *Passchendaele*
- As part of their spring 1918 offensive, the Germans again attacked the devastated ruins of the town, but again failed to capture them.

Ypres was important to the Allies since its successful defense blocked the Germans from the Channel ports. The defense was at a terrible cost, however, for during the First World War about half a million British and Commonwealth troops died on that part of the front.

Yugoslavia: formed after the First World War from the independent kingdom of Serbia and parts of the former Austro-Hungarian Empire. It contained many different nationalities, Serbs, Croats and Slovenes.

1919–45

Its best known political leader, *Pašić*, died in 1927, and its ruler, *Alexander I*, then set up a strongly pro-Serbian royal dictatorship as the only means to maintain order in the kingdom. In 1929, he named his country Yugoslavia. He was assassinated in 1934, and his young son, *Peter II*, succeeded, though the country was governed by his uncle Paul as regent, pursuing pro-German policies. When Peter took over power in 1941, the German army immediately invaded and he went into exile.

During the Second World War, the country was divided up by its German occupiers, who found increasing difficulty in maintaining their control in the face of an active partisan movement supplied and encouraged by the Allies. The Allies favored the effective communist partisan leader, *Tito*, who had recaptured large areas of the country, and the exiled Peter II was largely ignored.

1945–96

In November 1945, Tito proclaimed the foundation of the Socialist Federal Republic of Yugoslavia, which he led until his death in 1980. In 1963 and 1974, he had to meet the separate ambitions of the diverse peoples of the state by changes in the constitution which devolved more powers from the center to the constituent republics. After Tito's death in 1980, the six separate republics – *Serbia, Slovenia, Croatia, Bosnia-Herzegovina, Montenegro* and *Macedonia* – became even more important within the federal structure, at the expense of the central presidency, which was rotated between them. Communist ideas and practices were widely rejected.

The division of Yugoslavia

It proved impossible to quell the separatist demands of the different ethnic groups.

- In June 1991, the more prosperous, more Catholic republics of Slovenia and Croatia declared their independence. The federal Yugoslav army, which soon became the army of Serbia and its ally Montenegro, tried unsuccessfully to prevent Croatia from leaving until, after six months of fighting, the UN brokered a peace deal which gave Croatia independence in January 1992
- Macedonia proclaimed itself independent in September 1991, though the federal army did not withdraw, peacefully, until April 1992
- Bosnia asserted its independence in March 1992, but this led to four years of bloody civil war between Serb, Muslim and Croat inhabitants. An uneasy peace deal, dividing Bosnia along complicated frontiers and to be supervised by NATO forces, was put in place in 1996
- In April 1992, the two remaining republics of the old state of Yugoslavia, Serbia and Montenegro, announced the formation of a new Yugoslav federation, but this was not generally recognized internationally because of their aid to the Serbs fighting in Bosnia. It was the international economic pressure on the new federation which forced it first to end its aid to the Bosnian Serbs and then to put pressure on them to accept a

series of compromises on their territorial demands, which brought about the Bosnian peace deal.

Events in Yugoslavia after 1991 vividly exposed how artificial its unity as one nation had been, but also, by contrast, made clear how great was Tito's achievement in constructing the socialist state and then holding it together for 25 years.

18 The collapse of Yugoslavia

Z

Zaharoff, Basil: an arms dealer and manufacturer. He was regarded, pre-1914, as a sinister figure who encouraged war in order to increase profits. After the war, he was seen by some as part of the secret intrigue which had brought about the tension and the arms race leading to the First World War.

Zeebrugge Raid: a British First World War raid. In April 1918, the British navy blocked the entrance to the *U-boat* base at the German-occupied Belgian port.

zeppelins: German airships. They had limited commercial use before 1914 and played a part in the war by carrying out observation and bombing missions: both Paris and London were bombed. They terrified the civilian population, but were too slow and too inflammable to play an important part in the war. They were further developed between the wars, their use including a handful of flights across the Atlantic, reaching speeds approaching 100 miles per hour. Spectacular accidents, like the explosion on the HINDENBURG in 1937, limited both their commercial value and their military potential.

Zhdanov, Andrei: a Soviet politician who survived the 1930s purges to become the intellectual defender of Stalinism, attacking Western decadence in the arts and literature. He died in 1948.

Zhukov, Georgi: a Soviet military leader. He rose from a junior officer in the Red Army to become a general, and survived the 1930s purges to take the key role in planning Soviet strategy after the German invasion in 1941. He:

- defeated the Germans at *Stalingrad* in 1942–43
- lifted the siege of Leningrad in 1944
- led the attack on, and capture of, Berlin in 1945.

After the war, he was military commander of the Soviet *zone of occupation* in Germany. In 1947, he was demoted by Stalin but, in 1955, became defense minister. He had an equally uneasy relationship with Khrushchev, whom he at first supported, only to be dismissed. After Khrushchev's fall, his military rank was restored. His reputation as a military leader ranks very high, and he is seen as one of the outstanding military commanders of the Second World War.

Zimmermann Note: a dramatic espionage coup of the First World War. A secret telegram of January 1917 from the German foreign minister, Zimmermann, to the German ambassador in Mexico gave coded instructions for the latter to offer an alliance to Mexico. In return, if war broke out between Germany and the USA, Mexico would receive back the US territory taken from it in the nineteenth century. The British intercepted and decoded the telegram and passed it to the US government in March 1917, just as German submarine warfare in the Atlantic was causing serious US concern. The US government publicized the telegram, undermining the credibility of those American isolationists who wished to keep out of the war, and a month later the USA declared war on Germany.

Zinoviev, Grigori: a Soviet politician. He had been in exile with Lenin, and took part in the 1917 *October Revolution*. From 1919, he did much to establish the *Comintern*, which he led until 1926. He is famous in British history for a letter he is alleged to have sent during the 1924 election campaign urging revolutionary activity in the British army. It was claimed that this was a forgery which helped to lose the British Labour Party the election. On Lenin's death, Zinoviev combined with Stalin and Kamenev to prevent Trotsky from being elected leader. He was later outmaneuvered by Stalin and spent some years abroad, but on his return was accused of moral responsibility for the murder of Kirov and was, in 1936, the central figure in one of the great *show trials* of the Stalinist purges. He was then executed.

Zionism: the belief that Jews should create a homeland in Palestine. It:

- was a response to prevailing anti-Semitism in nineteenth-century Europe
- owed much to the advocacy of Theodor *Herzl*
- received a boost from the Allied ratification of the *Balfour Declaration* in 1917.

Many European Jews, however, preferred assimilation into European society, but between the wars there was a steady trickle of Jewish emigrants to Palestine. The experience of the *Holocaust* greatly increased the appeal of Zionism, and there was a flood of immigrants to Palestine after 1945. The state of Israel was founded in 1948, fulfilling Herzl's dream.

Zionist: a supporter of *Zionism*, the idea of creating a Jewish national homeland in Palestine.

zones of occupation: created in Germany by the Allies at the end of the Second World War:

- Germany was divided into four occupation zones controlled by Britain, France, the Soviet Union and the USA
- *Berlin*, which lay inside the Soviet zone, was also divided into four zones administered by the same four powers.

Within each zone, the military commander of the occupying power had full authority, and a control council of the four commanders acted in matters affecting Germany as a whole. In 1948, the Soviets, in the *Berlin Blockade*, cut the land routes between the Western zones in Germany and the Western zones in Berlin. This led to the *Berlin Airlift* and the Soviet withdrawal from the Control Commission. This in practice divided Germany between East (Soviet) and West (the Western Allies). In 1949, the three Western zones became the *Federal Republic of Germany* (West Germany) and the Soviet zone became the *German Democratic Republic* (East Germany).

Zog: the self-proclaimed king of Albania. He reigned from 1928 to 1939, when his country was invaded and occupied by Italy.

Z Plan: the Nazi German plan of January 1939 to build a large battle fleet. After the Munich Agreement, Hitler realized that Britain would not allow him to make vast territorial gains in Eastern Europe without going to war. His response was to give top priority to this plan and to launch a large expansion of the *Luftwaffe*. He probably still believed that he could settle his territorial claims on Poland without going to war with the Western Allies.